Top Down

POLITICS AND CULTURE IN MODERN AMERICA

Series Editors: Margot Canaday, Glenda Gilmore,
Michael Kazin, and Thomas J. Sugrue

Volumes in the series narrate and analyze political and social
change in the broadest dimensions from 1865 to the present,
including ideas about the ways people have sought and wielded
power in the public sphere and the language and institutions of
politics at all levels—local, national, and transnational. The series
is motivated by a desire to reverse the fragmentation of modern
U.S. history and to encourage synthetic perspectives on social
movements and the state, on gender, race, and labor, and on
intellectual history and popular culture.

TOP DOWN

The Ford Foundation, Black Power,
and the Reinvention of Racial Liberalism

Karen Ferguson

PENN

UNIVERSITY OF PENNSYLVANIA PRESS

PHILADELPHIA

340 8921

Published by
University of Pennsylvania Press
Philadelphia, Pennsylvania 19104-4112
www.upenn.edu/pennpress

Printed in the United States of America
on acid-free paper

2 4 6 8 10 9 7 5 3 1

Library of Congress Cataloging-in-Publication Data

Ferguson, Karen (Karen Jane)
  Top down : the Ford Foundation, black power, and the
reinvention of racial liberalism / Karen Ferguson. — 1st ed.
    p. cm. — (Politics and culture in modern America)
  Includes bibliographical references and index.
  ISBN 978-0-8122-4526-4 (hardcover : alk. paper)
  1. Black power—United States—History—20th century. 2.
African Americans—Civil rights—History—20th century. 3.
United States—Race relations—Political aspects—History—
20th century. 4. Liberalism—United States—History—20th
century. 5. Ford Foundation—History. I. Title. II. Series:
Politics and culture in modern America.
HV97.F62F47 2013
305.896'073—dc23
                                          2012048040

For Mike

Contents

Introduction

On August 2, 1966, McGeorge Bundy made his first major policy statement as Ford Foundation president in a speech to the National Urban League in Philadelphia. Entitled "Action for Equal Opportunity," Bundy's address was a clarion call for a new era at the Ford Foundation, by far the largest and most influential philanthropy in the world. Bundy declared that the Foundation's most prestigious and costly programs would experiment boldly by dealing with the ongoing black freedom struggle, especially black power's challenge to the nation. Pegged for Foundation president in 1965, the year of both the Voting Rights Act and the Watts riot, Bundy, along with his program officers and the Foundation's trustees, was keenly aware that the legislative victories of the civil rights movement had not solved what he still called the "Negro problem" of black assimilation into American society. In fact, as the struggle for equal opportunity had turned from "rights to reality," Bundy saw that "the agenda for the immediate future [was] as full and pressing as it [had] been at any time in the past."[1] Over the next ten years, the Foundation would ramp up its spending on "rights for minorities," granting more than $100 million in this area from 1965 to 1969 alone, in amounts reaching 40 percent of the entire budget for domestic programs by 1970.[2]

Making a speech about equal opportunity to the National Urban League, a venerable and unimpeachably mainstream and moderate black organization, was hardly controversial; however, what Bundy did next was. In a deeply counterintuitive move he sought to relegitimize racial liberalism's promise of color-blind opportunity and inclusion, not by attacking black power's repudiation of this American creed but by directly engaging black activists and their call for separatism and self-determination. As a result of Bundy's contrariness, the Ford Foundation played a pivotal role in establishing many of the hallmark legacies of the black power era, such as ghetto-based economic development initiatives, university black studies programs, multicultural and "affective" school curricula, and race-specific arts and cultural organizations.[3]

In fact, Ford played an instrumental part not simply in bankrolling such initiatives but in originating many of these projects itself, all of which served its interests in finding a way to deal with the challenge that the black freedom struggle presented to the nation's dominant ideas, practices, and institutions. In doing so, Bundy and his officers played a vanguard role in a nationwide effort by the so-called liberal establishment to engage black power.

The perplexing story of how elite, liberal whites, those from the Ford Foundation prominent among them, worked to institutionalize elements of a black power project seemingly antithetical to their worldview has fascinated a wide range of commentators over the last decades. This confounding relationship has held particular interest because it arose at a critical juncture for both white liberalism and the black freedom struggle that would ultimately see the decline of both. Scholars of black power most often blame, but sometimes credit, expedient white liberals and their institutions for neutralizing the threat of the movement's liberationist potential—essentially helping to kill it through soft power while law-and-order hard power attacked it from the right.[4] In return, many students of American politics and intellectual life have held black power, along with the Vietnam War, responsible for pushing liberalism beyond the brink, thereby resulting in the "unraveling" of the consensus that had unified the nation in the postwar period. As the story goes, liberals' variously motivated accommodation of bottom-up African American insurgency brought about the death of the postwar and civil rights period's incipient integrationism, equal opportunity, and color-blindness and ushered in the birth of multiculturalism, welfare entitlement, affirmative action, and identity politics—developments that in turn sparked a white backlash that helped propel the conservative turn in American politics.[5]

Even though these arguments are mutually opposed, they both have validity. However, as their contradiction suggests, they each miss the full story of liberalism's engagement with black power. In this book I seek to capture the complexity of this episode by widening the historical lens on the relationship between elite liberals and the actors and ideas that animated black power. This perspective has allowed me to uncover, among other things, strong and surprising affinities between Foundation officers' postwar formulation of racial liberalism and the racial separatism of Ford's black grantees, which helps to explain how and why Bundy's Foundation engaged so strongly with black power, beyond a straightforward emergency response. Similarly, moving forward from the 1960s to the 1970s and beyond permits a more complete understanding of the legacy of the Foundation's connection with black activists. As it turns out, while Ford's liberals were bloodied by this experience, they nevertheless survived the 1960s and went on to pioneer social policy deep into the conservative era, suggesting both their pragmatism and the ideological affinities that allowed them to continue to operate successfully in a new political climate. Indeed, mine is a story not of the death of racial liberalism but of its constant re-creation during the second half of the twentieth century.

Understanding how racial liberalism was remade from the top down is essential to understanding current American racial politics and its paradoxes.[6] To take an obvious example: How could an African American like Barack Obama, along with a tiny minority of his elite black peers, rise to the highest ranks of American government, business, and media, while a majority of his black brethren still face glaring inequalities? Why was it essential to his political success that the biracial Obama simultaneously assert his African Americanness culturally and establish his ability to thrive and rise in an ostensibly color-blind American meritocracy? How did his claims both to an Ivy League education and to grassroots community organizing operate together to legitimate his leadership potential as a black man within today's white liberal establishment? How is it that the first African American president came to office in the neoliberal era, when the egalitarian social democratic vision that animated the twentieth-century black freedom struggle has largely become a historical relic? I posit that a crucial element of the answer to these questions lies in the history of elite whites' engagement with black activism, beginning in the 1950s. Whites reshaped racial liberalism in their effort to forge a national consensus on race in the wake of the seismic changes wrought by both the legislative victories of the civil rights movement and the urban crisis of postindustrial, ghettoized cities that spurred black power. The Ford Foundation helped lead the way in this quest to manage racial conflict and inequality during the civil rights era and beyond.

The first black U.S. president was still a long way off in August 1966, when Bundy made his policy statement to the National Urban League. What made the issue of "Negro equality" the "most urgent domestic concern of this country" for Bundy and the Foundation's trustees and officers was not just the crisis of capital and white flight and black ghettoization that plagued postwar American cities.[7] Given the Foundation's and the larger American white elite's historic neglect of and ignorance about African Americans' lives, especially outside of the South, Bundy and his peers would never have responded to the urban crisis in this way if not for the fact that black people

were so vocally and actively fighting against their marginalization in an ongoing freedom struggle that white elites now understood to extend beyond
the South and to include far more than formal rights when defining equality.
Once African Americans had reestablished their formal, century-old consti-
tutional equality through the nonviolent direct action of the Southern civil
rights movement, the focus of the black freedom struggle moved into a new
phase, centered in and on the cities, most often outside of the South, and also
outside of the parameters of American liberalism. Black Americans began
to make their claims through methods like property damage and looting of
urban rebellions, and concepts like self-defense, anticolonialism, and racial
nationalism. Such actions and ideologies directly challenged the erstwhile
American promise of the perfectibility and egalitarian possibility of the nation, which had been reasserted in the postwar period by elite players like
the Ford Foundation but had so miserably failed ghettoized black urbanites.[8]

This challenge to the American "system" dealt a severe blow to the presumptions about social progress that undergirded postwar liberalism's promise, and it also girded the loins of white elites like Bundy to demonstrate that
these putative truths still prevailed in the context of the late 1960s. In their
optimism about the possibilities of the affluent society, most white liberals in
the 1940s and 1950s believed that the modernization inevitably wrought by
an ever-expanding corporate capitalism would be a rational and color-blind
process that would lead to the peaceful assimilation of all minorities into the
American mainstream, leaving behind the irrational practices of both white
prejudice and supposed black primitivism. From this worldview, racial inequality was an anachronism that would be inexorably dissolved with blacks'
and whites' incorporation into the industrial modernity of the city. However, instead of this inevitable, conflict-free process, African Americans either faced massive white resistance to their efforts to dismantle Southern Jim
Crow or found themselves further marginalized and impoverished if they
voted with their feet by leaving the rural South for the dead-end "second
ghetto" of postwar American cities. Thus, the relevance of race did not disappear as postwar racial liberals had imagined; instead, African Americans'
struggle against American society's postwar betrayal of their freedom dreams
resulted in their emergence as a visible and vocal public in American life as
well as in the advent of race as a potent and inescapable element in American
politics.[9]

This book examines the response of elite white liberals to the new racial politics spawned by the urban crisis and African Americans' claims to

power and self-determination. After exploring the crucial history of the Ford Foundation's postwar origins, I focus on the era between about 1965 and 1975, an interval that began with the seminal legal victories of the civil rights movement and ended with national economic retrenchment and political reaction. In this period, the critical national project for the American liberal establishment was to domesticate black power and its challenge to liberalism, reforging a social consensus on race. Not coincidentally, this period also corresponded to the endgame for what has been called the "long" civil rights movement, or that continuous strain within the twentieth-century black freedom struggle, including many elements of black power, that had sought social transformation outside the bounds of the nation's individualist, egalitarian creed.[10] While the iron fist of the emergent right surely played a decisive role in effectively silencing this radical vision, so did liberals' velvet-glove efforts to incorporate and ultimately assimilate the challenge of black power into the American way.

The Ford Foundation led the way in this liberal crusade, and what it did mattered. It was established in 1936 by Henry Ford, the founder and president of Ford Motor. However, the Foundation did not become a major national and international force until 1948, when Ford's grandson, Henry II, used a massive bequest of family-held Ford Motor stock to catapult it from a Michigan-based, family-controlled philanthropy to the largest private foundation in the world. It maintained this status throughout the period covered by this book; by 1966, its annual budget was around $200 million, and its $3.3 billion endowment was more than three times that of the Rockefeller Foundation, its nearest rival.[11] The younger Henry intended that this vast enrichment of the Foundation's coffers would allow it to act on the confident social-engineering ethos of postwar liberalism of which he was an adherent. Henry was not alone in his beliefs. He belonged to an elite formation of corporate, government, military, university, media, and philanthropic leaders, which played a pivotal role after the Second World War to perpetuate the nation's unprecedented prosperity and to expand its international dominance. Often called the "liberal establishment," based on their shared social, economic, and political vision, and presumed stewardship of the nation, these leaders held a whiggish faith in the postwar American "system" that they had helped create. They believed wholeheartedly in a boundless and beneficent corporate capitalism undergirded by the Keynesian security state and a technocracy of trained experts to manage the nation's social, economic, and political modernization. Henry Ford II and the group of philanthropic and business leaders whom he amassed to remake the Foundation as "the central agency of establishment philanthropy" were convinced that they had the resources and expertise to advance human welfare, as Ford's mission put it.[12]

In working toward these ends the Ford Foundation found itself in a very different position than its forebears, those industrial philanthropies like the Rockefeller Foundation and the Carnegie Corporation that had been founded during the Gilded Age, long before the expansion of the state and state provision during the New Deal and Second World War. Rather than big government supplanting the role of philanthropy in this new era, American foundations now led by Ford instead positioned themselves at the forefront of American foreign, social, and cultural policy during the pinnacle of the activist state of the Cold War and affluent society. For example, the Ford Foundation spearheaded philanthropic support for the most influential applied research that made modernization theory, behavioral science, and systems analysis the dominant conceptual tools for American policymakers in the postwar period. The Foundation partnered with the United States Agency for International Development as the most generous private institution promoting the Green Revolution and population control as major tools of so-called third world development. The Foundation also acted as a kind of domestic policy incubator for the Kennedy and Johnson administrations, initiating and testing out social programs, including those at the center of LBJ's Great Society, which were then applied nationwide. In addition, Ford led the way in spreading nonprofit culture throughout the United States, singlehandedly establishing symphony orchestras and dance and regional theater companies across the nation and playing a major role in the establishment of public television.[13] In all of these efforts the Foundation promoted its ideas and approaches as technocratic techniques to fix the roadblocks to what its leaders believed could become a perfect society of universal social peace, affluence, security, and cultivation, achievable through liberalism and corporate capitalism. In short, as the Board of Trustees boasted in 1962, the Ford Foundation fully exploited its position as "probably the only private institution which can . . . make a critical difference in the course of events" at home or abroad.[14]

Included in these events was the urban crisis. During the decade leading up to 1965, the Foundation's Public Affairs program garnered kudos for its pioneering initiatives to fix one of the kinks in the American system: the postwar migration of millions of poor, nonwhite rural folk, mostly from the South but also from the Caribbean and Mexico, to cities in the North and West. This urbanization created complex social and political problems centered on the "gray areas" of degrading, rapidly deindustrializing inner cities where the migrants settled. For the Foundation's officers, what made this rural-to-urban movement an issue was the challenge it presented to the migrants' assimilation into the American mainstream. How could impoverished former agricultural workers adapt to modernity, be accepted into America's institutional life, and experience the upward mobility of the American dream when the industrial city, the erstwhile crucible of immigrant assimilation, was gone or rapidly disappearing? African Americans' escalating protest against the ghettoization in which they found themselves trapped only steeled the Foundation's resolve that its officers must find an answer to this question. In pursuing this goal, the Ford Foundation became a preeminent postwar actor to work for the eventual incorporation of urban African Americans into the existing political economy. Consequently, while other agents of white power resisted all phases of the postwar black freedom struggle repressively and often violently, the Foundation found itself paralleling and even intersecting with the goals of black activism in an effort to shape the movement's outcome.

* * *

The Foundation made its engagement with the black struggle explicit with Bundy's appointment at Ford during the concurrent rise of black power. At that moment, Ford began applying a model to achieve its assimilationist objectives that intersected with some of the key goals, if not the ultimate aims, of the dominant strains of black power—most notably racial separatism and black leadership development. Thus the Foundation promoted a balkanizing ethic for the black urban poor that emphasized the need for the continuing isolation of minority communities so that they could experience a cultural revitalization that would lead to what Bundy called "social development" and eventual assimilation into the mainstream American political economy. At the same time, the Foundation fostered the creation of a new black leadership class that could be integrated into its elite model of American pluralism.

The Foundation's advocacy of ongoing racial separatism for all but a small black elite emerged out of experiences in the early 1950s when it faced political attack for advocating school desegregation even before the *Brown* Supreme Court decision. Cowed by the right-wing firestorm that resulted, the Foundation quickly abandoned racial integration as a policy choice. Actions like this one and others that followed demonstrated the Foundation's aversion to controversy and ultimately damaging unwillingness to face down its conservative opponents.[15] However, the Foundation's reluctance to stand up for desegregation also calls into question its leadership's commitment to this principle in the first place and, more broadly, the commonplace portrayal of assimilation through integration as a shibboleth of postwar racial liberalism.

Instead, the Foundation chose to address its ongoing commitment to racial assimilation through a counterintuitive and seemingly paradoxical policy of racial separatism. In fact, this strategy tapped into a long-standing reaction by white elites in the United States hoping to reconcile declarations of American freedom with the fact of the racial repression that imbued the nation. In fact, the white fantasy that African Americans could best develop into full citizens by being separated from whites stretched back to the Early Republic when many powerful white Americans worked to square the universalism of the Declaration of Independence with their distaste for racial mixing.[16] A century later, one of the first goals of industrial philanthropy in the Gilded Age was how to achieve this same goal within the context of African American emancipation. Almost two hundred years after the first expression of this ethos, Ford Foundation officers continued to look toward racial separatism as a key to solving this so-called "Negro problem" in the face of widespread black ghettoization and marginalization despite the victories of the civil rights movement. As with these earlier cases of American elites seeking this improbable goal, Bundy and his peers found allies among African Americans intent on the parallel, albeit very different, objective of self-determination through their separation from whites.[17]

This historical impulse dovetailed with the developmentalism of postwar racial liberals to reinforce the Ford Foundation's racial separatist and ghetto-based solutions to the urban crisis. While white liberals had abandoned a long-standing belief in African Americans' innate racial inferiority, notions of black cultural and psychological pathology that replaced biological racism served a similar function in buttressing the commonplace notion—stretching back to such diverse origins as Jim Crow segregation and the social ecology model of the Chicago School of sociology—that black people needed an indeterminate period of separate development before being able to assimilate successfully into mainstream American life. By the 1960s, a growing belief in the myth of white ethnic succession bolstered this apparent need for racial cloistering. According to this credo, the success of the grandchildren of the European immigrants of the industrial era could be attributed to the self-help and cultural resilience of the ethnic communities that their forebears had fostered in the new country. It followed that the black ghetto could similarly be a vital crucible for recent black migrants to the city, who like their now fully assimilated white-ethnic forbears, could benefit from a period of separate development in which to foster a strong cultural identity and contribute to American pluralism. Further, the model the Foundation chose to apply to racial minorities in order to overcome their "deprivation" and engineer the same success (which was supposedly experienced organically by white immigrant groups earlier in the century) connected the ultimate assimilation of minority racial groups at home to another of the Foundation's guiding tenets: the Cold War modernization ethos that ruled American third world development policy.[18]

Modernization theory developed in large part as a response to global postwar decolonization, a process that American policymakers repeatedly used to make sense of the situations of racial minorities at home. This tendency was especially pronounced in Bundy's Foundation given that the new president's expertise lay not in domestic race relations, about which he knew virtually nothing before 1966, but rather in foreign policy, because he had served as national security advisor for Presidents Kennedy and Johnson. Nevertheless, Bundy and his staff were not alone in comparing African Americans to third world nationals, suggesting how communities of color were perceived by postwar white liberals as foreigners to the nation and hence outside of its citizenry. In the United States and abroad, a key postcolonial issue for the Ford Foundation—which since 1950 had played just as vital a role in incubating American international development efforts as it did domestic social policy—was to play an effective role broadly in the national Cold War mission to attract the recently unfettered global masses to the American way. A Foundation solution in both cases was to accommodate the call for self-determination at home and abroad by identifying and training a cadre of indigenous leaders, whether in India, Indonesia, or Bedford-Stuyvesant, who would act as peaceful and rational brokers and spokespeople for their nation or race in a U.S.-dominated postcolonial global scene or the corporate capitalism of postwar America. Thus, from the Foundation's perspective, the African American community deserved representation in a pluralistic and meritocratic body politic, but such power should be exercised by the "best and brightest" of the black community as defined by the "best and brightest" of the white community.

A dynamic of racial brokerage was nothing new in African American history. However, the Foundation's leaders and the liberal establishment more generally were ready to afford this new black elite an unprecedented level of influence and power. They hoped to end the era's disunity by bringing about social peace in an American society that was increasingly complex, pluralistic, and corporate, in order to facilitate continued national prosperity and growth. Among the instruments the Foundation promoted to this end was the "systems reform" of American institutions so that they might better serve their role in the modern context. Most important for achieving this goal from the Foundation's point of view was the development of an expanded leadership class in the United States that had the managerial talent and expertise required to lead these reforms. The elite theory of pluralism to which the Foundation subscribed posited that this meritocratic expansion would also serve to deal with the conflicts wrought by African Americans' emergence in the 1960s as a visible and vocal political force; by expanding the notion of the nation's leadership class from white Anglo-Saxon Protestants, first to white ethnics and then African Americans and finally to other people of color, the Foundation sought to build consensus for its social vision through the diversification of the American elite. Thus it was no surprise that in 1979 the Ford Foundation chose a black president, Franklin Thomas, in a move widely seen by commentators at the time as a vanguard action in the opening of the American establishment. The growth of the black professional and leadership class since then, culminating in Barack Obama's election as president almost thirty years later, suggests that those observations were right.[19]

The Foundation's model of developmentalist assimilation and elite pluralism diverged sharply from the social vision of its black-power grantees. Broadly speaking, they, like other advocates of black self-determination, rejected the national democratic myth and individualist prescriptions for social reform that animated postwar liberalism. Instead, they advocated for collective action and group-based solutions, in the idealistic hope that they could emerge as potent political actors to transform the United States according to their redistributive social-democratic vision. However, despite the radical transformations they sought through black self-determination, the thinking of these black power activists was still often shaped by a mainstream liberal conception of pluralism, race, and social change, particularly as it pertained to their model of how the black community might be "developed" and mobilized to achieve their vision. This conceptual convergence brought the Ford Foundation and its black grantees together in the first place. However, the social conflict wrought by activism for black liberation pursued under the auspices of the Foundation demonstrated to Bundy and his officers that they would never be able to create racial consensus through grassroots black activism, resulting ultimately in their top-down and conservative strategy of leadership development to manage the black community.[20]

The relationship between the Ford Foundation and black power provides an opportunity to consider black power not only in terms of its radical vision and resultant activism but also in terms of what in 1969 a critical Robert L. Allen called the "domestic neocolonialism" that was its outcome, or what in 2009 a sympathetic Devin Fergus called "liberalism's capacity to reform revolution."[21] What both scholars were referring to was the domestication of black power through its accommodation within the confines of the existing social order. This was the "new regime of race relations management"—as Adolph Reed, Jr., put it—or more generally an example of the "incorporation of the restless and cheeky"—as Joan Roelofs has defined the role of philanthropy in American capitalism—that emerged out of the desire of powerful white interests, including the Ford Foundation, to restore social stability in the era of the riots not simply through the iron fist but also by the velvet glove of black leadership development.[22]

In short, the asymmetry of the power relationship between the Ford Foundation and its black grantees meant that the Foundation's social vision prevailed. Thus this book reminds us that black power developed within a larger American context that was shaped largely by the imperatives of elite white power, including the Ford Foundation's. What resulted from this process were the limited forms of institutionalized multiculturalism and diversity with which we live today, undoubtedly inspired by the call for black self-determination but also indelibly shaped by the prerogatives of powerful white interests and their deep investment in the status quo.

*   *   *

The period covered by this book represents a key period of transition in twentieth-century American history, as the Fordist, Keynesian, and statist New Deal era began to move into postindustrial, trickle-down, and laissez-faire neoliberalism. Among the consequences of this sea change was the end of the civil rights movement. Reliant upon a responsive, redistributive, and expansive federal government as the target of its most successful activism, the black freedom struggle began to fragment and shrivel into isolated community-scale struggles, just as outsourcing and globalization pushed the urban black poor further down into chronic unemployment or onto the bottom rung of the service sector. Meanwhile, as the economy restructured, conservatives skillfully repositioned the public discourse from the reasons behind black poverty and the urban crisis to notions of individual responsibility and morality.[23]

This intellectual and policy transition was predicated on a growing consensus about the utter failure of the larger 1960s urban liberal project, in which the Ford Foundation was a key player. In this telling, "limousine liberals," the Foundation's president and officers among them, had fomented black urban unrest in their unholy alliance with African American militants; according to this critique, liberal social engineering had deepened rather than solved the urban crisis. This narrative of mismanagement and wrong thinking produced a straw man for the conservative counterrevolution, which continues to use the trope of the "liberal elite" to explain what brought down urban America. This story of liberal-induced decline has helped the political right toward its goal of a new urban order that eschews statist solutions for free-market economics, the privatization of social services, law-and-order policing, and workfare to provide for the poor.[24]

Among the many historical inaccuracies of this account of liberal misrule is the fact that the Ford Foundation was actually an active participant in this transition by helping to establish the basis of a new urban and racial liberalism that was little different from what conservatives would claim as their new urban model. Bundy and his officers made this shift the hard way, when their active engagement with black power did not produce the assimilationist results that their developmental separatism had presumed. Learning from their putative mistakes, as their demonstration-based research was intended to allow them to do, Foundation staff refined and narrowed their vision and ambitions for creating black equality.

First, despite its instrumental role in the conception of Johnson's Great Society, the Foundation came to reject this plan for its failure to quell the urban crisis and the social conflict it created. For example, Bundy and his officers began to rethink their commitment to community action, a Foundation innovation that became a hallmark feature, and key source of criticism, of LBJ's War on Poverty. They came to this conclusion through a difficult experience: after the utter failure of their instrumental support of the decentralization and grassroots community control of ghetto schools in New York City based on a conception of community action through participatory democracy. Instead of creating an assimilating "reconnection" of the black community to the public schools as Ford intended through its support of community control, the Foundation found itself at the center of the political firestorm that was to become known as the New York City schools crisis, itself a key harbinger of a new conservative urban politics. While the schools crisis would prove to be an emblematic tipping point in the neoconservative backlash against 1960s urban liberalism, it was also one that led the Foundation itself to reconsider the underpinnings of its urban activism and to pull back from this short-lived experiment.

Furthermore, the backlash against community action, whether practiced by Lyndon Johnson nationwide or by McGeorge Bundy in New York City, obscured the many goals behind Ford's involvement in the schools—including the dismantling of an entrenched public bureaucracy and unionized workforce, and the promotion of local control, self-help, and private-sector involvement in the public schools—which presaged conservative urban public policy. In addition, the Foundation's engagement with black activists for control of their own schools was made on the basis of the same assumptions of black pathology and African Americans' inability to replicate the white ethnic pattern of upward mobility that also shaped conservatives' perspective and action on the urban crisis.[25]

Meanwhile, Bundy and his officers, like their political antagonists, began to look toward the private sector's resources and know-how for the solutions that the federal government had failed to create, an unsurprising direction for a philanthropy based on one of the nation's great industrial fortunes and on whose Board of Trustees in 1970 sat the presidents or chairmen of Ford Motor, Royal Dutch Petroleum, the World Bank, and the investment firm Donaldson, Lufkin & Jenrette. In making this switch, the Foundation also rejected the public turmoil and controversy stirred up by the participatory democracy of its community-action/control approach in order to move to an apolitical and elitist model of economic development to deal with the urban crisis from the top down. Joining with another establishment liberal, Robert F. Kennedy, the Foundation pursued this new strategy by pioneering the community-development corporation, an enduring hallmark institution of the devolved welfare state of competitive nonprofits that began in the Lyndon Johnson era and that has flourished from the Nixon presidency until today. Predating Nixon's election and his call for "black capitalism" to deal with ghetto turmoil, the Foundation's community-development corporations (CDCs) borrowed heavily from the corporate private sector, relying on it for its hierarchical and bottom-line institutional and management model, as well as for the public-private partnerships that became the bread and butter of community development in the neoliberal era.

In reducing its once expansive efforts to foster black equality to the community-development strategy, the Foundation became a leader in fostering other elements of liberalism after the conservative turn. Despite the fact that Ford acknowledged that its CDCs produced no appreciable benefit to the free-falling, postindustrial neighborhoods in which they were located, the Foundation celebrated these agencies for their success in cultivating individual black "public entrepreneurs," including its future president, Franklin Thomas, who then launched themselves successfully into the American meritocracy on the basis of their corporate apprenticeship in the ghetto. Thus the Foundation reduced its once lofty assimilationist goals for African Americans to one of elite development and individual upward mobility. In this way, along with other major Foundation initiatives for minorities, like its commitment to high-art black cultural expression, university black studies programs, and minority postsecondary and graduate education, the Foundation helped to foster the multiculturalism with which we live today, which has little to do with the racial equality that was the ultimate goal of black power advocates. In this formulation, diversity has become merely a value-added feature for elite educational or cultural institutions, or a source of competitive advantage for the private sector in a global marketplace. Meanwhile, back in the inner city, poor black children are fed the thin gruel of multiculturalism to foster racial self-esteem in a model of affective education, first promoted by the Foundation in the 1960s, which became a cheap substitute for policy and programs attacking the material and structural sources of academic underachievement.[26]

Thus, the ambivalent legacy of postwar American liberalism not only created many political opportunities for the conservative ascendancy but also allowed liberals to fit comfortably within the ideological and policy mainstream of neoliberal America. This surprising confluence reminds us that the differences between American liberals and conservatives play out within the narrow scope of the rhetorical conventions and policy alternatives of American politics, all of which have been inexorably shaped by the legacy of the paradoxes of American history, not least those of the eighteenth-century American liberalism from which today's putative "conservatives" and "liberals" are both descended.

Connecting the Foundation's legacy to the present political and economic context also helps to position American philanthropy today, which has reached an important juncture as a new group of West Coast philanthropists, whose wealth is based on the information economy, has superseded older, East Coast foundations, like Ford, whose wealth and influence were based on industrial fortunes gained during the nineteenth and twentieth centuries. In this new era, the Bill and Melinda Gates Foundation has taken the place of the Ford Foundation, both as the richest philanthropy in the world and in terms of its enormous policy influence at home and abroad. While the Gateses and other latter-day philanthropists claim a new model for U.S. philanthropy, on closer inspection their microfinance and charter-school schemes, their assimilationist goals for the poor and outcasts based on the principle of equal opportunity for individuals within the capitalist system, and their belief in themselves as catalysts for social change all resonate deeply with the Ford Foundation's experience and actions in the McGeorge Bundy era.[27]

*   *   *

New York City in the 1960s played an emblematic role in the historical processes explored in this book, both in being the nation's largest city and in its transition from an industrial center into the headquarters of global capitalism. First, New York was home to Harlem, the iconic "everyghetto" of the popular imagination and a metonym for black America.[28] Traditionally the biggest and most densely populated urban black community in the country, Harlem was formed by oncoming waves of black in-migration to New York City, along with the ongoing poverty and marginalization of its residents. Harlem became a symbol for the urban crisis and the so-called "Negro problem" of black assimilation to the city and modern life. Conversely, this very ghettoization made Harlem a most promising potential site of racial regeneration and African American self-determination. In fact, it was often credited for being the birthplace of black power, having been the site of the greatest successes of black nationalism to date, that of Marcus Garvey in the 1920s and Malcolm X in the 1950s and 1960s. While it retained its symbolic value, by the 1960s Harlem was not the city's only significant black community. However, the growth of enormous postwar "second ghettoes" in Central Brooklyn and the Bronx simply reinforced New York City's position as the capital of black America.[29]

Meanwhile, New York served an equally emblematic role in the history of liberalism. With a long history of labor activism and radical politics, a population made up largely of the white ethnic working class and their upwardly mobile children, and a highly unionized workforce, New York City embodied the statist and redistributionist New Deal liberalism of the Fordist era, as well as the electoral coalition that solidified this approach. All of that began to change during the period covered by this study, when deindustrialization and the city's rise as a center of finance capital radically transformed its economy. The response of John Lindsay, the liberal reform mayor swept into office in 1966 to deal with the resultant urban crisis, was very much in keeping with Lyndon Johnson's welfarist War on Poverty. However, by the end of Lindsay's tenure as mayor in 1973, this approach had been effectively discredited by its opponents for bankrupting the city and he left office with the electorate bitterly divided by race over the entitlement of the poor to state aid. The fiscal crisis that followed Lindsay's mayoralty ushered in a new era of political and policy conservatism, symbolized by the election of Mayor Edward Koch in 1977, which supported the city's repositioning as a preeminent hub of world finance and tourism. Thus, New York City encapsulated the tectonic shifts happening in cities all over the United States and the rest of the industrialized world in the last quarter of the twentieth century, in terms of both its global prominence and the extremity of its political and policy pendulum swing. In fact, as the embodiment of both liberal and neoliberal American urbanism, New York's narrative of transition has served as a morality tale for commentators from both the right and the left.[30]

Amid this transition, Bundy and his officers sought a solution to the urban crisis and black power's challenge to liberalism by using New York City as a high-profile testing ground. New York City performed a metropolitan function for Bundy's Foundation. It located demonstrations of new policy initiatives in New York, especially as they pertained to African Americans, in order to influence the rest of the nation. At the core of the book are case studies of three such demonstrations, which exemplified the political, cultural, and economic programs for "minority rights" actually initiated, and not simply funded, by the Ford Foundation. These were also the three focal points of the black power project for African American self-determination. The first case study examines the Foundation's fundamental and decisive role in the convulsive citywide crisis over school decentralization. In supporting black activists' bid for community control of New York City's school system, the Foundation fostered an educational model that was antithetical to school integration but still developmentalist and assimilationist in intent. The second case explores the Foundation's engagement with the Black Arts movement through the funding of all-black theater. In particular, I compare the Ford

Foundation experiences with the off-Broadway Negro Ensemble Company and the separatist and afrocentric New Lafayette Theatre in order to explore the Foundation's multiple agendas in fostering multiculturalism. The third case outlines the Foundation's role in pioneering community-development corporations, helping to create a nationwide model to deal with the crises of the inner city, primarily through the development of a strong leadership class. In this section, I examine grants to Brooklyn's Bedford-Stuyvesant Restoration and Development and Service Corporations, the Foundation's first and greatest commitment in its national CDC initiative.

This New York strategy worked for the Foundation in part because of the attention these grants garnered precisely because they were located within the city. Thus Bundy and the Foundation were able to collaborate closely with both John Lindsay and New York's Senator Robert Kennedy, the two most celebrated establishment liberals of the era. Dozens of other eminent figures were promoters of or commentators on Ford's New York efforts, or they found fame because of their involvement with them. President Kennedy's widow, Jacqueline Onassis, promoted an African textile business, and architectural superstar I. M. Pei designed a superblock in Bedford-Stuyvesant funded by the Restoration and Development and Services Corporations, on whose corporate board sat luminaries of the intertwined postwar policy, corporate, and financial establishment—C. Douglas Dillon, André Meyer, William S. Paley, Benno E. Schmidt, Thomas J. Watson, Jr., Roswell Gilpatric, and David Lilienthal. Virtually every prominent public intellectual in America, from the left's I. F. Stone to the right's Norman Podhoretz, had something to say about the New York schools crisis. Meanwhile, the Ford Foundation delighted in the success stories of the individuals its minority programs had helped bring to national attention. For example, Denzel Washington, Samuel Jackson, Phylicia Rashad, and scores of other prominent African American actors, playwrights, and directors first came to wider attention thanks to their work with the Negro Ensemble Company, whose New York City location meant that it was at the heart of the nation's theater scene. Meanwhile, Franklin Thomas, Bundy's successor, initially gained prominence in Brooklyn as the president of the Bedford-Stuyvesant Restoration Corporation, while the "graduates" of other Foundation CDCs from other parts of the country, including former mayors Wilson Goode of Philadelphia and Henry Cisneros of San Antonio and Congressman Esteban Torres of Los Angeles, followed in his footsteps to eminence.

Cisneros and Torres's inclusion on this list calls attention to the fact that

the Foundation dealt not only with African Americans in pursuing its pluralistic vision for the nation but also with other nonwhite groups as well as
women. However, the Foundation's work with African Americans largely set
the stage for these other groups. Just as New York City served as a demonstration area for Ford's programs, the Foundation's pioneering work on what
its officers once called the "Negro problem" remained their reference point in
work with other "minorities" and their claims. So, for example, Ford helped
found and underwrite the Mexican American and Puerto Rican Legal Defense and Education Funds, the Southwest Council of La Raza, and a number
of CDCs, all in recognition of Latino claims. However, these institutions and
initiatives were modeled on black "leadership" organizations like the NAACP
and its own Legal Defense and Education Fund or the National Urban
League or on the Foundation's existing community-development efforts in
black ghettoes, in an effort to help organize Hispanics into what Foundation
officers considered a "recognizable" interest group in the black mold. As late
as 1977, Bundy would still "shorten matters," as he put it, by making "black"
synonymous with "minority," even when referring to racial equality issues in
California, where Chicanos greatly outnumbered African Americans.[31]

*   *   *

The story of the Ford Foundation's engagement with the question of black assimilation begins in its formative years as a central institution of and actor for
the postwar liberal establishment, and thus this time frame is representative
of this powerful group's social-engineering ethos and vision for the nation.
At that moment, all social problems were solvable, at least according to the
Foundation's can-do trustees and officers, who believed wholeheartedly in
the ability of the modern American social and economic system to lift all
boats. Their self-confidence and optimism spurred the activism that by the
1980s would allow Foundation officers to boast that they and their predecessors had played an important role in diversifying the nation's highest reaches,
thus reinvigorating American institutional life and providing the black community and other minorities with representation in the American body politic according to their model of pluralism. In fact, this strategy could claim
its ultimate victory in the 2008 election of Barack Obama. The Foundation
could also boast that it had made an instrumental contribution to the diversification of mainstream American culture, thanks to its multicultural agenda
for education and the arts.

However, despite these achievements this book tells the story of racial liberalism's diminishing expectations in the post-civil rights era. Bundy's Foundation began its tenure seeking fundamental institutional reform through the redistribution of political power in order to pursue its assimilative model of social development for the ghetto. By the late 1970s, the Foundation had abandoned any notion of genuine transformation in the inner cities, where economic conditions and social marginalization had worsened since the 1960s. By that point, the Ford Foundation openly acknowledged its failure in this regard and had stripped down its objectives largely to bolstering its ongoing success in fostering individual minority leadership. In so doing, the Foundation was simply acknowledging the limitations of its racial liberalism, as well as its corresponding unwillingness or inability to confront the intractable structural problems facing the inner city. Economic and political power were not unlimited resources to be shared without conflict among all members of American society once the barriers to opportunity were removed, contrary to what the Foundation had once believed.

PART I

Sizing Up the Urban Crisis

Chapter 1

Modernizing Migrants

In 1967, the Ford Foundation's annual report included a special message from its president, McGeorge Bundy. Writing in the context of what he termed "the terrible riots of 1967," Bundy's essay nevertheless put forth a relentlessly positive argument about the nation's racial future, despite what he acknowledged were the dire facts of its past and present. Among these, he highlighted America's long and defining history of institutionalized racial exploitation, the white backlash that had met African Americans' freedom struggle, and the separatism of black power that marked their abandonment of the nation and its liberal promise of equality. Regardless of this dismal record, Bundy pledged that American society would "solve this problem." "The only possible final outcome," he claimed, was to emerge on "the far side of prejudice," to a future in which whites came to "regard as natural the equality" that today "many of . . . us see only as logical." "The preachers of hate" both black and white, he wrote, "who seem so much the men of the moment are in fact merely spume on the wave of the past." They were "temporary" obstructions to the march of progress for black people in a United States whose institutions "will have to be open to all" and in which "Negroes" would "take their share of leadership."

Bundy based his optimism on the "effort" that the Ford Foundation and other "leaders of good will and peaceful purpose" were willing to take to make his vision come true. "There is nothing automatic about any part of the American Dream," he told his readers. Instead, those "who want peaceful progress toward equality will have to work for it" with "speed and imagination, as well as steady determination." Even individuals and institutions, which "have done good work in the past will be found wanting if they do not do still more in the future," he continued, declaring that his "Ford Foundation expects to be measured by this test."[1]

Considering Bundy's promises from the perspective of a future that is much less than he prophesied despite much steadfast hard work, his vision could be dismissed as liberal bravado masking great uncertainty and fear, especially given the conflict-ridden moment at which he was writing. However, that interpretation would have to ignore the virtually unshakeable worldview, identity, and ethos of the postwar liberal leadership class of which Bundy was a dominant member and the Ford Foundation a dominant institution. Bundy's conviction about solving the "Negro problem" was consistent not only with the Foundation's leaders' long-standing ambition and ethos but also more specifically with their thinking and action on race in the United States. While the race issue did not become a singular focus at the Foundation until Bundy's presidency, nevertheless the situation of racial minorities in U.S. society had been one of Ford's central domestic concerns since its emergence as a major philanthropic force in the late 1940s. The "problem" of black assimilation to the mainstream had preoccupied postwar liberals, including those at the Foundation, as a predominant, yet fixable, roadblock to their preeminent goal: the ultimate modernization and flawless operation of the American "system." The activist, social-engineering ethos of this group that fueled this faith was bolstered by its members' elitist self-confidence that expert, technocratic management of state and society could lead to the nation's perfection. McGeorge Bundy's optimism in 1967 testified to the strength of the establishment creed on which the Ford Foundation was resurrected after the Second World War.

The Foundation and the Postwar Liberal Establishment

A fundamental paradox of the Ford Foundation's history was that the founder of the greatest philanthropy of the American century was an outspoken critic of institutionalized charity of any sort. The automobile magnate Henry Ford rejected the industrial philanthropy practiced by his forbears, like Andrew Carnegie and John D. Rockefeller, believing instead that his corporate system of mass production for mass consumption, later labeled "Fordism," had the greatest potential for solving social problems. Nevertheless, Ford felt compelled to create the Foundation in 1936 to shelter his fortune against the Roosevelt administration's antitrust Revenue Act, which threatened his and his family's ongoing control of the company through crippling inheritance taxes that would force them to sell their stock in a public offering. What resulted was the "first" Ford Foundation, a regional, family charity that limited itself in its first decades to building hospitals and museums in Michigan, bearing little resemblance to the behemoth it would become.

Henry's death in 1947, along with the earlier passing of his only child, Edsel, in 1943, would bring about the Foundation's transformation. Both these men's enormous fortunes had to be dealt with in order for the Fords to avoid the Internal Revenue Service and for family members to remain at the company's helm. Consequently, their estates bequeathed what amounted to 90 percent of the company's holdings to the Foundation in the form of nonvoting company stock, keeping the remaining 10 percent for family members. More important, in order to avoid ongoing scrutiny of the now hugely enriched Foundation from the IRS and Congress, Edsel's son, Henry II, changed the philanthropy's very nature, transforming it from a tax shelter serving the family's charitable pet projects into an independent, arms-length instrument of the public trust and a national and international force commensurate with its vast resources.[2]

While Henry Ford II faced considerable outside pressure to remake the Ford Foundation in this way, this move also reflected his own proclivities and dramatic postwar changes in American institutional and intellectual life. He played his part in this transformation at Ford Motor Company, a key player in a key postwar industry. After taking over the company in 1945, Henry II revived its dwindling fortunes by being one of the first corporate executives to latch on to systems analysis, a statistical method first used to assess the effectiveness of military weaponry that would soon become a powerful and ubiquitous corporate management tool. To do so, he brought in the so-called Whiz Kids to Ford's front office, a group that represented the ascendancy of technocratic experts as the key personnel to oversee the large public and private organizations that ran postwar America. This storied group of "organization men" comprised a number of former Air Force specialists, some with strong connections to the Harvard Business School, including Robert Mc-Namara, the future Ford Motor president, U.S. Defense Secretary, and World Bank president. These men's intersecting university, corporate, military, and government ties epitomized the links between these sectors and the growing consensus among their leaders about the path to American prosperity and power. The younger Henry also forged an accord with organized labor after decades of strife at Ford, thus ending the company's long-standing anti-unionism. He negotiated landmark postwar contracts with the United Auto Workers' president Walter Reuther, the quintessential "new man of power" in American labor. Reuther, like Ford, sought higher corporate profits—and hence for Reuther, higher wages and benefits—that labor peace could help bring about. Thus at Ford Motor, Henry II extended the new postwar social consensus about the unlimited potential of corporate capitalism to resolve social conflict and problems in American society.[3]

Ford's reliance on university-trained experts, his confidence in empirical research and analysis to solve management problems, his absolute faith in corporate capitalism as a force of good for all, and his drive for conflict resolution and social consensus all reflected the dominant worldview of those at the top of the system that wrought America's postwar affluence and global dominance. Indeed, he belonged to what sociologist C. Wright Mills called in 1956 the "power elite" and what opponents from both the New Right and New Left of the 1960s would come to label the liberal "establishment." This was the like-minded and interconnected group of American corporate, government, and military leaders who emerged during and after the Second World War to shepherd the nation's institutions, including philanthropy, to reflect, manage, and exploit the reality and complexities of worldwide economic and military dominance, Cold War conflict, and corporate ascendancy.[4]

While members of the establishment often abjured the label when applied to them, and despite the fact that the designation did not come into wide popular use until critics began to use it as a pejorative in the 1960s, it was nevertheless an apt descriptor for this group. Its members did not constitute a secret cabal, even though many of them and their influence were virtually unknown to the public given their behind-the-scenes role in the economy, public affairs, higher education, and the media. Nor did they control politics or policy. In fact, they often faced crippling opposition to their objectives, especially when it came to their aims for American society. They did not even make up a clearly defined social category. Nevertheless, they amounted to a dominant circle of exceptional influence whose ideology shaped a prevalent consensus on American foreign and domestic policy at the height of American world power, from the Second World War until the great anti-establishment rebellions of the Vietnam/black power era. They were not only corporate titans like Henry Ford II but also the leaders of other presiding postwar institutions—corporate law firms, investment banks, elite universities, news media, philanthropies, and think tanks—who often also served, as Robert McNamara and many others did, in executive or advisory roles to presidents and high military command.[5]

Beyond anything else, this group's members believed as Henry Ford II did, in corporate capitalism. After all, no one could deny that corporations had supplied and ensured the success of the "arsenal of democracy" that sealed the Allied victory in the Second World War. Why not assume, then, that the system that allowed this success would ultimately be responsible for securing a worldwide Cold War military and ideological triumph for the United States over the Soviet Union and the Communist system? At home, a widespread understanding that the corporate system had facilitated both the mass production and mass consumption that led to the astounding abundance and upward mobility of postwar American society bolstered the establishment's faith in American capitalism. Establishment members believed that this apparent economic miracle could save the world by lifting everyone out of poverty, thus erasing class conflict and other social differences through a universal, beneficent modernity that would result in world peace. They had no reason to be anything but entirely sincere in these convictions about the greatness of the American way; arguably they were among the most powerful people from the most powerful nation on earth, which had earned that distinction largely by hewing to their model for domestic prosperity and international influence.[6]

Given this faith in the corporate system, the overarching establishment objective for the postwar period was to create the social, political, and economic conditions that its members believed would best allow the American economy to expand. In doing so, they helped to shape a distinctive postwar liberalism that would dominate American public policy through the Lyndon Johnson era. Unlike earlier generations of elites in the industrial period, including figures like Henry Ford, Sr., leading figures in the postwar establishment, like his grandson, believed in the state as an ally in securing the nation's economic and social progress. Both the New Deal and the Second World War had taught establishment members that the government had an important role to play in corporate capitalism's smooth functioning. This belief in a "welfare-market society," a term used in the late 1940s by liberal public intellectual Walter Lippmann and his young protégé McGeorge Bundy, emerged largely through observing or, more likely for members of the establishment, participating in the war effort.[7] They had learned of the benefits of Keynesian pump priming through the system of wartime, publicly funded military contracts that cohered as the military-industrial complex during the seemingly endless crisis of the Cold War. They came to understand the importance of state-sponsored social security to the mass consumption that undergirded the postwar economy. Extending the connection between the government and the corporation, the Cold War bolstered the conviction of establishment members that American foreign policy should work actively to extend this American way throughout the world; indeed it was America's international duty to do so. At home, most of them supported the labor peace and economic benefits that would result from more widely distributed wealth if they treated with organized labor on its wage and benefit demands. Politically, they prized the social harmony that they believed would accrue from the meliorist social engineering possible in an expert-managed society free from political interference from below. They sought what historian Arthur Schlesinger, Jr., called the "vital center" that their welfare capitalism suggested, and they disdained any form of what they considered political extremism. Unsurprisingly, they eschewed any taint of Communism, but they also hated the demagoguery of the right. For them the right-wing populism of figures like Joseph McCarthy (who, in his antiliberal vendetta, often targeted members of the establishment in his witch hunt) demonstrated the dangerous irrationality of the masses and the disruptive social conflict inherent in mass politics.[8]

This group of expert managers and social engineers supplanted the older "Eastern" establishment of Mayflower-descended bluebloods and Gilded Age industrialists and their progeny, although a significant minority straddled both old and new elites. The postwar establishment was relatively plural and meritocratic—although virtually lily-white and all male—and its members would work to make it even more diverse in decades to come, at least compared to the hermetically sealed circle of Boston/Philadelphia/New York WASP "society" that had preceded it. A sampling from the inner circle of the quintessential establishment president, John F. Kennedy, gives a sense of this diversity. It included public school-educated Californians like Robert McNamara and descendants of working-class Jewish immigrants like MIT economist and modernization theorist Walt Rostow, as well as the Boston Brahmin, Harvard dean, and future Ford Foundation president, McGeorge Bundy. Thus this postwar formation constituted an aristocracy of talented men: some had worked their way into the establishment, and all had distinguished themselves in more than one of the key settings of the American century. This meritocracy reflected how aptitude and expertise had begun to supplant ancestry for the postwar establishment—an essential shift at the top for the effective functioning of the expansive institutions that now drove the nation.[9]

With the understanding that they were the best and brightest, and presumably the only ones with the know-how and talent to manage America effectively, establishment members regarded themselves as the guardians of the national interest. Given the enormous wealth at their disposal, as well as their collective identity as the clearheaded and expert stewards of the public good, this group sought private means in order to intervene independently in American society. In doing so, establishment members followed the lead of Gilded Age industrialists by using philanthropy as their activist instrument, remaking the first generation of industrial foundations—Rockefeller, Carnegie, etc.—to serve their postwar aims. Even more exciting was the prospect of an astronomically enriched Ford Foundation remade to their specifications.[10]

A brief narrative of the Foundation's postwar renaissance gives a sense of how completely it was the creation and tool of a diverse yet interconnected group of powerful men. In 1948, Henry Ford II began the Foundation's transformation by appointing a study committee and advisory panel to oversee the reorganization of the Foundation; this panel consisted of two nonfamily-member trustees: Donald K. David, dean of the Harvard Business School and recently appointed director of Ford Motor; and Karl T. Compton, president of MIT and a director of the Rockefeller Foundation. David and Compton chose H. Rowan Gaither, Jr., to oversee the reorganization. Gaither was a San Francisco lawyer who had government experience both in the New Deal and as the assistant director of the wartime Radiation Laboratory at MIT under Compton, where Gaither coordinated government and military contracts and liaised between academic science and industry in the development of radar, a transformative wartime technology. Gaither had recently become the president of the newly created RAND Corporation as it moved to become the most influential policy think tank of the postwar period. The Foundation trustees' acceptance of Gaither's report—which took a year to produce, and involved interviewing hundreds of academic, policy, and philanthropic experts nationwide—in turn led to the appointment of Paul Hoffman to be the first president of the "new" Ford Foundation. Hoffman was the former administrator of the U.S. government's Marshall Plan to reconstruct Europe, founder of the Committee of Economic Advisors (a powerful postwar policy institute), and the former president and future chairman of the Packard-Studebaker auto company.[11]

Hoffman and Gaither, who eventually succeeded Hoffman as Foundation president in 1953, answered to an active board of trustees, whose most prominent members were academic leaders like Compton and David and corporate chiefs like Charles E. Wilson, the president of General Electric, and John J. McCloy, a corporate lawyer who in 1953 became chairman of America's largest bank, Chase National. Wilson and McCloy's purview extended beyond their firms and the Foundation to the highest reaches of American domestic and foreign policy. Over his career, Wilson was the vice chair of the War Production Board during the Second World War, the chair of Harry Truman's postwar Committee on Civil Rights, and the director of the Office of Defense Mobilization, an enormously powerful agency established during the Korean War that set into place the federal policies undergirding the Cold War's military-industrial complex. Meanwhile McCloy, whom journalist Richard Rovere dubbed the "chairman of the American establishment," acted as FDR's Assistant Secretary of War, served as the postwar president of the World Bank, oversaw the creation of the Federal Republic as the U.S. High Commissioner to Germany, and, in 1954, when he joined the Ford Foundation's Board, assumed the chair for the Council on Foreign Relations.[12]

These snapshots of the reconfigured Foundation's leadership serve to underline these men's enormous influence in American public and foreign policy, as well as in business. They embodied the new postwar fluidity between the private and public sectors, helping to create links among the corporate world, the university, the executive branch of government, and the nonprofit sector. Most significant in this new dynamic was the faith that all these men had gained in the state and the possibilities of large-scale planning and engineering, a direct outcome of their experience with the powerful government agencies created to deal with the crises of the New Deal and Second World War. They now sought to broaden these instruments to oversee the expansion of the Fordist system and thus solidify American affluence and global influence.[13]

The accomplishments and authority of this new leadership also amply demonstrated the Foundation's place at the center of the American postwar public policy, where it functioned as a kind of private consultancy, advising decision makers throughout the Cold War state. Reflecting this role, the Foundation's officers felt an obligation to public service or, in other words, a desire to extend their values and goals to the nation and the world. They did so secure in a faith not only that their vision represented the public interest but also that they themselves and their protégés were the best stewards of that interest. Gaither would later tell a congressional committee that his Study Committee traveled from coast to coast in order to learn what the "people" wanted from the Foundation "in the interests of the public welfare." Instead, as journalist Dwight Macdonald pointed out, Gaither did not talk to the "people" but to "experts who . . . thought they knew what 'the people' wanted, or ought to want."[14]

So, according to those who drove the reorganization and mission of the new Ford Foundation, what should the people want? From its beginnings as a national philanthropy, the Foundation promoted a vision of domestic peace through socially engineered American pluralism to deal with the problems facing society. Thus, the ascendant policy elite who reconceived the Foundation turned it into the preeminent private advocate and funder of social science expertise in the United States. In doing so, they helped to catapult issues of "human relations" and nonviolent conflict resolution to equal significance as nuclear advantage for fighting the Cold War both abroad and at home. Such a focus clearly appealed to the professional interest and worldview of the closely knit establishment clique of university and foundation administrators, think-tank heads, and high-level public- and private-sector professional managers who made up Gaither's Study Committee. It also made particular sense in the wake of the Holocaust, amid the populist hysteria of the Second Red Scare, and on the cusp of the civil rights movement. Those who forged the new program for the Ford Foundation thus sought to promote expert social science as the right tool to contain the complex and potentially devastating threat that all of these elements posed to American prosperity, geopolitical advantage, and domestic peace.[15]

The Gaither Report

The expansive mission of the new Ford Foundation prompted national media attention, including prominent public intellectual Dwight Macdonald's lengthy three-part 1955 profile in the *New Yorker*, which he would then adapt and publish as a book, *The Ford Foundation: The Men and the Millions*.[16] Macdonald's fascination, in part, had to do with how the Foundation's men had used its enormous wealth to operationalize the activist ethos of postwar liberalism, thereby framing a new role for the philanthropy. That mission was encapsulated in Gaither's report, drily titled the *Report of the Study for the Ford Foundation on Policy and Program*. On the surface, this blueprint recalled the high-minded mission of the Foundation's philanthropic forbears to promote the well-being of all mankind. Thus like the Carnegie Corporation or the Rockefeller Foundation, the Ford Foundation's aim was not "merely to treat symptoms and temporarily alleviate distress, but rather to eradicate the causes of suffering" worldwide and at home. In short, as a powerful "catalytic agent," it would pursue its "general purpose of advancing human welfare."[17]

What was new about the Foundation was the way in which Gaither and the board of trustees intended to achieve this impressive ambition. Not "content to concern itself only with man's obvious physical needs," as older foundations had done through innovations in medical research, public health, and agriculture, the Foundation would focus on a new area, human behavior. Further, it would pursue this goal as a way to further America's global leadership and domestic peace in the Cold War era. Hence, the report called for "affirmative action," meaning in this case proactive grantsmanship by the Foundation, to eliminate "the basic causes of war," to advance "democracy on a broad front," and to strengthen democracy's "institutions and processes."[18]

The Study Committee's interpretation of these lofty goals and challenges in the Gaither report was a major, early articulation of the postwar modernization ethos, which was a key Cold War ideological formation that served establishment liberals' self-confident worldview and ambitions for America and the world. They believed that the methods of a technocratic state led by trained elites connected to the corporate sector, and perfected by Americans during the New Deal, Second World War, and the Marshall Plan, were required to spark, speed, and shepherd the tricky transition from agrarian tradition to industrial modernity everywhere, particularly in the postcolonial societies of the newly established "third world." America's postwar international role gave liberals the confidence, wherewithal, and mission to take on this work, while the Cold War lent this task urgency in the competition between American and Soviet forms of modernity for the hearts and minds of newly independent peoples.[19]

This developmentalist creed, which would be articulated formally as modernization theory, infused American social science and then foreign policy throughout the 1950s and 1960s, reaching its apogee with John F. Kennedy's rise to the White House. However, belief in and agreement on modernization stretched far beyond the academy or foreign policy circles; in fact, it was a fundamental driver of American postwar liberalism's activism in defining human progress and how it must best happen at home as well as abroad. Indeed, the Gaither report defined all of the Foundation's major aims in terms of modernization, not only internationally but domestically as well.[20]

American modernizers believed that the model of urban, industrial capitalism that had been inexorably transforming the United States since the Gilded Age represented the height of human achievement, or modernity. However, modernity for them represented far more than an economic system; it was a total social condition in which erstwhile agrarian "traditionals" were liberated from the fetters of race, tribe, superstition, feudalism, and the land in order to be assimilated into a homogeneous, rational, individualized urbanity. They would then be free to compete for the rewards of a technologically advanced, mass consumer society. While the transition process to modern life and selfhood might be difficult, ideally the end result was a society defined by the social peace wrought by consensus, particularly about the good life produced by modernity and the corporate capitalism and attendant political and social systems that had achieved it.[21]

Developing a model for how such adjustment could be achieved in order to overcome social dislocation and conflict became a major imperative for American philanthropy at the time of the new Ford Foundation's inception. Representatives from the Rockefeller Foundation and Carnegie Corporation who sat on the Study Committee's advisory panel intended that a significant portion of the Ford Foundation's bounty would be used to spearhead an effort in which their philanthropies would participate to create a new, interdisciplinary, and theoretically robust and unified social science to explain and ultimately shape human behavior according to the tenets of modernization. The Gaither report summarized the prerogative to create this macroscopic social science: "In the Committee's opinion the evidence points to the fact that today's most critical problems are those which are social rather than physical in character—those which arise in man's relation to man rather than in his relation to Nature." "Here," they concluded, "is the realm where the greatest problems exist, where the least progress is being made, and where the gravest threat to democracy and human welfare lies."[22]

Ultimately, the Foundation disbursed almost three-quarters of the approximately $86 million spent in a massive Ford-Rockefeller-Carnegie effort to build university social sciences between 1949 and 1958, and it served a similar role when it funded the Social Science Research Council. In doing so, it played a pivotal role in the postwar expansion, elevation, and prestige of social science. For example, the Foundation largely underwrote the Department of Social Relations at Harvard University, transforming sociologist Talcott Parsons's incubator of modernization theory into a full-fledged laboratory for the new field. It also provided start-up money for key international studies programs like the Russian Research Center at Harvard and the Center for International Studies at MIT, which shaped American foreign policy and development efforts during the Cold War. Foundation officers, like political scientist Francis X. Sutton, played important roles in the network of scholars working in the area of modernization theory, while McGeorge Bundy

worked hand in hand with Ford while he was Harvard's dean of arts and sciences so that the university's Department of Social Relations would become
the jewel in the crown of his faculty and indeed of the whole of American
social science.[23]

While the foreign policy objectives of the modernization approach were
obvious and laid out in a number of treatises, domestic goals were less explicit, given America's putative place at the peak of human progress. However, the Gaither report made explicit that a modernizing mission remained
for America, which explained in part the foundations' preoccupation with
understanding and shaping human behavior. In the highly advanced United
States, where, unlike within the "developing" world, the economy and technology had already achieved mass prosperity, modernization could be boiled
down to a problem of behavioral adjustment. As Gaither and his committee constantly reminded their readers, the American "social structure [was]
undergoing profound change," "from a rural, agricultural, and relatively simple society to one which is urban, industrial, and highly complex." Unfortunately, "the slowness of people to adjust themselves to such vast and rapid
changes" had resulted in "dislocations and breakdowns." This "transition" resulted in both "political, economic, and social unrest" and the "re-examination
and challenge" of "basic political and moral principles." Indeed, there existed
a "backlog of situations" creating this unrest, thus demonstrating the need
for Americans and their institutions to adjust to modernity.[24]

Liberal social scientists and their benefactors found plenty of "situations"
in postwar society that confirmed their thesis about Americans' maladjustment to modernity. The Gaither report's authors, for example, writing on
the brink of the right-wing populism of the Second Red Scare, warned that
through "suspicion, hysteria, or expediency, we may compromise [demo-
cratic] principles," thanks to the vulnerability of an unsophisticated populace
to the allure of mass politics.[25] At the other end of the political spectrum, the
"lack of industrial peace" of the immediate postwar period demonstrated the
"destructive instability" created by a restive workforce that was seduced by
socialism and had failed to understand the promise of Fordism.[26]

Finally, the wartime and postwar urban migration of African Americans
out of the rural South and into American cities presented the classic peasant-
to-proletarian problem of modernization around the world. More specifically,
ongoing Jim Crow in the South and white opposition nationwide to African
Americans' movement out of peonage also demonstrated both the uneven
development of the United States as well as the irrationality of white racism

in its blockage of black progress, and hence full American modernity. What brought this "problem of minority tensions and race relations" together with right-wing populism and class conflict in the minds of the Study Committee's liberals was its potential for unrest.[27] "[I]ntergroup hostilities weaken our democratic strength by dissipating important resources of energy in internal conflicts," Gaither summarized, "and by swelling the ranks of malcontents who constitute the seed bed for undemocratic ideologies." Furthermore, such conflict blocked "positive opportunity for the development by individuals of their full potentialities."[28]

As these excerpts suggest, while the Gaither report identified the conflicts over African American assimilation as one of the central challenges to national development, it did not consider this issue to be unique, but rather only as part of the larger matter of the conflicts blocking American modernization. For the modernizers of the liberal establishment, any kind of sectarian conflict or minority claim, including those involving race and ethnicity, represented an irrational diversion from the nation's mission to promote an expansive corporate capitalism that would ultimately lift all boats and erase all differences, at home and worldwide. In fact, it was precisely the geopolitical importance of convincing the world's people of the beneficence of the American way that had first brought postwar white leaders' attention to the problems of racial inequality, an issue that they had previously almost entirely ignored. White Americans' acceptance and perpetuation of racial inequality in the face of the black struggle against Jim Crow presented a particular public relations problem for the nation's modernizing mission in the nonwhite third world. These Cold War imperatives, beyond any other factor, impelled the Foundation's leaders, like other white elites, including Presidents Truman, Eisenhower, and Kennedy, to take action on the issue of racial inequality. As the Gaither report decorously put it, "The attitudes and actions of Americans sometimes seem incomprehensible to our friends and allies abroad, who speak of their confusion at the disparity between the words and deeds of our democracy." Supplying them "with examples of democratic philosophy at work may in the long run prove to be the most important part of our logistics in the ideological war."[29]

While the Foundation's creators recognized the internal and external perils caused by racial conflict among other problems of modernization, Gaither's report reflected a supreme confidence in overcoming all challenges to American democracy, including those presented by the black freedom struggle. Like all snags to national progress, racial conflict and differences could be solved through a universal understanding of human relations, a key conviction that operationalized modernization theory both at home and overseas. From this perspective the "Negro problem" was a difficult one, to be sure, but no different than any other, either in its root of premodernity or in its solution of a predetermined modernization.

In seeing racial conflict and other challenges to American progress in this way, Gaither and his committee betrayed what scholars have recognized variously as the dominant attitudes of "pessimistic" or "paranoid optimism" and "believing skepticism," from which liberal policymakers approached all social issues in the modernization era.[30] A postwar affluent society, brought about through the technical and managerial mastery of corporate, government, and university leaders like those who had shepherded the Foundation's remaking, meant that the United States now had both the expertise and wherewithal to move up the hierarchy of human needs, from solving physical and material conflicts and problems to social ones. In this "postcapitalist" and "postideological" society, liberals believed that the conflicts of industrial capitalism had been ironed out and a permanent prosperity had been made possible for everyone, in what historian Howard Brick called a newly dominant "wishful theory" of human relations.[31] Thus for the Study Committee, social problems and their solutions were not structural, but rather bureaucratic or therapeutic. So, for example, sharing the optimism of liberal labor economists of the day, the committee saw one of the key sources of conflict in the United States, "the problem of industrial relations," not as a contradiction inherent in capitalism, as it had been interpreted before the war, but as one of "organization and administration in business firms and unions" as well as one of "human behavior," which could be mediated once understood.[32] Similarly, the Gaither report intimated, other intractable issues like African Americans' modernization and assimilation could be successfully managed.

This interpretation of industrial or racial conflicts as organizational and behavioral issues encapsulated the Foundation's understanding of and solution for all American social problems. They were matters of maladjustment, inefficiency, and underdevelopment, of both individuals and institutions that had failed to assimilate to modernity. These vexing, if putatively anomalous and isolated, hitches in an otherwise well-oiled American system could be resolved by pragmatic social scientists acting as social engineers. The Foundation was not alone in this attitude, although it played a key role in promoting it. Understanding society and institutions as fixable "systems" dominated American social science and policy thinking in the postwar period, from business, to the military, to the welfare state.[33] Conceptualizing social problems in this way spurred the Foundation's founders' activist ethos that they could and should work confidently and aggressively to reshape American democracy in order to perfect it. "When morale is high, when men are free, when life is enriched, when self-government operates well, when production flourishes, when there is a pervasive sense of individual dignity and of national unity," the Gaither report intoned, "only then is democracy internally strong and well armed."[34]

Such a flourishing, smoothly functioning system required wise oversight. Thus the Study Committee report was imbued throughout with a focus on developing technocratic expertise, which the Foundation defined as "leadership," and which it found wanting in an American polity that sorely needed it. As Peter Odegard, head of the Political Science division of Gaither's Study Committee, bluntly put his elitism: "One of the characteristic features of Jacksonian democracy . . . was the belief that any citizen of reasonable character and intelligence was qualified to discharge the duties of almost any public office from President to messenger boy." "This democratic 'myth,' false even in Jackson's day," Odegard concluded, "has become grotesque today."[35] Gaither's report elaborated more diplomatically that as the American polity had grown in complexity, "[s]uccessful self-government" meant more than ever that "[a]t every level of government," leadership must be "in the hands of those best fitted to serve." Only by attracting and training "sensitive and intellectually gifted men and women" to become "the nation's more competent technicians and administrators" could the United States ensure that the state worked for "the welfare of the general public" rather than "the special interests of particular groups."[36]

The Study Committee made the "leadership problem" a focus of its educational objectives, believing that university-trained public policy professionals like themselves were at a critical shortage in the United States and that the Foundation was in a unique position to develop these leaders. They were of a certain type, stamped from the mold of the liberal establishment and the self-confident and self-referential group of policy intellectuals who manned the Study Committee. These leaders were to be nonpartisan and nonelected, expert, and "rational," according to the precepts of the mainstream of liberal social science. In short, the leaders were expected to provide, on a smaller scale, the same kind of direction that the Foundation itself believed that it offered to the nation. They would both define and represent the "national interest" as those best able for these tasks.[37]

This form of leadership connects directly to the postwar American establishment's formulation of an ideal American democracy, which was striking in its emphasis on strong, rational, and expert leadership. For America's Cold War elite, democracy was pared down from the expansive populist vision of the New Deal—not to mention the fearsome mass politics that led to the totalitarianism of fascism and Stalinism, and at home the hysteria of McCarthyism—and reduced simply to the electoral sphere. Rational, technocratic experts, bolstered by new management techniques like systems analysis, controlled all other decision making; from on high the best and brightest competed among themselves for votes or, better still, for powerful policy positions outside of electoral oversight. For proponents of this meritocracy, the health of a democracy was based on consensus and consent. Open conflict on substantive issues among elites or dissent from voters marked a democracy gone awry.[38] The Gaither report made this point clear when it warned that while democracy "accepts the fact of conflicting interest" and even promotes the "positive expression of divergent views, aims, and values," "intergroup hostilities weaken our democratic strength by dissipating important resources of energy in internal conflicts and by swelling the ranks of malcontents who constitute the seed bed for undemocratic ideologies."[39]

According to the Gaither report, these hostilities did not originate in systemic problems in American society; instead they were "both a cause and a result of individual maladjustment" to urban-industrial modernity. In fact, the report asserted that the "continuing movement of the great majority of our population to cities has undoubtedly contributed to the spread of personal maladjustment," an individual disorder which "some authorities," according to Gaither, felt was "the most characteristic and widespread ill of our civilization."[40] While this maladjustment had individual consequences, such as unsuccessful personal relationships, it also lay at the root of social conflict.

Therefore, while there was an "urgent demand for a rational basis for planning and responsible decision making," Gaither's report found that an "understanding of human behavior" was just as essential as finding the elite leadership to "maintain the democratic nature of such planning and control" if Americans were "to make adequate personal adjustment to the conflicting and changing demands of modern living."[41] Hence, the Gaither report sowed the seeds for the rise of behavioral science, much of it underwritten by the Ford Foundation, premised on the belief that social unrest was a matter of individual "maladjustment."

Desegregation as Modernity

The Gaither report's finding that the bottlenecks and conflicts of Cold War America were due to the growing pains of modernization drove the Foundation's conception of the problem of racial inequality, along with its solution. In other words, this problem like all others could be cured through a two-pronged social-engineering approach of elite, expert management of American institutions and of individual adjustment to modern society. Furthermore, the challenge of black assimilation in the age of migration was not a unique or intractable problem for the report's authors; it was simply one of many possible "laboratories" for behavioral research to deal with America's crucial transition to modernity.[42] This mass movement, which brought up difficult questions of equal educational opportunity and the "political participation of racial minorities," was just symbolic of many "stubborn life problems," which the Gaither report listed as also including "industrial relations," "old age," and "international and intercultural understanding" in the postwar United States, for which the "swift pace of social invention" required that "the democratic rules be modified."[43]

The report's reassuring complacency in framing the "problem of minority tensions and race relations" obscured the fact that establishment liberals, including those at the Ford Foundation, were already coming to understand racial inequality as a fundamental threat to the national interest, as they defined it.[44] Between 1940 and 1950, about 1.5 million African Americans left the South for northern, midwestern, and western cities, and this migration would continue unabated until 1970. Most of these migrants were the quintessential "traditionals" by the standard of the modernization ethos—former farm tenants struggling to assimilate to urban-industrial modernity. Not only that, but their migration was causing major social conflict from recalcitrant whites throughout the country who wished to prevent any upset to the racial caste system, despite what Gaither and his committee called the major assumption of "democratic theory," that "discrimination and hostility between various groups on the basis of race, national origin, or religion can be kept below the point where the basic well-being of society is threatened."[45] Meanwhile, those black Americans who remained in the South continued to be constrained by the anachronisms of Jim Crow, which prevented the region's social and economic progress, thereby stunting the nation's overall modernization process and presenting a glaring contradiction to the promise of democracy at just the moment that the United States was most fervently trying to sell this pledge to the postcolonial world. Furthermore, American liberals, like most overseas observers, interpreted these racial dynamics from a new, postwar position of resolute antiracialism arising from the worldwide reaction to Nazism and its culmination in the horrors of the Final Solution. No wonder, then, that dealing with America's "Negro problem" became a central aspect of postwar liberalism.[46]

Thus, the Ford Foundation joined other establishment liberals in this period to understand the nation's race problem and to solve it, according to their elite and activist social-engineering vision. This project was undergirded and motivated by the recently published work of Swedish economist Gunnar Myrdal. His magisterial study, initiated and funded by the Carnegie Corporation philanthropy and published as *An American Dilemma: The Negro Problem and Modern Democracy* in 1944, would become the founding document of postwar racial liberalism. Myrdal understood Jim Crow as a pathological distortion of the nation's fundamental creed of democracy and equal opportunity, which was now becoming a national problem in the wake of black migration beyond the South. The result of this contradiction, or dilemma, for Myrdal, was a behavioral one of white prejudice that in turn cramped and distorted African Americans' psyche by preventing them from assimilating into the American mainstream.[47] Myrdal thus called for a program of state-sponsored social engineering based on social-scientific research to facilitate black economic, social, and cultural assimilation through top-down institutional reform to integrate American life, the psychological development of whites and blacks, and intercultural education. Myrdal's thesis and program appealed to what his biographer Walter Jackson called the "immediatist liberal orthodoxy" of the postwar American establishment, which prompted its members to attack even the most intractable social conflict and problems with a self-confidence that betrayed their faith in both technocratic solutions and the truth of the American creed.[48] For a generation of racial liberals, *An American Dilemma* served as the incontestable intellectual foundation on which they validated their beliefs about the white and black behavioral sources of the "Negro problem" and the assimilationist program that would solve it.

This top-down activism began right after the war, when President Harry Truman took unprecedented steps in explicitly recognizing black civil rights as a federal issue. In 1946, he appointed a Committee on Civil Rights, chaired by future Ford Foundation trustee Charles E. Wilson. The committee popularized Myrdal's findings and recommendations by interpreting the rampant racial conflict and violence that followed demobilization and black migration according to the book's central arguments. The widely circulated report of findings, *To Secure These Rights*, recommended, as Myrdal did, a series of public policies promoting civil rights, including the creation of permanent fair employment practices and civil rights commissions, federal protection against lynching, abolition of the poll tax, and a civil rights division for the Justice Department.[49] Truman and his political allies could not get these recommendations past hostile Southern Democrats in Congress, but that did not stop the president from using his executive powers to order the desegregation of the armed forces, as well as to end employment discrimination in the federal civil service and by government defense contractors. Secretary of State Dean Acheson openly supported Truman's domestic civil rights agenda on the grounds of Cold War foreign relations, and Justice Department officials took the unprecedented step of filing amicus curiae briefs for plaintiffs in the civil rights court battles that proliferated during and after the Truman era to overturn legal segregation. Wilson, Truman, and Acheson were no radicals in their civil rights activism; they acted with virtually complete support from a liberal establishment convinced by Myrdal's thesis and were compelled to act on it both by postwar exigencies and by their belief in elite, statist solutions to complete America's modernization.[50]

The Ford Foundation first played its part in this campaign through the Fund for the Advancement of Education (FAE), the most lavishly endowed of a number of quasi-independent subsidiaries into which the "new" Foundation was at first organized in a decentralized structure.[51] Guided by its mandate and soon to be followed by another offshoot, the Fund for the Republic, the FAE worked to effect the peaceful desegregation of American life, both before and after the landmark *Brown v. Board of Education* Supreme Court decision.[52] Along with working to professionalize curriculum development, teacher training, and school-board management nationwide, the FAE advocated for the "equalization of educational opportunity," both in theory and practice. Headed by Clarence Faust, a former dean at Stanford University, and Alvin Eurich, who had been the president of the State University of New York, the FAE's distinguished executives and trustees forged a consensus that sparked the fund's liberal activism on behalf of desegregation.

Like their confrères in the liberal establishment, the FAE's leaders agreed that working to end segregation would be one of their priorities, not primarily because of an ethical impulse to right a wrong, but because of their desire to defend against what they considered racial segregation's manifold threat to

the national interest, as they defined it. The diverse board that conceived the
FAE's priorities encapsulated this rationale. It included Walter Lippmann, the
internationalist intellectual, nationally syndicated columnist, and preeminent advocate of antipopulist elitism; Frank Abrams, chairman of Standard
Oil (now Exxon); and Ralph Bunche, the African American political scientist
and diplomat, 1950 Nobel Peace Prize laureate, and chief researcher for *An
American Dilemma*. These three men were variously inspired by different aspects of the potential benefits of desegregation, but all had a shared faith in
corporate capitalism and the nation's Cold War imperatives. Lippmann, who
had popularized the term "Cold War," saw the FAE's desegregating mission
in geopolitical terms—as a tool of national security that would ultimately develop a broader cadre of experts needed to run the security state, and more
immediately to remove the thorn of educational Jim Crow that was hurting
the United States in its anti-Soviet global mission. Abrams, the corporations'
man, sought to expand access and opportunity to education based on his application of the national manpower approach, which saw the nation's schools
as serving the corporate economy by providing the skilled workers needed
to maintain productivity. According to this model, school segregation simply wasted a potentially valuable labor force by excluding African Americans
from full educational opportunity. Bunche, one of the few nonwhite members
of the postwar establishment, was a stalwart racial liberal by the early 1950s,
belying his earlier leftist beliefs that conjoined racism with capitalist exploitation. He supported the FAE's activism in order to support the NAACP's legal
victories leading to *Brown*, take advantage of the opportunities presented by
the Cold War to promote racial democracy, and open the ever-expanding
corporate economy to African Americans. These motivations connected
Bunche to Lippmann and Abrams and provided the dominant establishment
rationale for the necessity to desegregate American society.[53]

The FAE's activities reflected these men's and the Foundation's belief in the
inevitability and necessity of racial desegregation in a modernizing America.
Two FAE-initiated research efforts, *The Negro and the Schools*, published one
day before the 1954 *Brown* decision, and 1958's *The Future Is Now: The Puerto
Rican Study*, encapsulated the Foundation's position that the modernization
of American society would make African Americans' and other nonwhites'
assimilation into the American mainstream inevitable, if it were managed
rationally. The FAE undertook *The Negro and the Schools* in 1953, when the
NAACP's challenge to public school segregation had reached the Supreme
Court and the end of Jim Crow in education seemed possible. FAE leaders

approached this controversial topic gingerly, most obviously by hiring Harry
S. Ashmore to lead the effort; he was a white Southerner with Confederate
forbears who was a newspaper editor at the *Arkansas Gazette*. Despite his
background, the liberal Ashmore approached desegregation as both an inevitable and necessary endpoint for American modernization. According to
his study, the "great migrations" within the United States since the beginning
of the Second World War had acted "as though a giant egg beater had been
inserted into the center of [the American] population," with enormous consequences for the racial status quo. First and foremost for Ashmore, black
people's internal migration from the premodern rural South to cities around
the nation had "profound meaning for the Negro." "If it did not dislodge him
from the bottom of the economic and social scale," Ashmore explained, "it at
least opened up great gaps above him."[54] Meanwhile, as millions of blacks left
the South, "a substantial number of managerial migrants" had come South
as the "economic time lag"—which had "kept the region at the rear of the
great American industrial march"—was being "wiped out." This latter white
migration meant that in the South "the concepts of an industrial society are
now contesting with those of the agrarians" and that the "isolation . . . necessary to the preservation of the region's special identity is breaking down."[55]
It was only a matter of time, Ashmore intimated, before African Americans
and white Southerners would be integrated into a rational, industrial, and
egalitarian modernity.

Thus Ashmore's study reflected two tenets of postwar racial liberalism—
that American racism was a Southern problem, and that racial inequality was
a product of social retardation that would be dissolved with the wholesale
modernization and rationalization of American society, particularly in the
"backward" South. Ashmore hardly originated these tropes, whose dominance reflected their inherent importance to managing race in the Cold War
era.[56] In fact, they were an intrinsic part of the public relations campaign to
sell the promise of American freedom and democracy around the world, despite the nation's ongoing and growing racial conflict sparked by the African American freedom struggle. By casting the Jim Crow South as the site of
American racism and racists, American racial inequality could be considered
a pathological aberrance, a tumor that could and should be excised from an
otherwise healthy body politic and egalitarian national creed. Furthermore,
if racism were an exclusively Southern problem, it could easily be cast as one
to be solved by social-engineering the region's modernization. Ever since
Franklin Roosevelt, during the New Deal, had labeled the region's under-

development as the "nation's number-one economic problem" and had then launched programs like the Tennessee Valley Authority's ambitious hydro-electric and social engineering program to fix it, American modernizers had been seeking to assimilate this agrarian region into urban-industrial moder-nity. Now it was time to extend this process to the South's racial conventions.[57]

While Ashmore mapped out a reassuringly inevitable process of social modernization for the South, he acknowledged that with African Americans' migration, their "special problems" were "for the first time genuinely national rather than [of] a regional character."[58] He suggested that the root of these problems lay with those who would try to stop modernization's inexorable march, or, in other words, those whites, North or South, who were resisting the "legal and extra-legal pressures against segregation" launched by African Americans.[59] He pointed to the successful desegregation of the armed forces, as well as the largely peaceful incorporation of black voters in the political process as they moved out of the rural South, as hopeful precedents for the possibility of conflict-free school integration. However, first, resistant whites had to understand what Ashmore claimed rational and forward-thinking Southern school officials and politicians already privately acknowledged; they knew, according to Ashmore, that "integration was coming—not over-night and not necessarily as a direct result of court action, but as a result of the larger trends of which it is a symptom."[60] Faced with this apparent inevit-ability, it was in the best interests of white Southerners to embrace reason over ideology and to desegregate their schools before they were compelled to, and to do so as systematically and completely as possible.

Thus, Ashmore's study concluded that African Americans' quest for racial equality marked the logical next step for them in the modernization process, while recalcitrant and irrational whites resisted this unavoidable outcome and thus held up American progress. As Ashmore wrote, "Change must be the central theme in any appraisal that touches upon the relationships be-tween the majority and minority races—but the mere recording of change can be controversial when emotions cancel out the laws of logic."[61] Given the centrality of black pathology that would soon mark racial liberalism, this finding is striking in its making of white irrationality cum behavioral malad-justment as the key roadblock both to black, and hence national, modernity. Nevertheless, it was entirely consistent with the FAE and the Foundation's modernizing and social-engineering missions.

As the FAE worked to convince recalcitrant whites of the unavoidable approach of school desegregation and its modernizing benefits, it also sought to use the schools to engineer the smooth assimilation of migrants to urban modernity. The problem for the FAE was that when migrants were "'different' in race, creed, color or other noticeable characteristics from those in their new neighborhoods, the newcomers will have troubles and they will cause troubles," especially when the newcomers were poor and came from "underdeveloped areas" of the United States, like "the South and Southwest and Puerto Rico."[62] The FAE believed that public schools could play a vital assimilationist role in overcoming this friction, especially if the talents of social workers, psychologists, and other mental health experts could be brought to bear to ease the transition and "adjustment" of new migrants.

These assumptions underlay the FAE's most ambitious grant to deal with this issue: a collaboration with the New York City Board of Education, which began, like the Ashmore study, in 1953. This project, known as the Puerto Rican Study, was funded by grants that amounted to almost $500,000; it sought to develop a behavioral approach to promote assimilation—the ultimate goal of the Ford Foundation's desegregationists—for the tens of thousands of migrants who began streaming from the island into the city every year after the war in the first airborne mass migration in American history. This movement would continue unabated until the end of the 1950s, increasing the Puerto Rican population of the city to an estimated nearly 500,000 by 1956, an eightfold increase since 1940. Puerto Rican migration was roughly comparable to the more than half million African Americans who had arrived in New York City in the 1940s, but that influx had only resulted in a 60 percent growth in the black population. Furthermore, Puerto Ricans were the first large group of offshore newcomers who had landed en masse in New York or any other mainland American city since the imposition of immigration restriction in the 1920s. While Puerto Ricans were U.S. citizens, they were received as unassimilated aliens to American society and culture; they did not speak English, were not considered white, and were erroneously perceived by outside observers as an undifferentiated mass of ill-educated former peasants. Policymakers and social scientists obsessed about this "Puerto Rican problem" because of its specific implications for New York City and also because it was the ultimate test of the possibility of modernization and assimilation in an age of mass, nonwhite migration to American cities. From the universalizing perspective of American modernizers, if a way could be found to manage and execute Puerto Ricans' assimilation, with their extra language barrier, then it would undoubtedly work for other nonwhite groups as well, including black newcomers from within the continental United States.[63]

The final report of the Puerto Rican Study framed the language-learning and cultural-assimilation needs of the migrants as an immediate and imperative challenge to facilitate the "adjustment of Puerto Ricans to a happy citizenship on the mainland." Entitled *The Future Is Now*, and with an image of an empty hourglass as its predominant graphic motif, the study warned that "tomorrow" was "too late" to deal with this problem; if Puerto Rican schoolchildren were "to become contributing members of the community tomorrow, we must help them now to adjust to their new home and language and their new culture."[64]

This was a deliberate effort in social engineering, to develop "effective techniques with which the schools could promote a rapid adjustment of Puerto Rican children and parents to the community and the community to them." While the study's authors believed that "like all other groups that have entered New York City, by the third generation the Puerto Ricans will become socially and educationally assimilated," it sought "acceleration" of this process through a "unified attack on many fronts" by a full spectrum of educational and psychological specialists, including Puerto Rican and other Spanish-speaking professionals. The research findings focused on language acquisition "as the primary method of adjustment," and the study promoted cutting-edge educational assessments and pioneering theories and methods in the new field of English-as-a-second-language instruction. However, the report also recommended fostering "family adjustment" to "new cultural patterns" through psychological testing of students, as well as counseling and housing clinics, and other outreach services for Puerto Rican parents.[65]

While these educational and behavioral efforts went beyond the "normal functions" of the schools, particularly when they offered "counsel and advice to the parents," the authors nevertheless saw these programs as crucial to the "cultural adjustment" of Puerto Rican children, a preoccupation of the study. To further this latter-day Americanization, the study insisted that migrant students attend integrated schools, declaring, in bold, that "to learn English and to adjust to new surroundings . . . is best accomplished in mixed classes of Puerto Rican and native-born children." Thus the study proposed that the schools become the total institution of assimilation, with American-born and English-speaking learning and psychological specialists leading the migrants and their parents to their incorporation. "Whether testing the children or teaching the children, whether meeting the parents or guiding the parents," the study boasted, "the New York schools are provided with materials and approaches to launch the non-English-speaking newcomers to our City into the mainstream of life."[66]

Thus, like Ashmore's work, *The Future Is Now* reflected and reinforced modernizers' faith in the inevitability and desirability of racial desegregation wrought by the force of migration. It also evinced the belief that this resettlement's potential to create racial assimilation and equality would be best, and most quickly and peacefully met, if it were managed by dispassionate experts who deployed the latest in social and behavioral science to smooth the way.

However in the end the FAE's schools projects were brought down by exactly the kind of "irrational" social and political conflict that they were intended to prevent. Between 1952 and 1955, the Ford Foundation was the target of the Cox and Reece committees, two right-wing congressional investigations seeking to connect large American foundations and their grantees with Communist subversion, precisely because of activities like the FAE's promotion of school desegregation. This conservative, populist revolt against postwar philanthropy was indicative of the broader cleavages and confrontations that characterized Cold War America, and this belied liberal modernizers' sanguine view of their society and how to heal what they characterized as its eminently solvable problems. President Truman's failure to pass civil rights legislation thanks to the obstruction of members of his own party, the Second Red Scare—including the Cox and Reece committees—and white Southerners' anger at U.S. Cold War propaganda portraying desegregation as an essential part of America's unfinished business and their region as the nation's primitive backwater were all indicative of an insurgent, postwar American conservatism. Adherents to this creed rejected the elitist, statist, and assimilationist project of social modernity promoted by the liberal establishment, including its definition of white supremacy and racial segregation as a fundamental social problem, and one for which they were the guilty party as the "traditionals" who needed to be fixed. Unsurprisingly, then, a key flashpoint in this ideological conflict was the future of race relations in the United States at the cusp of the Second Reconstruction of the postwar black freedom struggle. Conservative obstruction of modernizers' desegregationist aims may have reinforced the antipopulist elitism of the liberal establishment as well as its members' conviction that they were the nation's only truly modern subjects and hence its best rulers. Nevertheless, liberals were placed on the defensive, if they did not actually capitulate to the right.[67]

During the 1950s, institutions of the liberal establishment like Harvard and Yale purged faculty, administration, and students based on anti-

Communist accusations and in league with the FBI or other government authorities, despite these universities' leaders' professed antipathy to the populist hysteria of McCarthyism and public affirmations of academic freedom. Given this environment, American social scientists focused their attention on the better-funded and less-contentious tasks of modernizing the third world or of apolitical and race-neutral behavioralism, instead of politically suspect social engineering of race relations at home. Meanwhile, the Foundation's trustees were unnerved by attacks from Congress and the conservative press. While these tirades were directed mostly at Ford's other subsidiary, the Fund for the Republic, which dealt more explicitly with issues of civil liberties during the Second Red Scare, in the end these investigations only really affected civil rights activists who came to be blacklisted. In 1958 Foundation leaders shut down the FAE as an independent entity. Furthermore, the Foundation's vice chair, Donald K. David, appeased conservative critics by coming up with an expensive, but effective, public relations scheme in which Ford gave away $500 million in innocuous, blue-chip grants to universities and hospitals. Meanwhile, the Foundation's work in international affairs became its most prestigious grant area and de facto refuge for modernizers, who could no longer safely work within America's own "backward" areas. These concessions spoke to both the power and ubiquity of postwar anti-Communism among liberals and conservatives and the weakness of the Ford Foundation and other establishment players' commitment to racial equality as an issue in the face of the conflict and blowback created by activism that promoted desegregation.[68]

Thus ended the Ford Foundation's short-lived campaign to desegregate American life and, for a time, its activism toward modernization through black assimilation. However, after only a few years the latter goal would be reanimated by the Foundation's ongoing commitment to the principles of the Gaither report, which would continue to guide its grant making for at least thirty years, including its growing commitment to African American assimilation, albeit without integration. As a document identifying modernization as a key national goal, the report provided a road map for the Foundation's ongoing strategy for African Americans: a plan to develop expert leadership to guide the behavioral change necessary to complete migrants' transition to the urban, modern mainstream; a commitment to social engineering and the elite theory of democracy to manage the shift peacefully; and an understanding of social conflict as an irrational, pre- or antimodern reaction to the inevitable progress to modern times.

Chapter 2

The Social Development Solution

In 1962, the Ford Foundation's trustees released *Directives and Terms of Reference for the 1960s*, an implicit call to action against Henry Heald, the Foundation's president. Heald's conservatism and top-down management style had been very attractive to the board just a few years before in the wake of the 1950s Red Scare, but now he seemed stodgy and ill suited for stewardship of Ford's almost limitless resources and the activist ethos of its founding mission. John F. Kennedy's election in 1960 emboldened the Foundation trustees and the rest of the postwar liberal establishment to act on their ambitions for the nation and the world. Modernization and the other, attendant ideological foundations of postwar liberalism reached the peak of their influence during the New Frontier, restoring the trustees' confidence and impatience to make a real mark on American society. In the Kennedy era, the trustees felt that they could and must reaffirm the Foundation's purpose. In the *Directives*, they recommitted themselves to the Gaither report's mission of conflict resolution at home and abroad. They advocated for a program of "courageous experiment," in which the Foundation took "affirmative action" in dealing with an enormous range of domestic and international social problems through demonstrations of new programs and the creation of new institutions, some of which they fully expected might fail but should nevertheless be tested.[1]

The trustees' renewed activism was also prompted by the Foundation's ever-ballooning coffers, a product of the Foundation's 1955 sale of more than $600 million in Ford Motor stock and of ongoing postwar national prosperity. By 1966, the Foundation's $3.3 billion endowment was more than three times that of the Rockefeller Foundation, its nearest rival.[2] In short, like the Bill and Melinda Gates Foundation today, Ford in the 1960s could afford to be ambitious and experimental, and even to make mistakes. As the trustees boasted in the *Directives*, the Ford Foundation was "probably the only private institution which can mount an effort sizable enough to make a critical difference in the course of events," either at home or abroad. [3] Furthermore, ongoing national prosperity had bolstered elite liberals' trust in the American system even beyond the Gaither era's confidence. Such faith, along with growing social-scientific knowledge, meant that they believed more than ever before in the possibility of peaceful social change through systems reform leading to modernization.

This worldview prompted the trustees to address the challenge of the black freedom struggle, and it also shaped their response for how to solve it. Now a key social tension, and not just one of many it had been for Gaither and his committee, the trustees felt a special obligation to address "the social and political implications of the American Negro population's growing dissatisfaction with second-class citizenship."[4] This was a cause that Ford had abandoned in the mid-1950s, but a small number of other philanthropies had continued to support black equality, particularly in the South. As African Americans' self-assertion had grown into a full-blown social movement prompting massive white resistance, the Foundation's trustees and officers, compelled by their animating beliefs, sought to regain the ground they had lost in this field, not by funding the Southern civil rights movement, but by supporting systems reforms from above that would resolve racial conflict, achieve equal opportunity, and restore the nation's equilibrium, particularly in American cities outside the South. The ongoing emergence of a visible and vocal black public made clear the inequities faced by African American communities throughout the nation, which were a stark exception to the aggregate upward mobility of the period. In the affluence of an era that President Kennedy proclaimed the "Decade of Development," modernization once again became a crusade, at home as well as abroad, based on the belief that all could partake in the good life, given the right technocratic tweaks to the system and the appropriate behavioral adjustment.[5]

However, this return to activism did not mean that the trustees had regained confidence in their own early convictions that white racism was at the heart of the "Negro problem" or that desegregation was the solution. Rather, in their zeal for action on this matter, they accommodated their ongoing proscription on desegregationist solutions by supporting an improbable strategy of black assimilation through ongoing racial segregation—namely through an approach that I label developmental separatism—and which the Foundation ultimately called social development. This decidedly counterintuitive strategy exposed the Foundation's brand of liberal reformism; Ford's leaders reliably beat a retreat from "race mixing" at the first hint of the white backlash and social turmoil that this strategy might produce. However, ongoing racial separatism also made sense to Ford's leaders thanks to postwar American liberals' adherence to modernization theory and notions of cultural and behavioral lag among African Americans as the reason for blacks' ongoing poverty and alienation from the mainstream of American life. Both the separatism and developmentalism of its approach, if not its impetus, would provide the Foundation with a link to the demand for black self-determination voiced by black power advocates.

Paul Ylvisaker Confronts the Urban Crisis

Paradoxically, the conservative Heald era at the Foundation had seen the birth of the program that would serve as the template for the kind of bold activism on racial inequality that the trustees were seeking in 1962. While the Foundation deliberately turned its focus away from confronting civil rights in the late 1950s, the Southern struggle and black mass migration out of the region meant that these issues were at the very center of American life in the postwar period. In fact, they were an intrinsic aspect of virtually all domestic concerns. The specific issue that reconnected the Foundation back to the "Negro problem" and the liberal activism needed to deal with it was the "urban crisis" of postwar white and capital flight from cities just as impoverished African Americans were streaming in from the rural South. The man responsible for this revival was Paul Ylvisaker, who joined the Foundation in 1955 to lead the newly created Public Affairs program, at first a relatively obscure and poorly funded initiative to deal with the problems of governance identified by the Gaither report. Ylvisaker's innovative grant making to address the urban crisis would soon transform Public Affairs into the Foundation's prestige domestic effort, thanks particularly to his Gray Areas program and the philosophy of community action that undergirded it, both key progenitors to Lyndon Johnson's War on Poverty.

Ylvisaker was a Swarthmore College political scientist when he went on leave in 1952 to become the executive secretary to Mayor Joseph S. Clark of Philadelphia, the blue-blood "good government" candidate who swept into city hall on a nationwide wave of municipal reform. Clark hired Ylvisaker as part of his team of "best brains" to effect Philadelphia's transformation from a city driven by a patronage-heavy political machine into a modern metropolis managed by academic and technocratic experts, including Ylvisaker. Ylvisaker, whose dissertation was a case study of the political consensus building that achieved the modernization of county government in New Deal-era Minnesota, was the ideal specialist to act as the mayor's right-hand man. As such, Ylvisaker participated in a remarkably well-informed and prescient urban administration that understood the complexities of the era's industrial decline, suburbanization, and in-migration better than most city governments of the day. Philadelphia's experts were also at the cutting edge of thinking about and acting on municipal systems reform, industrial planning, and urban renewal, which, in their postwar confidence, they believed would achieve a seamless urban overhaul. As an optimist, pragmatist, and activist at the center of an administration that symbolized the best practices of effective governance as defined by the Gaither report and establishment liberalism in general, Ylvisaker would have been a deeply attractive candidate for the Ford Foundation's Public Affairs program.[6]

Ylvisaker left Clark and Philadelphia for the Foundation and New York City in 1955. This timing shaped his work at Ford in several ways. It meant that he only experienced Philadelphia's heady honeymoon of modernization and was not a part of city government when Clark's ally and successor, Richardson Dilworth, as well as other reform mayors around the country, had to contend with the considerable political blowback to the implementation of their plans for urban renewal, public housing, and desegregation.[7] It also meant that he arrived at the Foundation at a contradictory moment, at least in hindsight. The mid-1950s marked the Foundation's self-imposed retreat from politically contentious social issues after the controversy over its school-desegregation and civil liberties efforts; the windfall from its sale of Ford Motor stock would ultimately end this moratorium, albeit with a proscription on racial integration still in place.

Ultimately, Ylvisaker's insight, experience, and idealism, as well as the constraints and opportunities that he faced at the Foundation, would lead him to interpret the urban crisis and its attendant "Negro problem" in terms of the assimilation of rural migrants to urban modernity. He also came up with technocratic and behavioral solutions to speed assimilation, thus sparking again the modernizing goals of the Gaither report and the suspended social-engineering activism of the FAE. His 1963 speech to the Citizens Conference on Community Planning in Indianapolis encapsulated Ylvisaker's preoccupations. In describing the Foundation's recent activities on the urban front, he described the American city's role as "a continuous system" of assimilation for newcomers, who once had been Eastern and Southern

Figure 1. Responding to the urban crisis in the Kennedy era, Paul Ylvisaker, an upstart Foundation program officer, established the intellectual and programmatic blueprint for the Foundation's work with racial minorities throughout the 1960s and 1970s. Ford Foundation Archives. Courtesy Rockefeller Archive Center.

Europeans but were now largely domestic migrants from the countryside, "the Negroes, the Puerto Ricans, the mountain Whites, the Mexicans, and the American Indians." He was precise about both what this assimilation process entailed for urban migrants—the movement from "central-city tenement to suburban ranch house, from menial employment to the club-for-lunch, from the sheer necessity of ethnic-bloc voting to the relaxed assurance of nonpartisan elections"—and what amount of time—three generations—it had heretofore taken to "climb the totem pole of urban culture."[8]

Ylvisaker praised what he saw as the indubitable historic success of this organic "system of producing first class citizens." However, unlike other poverty experts of the era, he was not ready to leave to chance the assimilation of this last group of rural migrants. He told his audience that "as any production expert could tell you," to do so would be to abandon the newcomers to a process that was "dangerously slow, full of inefficiencies, and in many respects primitive and barbaric" and that might even be falling apart, given "the unskilled and unemployed piling up in the population of . . . central cities across the country." He sought to extend the program of the Puerto Rican Study beyond the schools by "put[ting] systems analysts to work on the social production system of the modern metropolis to . . . increase social output," so that the city might be restored to its assimilative role and to "do in one generation for the urban newcomer what until now has taken three."[9]

Ylvisaker had not been hired to focus on the problem of assimilating nonwhite migrants to urban modernity. Rather, in the race-averse Foundation of the 1950s, his task was to deal with a more generalized concern about how cities nationwide were mushrooming beyond their limits, far into the suburban hinterland. The Foundation's 1957 annual report went so far as to predict that, within twenty years, massive and unbroken "linear cities" might stretch from Boston to Norfolk, from Los Angeles to San Francisco, and from Milwaukee and Chicago to Pittsburgh. The Foundation helped to frame the development and governance of these potential megalopolises into a major urban policy issue in the 1950s, and it advocated expert leadership and modern management techniques from on high in order to make these massive regions work and prosper. Ylvisaker's experience in and research on regional governance and intergovernmental cooperation made him an expert in this field.[10]

When Ylvisaker began focusing on this issue, the racial dimensions of black urban migration and white suburbanization inevitably emerged as crucial macro problems of regional growth and governance, bringing his attention back to the Foundation's erstwhile interest in overcoming white re-sistance to racial desegregation in order to facilitate national modernization. As his 1963 speech clearly demonstrated, Ylvisaker agreed with his Foundation predecessors that assimilation through desegregation was both inevitable and essential to this goal. Thus he at first focused on white suburbanites. Since the end of the Second World War this group had been flocking to a racially exclusive, privatized, and inward-looking urban hinterland composed of balkanized and self-interested municipalities that deliberately turned their backs on the increasingly nonwhite central cities around which these new communities had formed. Returning to the Foundation's earlier preoccupations about the essential assimilationist role of the city, Ylvisaker feared that this self-interested segregation would destroy the city's erstwhile first and "noble" social function to guide its newcomers to modernity and to provide opportunities for their upward mobility. In his numerous writings on the subject in the late 1950s, Ylvisaker frankly addressed the bald racial considerations and segregationist impulse behind white flight. He blamed this "search for homogeneity" for turning the inner-city neighborhoods, from which the new white-ethnic suburbanites had moved up and out, into deteriorating, dead-end ghettoes, or what he termed "gray areas" by "blocking the suburban exit" for the largely nonwhite migrants who had taken their place.[11] This was a classic systems problem in which a solution would have to be found to unplug the bottleneck of irrational white behavior in order to reestablish the city's assimilationist function.

Thus, like Gunnar Myrdal, or Harry Ashmore in his FAE school desegregation study, Ylvisaker blamed white racism for obstructing the incorporative process so necessary to African Americans' and America's ongoing modernization. Also, like other postwar racial liberals, he believed that this "sin of segregation . . . against the spirit of the city" could be reversed through the panacea of rational, top-down leadership for systems reform.[12] He called for a new urban federalism, in which a "strong metromayor," buttressed by an executive team of progressive social planners and expert urban researchers would be able to engineer a new metropolitan consensus or "mutuality of concern."[13] They would do so through innovative, expert-run civic engagement processes that would integrate the interests of the city and suburb, thus returning the city system to its natural role as the great machine of assimilation.

This moment in Ylvisaker's thinking was striking in its indictment of white suburbs and suburbanites for the urban crisis—even consigning them in one 1959 article to a special circle of hell for their transgressions—an argument that would not regain traction for almost another forty years.[14] In fact, even as he published this condemnation, Ylvisaker had shifted his thinking, and in doing so he helped to cement what was becoming the dominant interpretation of the urban crisis—one that ignored white racism by focusing on black deprivation and pathology, and would drive public policy for decades to come.

Ylvisaker made a pragmatic choice in shifting his focus from perpetrator to victim. While he continued to view the self-segregation of suburban whites as an important aspect of the urban crisis, the studies that Ylvisaker commissioned to study the viability of his solution revealed the political roadblocks that would emerge by challenging the racial privilege of the most powerful metropolitan demographic groups. Furthermore, Ylvisaker withdrew from his goal to create and manage a consensus of interest between black and white city dwellers once he observed how the polarizing issue of urban renewal had sparked political conflict nationwide, including back in Philadelphia, between black communities and their cities' white political and business establishments. While Ylvisaker had once imagined that new "civic processes" that encouraged "discussion, debate, and participation" would create effective metropolitan governance, his observations of real-life political realities quickly changed his mind.[15]

In a conceptual about-face, Ylvisaker abandoned what he now called the naïve, "ethical Shangri-La" of his former intention to create a public-interest consensus through metropolitan government, and he instead began to naturalize the segregationist impulse.[16] He no longer framed white flight as a deliberate and ignoble practice but as part of a forgivable and inevitable human instinct shared by suburbanites and ghetto dwellers alike to create, out of the modern city's new diversity, "understandable and manageable pieces of homogeneity" in which in his calculation, "class and taste differentiation" between and within groups were as important as racial considerations in dividing the metropolis.[17] For Ylvisaker and the Foundation, the core of this social fracturing was no longer the behavioral maladjustment of segregationist whites but, remaining with the behavioral explanations for social conflict of the Gaither report, that of an alien lower-class migrant population. These newcomers were unprepared for urban modernity, according to Ylvisaker, who called them un-"housebroken" to the bourgeois values that would allow them to become what he called "first-class citizens" by participating productively in their own uplift and in forging a metropolitan consensus.[18] Thus, he began to interpret the conflict over urban renewal as irreconcilable, not because of the racist behavior of white proponents of slum clearance and redevelopment, but because of what he disapprovingly called the confrontational "new black." According to Ylvisaker, these recent migrants had illogically rejected the implicitly rational leadership of the "old black coalition" and its putatively pragmatic and logical willingness to compromise with the city's white elite in its brokerage for the black community.[19]

Community Action and the Origins of Developmental Separatism

Ylvisaker called this reconception of the urban crisis the most important intellectual and strategic breakthrough of his career. The root cause of what made the metropolis ungovernable, in his mind, was no longer white flight and the lack of "metropolitan organization" to fight it but the behavioral "people problems" of nonwhite "migrant flows" into the city.[20] In this new conception, Ylvisaker shifted the locus of reform from the metropolitan region at large, and the suburbs and suburbanites in particular, to the ghetto or "gray area" and its premodern settlers. In doing so, he developed a separatist and developmental model of assimilation that would drive the rest of his career at Ford and the Foundation's solution to the urban crisis for more than a decade to come.

Significantly, like in the earlier example of school desegregation, Ylvisaker's reversal meant that once again the integrationist impulse was quashed at the Ford Foundation, along with articulations of white responsibility for black inequality, just at the moment at which the social conflict they promised to generate became clear. However in this case, Ylvisaker's conceptual shift did not represent a crisis of confidence; rather, it was a strategic way forward to allow him to ramp up the Public Affairs division's social-engineering activism, instead of shutting it down. The narrower focus on the myriad "deprivations" of urban migrants and their ghettoes avoided what Ylvisaker knew from his political experience were "verboten" race and structural issues, in favor of a behavioral and systems-reform approach that conformed to both the Foundation's institutional caution and its activist ethos. Thus, it was no surprise that Ylvisaker used the euphemistic term "gray areas" instead of "ghettoes" to describe the nonwhite and largely black, migrant inner cities that formed in the postwar period; the latter term was simply too redolent of

deliberate white exclusion and marginalization of black residents to suit this
new framing of the urban crisis.[21]

In making this conceptual shift, Ylvisaker plugged into a strategy that had
proven politically successful for racial liberals since the *Brown* decision in
order to focus on African Americans' social and cultural privations without
attaching guilt to whites.[22] The putatively universal schema of the modernization process facilitated this blamelessness by making African Americans'
troubles in the cities part of the inevitable challenge of relocation for rural
folk, no matter their race or who they were. Thus Ylvisaker's first task in developing the Gray Areas program was to define and promote the problem of
migration to his superiors as the central problem for American cities. So, in
the late 1950s, he hired consultants to study the internal cultural dynamics of
various migrant groups. This research helped to sum up the urban crisis for
the Foundation in the familiar terms of maladjustment to urban modernity,
or as the problem of a "deprived poverty class migrating in increasing numbers to the city, filling its old slums and creating new ones."[23]

In a 1973 interview, Ylvisaker discussed frankly how this project deliberately and explicitly pathologized the migration and migrants, allowing
him to define urban gray areas as the nation's "Calcutta" and thus sell this
problem to the trustees as an area of urgent national concern. In doing so,
he advocated expert intervention on behalf of the poor on the basis of the
poor's ostensible behavioral debilitation.[24] He portrayed the recent arrivals,
the newest waves of African Americans from the "deep, deep South," as so
countrified that even a black Foundation monitor, the Rev. Leon Sullivan of
Philadelphia, who ministered to a large, urban congregation, resigned from
his task, feeling, according to Ylvisaker, that he had no "beginning points"
from his own, presumably more modern "cultural stream" to use in com-
municating with and understanding these new, rustic city dwellers. Likewise,
Ylvisaker's study group reinforced the now-familiar notion of the "Puerto
Rican problem," defining it as a "family syndrome" of chain migration that
was responsible for concentrating Puerto Rican communities in a few neighborhoods in a few East Coast cities and perpetuating their supposed cultural
deficiencies through the persistence of kinship networks. Demonstrating that
this pathology was not just a problem of nonwhite racial groups but one of
migration and modernization, Appalachian whites fared no better than African Americans and Puerto Ricans in Ylvisaker's analysis. Urbanization was
"ruining" even those "sturdy oaks of our culture," as Ylvisaker characterized
them; in fact, in his words, these white mountain people were "worse prob-

lems" for their host cities "than were the blacks."[25] In short, Ylvisaker and his crew of consultants and monitors made the implicit case that postwar urban migrants might just be the toughest cases for assimilation to urban modernity that the American city had ever faced.

Even more problematic, according to Ylvisaker, these late arrivals were landing in the city just at the time when deindustrialization, urban renewal, and suburbanization had stripped ethnic enclaves of their capacity to assimilate newcomers within three generations. Having effectively framed the problem as one of migrants' cultural pathology and the city's lack of opportunity, Ylvisaker returned to his and the Ford Foundation's perennial solution of systems reform and social engineering, claiming that it could restore, improve, and actually speed up the assimilation process in the gray areas or, as he put it, that the "urban social system" could be "perfected [largely] by rational means and specific devices."[26]

His program first and foremost sought a comprehensive overhaul and harmonization of the city's public education, social welfare, and justice systems—the traditional "enabling institutions of assimilation," as two early scholars of gray areas, Peter Marris and Martin Rein, characterized them—and the coordination of these systems with federal and state agencies and programs, higher education, local industry, and philanthropy.[27] These were steps intended to rehabilitate the gray areas' critical social "production processes," which had become, in Ylvisaker's mind, "bottlenecks in the process of citizen-building."[28] This approach was a more ambitious version of the sweeping remediation recommended for migrants by the Puerto Rican Study, but minus its focus on racial integration. With gray areas, Ylvisaker invented a "new instrumentality," the independent community-action agency that, from above and outside, could see all the systems affecting the gray area neighborhoods and imagine how these might best be reformed and coordinated to facilitate the assimilation process from within the migrants' own neighborhoods.[29] Expert gray area managers would act upon that vision through the "art of jujitsu," as Ylvisaker put it, or the power of "exerting smaller forces at points of maximum leverage to capture larger forces" that might otherwise work against the task at hand.[30] In the end, the Foundation funded these independent "community-action" agencies in four cities: Oakland, Philadelphia, Boston, and New Haven. These projects garnered enormous attention and traction in social policy circles, resulting ultimately in the Johnson administration modeling its own community-action strategy for the War on Poverty on Gray Areas demonstrations.[31]

The "community action" of the War on Poverty has been characterized as an experiment in "maximum feasible participation" by the nation's poor. However, the Gray Areas program's pioneering iteration of this approach was entirely in keeping with the Ford Foundation's elitist, top-down notions of governance, assimilation, and social change, and in fact it resembled nothing so much as a miniaturization of Ylvisaker's earlier vision of metropolitan consensus engineered by a new, executive-led, technocrat-run metropolitan level of government. The gray area community agencies were hierarchical and paternalistic, with residents left almost entirely out of developing and implementing programs, which were controlled by planners, economists, psychologists, and sociologists. Such exclusion was based on the Foundation's preoccupation with the need for strong leadership at all levels of American governance, compounded by notions of the "vicious cycle of poverty" plaguing the gray areas' residents.[32] In this model, grassroots participation was conceived as a kind of necessary group therapy initiated by outside experts for neighborhood people otherwise unable to think and act on their own behalf and best interests. Returning to one of his favorite metaphors, Ylvisaker wrote that these "human beings . . . crushed at the bottom of the community's totem pole" first and foremost needed programs to "develop [their] latent potential"[33] before they could claim the responsibilities of full citizenship in the society at large. The isolation of gray areas was supposedly so complete that, in Ylvisaker's mind, any attention paid to these neighborhoods by outside experts could help to peel "a couple of layers of hopelessness off the morale of . . . residents." What also helped was a simple "symbolic act of respect" like the Detroit public schools' inclusion of "Negro faces and situations in first-grade primers."[34] These therapeutic gestures constituted "community action" for and not by local residents in inner-city districts who, according to Ylvisaker's reckoning, were not yet ready for the mainstream. Instead they had first to be prepared for their assimilation by experts through a period of separate development in their own neighborhoods.

Despite this portrait of passivity borne of crushed spirits, Ylvisaker would never have been spurred to create the Gray Areas program without widespread and organized African American activism against urban renewal, deficient public schooling, and other issues involving unresponsive and discriminatory urban public services. This paradox was part of the central contradiction undergirding racial liberalism's damage and deprivation thesis.[35] In Ylvisaker's case, this inconsistency was partially resolved by the Foundation's larger conception of consensus and consent as a marker of a healthy society, one in which any open social conflict was behaviorally suspect. Ylvisaker believed that while protest had a necessary, catalytic role to play in instigating social reform, ultimately a "middle ground" had to be found, "neither . . . of complete acceptance nor of unrelenting hostility," in order to create "the domestic tranquility and search for the common welfare which have become the American heritage."[36] This, as always for the Foundation, was the fundamental goal for "social engineers" and "public entrepreneurs" as Ylvisaker called them. Ideally, they would both find innovative and effective means to correct the cause of the protest and "convince . . . the man in the Gray Area Street" that their programs were "for real" and not "window-dressing for the status quo."[37] Thus, the public entrepreneur would create social change through social peace. Nevertheless, Ylvisaker knew that the city's "social system" could not be "perfected by clever manipulators, no matter how well trained, nor for that matter by eager philanthropists working alone and from the outside." Instead, the linchpin of his program was the "toughest" urban problem, that "of generating indigenous leadership and the spirit of self-help" among the migrants themselves.[38] Hence, finding and developing local black leaders who could lead their people's therapeutic uplift and ultimate assimilation formed the second thrust of Gray Areas program's developmental separatism.

For Ylvisaker, developing black leaders would moderate social unrest and build legitimacy for the Foundation's assimilationist efforts by turning "militancy" into "integrity and concern" and "people who . . . hate" into "persons ready to build and create."[39] While building indigenous leadership had the therapeutic aim of addressing alienation, and the political aim of conflict resolution, it also represented Ylvisaker's meritocratic vision. The Harvard-trained Ylvisaker, a Minnesota-bred Norwegian American who had begun his studies at Bethany Lutheran College and Mankato State University, was himself a direct beneficiary of the postwar opening of establishment institutions to brilliant erstwhile outsiders. Ylvisaker reminisced with pride about extending this model even further at the Foundation. He boasted about building a "diverse" staff in Public Affairs, which was one of the only places at the Ford Foundation where non-Ivy League graduates, let alone non-New England WASPs, could be found in the late 1950s and early 1960s, at least in professional positions. He noted with pride that two of his most valued underlings, Bill Pincus and Henry Saltzman, were Jewish and had what he called immigrant "ghetto" origins, thus suggesting the assimilative achievement of the American city. Extending his cosmopolitanism even further,

Ylvisaker hired the Foundation's first African American professionals: Robert C. Weaver, the eminent economist and former and future federal official, as a full-time consultant on black migration in the late 1950s; and Christopher Edley, lawyer and former chief administrator of the U.S. Commission on Civil Rights, as Ford's first black program officer in 1963.[40]

In opening up his unit to the best and the brightest, no matter their origins or color, Ylvisaker extended the elite pluralism that lay at the heart of postwar democratic theory. This brand of pluralism, like all others, was intended to give minorities a voice in the American system. However, it was also a model favored by the liberal establishment in the 1950s and 1960s because it was thought to prevent the foolish, ignorant, potentially tyrannical majority from getting its way, as it had in Nazi Germany and the McCarthy-era United States. Antipopulist pluralism achieved this end on a broad scale by providing room for a wide diversity of minority voices in the political forum. The interest groups themselves avoided the folly of the masses by being controlled by elites who represented their particular constituencies while sharing the worldview and leadership style of their fellow members of the inner circle of American leadership.[41]

Indeed, Ylvisaker pioneered what would soon become an important Ford Foundation corollary to the developmental separatism of gray areas. He worked to extend pluralism among the nation's decision makers, who until now had had a decidedly white and upper-class cast. He hoped to identify and develop a new cadre of black leaders who could manage the social conflict arising from the "new black" urbanites and their freedom struggle. These men—and they were always men—mirrored the liberal establishment's own self-perception as the natural born leaders of America in terms of education, leadership style, and even outward appearance; they tended to place inordinate favor on physically imposing black men who dressed like they did, in the sober yet sharp style of the Kennedy era. The fact that there were such figures was a revelation and relief to the Foundation's trustees in Ylvisaker's era, who had little or no understanding of the African American community beyond the picture of pathology painted by him while promoting the Gray Areas program.

Ylvisaker told a revealing anecdote that may have marked a turning point for the Foundation's board of trustees in terms of its understanding of the black community and its leadership potential. In the early 1960s, Ylvisaker met Leon Sullivan, a black minister from Philadelphia who ran a number of groundbreaking local vocational and economic development programs

that were by any measure far more successful than the city's underperform-
ing Gray Areas agency. Despite Sullivan's impressive achievements, Ylvisaker struggled in vain against his recalcitrant Foundation superiors to fund
these innovative projects. Meeting one roadblock after another, Ylvisaker
resorted to what he called the "Machiavellian act" of "arrang[ing] for Leon
to come over and meet me just at the time the trustees broke up their meeting." Purposely encountering them at the elevators, Sullivan, "from six feet
six . . . looked down at Henry Ford [II] and [John J.] McCloy and all these
guys." "In a few seconds," Ylvisaker gleefully recounted, Sullivan "had the . . .
trustees around him like the Sermon on the Mount." According to Ylvisaker,
the encounter ended with Henry Ford II asking Sullivan, "My God, how
do we manufacture more of you?" and Sullivan reportedly responding, "By
giving me some money."[42] Give money they did to Sullivan's community-
development projects, and he became the Foundation's pioneering model of
"indigenous" leadership.

In this incident, like so many others, Ylvisaker demonstrated the pitch-
perfect political intuition that would move Public Affairs from being a "rag-
tag bunch" at the Foundation's margins to representing its most renowned
and influential domestic program. His timing was perfect, too. Ylvisaker acknowledged that the Gray Areas program benefited from its "beautiful running time" at the height of the Development Decade, when the Foundation's
antipoverty demonstrations became a fountainhead for federal social and
foreign policy activism.[43] It played a vanguard role in developing programs
and funding the applied research that would lead directly to both Lyndon
Johnson's Great Society and the ascendance of modernization theory as the
driving force behind the work of the United States Agency for International
Development (USAID).[44] The modernizers at the heart of the Kennedy administration were inspired particularly by the Foundation's international
"population" programs and Gray Areas, both of which focused largely upon
the "urban crisis" of the economic and psychological adjustment problems
of displaced rural migrants to cities, at home and abroad.[45] On the domestic
front, Gray Areas along with another closely allied Public Affairs community-
action demonstration, New York City's Mobilization for Youth (MFY), became key progenitors of the War on Poverty, after the Kennedy administration had already joined with the Foundation to fund MFY through the
President's Committee on Juvenile Delinquency (PCJD). The ideas behind
Ylvisaker's programs traveled with the steady stream of Ford Foundation
staffers and grantees who went to Washington, D.C. in this era, forming a

kind of farm team for federal policymaking. These figures included people like Mitchell Sviridoff, who helped draft the Economic Opportunity Act. He headed New Haven's Gray Areas agency after being recruited away from the Alliance for Progress, Kennedy's ambitious modernization effort in Latin America. Lloyd Ohlin, the chief research consultant for the PCJD, helped develop "opportunity theory," the key idea behind the War on Poverty, when he worked at MFY. Lyndon Johnson appointed Robert Weaver as the first ever African American federal Cabinet Secretary of the new Department of Housing and Urban Development (HUD), a position chosen for him first by Kennedy in 1961 during the initial, unsuccessful bid to create HUD.[46]

The Foundation's direct influence on the Kennedy administration bolstered the trustees' faith in Ylvisaker's approach, which, like in the case of developing black leadership, stretched but did not overreach their worldview or ideology. Further, in devising developmental separatism, Ylvisaker found a way for the Foundation to pursue its assimilationist and modernizing goals without pushing the political hot button of racial desegregation or integration, freeing conflict-averse trustees and officers to pursue the activism promised by Ford's mission. In sum, the Gray Areas program, and its model of behavioral and systems reform in the ghetto through indigenous leadership development, offered the trustees exactly the approach and solution that they were looking for to manage and solve the Negro problem and its latest iteration, the urban crisis.

McGeorge Bundy's Ford Foundation

Buoyed by the policy ambitions of the New Frontier and Great Society, as well as the Foundation's indelible mark on both, in 1965 the Foundation's trustees sought a replacement for Heald. They wanted a man who shared their ambitions to make the Foundation into an instrument of liberal social transformation modeled in part on Ylvisaker's pioneering example. McGeorge Bundy fit the bill. Despite the controversy to come over his focus on and explicit involvement with racial issues—especially when they seemed to jibe with some forms of black power—Bundy's approach and solution were deeply rooted in the Foundation's assimilationist creed, albeit adapted to address the assertions of the black freedom struggle. The path he outlined for American "minorities" thus owed a great deal to the Gaither report's articulation of modernization ideology and the elite theory of democracy, along with Paul Ylvisaker's programs of community action and developmental separatism.

These precedents were clear in Bundy's outline of the Foundation's plan of action for African Americans, which he debuted in a 1966 speech to the National Urban League in Philadelphia. In it, he announced that the primary focus of his presidency would be to create the conditions for "full equality for all American Negroes," which he proclaimed was "now the most urgent domestic concern." Among Bundy's priorities in this area were "research as a weapon," or the application of demonstration-based social science experiments to determine the best possible programs to "turn the tide of hope upward in the ghetto"; better communication between whites and blacks "in the face of enormous social problems and rapid social change" in order to foster "peaceful progress"; an activist conception and practice of racial justice that moved beyond legal rights to a "larger" definition that called "for *urgency*, and *priority*, and *preference* for what helps to end *injustice*"; and strengthening leadership of "Negroes who work for peaceful progress," thus building "the hope and self-confidence of the Negro American." Finally, he emphasized that the city must be the crucible for forging racial equality, given an ongoing urban crisis in which what the Ford Foundation officers now explicitly called "the ghetto," created by white barriers to black opportunity and mobility, threatened to "[pull] the central city down."[47] In short, this social-engineering and therapeutic approach to the ghetto largely replicated Paul Ylvisaker's vision of gray areas, itself borne of the Gaither report's priorities. Bundy's innovation was to move this strategy for African American modernization and assimilation to the forefront of the Foundation's mission.

While Bundy's approach was not a new one for the Foundation, the messenger certainly was. In him, the trustees had found a high-profile leader who showed complete confidence in handling the Foundation's growing endowment and concomitant prestige as the largest private foundation in the world and who promised to exceed even the public policy success of Ylvisaker's Public Affairs program. A Republican from a patrician Boston Brahmin family, Bundy epitomized the American liberal establishment.[48] His lineage alone put him in line for leadership of the nation's upper crust. As the *New York Times* gushed, Bundy was a "Lowell on his mother's side" and thus "scion of the poetess Amy, the astronomer Percival, [and] Harvard's president A. Lawrence" in addition to the family's patriarch, pioneering industrialist and textile-mill owner Francis Cabot Lowell. Bundy was also a "product of Groton [boarding school], classmate of Henry Ford [II] and member of

[the] Skull and Bones [ultra-select secret society] at Yale University."[49] As a Yale undergraduate, he was already cogently articulating establishment ide-ology, appropriating the vital center liberalism of two key American public intellectuals—his friend, historian Arthur Schlesinger, Jr., and his Progres-sive mentor, public intellectual Walter Lippmann. Bundy shared their anti-Communism, but even more importantly the elite theory of democracy, in which the public interest could best be served by an educated elect forging a rational middle path, as opposed to the populism of mass politics. He first distinguished himself after the war at Harvard University, where in the 1950s he was the youngest Dean of Arts and Sciences on record, not to mention the only one without a graduate degree. There, he took a leadership role in the postwar disciplinary and meritocratic transformation of the Ivy League, making Harvard a powerhouse of social science and opening it up to brilliant minds, whatever their ancestry.[50]

From Harvard, Bundy moved on to become a national security advisor to John F. Kennedy, a position at the pinnacle of power at the height of the Cold War. Representing the liberal establishment's ascendant intellectual wing, he joined in with other young elites to imbue the Kennedy White House with the indefatigable spirit of technocratic optimism and can-do social-engineering know-how that undergirded the spirit of the New Frontier and then the Great Society. Even within Kennedy's exalted inner circle, Bundy stood out; one of his peers characterized him as the era's own John J. McCloy, comparing him to the establishment "chairman" and family friend.[51]

Bundy had a special rapport with the president; both men shared a cool, pragmatic, and activist ethic, which Kennedy liked to call "balls," or the cour-age to take action. This modern machismo indelibly shaped the putatively objective and expert decision making of the Kennedy administration. So did an ironclad belief—first cemented in the Second World War and bolstered by the Cold War's political and ideological imperative to fight Communism—in America's responsibility for the world. What this meant for Bundy as Kenne-dy's national security advisor was an obsession with demonstrating that the United States was living up to its role as global watchdog. Using the historical example to which he constantly returned, he warned that the United States must never be guilty of appeasing Communism the way British Prime Min-ister Neville Chamberlain had conciliated Adolf Hitler. Hence Bundy was almost always a voice for action in the Kennedy and Johnson White House, much of which was or could have been disastrous if carried out. He advo-cated for airstrikes against Cuba during the missile crisis; supported covert operations like the Bay of Pigs and Operation Mongoose to overthrow or assassinate Cuba's Fidel Castro, as well as the ultimately murderous plot to instigate a coup to depose South Vietnamese leader Ngo Dinh Diem; and, most fatefully, pushed for the sustained bombing of North Vietnam, which would escalate American involvement into all-out war. Secure in his establishment identity as the best possible servant of the national interest, he was loyal to the end to both Presidents Kennedy and Johnson, believing that they had the right men advising their decisions. When he left the Johnson White House in 1965, it was not due to any fundamental policy differences over Vietnam like it would be for other key figures, but because of the U.S. president's unwillingness to be *more* confident and open in promoting his foreign policy decisions to the public. In fact, Bundy remained a key foreign policy advisor to LBJ after leaving Washington for the Ford Foundation.[52]

Given his ongoing faith in American foreign policy, Bundy was very lucky in timing his departure from Washington. His pivotal role in creating the Vietnam quagmire could very well have torpedoed his career. The Foundation's offer provided him a life raft in the nick of time, allowing him to jump ship from the Johnson White House before the credibility gap would sink it. Once in New York, he turned his attention to domestic issues, hitching his star to Paul Ylvisaker's celebrated Public Affairs program, whose agenda Bundy moved to the center of the Foundation's program. Signaling this shift, after much deliberation Bundy declined to appoint Ylvisaker as vice president of National Affairs, the new Foundation division that subsumed the Public Affairs program as its centerpiece. Ylvisaker's extraordinary success in conceiving, demonstrating, and selling community action made him an unacceptable rival to Bundy as the new president sought to make his mark in the same area. Nevertheless, Ylvisaker's legacy persisted, as Bundy's own appointments demonstrated. After a brief stint as his own VP of National Affairs, in 1967 Bundy named Mitchell Sviridoff, the former director of New Haven's Gray Areas program, as his replacement. Then, in 1968, Bundy hired Roger Wilkins, who had been running a community-action program for the U.S. Departments of Commerce and Justice inspired by the Foundation-funded MFY. Wilkins ran the Foundation's Social Development program, which commanded nearly one-half of National Affairs's budget in an effort to put Bundy's Urban League speech priorities for minorities into practice. In short, Ylvisaker's influence was far-reaching and indelible.[53]

Yet the context for Bundy's appointment and decision to draw on and expand the Public Affairs program had changed dramatically since Ylvisaker's

rise to the top of American social policy circles. While Ylvisaker had operated at the pinnacle of American liberalism's self-confident activism, Bundy
came to the Foundation's helm at the point at which the postwar consensus
had begun its precipitous unraveling, thanks to the Vietnam crisis that he
left behind in Washington and the black freedom struggle and urban crisis
that he intended to engage from New York. By 1965, members of the liberal establishment—especially those outside Washington and in academia
and the media, including Bundy's mentor Walter Lippmann—had begun to
object openly to further American involvement in Vietnam. By 1968, these
doubts had spread even to the most conservative and powerful Wall Street
figures and "Wise Men" foreign policy advisors to the president—a circle that
included figures like Foundation trustee John J. McCloy—who had reached
the limit of their support of the nation's involvement in Vietnam, helping to
prompt Lyndon Johnson's decision not to run for reelection.[54]

Americans' reasons for opposing the war were varied, but a predominant
one was what would come to be called the "credibility gap," in which the reality on the ground in Vietnam gave lie to the establishment assumptions
about the rationale and mission for American military intervention, prompting the New Left and antiwar movements to tear apart not only establishment
institutions like elite universities but also what had been for decades unquestioned reasons for America's predominant role in the world. Meanwhile, the
credibility gap had another, domestic dimension, when the urban crisis intensified as the black movement moved out of the rural South and into a new
phase of black power and open rebellion, despite the developmental and assimilationist promise of Lyndon Johnson's Great Society and War on Poverty.

This "social revolution" at home, as Bundy would put it, would drive his
Ford Foundation presidency. According to one Foundation document, "the
word that most nearly explains both the shifts of priorities and the change
in overall spending level" in the Bundy era was "Negro."[55] The issues of ghettoization and assimilation that Gray Areas addressed so confidently had
become critical by the time Bundy came to the Ford Foundation. Unlike
Ylvisaker, Bundy was forced to talk explicitly about the urban crisis and its
racial, and particularly African American, dimension—including by using
the term "ghetto"—thanks to the radical critique of black activists undergirded by the rebellions in urban black communities throughout the United
States. It is difficult to underestimate the American establishment's anxiety
in face of rioting that, escalating between 1965 and 1968, hit dozens of cities,
cost hundreds of lives, and laid waste to hundreds of millions of dollars in

Figure 2. Foundation President McGeorge Bundy (pictured here in 1974) made the "social development" of racial minorities, particularly African Americans, the hallmark of his time at Ford. Ford Foundation Archives. Courtesy Rockefeller Archive Center.

property. Although Foundation program officers and staff might rationalize the unrest in comforting and patronizing liberal terms, such as one characterization of it as representing "the entrance pains of the American Negro into full citizenship," they nevertheless had little idea about how to stop the rebellions or their negative impact on "the American body politic," which they felt consequently was "suffer[ing] most acutely" from its effects.[56] Fear of the destabilizing impact and revolutionary possibility of a sustained black revolt drove virtually all American social policy, public and private, during this crisis.

Bundy joined this battle with almost zero preparation. Before coming to Ford he had no previous experience and displayed no interest in African American or race issues in the United States, beyond a long-ago, requisite reading of Gunnar Myrdal's *An American Dilemma*. His lack of concern for the situation of African Americans would lead him to actions like joining Washington, D.C.'s Metropolitan Club in 1961, *after* both his brother William and Robert F. Kennedy had left it for its whites-only membership policy. He had little opportunity to become more engaged in the issue of racial equality before leaving the White House, given his singleminded focus on foreign policy. So, for example, his critical February and March 1965 decision making to support an escalating bombing campaign against North Vietnam happened in tandem with another crucial turning point: the civil rights activism in Selma, Alabama, that would lead to the Voting Rights Act.[57]

In the face of his ignorance and the general panic over the riots, Bundy decided with characteristic speed and confidence to focus his energies on ending racial inequality and solving the urban crisis. He declared his intentions with high-profile announcements, like the Urban League speech, followed up by a cluster of grants to a full range of black rights organizations. This funding represented the Foundation's first explicit re-engagement with racial politics in the United States since the 1950s. It included what would become a long-term and large-scale commitment to mainstream black organizations—the NAACP and its Legal Defense and Educational Fund (NAACP LDF), as well as the even more mainstream and venerable National Urban League. However, it also provided smaller, more controversial short-term grants, including one to the advocates of nonviolent direct action in Martin Luther King, Jr.'s Southern Christian Leadership Conference for a minister education program, and another to the black power incarnation of the Congress of Racial Equality (CORE) for a voter registration campaign in Cleveland.[58]

Despite supporting this array of black-led efforts to demonstrate the Foundation's new energy and concern in this area, Bundy's approach to educating himself on racial issues betrayed his ongoing faith in postwar racial liberalism and its establishment adherents, despite the challenges both were facing, including from the African Americans he now made his cause. In his quick study of the race problem, Bundy depended on experts from the mainstream of liberal social science, almost all of them white. For example, in preparation for his Urban League speech, Bundy supplemented his reading of Myrdal by relying largely on *The Negro American* (1966), a comprehensive anthology edited by the white sociologist and father of modernization theory, Talcott Parsons, and black psychologist Kenneth Clark that attempted to rework the faltering Myrdalian orthodoxy in the face of black and New Left rejection of the promise of the American creed. The compendium included more than twenty chapters by the likes of Harvard psychiatrist Robert Coles, public intellectual Daniel Patrick Moynihan, Urban League leader Whitney Young, and Keynesian economist James Tobin, among many other established figures. In 1967 Bundy added to his reading list white novelist William Styron's book *The Confessions of Nat Turner* (1967), which imagined the slave revolutionary in terms of behavioral pathology that racial liberals believed white prejudice and exploitation had wrought in the black community. Bundy used Styron's thesis to shape his next major policy statement on racial inequality in the Foundation's annual report of that year. When Bundy finally did meet in person with select black movement leaders, including Martin Luther King, Jr., and CORE's James Farmer, he almost always did so on his own turf—at home, at the Foundation, and at the exclusive Century Club.[59]

This selective, whirlwind preparation to join the fight for racial equality resembled nothing so much as Bundy's first trip to Southeast Asia—what was termed a four-day "fire-brigade mission" to Vietnam, years after he had begun forging U.S. foreign policy for the region—in which he readied himself to help LBJ make a decision on U.S. military escalation. Where did Bundy find the confidence to make such leaps into the unknown? Journalist David Halberstam interviewed one informant who talked about Bundy's belief that he was "part of a line starting with Teddy Roosevelt and continuing with [Franklin Roosevelt's secretary of War, Henry] Stimson and [Harry Truman's Secretary of State, Dean] Acheson[,] which best understands the goals, responsibilities, and interests of the United States" and hence "know[s] what is right for the country."[60] Historians Steve Fraser and Gary Gerstle have called this entitlement a "sense of social trusteeship" held by public-minded members of the American elite, in which they "self-consciously took up the challenge of ruling on behalf of the whole commonwealth,"[61] including by sometimes moving from their focus on foreign affairs and engaging subordinate groups, especially during those grave crises, like the riots, that endangered the domestic status quo. Indeed, Bundy and his Foundation officers clearly felt that it was their unique responsibility to deal with the challenge of the riots and of black power. Just as Bundy felt so strongly that it was the establishment's responsibility to save South Vietnam from Communism, he felt a duty to do something about racial inequality, lest it rend the nation. As one Foundation official maintained, it was essential that the Foundation "show that the establishment was not turning its back on black militant organizations."[62] In fact, it was the Ford Foundation's duty "to have the patience, and the skill, to channel this rage, and . . . to be able to take a deep breath and ignore the bluster."[63] Further, Bundy urged white critics to consider the moderating influence of treating with black nationalists and disaffected ghetto dwellers. In defending the grant to CORE, which had recently become an explicitly black nationalist and racially exclusive organization, he quipped, "Motherhood, boy scouts, voter registration . . . everyone's for it, as an alternative to rocks and fire bombs."[64] In his mind, Bundy had found the vital center that would lead the nation out of this crisis.

Thus while he might have lacked preparation to lead the battle, his ambition at the Ford Foundation was far greater than simple firefighting. He was determined to curb conflict and to solve the enduring American problem of racial inequality. Bundy vowed in his first Foundation annual report that "the country of Abraham Lincoln" was "not going to become a no man's land for an apocalyptic contest between white and black fanatics." Instead, mustering all of the confidence of Cold War liberalism's progressive promise, he prophesied that the nation "is inevitably going to right these ancient wrongs, and this time by peaceful means."

Nevertheless, Bundy did not trust that this predestination would come to pass without heavy lifting; as he put it, "the mode by which the inevitable comes to pass is effort."[65] This contradictory credo, which reflected the ethos at the heart of modernist social engineering and the systems-reform method, also expressed Bundy's mission at the Foundation. The effort that Bundy proposed was to be made largely by technocratic experts who engaged in the kind of action-based social-scientific research that had become a Foundation specialty and which Bundy had promoted at Harvard and in Washington. As one of his former government colleagues wrote about his approach to Vietnam, Bundy held a fundamental belief that "a group of experts" could take a "rational approach" to virtually any problem "and come up with a workable plan, and that because it is rational, it will work."[66] Or, as Bundy himself put it, he admired "those who can reduce great qualitative issues to practical questions of choice in the use of resources."[67] Thus, in promoting "research as a weapon" to solve racial inequality, he distilled the issue into a series of practical and putatively solvable research problems in his Urban League speech: "What kinds of better schools will help most to turn the tide of hope upward in the ghetto? What patterns of cooperation . . . among whites and Negroes . . . can bring new levels of investment to both the city center and the Southern rural slum? What really are the roots of prejudice and how can we speed its early and widespread death?"[68]

For Bundy, these were solvable problems if tackled by dispassionate academic experts or those trained by them. Accordingly, he held that the civil rights movement would have been better fought had its leaders had the opportunity to be trained by leading scholarly authorities at an institute like the Russian Research Center, whose growth Bundy had overseen as Harvard dean in order to play that role for American diplomats during the Cold War. Indeed, Bundy's Foundation established just such a center for black leaders, the Metropolitan Applied Research Center (MARC), as one of its first actions on behalf of racial equality. It was led by Kenneth Clark, the distinguished City College psychology professor and public intellectual who was one of the nation's preeminent black liberals. Staffed by university-based social scientists, MARC offered fellowships to Martin Luther King, Jr., CORE's Floyd McKissick and Roy Innis, and former Student Nonviolent Coordinating Committee leader and Georgia legislator Julian Bond, among others.[69]

As MARC's founding suggests, Bundy privileged academic bona fides over indigenous, experiential expertise, including when dealing with the urban crisis. According to the *Times*, Bundy had consulted with black leaders as an afterthought, "in the hope that some idea" would "arise . . . that has not already been uncovered by the . . . very capable staff Ford has had working on these problems for a decade."[70] Even an African American like Roger Wilkins who had expert qualifications in the way that Bundy and his officers defined them— law degree from the University of Michigan, high-level administrative posts in the Kennedy and Johnson administrations, and membership in African Americans' own establishment as nephew to NAACP executive secretary Roy Wilkins—felt stifled by the "assumption about their omniscience" shared by the "successful, middle-aged white males" who ran the Foundation.[71] Wilkins never saw any evidence that his intrinsic experience as a black man in America had any value for most of them; despite his experience as a New Frontiersman and even though he was hired to run the Foundation's largest program attacking racial inequality, he always felt like an outsider and a token.

Not surprisingly, then, in Bundy's opinion, the solutions to racial issues were largely a matter of top-down social engineering. As he told an audience at Harvard in his 1968 Godkin lecture on "the essentials of free government," "I believe that it is precisely because it is so hard for anyone to change the minds of men" from their ingrained racial attitudes "that we must turn to the instruments of government" to do it, citing as precedents Truman's desegregation of the armed forces and the activist Warren Supreme Court's *Brown* school-desegregation decision. Similarly, "[w]e are rich enough" as a nation, he continued, "to end poverty and racism, " but such action could only happen through federal law written and federal policy conceived by the most expert public servants available. This top-down authority, defining and serving the public interest would produce a "federal government for freedom."[72]

Black Power and the Social Development Solution

The apparently defiant elitism of the Godkin lecture flew in the face of the decade's social movements, all of which recoiled against the elite theory of democracy and what it had wrought, and instead promoted participatory democracy and minority self-determination. Even more curious, Bundy made the speech at a time when the Foundation, at his direction, was in the midst of engaging one of those movements, black power. Despite this apparent contradiction, Bundy and his officers met the challenges of escalating urban conflict and the call for black self-determination in an approach entirely consistent with their long-held worldview.

First, they deepened their commitment to Ylvisaker's developmental separatism. They saw this approach as a crucial solution to black insurgency, which they now interpreted explicitly in terms of the liberal consensus about the cultural pathologies that had kept black migrants from the assimilationist success of the European immigrants of yesteryear, and, in a new twist, the "problem" of global postcolonialism and international development. Since the era of the Gaither report, the Ford Foundation had interpreted social unrest as an indicator of social maladjustment, particularly among recent migrants to the city who had not yet fully assimilated to urban modernity. By the time Bundy joined the Foundation, this formulation had become part of a deeply engrained national consensus that African Americans' troubles were due largely to a racially specific culture of poverty. Even Christopher Edley, the Foundation's only black program officer before Bundy's arrival, echoed this view when he wrote that the "the problems of the Negro in northern cities must be understood and dealt with in terms of a total pattern of deprivation and pathology which dominates their [sic] lives"; according to Edley urban African Americans' "eroded human agency" meant that they lacked the "power . . . to deal effectively realistically and rationally with their problems," as made evident for him and his colleagues by the apparent nihilism of the riots. These uprisings were, in his words, "the northern folk Negro's version of the more disciplined demonstrations of the southern Negro."[73]

This perception of northern blacks was particularly disturbing to Foundation officers when it was compared to the widespread glorification of an ostensible ethnic pattern in which the twentieth-century Ellis Island immigrant experience of assimilation and upward mobility from the urban ghettoes of cities like New York, supposedly achieved without government handout or special pleading, became the normative American story. Ylvisaker had hopefully imagined this process as potentially universal and sought to restore it for African Americans through the systems reform undergirding gray areas. However, that line of thinking led to a political dead end when it forced him to deal with the thorny political issues connected to the racialized structures of American society. So by the time of Bundy's tenure at the Foundation, both liberal and conservative policymakers and pundits instead used this white success story as an emblematic counternarrative to explain persistent African American failure to assimilate, emphasizing black differences from the supposed white norm.[74] This interpretation saw white-ethnic immigrant groups' upward mobility as a product of the strength of their respective cultures relative to African Americans' supposed weakness. Similarly, from this perspective black failure was not rooted in deindustrialization or labor and housing market discrimination but in slavery's dehumanizing legacy and the experience of urban migration. As the story went, these experiences had left the African American community rudderless by stripping it of the cultural foundations that had protected other immigrant groups and by emasculating black men, thus depriving the black community of the anchor of patriarchy within the family and community leadership believed to have formed the foundation of white-ethnic communities' success.[75]

These hegemonic ideas about black poverty being a product of African Americans' distinctive cultural damage imbued the thinking of racial liberals in the mid-1960s and drove their policy solutions. Thus the inspiration Bundy derived from reading Styron's *Confessions of Nat Turner* corresponded to Lyndon Johnson's deployment of Daniel Patrick Moynihan's infamous work on the unique "tangle of pathology" ailing black families; both provided a politically expedient and palatable justification for race-conscious social policy, largely unheard of in the United States until the Great Society.[76] So, for example, Ford Foundation officers proclaimed that there was a "striking difference between conventional philanthropy and philanthropy directed to overcoming deprivation." For them, the "contributions of the latter include a large ingredient of 'technical assistance' in the form of ideas, methods, and informed sympathy supplied by staff and other specialists."[77] As Christopher Edley put it, given their cultural deprivation and pathology, these "specialists" were needed to "function on behalf" of the black poor "in ways similar to the ways in which more privileged middle class individuals and groups function for themselves."[78]

Foundation officers most often explained this paternalist approach to the ghetto in terms of the Foundation's international development efforts, the "parallel" to which one Foundation document claimed "was almost complete" now that Ford's domestic divisions were working with what another report called "'developing areas' here at home" in "urban ghettoes and rural depressed regions."[79] This coupling of black ghettoes and "developing" nations suggested Bundy's propensity to explain domestic issues in terms of his expertise in foreign affairs. However, he was not alone in making that connection. Since the 1950s the Foundation's officers and grantees had echoed other modernization ventures by making implicit connections between the tasks of international and domestic development. These non-Ford efforts included those of the Peace Corps, which in the early 1960s sent volunteers to black ghettoes and Indian reservations to prepare them for overseas work in international development under the assumption that African American and Native American communities were somehow foreign, outside of the nation and modernity, and needed to be incorporated through the process laid out by modernization theory. This supposition imbued President Johnson's War on Poverty, an effort that he chose Peace Corps director Sargent Shriver to lead.[80]

Similar interchange between international and domestic development happened during the Bundy era at the Ford Foundation. Bundy often consulted on domestic programs with his closest confidant at Ford, David E. Bell, whom he had appointed as the vice president of the Foundation's International Division and who had been administrator of USAID, overseeing such modernization projects as the Strategic Hamlet program in Vietnam. Bundy's handpicked vice president of National Affairs, Mitchell Sviridoff, had experience both in Kennedy's Latin-American Alliance for Progress and as the head of New Haven's Gray Areas agency. Bundy-era Social Development program officers Roger Wilkins and Sol Chafkin came to the Foundation with prior experience as bureaucrats in both federal international and domestic development agencies. Another, Eamon Kelly, would go on to work in international development based on his experience with "minority" programs at the Ford Foundation.[81] This interchange reflected the commonplace notion that, like third world nations, the African American community as a distinctive, "developing" subculture in the United States had to undergo a kind of separate, carefully engineered nation building of its own in order to be prepared to assimilate fully into the highest stage of modernity, epitomized by mainstream American society.

Thus, by the mid-1960s those pondering the issue of black assimilation at the Ford Foundation believed even more firmly than their predecessors that a period of black separatism was a vital prelude to full participation in American life in order that African Americans might build the institutions and leadership class needed to compete with other groups within society. As early as 1965, the Ford Foundation's domestic program directors had moved away from an approach stressing "social integration," indeed declaring "that these forms of integration have a lower (if not the lowest) [Foundation] priority." Instead, it would focus on programs that stressed "economic and educational advancement of disadvantaged minority groups" even when in segregated settings, believing that these programs would "in time normalize social integration."[82]

These separatist and developmentalist assumptions quickly became explicit with McGeorge Bundy's ascension to the helm of the Foundation. Throughout the spring and summer of 1966 Ford Foundation staffers, as part of Bundy's rejigging of the Foundation's organizational structure, began the task of bringing together the discrete programs scattered throughout the philanthropy that dealt with "minority group problems" into a coordinated effort that better represented the interrelated issues facing African Americans and other nonwhite groups.[83] After long discussions about this program the group named it "Social Development," at once an obfuscating moniker for a program that would deal exclusively with racial minorities—and overwhelmingly African Americans—and an extraordinarily revealing label representing precisely the Foundation's aims for the inner city. The Foundation's fundamental goal was to build a separate "society" among African American migrants in order to ready them for its model of assimilation in a process deeply reminiscent of that of third world development.

While the developmental separatism of the Social Development program might have represented the culmination of its preoccupation with modernization and assimilationist efforts on behalf of "deprived" people at home and abroad, the activism of those black ghetto dwellers, Chicano farmworkers, and Vietnamese peasants, among other postcolonial peoples, had shown Bundy that efforts on behalf of the passive and pathological had often faltered in the past, failing to prevent powerful movements for self-determination deeply antithetical to the ethos and interests of the American establishment. He would continue to insist, notably in a *Foreign Affairs* article written at the end of 1966 that argued forcefully for America to wage both the war against North Vietnam and racial inequality at home, that there "was no safety yet for free men anywhere without [Americans]" and that American political and economic interests were in the best interests of the world. However, he knew from direct experience that his was a minority position globally. Like the European colonizers before him, he had been confounded by what he called the "stubborn insistence" of the Vietnamese and other third world peoples to resist assimilation into the American empire and to insist upon "doing things their own way," as Bundy put it. Consequently, he believed the crucial "political" or hearts-and-minds aspect of the war in Vietnam would only be as effective as its ability to engage "the energies and convictions of the Vietnamese people themselves." In fact, the black freedom struggle, and particularly calls for black power in the United States presented the same dilemma for Bundy as America's "political" problem in Vietnam and in the rest of the postcolonial world: how to find the "olive branch" that would bring the free-thinking Vietnamese and other newly independent peoples to accept the American way. [84]

Bundy's solution to this problem in Vietnam, especially when he acted as an external advisor to Johnson after joining the Ford Foundation, was a program of pacification and what would come to be called "Vietnamization" of the war, whereby he hoped, respectively, that the good intentions and works of the Americans would overcome the nationalist appeal of the Viet Cong, and that building the capacity of the South Vietnamese to rule and fight for

themselves would allow U.S. troop withdrawal. In promoting these policies, Bundy attempted to deal with what he saw as a central dilemma of the
war: while, according to Cold War logic, the "loss" of South Vietnam to the
North could not be countenanced, the South Vietnamese could not be "won"
through what he called an anachronistic "white man's war" against "brown
men."[85] Such a battle would only build antipathy to the United States and its
anti-Communist mission in the postcolonial world, not to mention aggravate
the enormous social conflict over Vietnam at home, which Bundy compared
to the Civil War in terms of its threat to the nation. Thus, more and more,
he advocated for a kind of guided development and self-determination in
South Vietnam, in which under the military protection of the United States
and its "massive support for relief, for rehabilitation and for economic and
social advances," the region would experience "growing military and political
strength and self-confidence." Significantly, he even compared such efforts to
Johnson's domestic Great Society. [86]

The logic behind this strategy corresponded directly to Bundy's controversial decision to engage at home with the demands of black power advocates. In fact, Bundy conjoined the war in Vietnam to the black freedom
struggle as similar and equally important national responsibilities. As he
suggested at the end of his *Foreign Affairs* article, both were essential to the
crucial "construction of a stable peace," quoting from his hero, Franklin Roosevelt's Secretary of War Henry Stimson, who set this global goal as America's
responsibility in the postwar world.[87] So while critics may have seen the
Foundation's actions in the black power era as dangerous flirtations with
black "revolutionaries," Bundy was simply adjusting what were for him intertwined domestic and international "development" strategies to the age of
self-determination, without altering their goals. Like Bundy's aims for Vietnam, abroad the Foundation sought to shape a new postcolonial reality in
which independent third world peoples were made available for incorporation or assimilation into a global order dominated by the United States—that
is, if their call for self-determination could be engaged while still protect-
ing the American interests. At home, black sociologist Robert Allen wrote
in 1968 about the Foundation's "domestic neo-colonialism"[88] in manipulating
the black movement at home to precisely these ends.

Thus, in the United States, the Foundation approached the dilemma of
the peaceful incorporation of African Americans into the American political
economy from a perspective that emphasized racial separatism so that African American communities could mature to assimilate into the American

mainstream with the least conflict possible. The separatism of this approach and also its emphasis on building black cultural identity and developing strong black leadership intersected with the black power project for black self-determination, even if its ultimate goal of assimilation was deeply antithetical to those of the black freedom movement. From the beginning, Bundy believed that a strengthened black identity would ultimately buttress African Americans' "membership in society as a whole."[89] Consequently, the Social Development program fostered "grant proposals directed at increasing the group identity and power of minorities" insisting that "in black identity (at least those manifestations free of reverse racism and destructive apartheidism) may lie the social strength that played so critical a part in the rise of other urban ethnic groups to political and economic status."[90] This therapeutic emphasis connected to the Foundation's desire to replicate white ethnics' urban success among African Americans and Ford's historical emphasis on the behavioral aspects of the modernization process. More immediately, it also reduced black power to a psycho-cultural and therapeutic issue of black identity without having to deal with the structural and material issues that initially fostered the call for black self-determination. Nevertheless, despite the assimilationist and pacification objectives behind the Foundation's focus on building black identity, it converged directly with the cultural focal point of black nationalism.

Given both the Foundation's ongoing assumptions of black cultural "deprivation" and incapacity, and African Americans' calls for black power, the other essential aspect of developmental separatism was the creation of indigenous, grassroots leaders who could organize and control the urban black masses and with whom it could broker. Such an orientation jibed with the Foundation's changing focus in its modernizing international development work. Where in the 1950s and 1960s it described itself as having emphasized the top-down "transfer of knowledge, skills, and resources from the advanced countries," consistent with modernization ideology and paralleling the Gray Areas approach, by the 1970s it sought to develop "institutional resources," "individual skills," and "professional competence" among "third world nationals" themselves. These self-help efforts, according to the Ford's International Division, were state-building programs aimed at increasing "national capacities" to deal with their own problems.[91] Hence, the locus of help moved from the First World United States to Third World nations themselves and particularly to expert indigenous leaders who would shepherd their people out of the doldrums.

While these postcolonial measures can be read as fostering self-determination, they also promised the incorporation of a third world elect into an international model of elite pluralism led by American liberals, like those at the Ford Foundation. First, the Foundation funded the training of these experts, either at prestigious American universities or at research centers established in developing nations themselves. Second, the Foundation sought to create linkages among those third world experts who were working on similar development issues around the world and to facilitate their participation in "international forums" where they could "articulate the needs of their countries."[92] Thus, a cadre of Ford Foundation–funded and fostered leaders were legitimated to act as peaceful and rational brokers and spokespeople for their countrymen and women in a U.S.-dominated postcolonial global scene.

The origins of this two-pronged approach to international development might very well have begun with the Foundation's developmental separatism, which saw indigenous leadership as pivotal in guiding the assimilation process from the top. As Bundy's officers worked to establish the Social Development program their one point of clear consensus was that black leadership development must play a central role. The Education Program was to "concentrate on the most promising Negro youngsters and on development of leadership in educationally deprived areas."[93] It seemed obvious that "the minority group organizations in this country need help in developing top-, middle-, and lower-level leadership."[94] The Public Affairs division hoped to expand the pool of "trained leadership in minority organizations in order to help these groups achieve the competence and sophistication they will need in negotiating programs of improvement in education, housing, and employment."[95]

This strategy would result in tangible dividends in terms of Bundy's preference for expert, top-down interventions in dealing with racial inequality. The black freedom struggle's turn from the turbulence of the 1960s to the mediated conflicts of public-interest judicial activism of the 1970s can be attributed in part to the Foundation's funding of organizations like the NAACP LDF along with other comparable organizations—including the Mexican American and Puerto Rican Legal Defense and Education Funds (MALDEF and PRLDEF), both created out of whole cloth by the Foundation as Latino versions of the NAACP LDF. The Foundation founded these advocacy organizations, which had no grassroots membership, to extend the legal civil rights strategy that had resulted in the *Brown* decision, postwar racial liberalism's greatest achievement. They acted on behalf but not with their respective racial communities in the courts, not the streets, to achieve public policy victories, including ones involving bilingual education, affirmative action, fair employment practices, and enforcement of school desegregation, all through the expert legal intervention of their largely nonwhite lawyers, often cultivated through Foundation support of minority legal education.[96]

Expert, indigenous leadership would also help to resolve the challenge to the elite theory of democracy posed by black demands for self-determination through participatory democracy. In the Godkin lecture, Bundy suggested a solution to this quandary. While largely a defense of top-down authority to serve the public interest, he also acknowledged in his speech that the populist challenge of 1960s social movements meant that a "theory and practice of a government" was needed "which reconciles executive authority and popular participation." His ideal was to place "a heavy premium on the kind of leadership, like that of John Kennedy . . . which allows the citizen to participate by a serious identification of his concerns with those of a political leader." While he acknowledged that "there is a fine line between democratic leadership and mere personalism," he found "no good case for giving up on the former for fear of the latter" in an effort to reconnect authority and participation "in a system of power that is both strong and responsively shared."[97] Extending Bundy's logic to the specific instance of African Americans, their calls for participation could be best served by rational and responsible leaders of their own race to guide their social development. While a frankly elitist notion, in a society that had denied African Americans real power, such a premium on the creation of black authority and leadership nevertheless resonated deeply with black power's call for self-determination.

So did the Ford Foundation's separatist vision for African Americans. Bundy and his officers believed that a period of separate "social development" was a necessary stage in African Americans' eventual assimilation into the mainstream. Eventually, as he promised in the Foundation's 1967 annual report, members of the black community would take on their proportion of leadership positions in American society, and they would do so without having to deny their blackness. He declared that "the destiny of the Negro in America is to be both Negro and American, and . . . as he makes progress he is likely to do what the rest of us do: he will take pride in his particular group at the same time that he insists on full membership in the society as a whole."[98]

White Power in the Black Power Era

While Bundy was ready to treat with black power advocates in order to bring about racial equity, his goal was always the perpetuation of an American system in which a like-minded liberal establishment remained in control at the very top. For example, while he could imagine individual African Americans sharing in the nation's leadership with whites—and in fact in 1980 a black man, Franklin Thomas, would replace Bundy as the Foundation's president—these new decision makers were not to transform the country; rather, their individual social mobility in American society would represent their successful assimilation into its mainstream. Furthermore, Bundy and his establishment peers would determine and oversee the process by which this incorporation would happen to best serve the interests of corporate capitalism. In November 1967, one year into McGeorge Bundy's presidency and the Social Development program, the Foundation opened its new headquarters on 43rd Street, near the United Nations headquarters and Chrysler Building in midtown Manhattan. An architectural marvel, the hugely expensive building boasted rose-tinted granite cladding, two ten-story glass exterior walls, luxurious fixtures, and, most spectacular, an indoor tropical garden, reaching up into the expanse of a soaring atrium. The *Times* architecture critic Ada Louise Huxtable proclaimed it a masterpiece of understated extravagance, "a splendid, shimmering Crystal Palace" for America's "corporate Medici," in which "grants will be made and programs pursued in a virtual hothouse of standardized, suave elegance."[99]

Both the Medici and hothouse analogies were apt. A monument to the Foundation's wealth and power, the new headquarters also symbolized Ford's elite privilege to foster a worldview sheltered from real-world constraints and to pursue its social vision as it saw fit. Two aspiring grantees learned this about the Foundation from Social Development program officer Roger Wilkins when he took them to lunch in the headquarters' expansive, penthouse dining room. They were black, grassroots community activists whom Wilkins characterized positively as "working idealists" embodying "the purified essence of the black consciousness movement of the late '60s." According to Wilkins, after looking down at the atrium, dizzy from the height and from the luxury of their surroundings, the pair explained to him that all they needed was $25,000 to sustain their successful inner-city preschool for another year, after which they would be in line for public funding. Wilkins had to tell them no; their program simply did not fit within the current priorities of the Foundation. As the elevator doors closed on the disappointed couple, Wilkins overheard the man say, "We could run our school for three years with just what it cost to build this elevator."[100] Through the Foundation's rejection these aspiring grantees learned—or most likely relearned—the lesson of white power in the black power era the quick and easy way; this inevitable realization would be a longer time coming for the Foundation's successful black power grantees in the chapters that follow.

PART II

Transforming the Ghetto

Chapter 3

Developmental Separatism and Community Control

When the Ford Foundation's Fund for the Advancement of Education and the New York Board of Education joined forces in the early 1950s to deal with the "problem" of Puerto Rican migration to the city, their solution was clear. The authors of the study that resulted from their collaboration were confident that the "rapid adjustment of Puerto Rican children and parents to the community and the community to them"[1] would result from a conflict-free integration of these children into racially mixed public schools where they would have access to a wide array of cutting-edge enrichment programs aimed at their acculturation to city life. This rosy view of a desegregated future in New York City's schools was based on two core assumptions undergirding postwar racial liberalism. The first was that school segregation was a Southern, regional problem of Jim Crow law and premodern irrationality that would be dealt with through the landmark 1954 *Brown* Supreme Court decision. The second was that racial liberalism prevailed among whites in the modern, industrial North and that any racial segregation that did exist there was natural or accidental, not the result of deliberate policy. Instead, the key racial issue in New York City was one of assimilating the largely nonwhite and rural migrants streaming into cities from the Puerto Rico and the U.S. South into the modern mainstream.

However, in the years to come, this worldview and hypothesis would be sorely tested in New York City and other cities round the nation. Recalcitrant officials, spurred on by white citizens' resistance, stymied desegregation in the South *and* North. Meanwhile, instead of becoming centers of migrant assimilation, ghetto schools deteriorated nationwide. In New York City specifically, the Board of Education that cosponsored the Puerto Rican Study belied its commitment to integration and acculturation. It refused to acknowledge

and then failed to act decisively on the racial segregation and inequality created by its own racialized zoning of school districts and its tolerance of a personnel policy that filled the city's de facto black schools with the system's least
experienced teachers. Meanwhile, the Ford Foundation itself lost the courage
of its convictions after the right-wing congressional scrutiny of the Reece and
Cox commissions, bowing to political pressure by abandoning desegregation
as a policy solution and ignoring the ongoing crisis in inner-city education
caused by policies like those of the New York City Board.[2]

Given this history of wholesale white disregard, resistance, and prevari-
cation, the only reason that school desegregation did not die as a political
issue in New York City and elsewhere was because of the Sisyphean struggles
of civil rights activists. In the 1950s and early 1960s, this group saw school
integration as the most likely course to make the public schools answerable
to the nonwhite parents and children for whom they were, in large part, failing miserably. In New York City, this crusade began right after the *Brown*
decision, led by black psychologist Kenneth Clark, one of the crucial expert
witnesses in the case. He and his supporters knew full well that segregation
was a problem for the North and New York City, and they used *Brown* to
fight the board's defense and justification of the status quo, forcing it to establish a commission on integration in December 1954. While the commission published recommendations for desegregation, the board did virtually
nothing about them. This inaction established a pattern of equivocation and
foot dragging that would continue for the next decade, stimulated by a level
of organized white-citizen resistance to school integration in New York City
comparable to that of many Southern cities.[3]

By the mid-1960s, New York City's black school reformers had reached
the end of their tether. Frustrated and angered by the official reaction to their
claims to educational democracy and simple justice, they turned away from
seeking the white cooperation required to achieve desegregation, and they
instead decided to go it alone by shifting the direction of their fight to the
community control of ghetto schools. Like other claims to black power and
self-determination in this period, this one emerged out of African Americans' lived experience in cities where they were marginalized by a majority
that profited from their exploitation; no wonder, then, that many black New
Yorkers described their situation in terms of colonialism.

It was at this crisis point for racial liberalism that the Foundation rein-
serted itself into the affairs of the education of nonwhite groups in New York
City's public schools, this time by focusing on African Americans. However,

the Foundation no longer partnered with the Board of Education, as it had for the Puerto Rican Study; instead it joined forces with activists calling for black power through community control. In making this switch, McGeorge Bundy and his officers began to revise the Foundation's strategic approach to the urban crisis, but without abandoning the focus on the "problem" of black migration to dead-end ghettoes and the urgent task to create opportunity for black assimilation into the mainstream. Driven simultaneously by the fear of urban unrest and Bundy's overweening confidence that he held the formula for a successful postcolonial transition, whether in Vietnam or post-civil rights America, the Foundation's involvement in the New York schools crisis ushered in a new phase of its developmental separatism. Now the Foundation worked directly with black power advocates, albeit to achieve its and not their objectives.

Bundy and the Foundation's direct involvement in New York's public education system was central to the city's schools crisis of the late 1960s, which resulted in student boycotts, sit-ins at the Board of Education, three citywide teachers' strikes, and, many argue, the permanent realignment of the city's politics along racial lines. Indeed, the Foundation's involvement in the crisis was a predominant way in which Bundy's presidency has been remembered, and for good reason.[4] Bundy played a key mediating role in the first volley in the community-school movement—the high-profile controversy over the appointment of a white principal at the all black and Puerto Rican Intermediate School (I.S.) 201 in East Harlem. Then Bundy was named chair of the Mayor's Advisory Panel (MAP), which developed a plan for the decentralization of New York City's school system that was deeply influenced by his experience in the I.S. 201 affair. Finally and most controversially, the Ford Foundation under Bundy's watch played a key role in the creation of—as well as devising the plans and providing the only operating funds for—three demonstration school districts in impoverished, minority areas of the city. So, although black activists may have initiated the notion of community control from below, from above the Foundation, by virtue of its political influence and financial power, not only played an essential role in this idea's conception but also indelibly shaped its execution according to its assimilationist aims. In fact, Bundy and his officers were among community control's most fervent white supporters and its most instrumental advocates, bar none.

They dove head first into the schools crisis without really considering or understanding the dangers or implications of involving themselves in New York City's racial and school politics. Nor did those at the Foundation fully grasp or appreciate the vision of black self-determination held by the community-control advocates whom Bundy and the Foundation supported in the battle over public education in New York City. These misunderstandings put the Foundation at the center of an iconic political battle that symbolized the culmination of the twentieth-century black freedom struggle in which African Americans sought to use their new voice and visibility to push beyond the formal equality they had recently attained through the postwar civil rights movement to a more expansive notion of freedom that stretched beyond liberalism's limits. The lessons Bundy and his officers learned from this experience would be the touchstone for the Foundation's subsequent efforts to forge a new consensus on race and to find a liberal solution to manage the ongoing and worsening crisis of inner-city poverty and alienation.

The I.S. 201 Controversy and the MAP Solution

In November 1966, Columbia University launched a $200 million fund-raising campaign by announcing a $35 million grant from the Ford Foundation. Of this amount, the Foundation earmarked $10 million to support new initiatives in urban and minority affairs as one of McGeorge Bundy's first efforts to deal with the urban crisis. Included in this smaller sum were special funds set aside for improving "minority relations" in Harlem's Morningside Heights community, adjacent to the campus. Around the same time, the Foundation suggested that Columbia faculty supervise the Urban League's innovative Street Academy program, an established Ford-funded initiative that brought black juvenile delinquents and truants back into the education system.[5]

In retrospect, Ford staff admitted that this grant and proposal were "both poorly-timed and insulting."[6] In recent years, Columbia had been on a collision course with its neighbors in Harlem, who had mobilized against the white institution's high-handed and unilateral development schemes in the largest and most significant black community in the United States, most recently for a gymnasium on the public land of Morningside Park. Harlemites were in no mood to accept such "colonial" expansion, elitist sops, or the white usurpation of black-led initiatives like the Street Academies, especially at a time when calls for black self-determination were reaching their height.[7]

By all accounts McGeorge Bundy was blindsided by the black outrage that followed the Foundation's maladroit move. In seeking a way for the

Foundation to make a mark in solving the "urban crisis," the new president had simply turned, as he and postwar American philanthropists always had, to universities and their experts to address the social issues of the day. Historically, this reflex was particularly strong when it came to white engagement with the "Negro problem"; even the most liberal of America's white race relations experts could not conceive of black self-determination given their understanding of African American underdevelopment in terms of behavioral and cultural deficiency. That is why Bundy had been so pleased that the "great university on Morningside Heights," as he put it at the press conference announcing the grant, was positioned to help out black America, "neighbor" as the school was "to one of the greatest problems and opportunities of American life—the problem and the opportunity of Harlem."[8]

However, the Columbia grant would be the last time that the Foundation failed to acknowledge African Americans as a distinct public within the body politic, a hard-won and most consequential result of the postwar black freedom struggle. Within months both Bundy and the Foundation appeared to have made an about-face in their approach to the so-called problem and opportunity of New York's black ghettos by publicly placing themselves at the center of a bold experiment in black self-determination: the decentralization of the New York City school system in order to facilitate what black power activists termed the community control of ghetto schools.

The call for community control began as the culmination of a long effort in New York City to reverse the astounding record of student underachievement and failure in ghetto neighborhoods in which by the mid-1960s black students read on average two years behind and dropped out at twice the rate of their white counterparts.[9] For a decade, black activists addressed these inequities as Kenneth Clark originally did in 1954, by using the *Brown* Supreme Court decision as a political tool to end de facto racial segregation among the city's public schools. The Board of Education, consistent with the liberal integrationism of the Puerto Rican Study, agreed readily to the principle of desegregation. However, it rarely moved on this belief without the prodding of a citywide group of grassroots activists led by black minister Milton Galamison, first through the NAACP, and then through his independent organization, the Parents' Workshop for Equality in New York City Schools.[10] What resulted from this pressure was a series of ineffectual, laissez-faire open enrollment and school choice plans that only managed to attract a tiny minority of black children

to majority white schools, while more forceful directives to achieve desegregation through the rezoning of school districts, school pairing, and
the creation of new "intermediate" (i.e., junior high) schools sited on the
borders between black and white neighborhoods, resulted in vociferous
reaction and mass protest from well-organized white parents and citizens
and their umbrella organization, Parents and Taxpayers (PAT).[11]

Like white opponents to the desegregation of public facilities nationwide, PAT's members saw themselves as entitled taxpayer/citizens who, in
this case, were defending the putative academic, racial, and "neighborhood"
integrity of their local schools against both the forced desegregation of their
children to "black" schools and of black and Puerto Rican interlopers to
"their" schools. The political effectiveness of this opposition, along with the
institutional inertia of the city's behemoth schools bureaucracy and the dramatic demographic shift caused by white flight from and black migration to
the city during the 1950s had significant political and policy consequences.
By the mid-1960s the Board of Education had effectively abandoned school
integration as a possibility in a system and city that was more segregated than
it had been in 1954 and whose public-school student population had become
more than 50 percent nonwhite.

Black school activists learned decisively of both the board's change of
heart and the limits of white racial liberalism in February 1964 when the
Parents' Workshop, along with a broad coalition of the city's civil rights and
school integration activists led by Galamison, carried out a one-day school
boycott that resulted in the absence of 450,000, or 44 percent, of the system's
students. Despite being one of the largest grassroots protests in U.S. history,
the boycott failed either to result in a board timetable for desegregation or
to gain the endorsement of the powerful white majority teachers' union, the
United Federation of Teachers (UFT), and other prominent white liberals
and their organizations, which had once publicly claimed a commitment to
integration.[12]

In the face of this ongoing rejection from the board, teachers, and their
white fellow New Yorkers, black school activists finally abandoned desegregation as a viable strategy to achieve educational equality. Instead, they began to call for a withdrawal from the system that had betrayed and rejected
them: ghettoized African Americans should control their own "community"
schools. This argument was not surprising; while Galamison and his inner
circle were devoted to a radical vision of racial integration, the rank and file
of involved black parents had always been most interested in improving their

children's education, preferably in their own community schools, racially mixed or not. Desegregation had clearly failed as a strategy to produce that pragmatic goal, and the indifference and hostility of white officials and parents to integration made it clear to many black New Yorkers that they were alone in their quest for quality education for their children.[13]

The struggle for community control first became public in East Harlem, where in September 1966 a cross section of local parents and activists prevented the opening of the brand-new I.S. 201. This protest was the culmination of months-long activism on the part of East Harlemites after the school board, in the face of white parents' rejection, had abandoned its ambitious plan for an integrated school, leaving the student body entirely black and Puerto Rican, and then, adding insult to injury, had appointed a white principal, Stanley Lisser. In response, mobilized black parents demanded that unless white children were brought in to integrate the school, the East Harlem community should be allowed to run I.S. 201 itself, including by making personnel decisions. If the board did not grant them their wishes, they promised that a student boycott would prevent the school's opening. What resulted was a political firestorm and impasse that pitted black activists, now joined by black nationalists from Malcolm X's Organization of Afro-American Unity (OAAU) and the black power incarnation of the Student Nonviolent Coordinating Committee (SNCC) against the school's and city's teachers and principals. These school professionals vigorously defended the established, ostensibly color-blind, seniority and placement policies that had put Lisser in place, as well as their autonomy from parental or community oversight. Meanwhile, the Board of Education vacillated between appeasing both groups, satisfying neither, and intensifying the high-profile crisis, which stretched on for many months.[14]

The call for community control was not solely an East Harlem affair, as the Board of Education and all New Yorkers would find out a few months later when Lillian Wagner, a poor black parent from Ocean Hill-Brownsville in Brooklyn, was prevented from speaking at one of the board's public hearings. As it turned out, that day the gallery was filled with a diverse group of school activists from around the city who had been organizing their neighborhoods for educational self-determination. After Wagner was silenced, this group rose up in solidarity and protest, occupying the board's chambers for two days as the "People's Board of Education." They named Milton Galamison and Wagner its president and superintendent of schools, respectively, and called for community control of the New York City public education system.[15]

These well-publicized and effective efforts to destabilize and delegitimize one of the city's key public institutions would ultimately spark enmity for black school activism not only at the Board of Education and within the UFT but also among much of the city's white working- and middle-classes. However, this strategic about-face to improve ghetto schools would also attract influential white support from other quarters, which the decade-long effort for desegregation had never managed to secure. Prominent left and liberal intellectuals and commentators like I. F. Stone, Alfred Kazin, and Dwight Macdonald; members of the city's business elite who coalesced around the New York Urban Coalition in the wake of urban rioting; and the city's mayor, John Lindsay, and his administration all championed decentralization and some form of community involvement as the best model to deal with the urban crisis. Above all of these stood the Ford Foundation, which through its support of and direct engagement with black activists would shape the movement for community control.

This heterogeneous coalition was part of a dominant impulse in the 1960s to reject the "old" modernist reform ethos that had ruled left and liberal thinking since the New Deal. Where universal bureaucratic state solutions had once seemed to offer the path to equal opportunity and an expansion of the good life throughout American society, now they seemed like authoritarian methods that threatened democracy by destroying communities through policies like urban renewal and freeway building and through unresponsive and inflexible bureaucracies, like New York City's Board of Education, that had no capacity to understand the diverse lives or needs of the people they served. Black activism, including the call for community control, was a critical element in this broad backlash against autocratic state systems, as were the New Left's call for participatory democracy, the anti-urban renewal and gentrification movement spawned by writers and activists like Jane Jacobs, and the community-action approach of the Ford Foundation's Gray Areas and Lyndon Johnson's Great Society. Like many members of the postwar liberal establishment, McGeorge Bundy joined this movement, despite his erstwhile faith in an elite-led technocratic state. Consistent with other hallmarks of his liberalism, he supported and directly engaged black activists against the Board of Education as a matter of systems reform and of conflict resolution.[16]

Bundy became directly involved with the I.S. 201 affair in the fall of 1966, when he was invited by the Board of Education, at John Lindsay's suggestion, to head up a blue-ribbon taskforce to iron out the details of a plan for the school announced by the board in October 1966. This plan responded to the demands of black school activists by agreeing in principle to decentralizing the schools, but it maintained that local people could merely become advisors to board administrators who would retain the real decision-making power.[17] The task force was to be made up largely by the presidents and deans of New York–area schools of education and by elite, national black brokers like civil rights and labor leader A. Philip Randolph and psychologist and iconic school integrationist Kenneth Clark, without any representation or participation from the new community-control movement.[18]

Black school activists in New York reacted with outrage to this plan, which, much like the Foundation's grant to Columbia, represented business as usual. After years of foot dragging and betrayals by the Board of Education on improving the education of black students, including through integration, black New Yorkers were impatient for action that would allow them to force real concessions from this inveterate opponent. As the activists negotiating on behalf of parents and students of I.S. 201 insisted, "The community must have a significant voice to force the Board to assume its responsibility to educate its children."[19] There was no way that black school activists would accept an advisory role only, let alone follow a board-led plan for decentralization that its members had no role in devising and in which they had no faith. Thus, the Board of Education's recalcitrance in ceding any control intensified black opposition, further fueling the schools crisis and leading Bundy to openly reject the taskforce idea. Meanwhile, Bundy and his staff engaged in a nine-month, behind-the-scenes effort to mediate the crisis independent of the school board, focusing particularly on the demands of black activists, "with the hope" that the Foundation's representatives would connect community groups "with school officials."[20]

The negotiated settlement that finally resulted from Bundy's "invisible taskforce"[21] was hammered out between black community-control activists and representatives of the UFT who were brought to the table by the Ford Foundation. It proposed a coalition of parents, community members, and teachers to rule the schools in East Harlem—a power-sharing agreement between the black community and teachers that would ultimately become the basis of the three community-control demonstration districts that the Foundation would fund, of which the I.S. 201 neighborhood was one.[22] More immediately, Bundy's colleagues and allies congratulated him for his apparent success in negotiating the crisis and developing a potential new consensus for school governance in the age of black power.

The most important of these partners was Mayor John Lindsay, who fully supported Bundy in the I.S. 201 affair. A patrician and liberal Republican like Bundy, Lindsay had won the mayoralty in 1966 by hewing to the emerging antibureaucracy orthodoxy. He endeavored to transform the city's entrenched civil service in the schools, police, and city services—on which he blamed the city's multiple failures in tackling the urban crisis. To these ends and from the top, Lindsay contracted outside organizations, including the Ford Foundation and RAND Corporation, to draw up plans to overhaul the city's agencies, and he then hired outsiders to run them. From below, Lindsay mobilized black and Puerto Rican leaders and residents to work and vote on his behalf, not only because they could help quell urban unrest but also because they were a new and potentially powerful political bloc that the mayor could employ against the city's established leadership.[23]

As part of this ambitious program of systems reform Lindsay succeeded in a campaign to get New York State's permission to break up the city's school system into multiple boards, which would entitle the public schools to additional funding and would facilitate the dissolution of an entrenched school bureaucracy that Lindsay saw as responsible for the inner city's educational failure. Lindsay's mandate from the state in March 1967 was to decentralize the system into separate borough boards based on a plan devised by him and not the superintendent of schools, Bernard Donovan. This authority allowed the mayor to begin to wrest control from the Board of Education, which had been operating virtually free from city hall.[24] Armed with the means for fundamental school reform, Lindsay appointed Bundy, fresh off of his I.S. 201 victory, as the chair of the mayor's advisory panel created to come up with a plan that Lindsay intended would far exceed Albany's minimal requirements to decentralize the system, thus further diluting the power of the existing Board of Education and giving some measure of control over schools to local communities.

Bundy's direct and active role in New York's school politics marked the unprecedented involvement of the Foundation in public affairs. Since its postwar reincarnation, the Foundation had steadily extended the meaning of its mission to be a vital, independent catalyst or "change agent" in American public policy. However, the Foundation, let alone its president, had never so directly involved itself in such a high-profile controversy. The specific details surrounding Bundy's intercession in the I.S. 201 conflict are murky, but what is clear is the enormous excitement Bundy's involvement created among those at Ford who knew about this "unaccustomed but productive role for Foundation influence."[25]

Figure 3. Mario Fantini, the behind-the-scenes architect of the Ford Foundation's support of school decentralization and community control in New York City, was a specialist in "affective" and multicultural education. Ford Foundation Archives. Courtesy Rockefeller Archive Center.

For supporters within Ford, the most exciting aspect of Bundy's involvement was its potential to demonstrate how the Foundation could employ its people directly, and not simply its programs, in order to effect peaceful social reform. The Foundation was, as one unnamed enthusiast put it in language that reaffirmed and extended Ford's charter commitment to activist leadership in public issues, the only "independent agent" in this case "with enough power, status and autonomy to bring the alienated groups together around a common agreement." For this commentator, Bundy's ostensible success in brokering an agreement among all the antagonists in the I.S. 201 controversy resulted in a new direction for the Foundation in which it not only "solve[d] problems by giving away money" but also could do so through direct and active involvement with them, thanks to "the prestige of its president and the know-how of the people in it."[26]

One major supporter of such a role was Mario Fantini, Bundy's right-hand man on the schools issue. At the beginning of Bundy's involvement in the I.S. 201 controversy, he had picked Fantini, a young, recently named program officer in the Foundation's Public Education Division, as the in-house expert who could help him negotiate the controversy and his role in it. Fantini quickly became Bundy's most trusted sidekick. He had the expertise on public schooling and on the education of the poor that Bundy lacked, and he also shared Bundy's change- and action-oriented perspective. A "hand-in-glove"[27] relationship developed between the two men during the I.S. 201 negotiations in which Fantini often acted as Bundy's proxy in negotiating with the black community, the Board of Education, and the mayor's office.

Indeed, Fantini played a key part in egging Bundy on to play a direct role in this public issue, laying out his case to the president in a memo early in the I.S. 201 controversy. For him, Bundy's involvement would achieve three important breakthroughs for the Foundation. It would "identify the new leadership of the Ford Foundation with the most vital domestic issue of our time" and "project to all the image of a new role for the Foundation in areas of high risk." Second, "it would stimulate certain members of our staff to assume a new modus operandi in which they actively 'make things happen' rather than wait and reflect on the proposals from the field." Finally, "it would give the Ford Foundation an unmistakable leadership role in the important problems of the day, a role that goes beyond merely making money available."[28] In making this pitch-perfect case for Ford-initiated action, Fantini demonstrated the insight into Bundy's style and objectives for the Foundation that had brought him into the president's inner circle.

Such boosterism was vital to the Foundation in the mid-1960s, when Bundy sought a mandate for his presidency while the nation was racked by urban rebellions. In this vexing context, the schools crisis provided the Foundation with a hook on which to demonstrate that even in the supercharged and explosive environment of American cities in the late 1960s it still had the right stuff to steer the course of peaceful social change through its activism. However, in order to do so, the Foundation had to engage with rather than dictate to the black urban public, as the furor over the Columbia University grant had shown. This was a step the Foundation had yet to take, despite its previous community-action programs, such as Gray Areas or Mobilization for Youth.[29]

This shift at the Foundation actually began, as with so many of the Bundy-era initiatives, during Paul Ylvisaker's tenure. In the wake of the Watts riot in 1965 and in the months before his resignation, Ylvisaker invited "some of those who had burned Watts," as he identified them, to help manage an employment program Ford had established in the community.[30] Ylvisaker's intention, like Bundy's in his sympathetic negotiation with black school activists at I.S. 201, was to answer the question of whether philanthropy might stretch the "established order that we live in . . . far enough to shelter and to include those who are outside, or who feel outside this system."[31] If it could, Bundy and Ylvisaker surmised from their liberal, activist perch, the urban crisis might be solved. Buoyed by encouraging signs from their efforts to this end, both men answered a decisive "yes" to the question of whether there should be direct engagement with black activists in order to create social peace.

The success of this approach was confirmed for Bundy when, in the midst of the supercharged controversy over Lisser's appointment, he and his staff were able to negotiate a settlement in the I.S. 201 controversy. Praising them for rejecting the Board of Education's old-fashioned "task force" idea, an in-house Foundation assessment found that "one of the big lessons" of Bundy's involvement was that Ford officials could no longer "develop new ends with old means" when dealing with the black "public." Instead, Bundy and his aides had jumped into the deep end and dealt directly with what this analysis called the "hard core" black power activists of the "last layer" or "bottom" of the black community, rather than depending on elite black brokers from the Urban League or NAACP as they would have in the past, if they dealt with African Americans at all. Implicitly presuming the anger and confrontational tactics of these grassroots black school activists to be irrational, Bundy and his aides applauded themselves on their success in pacifying this "emotionally oriented group" by getting them to "think through decisions that require compromise" while forging the negotiated settlement at I.S. 201.[32]

Bundy relished this secret role, which for him, according to one commentator, was "part self-education, part mediation, and part searching for a useful foundation role."[33] The schools issue brought him back to a familiar place, at the center of a bona fide emergency in which he could take decisive action, just as he had as part of Kennedy's and Johnson's inner circles. This drive to take a leadership position in creating consensus out of the urban crisis, all the while learning on the job, would characterize Bundy's role throughout the Foundation's involvement in the reorganization of New York City's schools. In another familiar pattern for Bundy, by January 1967, just a few months into his involvement with the schools issue, he and his staffers felt that they had been fully "educated to the urban problems and the role of the school and complexities of running a big city system and the pushes and pulls of different publics."[34] Confident that their brief experience had made them experts and unwavering in their commitment to fundamental reform of the Board of Education, Bundy and his staff's stance solidified into what he called the "essentials" for improving the school system—"decentralization, and the autonomy of decentralized, community school systems."[35]

This was the position from which Bundy operated and did not deviate after accepting John Lindsay's April invitation to chair MAP, whose mandate was to establish a decentralization plan. Now secure in what he believed was his mastery of the schools situation and his thinking on it, Bundy readily took on this high-profile and very public role that offered him an opportunity to put his wisdom into practice. While MAP was ostensibly a city hall initiative, it was at least equally a Foundation project. Bundy chaired the panel, and its second most influential member was Mitchell Sviridoff, the former head of New Haven's renowned, Ford-funded Gray Areas project. Sviridoff, whom John Lindsay had just appointed as his head antipoverty bureaucrat, was only months away from being named Ford's Vice President of National Affairs. Furthermore, the panel staff, which did virtually all of the empirical, conceptual, and political legwork for MAP, including writing the final report and recommendations, was led by Mario Fantini, who was aided by Richard Magat, the Foundation's communications head. The Foundation even housed the MAP staff at its headquarters. [36]

All of this involvement pointed to the enthusiastic desire within Bundy's Ford Foundation to be a "lever" as an "influential . . . source of professional and financial support"[37] so that it might impose its vision of educational reform in New York against a recalcitrant Board of Education. In a remarkable inversion of a—mostly pejorative—label with which it was defined in the 1960s, the Foundation identified itself as anti-"establishment" during the schools crisis, arrayed against the "establishment" of "professional educationists," a term Mario Fantini used for the Board of Education's teachers and administrators who were unable or unwilling to disturb the system's status quo, despite its dysfunction.[38] By contrast, Foundation officers believed that they could cut across politics and business as usual through their expertise, money, and supposedly disinterested understanding of the public good. Fantini responded to a journalist's questioning about the Foundation's lack of public accountability, especially in relation to the crisis of the public school system, by asserting that the Ford Foundation's "strength" was in its "independence," meaning that "it can absorb the jolts that naturally emanate from social changes challenging the power structure."[39] In another internal document, an unnamed Foundation staffer defined the impact of this purported independence in more self-important terms. Describing Bundy's success mediating between the antagonists in the 201 crisis, he or she wrote, "Everybody else has a vested interest in domestic issues. . . . What we brought to [the 201 crisis] was our own independence and our own know-how and we could see things more clearly than anyone with a vested interest."[40]

Given this remarkable self-confidence, MAP's final report unsurprisingly simply fleshed out the plan for the schools that Bundy and Fantini had articulated before joining the panel. In its report, MAP proposed the Board of Education's reorganization into a federation of thirty to sixty independent school districts. Each of these would have its own board: some board members would be selected by the parents of district students, while the rest would be chosen by the report's replacement for the old Board of Education, a much weakened "central education agency."[41] These community-based local boards would have broad powers over budgets, curricula, textbooks, building maintenance, and, most controversially, personnel, including the hiring and firing of teachers, principals, and district superintendents.[42]

The Foundation's Case for Decentralization
and Community Control

Why were the Foundation's school reformers so committed to the solution of decentralization from the top and community control from below? The MAP report's title, *Reconnection for Learning*, provides one hint. Its focus on connection gestured toward the dream of conflict-free assimilation that had always been the Ford Foundation's aim in dealing with the "Negro problem." Decentralization and community control could bring African Americans into the national fold by reconnecting the public school system to its role as a gateway of opportunity for poor children. Meanwhile, the schools would be transformed into the setting where ghetto-bound adults could, from the shelter of their own neighborhoods, overcome their supposed behavioral deficiencies and experiential deprivation through their active participation in a key neighborhood institution that would serve as their connection to the rest of society.

These were not entirely new ideas, either at the Foundation or in broader education circles. In fact, Fantini, who led the MAP staff, had spent his career working on the public education aspects of the urban crisis. As the son of working-class Italian immigrants, Fantini had attended Philadelphia's public

schools, and this experience impelled his life's work to develop more em-
pathic and culturally appropriate schooling for the urban migrants streaming
into postwar American cities. After pursuing this goal as a schoolteacher in
Philadelphia, as chair of the teacher-training program at Temple University,
and through an Ed.D. from Harvard, Fantini moved to Syracuse, New York
to head up the innovative Madison Area Project, a centerpiece of the Foundation's Elementary School Teaching Project, a large-scale action-research
initiative that sought more effective pedagogy and curricula for poor, minority children. Having impressed the project's patron, Fantini moved on to
become a program officer in the Foundation's Education program. [43] This last
career move proved to be most propitious for a man of Fantini's passions and
experience when the schools crisis gave him the unexpected chance to engage his experience and apply his thinking at the center of an urgent effort to
reform the nation's largest school system on behalf of the demands of its most
marginalized communities. Understanding that he had been presented with
a once-in-a-lifetime opportunity, Fantini worked tirelessly for MAP, whose
final report his staff facetiously proposed to call "Fantini Power," so great was
his imprint. [44]

Nevertheless, Fantini did not work alone in developing a model for school
reform. In order to implement the political and systems reform required to
bring change to ghetto classrooms, Fantini chose a key ally and fellow action
researcher, Queens College political scientist Marilyn Gittell, whom he hired
as MAP's chief consultant. The controversy over community control had also
provided Gittell with an exceptional opportunity to act on her longtime animating concern—to make municipal government truly representative and
accountable through participatory democracy. Her academic inspiration for
this focus was the liberal mainstream of postwar political theory, which held
that American democracy was based on an open and representative pluralism based on the competition of interest groups. Gittell accepted that orthodoxy at the national level, but, based on her observations of New York, she
knew that it did not hold for the postwar city, where the huge constituency
of poor, recent migrants lacked power over the state institutions and services
that deeply affected their lives. Working from postwar liberalism's commonplace that American corporate capitalism had infinite capacity to expand
the circle of opportunity—she claimed that in the United States "power is
constantly increasing as a result of modernization"—she blamed monolithic
municipal bureaucracies for blocking political influence from American cities' new nonwhite constituencies. [45] Reforming this system would require the

Figure 4. Queens College political scientist Marilyn Gittell—pictured here in 1980 with her foe in the 1960s schools crisis, United Federation of Teachers president Albert Shanker—partnered with the Ford Foundation in developing plans for the decentralization of New York City's schools and the Foundation-funded community-control demonstration districts. Paul Hosefros/The *New York Times*/Redux.

restoration of a genuine pluralism in which political power was distributed vertically as well as horizontally, expanding from the highest to the lowest levels in society. Without the political participation of all groups, entrenched interests would remain in place and the social and political change needed to respond to cities' new demographic and social realities would be impossible.[46]

Gittell was not a radical. Nevertheless, she was a relentless reformer whose argument presented a fundamental challenge to the status quo. It gained some purchase among policymakers in 1964 when she was hired as a consultant on Mayor Robert Wagner's Temporary Commission on City Finances to make the political case for school decentralization. In her groundbreaking report, she exposed in exhaustive detail the enormous re-calcitrance of the Board of Education to change and the negative implications of this stonewalling for urban education just at a moment when the schools' effectiveness was critically important, given the influx of poor mi-grants into classrooms. She advocated for the politicization and democra-tization of the school system as a solution, recommending that the mayor, rather than the nonelected and hence unaccountable superintendents, have control over the schools, and that the system be decentralized in order to foster participatory democracy, especially among the city's poor and disen-franchised nonwhite communities.[47]

At first her decentralization solution found few followers. Mayor Wag-ner did not want to deal with the political hot potato of the schools, and the city's black school activists depended on a citywide school system in order to achieve their desegregation aims. That changed rapidly with the call for community control, when breaking down the school system and community involvement in the schools became de rigueur, both among school activists and in liberal systems-reform circles, including at the Ford Foundation and in John Lindsay's city hall. Nevertheless, the schools bureaucracy and the teachers' union remained powerful antagonists and Gittell remained such a controversial figure that at first Bundy reportedly met with her only in secret. Nevertheless, like Jane Jacobs, another urban affairs gadfly of the era, Gittell ultimately became an established and nationally respected figure. Only eight years after beginning her academic career, Gittell by 1968 had become a full professor and the founder-director of the Institute for Community Studies, initially created through almost $1 million from Ford to supervise and sup-port the Foundation-initiated community-control districts, and then funded over the years by a multitude of generous grants from liberal philanthropy; she spent the rest of her life as a prominent scholar and advocate for participatory democracy in the fight against unrepresentative and undemocratic government services that marginalized the poor.[48]

Together Fantini and Gittell, along with the help of Richard Magat, Sviridoff, and various other allies within the Foundation and without, would flesh out the MAP blueprint for decentralization. In the voluminous archive that remains of their work lies the story behind the paradox of the Foundation's direct engagement with the community-control movement—one of the signal efforts for self-determination of the black power era—in order to achieve the contradictory aim of black assimilation into the American system.

First and foremost, Ford's school reformers joined with black school activists because of their shared outrage over the failure of the city's public schools. In 1966, the Foundation's Education division noted that in the previous fifty years "the position of the city relative to educational opportunity has been reversed." Where parents had once "moved into cities to provide for their children's education," now if they could they left for the suburbs or sent their children to private schools, leaving a dysfunctional and underfunded public school system to the neediest children, the majority of whom in New York City were black or Puerto Rican.[49] Foundation officers knew that black parents shared their understanding "that without success in education all avenues to mobility are closed."[50] Thus they interpreted the schools crisis to be the result of the betrayal of an important aspect of the American social compact, which was that public education had a crucial role in providing access to equal opportunity in a free society. Only a radical reorientation of the schools to serve students' needs could regain the black community's faith in the "system" and avoid social rupture.

Fantini and Gittell's starting point in achieving this goal was decentralization to restore the "sick" school system to its role as an "agency of opportunity."[51] In choosing this focus, MAP's members and staff worked within the paradigm of one of the key trends in postwar organization theory. Systems reform that could come about by breaking down large institutions into smaller, semiautonomous, and largely self-regulating units could potentially quell the Cold War cultural panic surrounding the loss of the accepted hallmarks of the American way—free-market competition, and individual freedom and opportunity—in the face of stultifying postwar corporate and bureaucratic consolidation. Although the "small is beautiful" ethos is often attributed to the 1960s counterculture, its origins can also be found among mainstream business leaders and intellectuals in the Cold War period who searched for a way to restore American opportunity and freedom from within corporate capitalism and in opposition to the centralized tyranny of the Soviet Union.[52] Indeed, Marilyn Gittell's call for decentralization was part of this larger trend; she sought to ensure that the pluralism that was theoretically at the heart of American democracy actually existed.

McGeorge Bundy had himself become a fan of meritocratic decentralization prior to joining the Ford Foundation. At the National Security Council he cut down on its bureaucracy and strict chain of command. Instead, his biographer wrote that Bundy held "smaller, freewheeling NSC meetings" where participants could "argue the merits of each policy course based on substance," unstymied by bureaucratic prerogative.[53] He extended this style to the Ford Foundation, where, in a major shake-up, he fostered the kind of pluralism and participation advocated by Gittell for the school system. He reorganized the Foundation to privilege a free flow and competitive market of ideas between and within divisions, loosening an institutional structure that had created both vertical and horizontal barriers. As he told *Business Week*, "[T]hings are crispier around here. . . . We had a hierarchical organization before—the bright ideas came from below, and the higher you went the more they said 'no.' Now . . . there's more interchange. Now bright ideas come from all over the place."[54] In this atmosphere, young, expert, action-oriented, and forward-looking men like Fantini, whom the magazine chose to profile as one who had caught Bundy's ear, could work with him on innovative schemes.

Ford's school reformers advocated an even more radical decentralization for New York City's school system, which they aspired to hollow out by creating a multitude of largely independent districts, custom-made for the needs of individual communities, and bringing new, nonstate players into the public education system.[55] For example, Sviridoff advocated for "hundreds of independent systems with no more than 15,000 pupils in each."[56] In a plan that presaged the public-private partnerships of the neoliberal era's charter school movement, an approving Fantini reported that Sviridoff envisioned these "competitive" subsystems as being ones in which "the School Board sub-contracts for the actual operation of schools with such groups as universities, industrial firms, teachers' unions, parents, etc."[57] Fantini even worked with some of the I.S. 201 activists, along with Kenneth Clark and other consultants, to come up with a plan for an independent school in Harlem that would demonstrate this approach.[58]

All of these ideas about decentralization involved retooling and reinvigorating hallmarks of liberalism for the necessary organizational complexity of modern America. Similarly, for Ford's education reformers decentralization harkened back to an "American tradition" of "public control of public education," and a "Jeffersonian" concept of localism in which community members had a great deal of power and autonomy over their children's schooling.[59] In fact, in demanding community control, the decentralizers repeatedly claimed the urban poor were only asking for what the American middle class had in the form of "the intimacy, flexibility, and accessibility" of "innovative suburban school systems."[60] By invoking the postwar cult of localism, this rationale for decentralization paradoxically tapped into an ideology driven by the segregationist impulse of whites who had used it to maintain the racial and economic homogeneity of "their" neighborhoods. This included PAT members' efforts in New York City to ensure that African Americans did not attend "their" public schools.[61]

Given its history of shying away from the racial conflict promised by school integration, it is not surprising that the Foundation's support of black school activists began once they had adopted the separatism of community control. In fact, in their promotion of school decentralization, Fantini, Gittell, and Magat all explicitly rejected school integration outright as a realistic means to improve black educational achievement and opportunity within American society. As Gittell put it, "[M]ost American cities are increasing in racial segregation, and within a generation will have a majority black population. School integration simply is neither feasible nor foreseeable in the near future."[62] Fantini told Bundy that because of this growing black/white, urban/suburban split, school integration would require "metropolitan cooperation" between suburban and inner-city jurisdictions, a model that he, like Paul Ylvisaker before him, rejected as "highly unrealistic."[63] Magat shared this dismissive attitude on integration; while in the years leading up to the schools crisis he had been involved in a school desegregation lawsuit in his family's home town of Mount Vernon, New York, he nevertheless boasted to an interviewer that by the time of his involvement in MAP, he and his panel colleagues had rejected this shibboleth of civil rights racial liberalism. They "called attention to the emperor's clothes," Magat claimed, by openly declaring that "integration never has been, or hasn't worked, hasn't happened, and it's not going to."[64]

While the passivity of this response to ongoing and deepening racial segregation might seem anomalous given the Foundation's identity as a social engineering "change agent," it actually opened up another, more palatable avenue for Foundation activism to that end, the developmental separatism of Bundy's social development program to deal with the urban crisis without the conflict inherent in desegregation. Furthermore, Bundy and his staff supported decentralization because they believed that local black parents' and community members' meaningful and even central role in their neighborhoods' schools would overcome the social alienation borne of ghettoization and prepare them to join the American mainstream.

Since the inception of Gray Areas and Mobilization for Youth in the early 1960s, the Foundation had promoted the concept of community action in poor urban communities to these ends by facilitating local people's involvement in the programs that most affected their communities, with the goal that their grassroots participation would train poor people in citizenship, ultimately helping them to catalyze the systems reform needed to overhaul urban institutions, such as public education, and in the end return the city to its opportunity role.[65] Thus the Foundation welcomed African American school activism, even when it spilled over to calls for black autonomy, believing that it would ultimately bring the reform that would facilitate black communities' peaceful acceptance of and incorporation into the system. Ford's school reformers interpreted "Negro demands for participation in public education" through community control as being a quest for "attaining greater *connection* to society, not separatism."[66] Indeed, the Foundation's school reformers believed community control would ultimately result in more meaningful black assimilation than any efforts at desegregation. Therefore, unlike many white commentators, the Foundation's school reformers did not fear the active participation of presumed "radicals" in the school system. They reassured community-control critics on this point by reminding them that the "classic pattern of the revolutionary is that, when he takes power, he shifts from destroying institutions to building order and new institutions."[67]

However, in order to achieve this conflict resolution, these "revolutionaries" had to learn the fundamental responsibilities and skills of political involvement and institutional management. That this social-development process could begin in the familiar environment of African Americans' own neighborhoods, among their own people, and through a public institution that bridged the ghetto and the wider world, made community control of the schools the perfect training ground for the Foundation's developmental separatism. As one MAP discussion paper put it, "The great need at this time is to enable neighborhoods and ethnic groups, particularly in the ghettos, to develop strength, self-confidence, and a feeling of control of their destiny. Requiring interaction with other groups at this time would not only make this difficult but might generate strife and factionalism."[68] In other words, like black students, black communities were in the childhood of their development, and they needed the shelter of the ghetto to build the necessary skills for full political and social participation. In promoting racial separation, the school reformers were shunning the "integration of vastly unequal parties" in exchange for a period of separate social development and the potential for a more equal incorporation of African Americans into the polity in the future.[69]

This social development through the separatism of community control was particularly important to the Ford Foundation during the schools crisis when African Americans would not accept guidance from nonblack outsiders. Exogenous white leadership had been a hallmark of the Foundation's earlier community-action interventions because of its presumption of ghetto dwellers' incapacity for effective self-rule.[70] These beliefs about black incompetence did not disappear in the black power era, but community control promised to help train African Americans to be responsible leaders. Ford's school reformers believed that experience was "the great teacher" and that community participation in the schools would "instill in parents and the community a new respect for the complexity of the professional problems in urban education."[71] The responsibility that accompanied "the power of effective voice" would result in "judgment, stability, and dedication to constructive purposes."[72] Hence, MAP staff always emphasized the "responsibilities" of community control in terms of local board representatives acquiring the competence and knowledge required to run their community schools. Only through this experience and responsibility could effective "political integration of the disadvantaged" occur.[73] In short, as Fantini put it, "Kids grow through participation; people learn through participation," and hence "[p]articipation is a growth mechanism" that would lead to the political development of ghetto communities.[74]

However, this would depend utterly on overcoming African Americans' behavioral problems, which racial liberals in the 1960s believed to run deep and to be at the core of black underachievement and marginality within society. Linking black achievement to psychological and cultural health was nothing new at the Foundation, which had been at the forefront of funding and promoting the behavioral sciences after World War II and whose researchers in the 1950s had pioneered theories of cultural deprivation and pathology to explain black delinquency, leading to school reforms like compensatory education to "fix" black children's supposed deficiencies so that they might learn. However, in the mid-1960s, the Foundation changed tack with Fantini's groundbreaking research in Syracuse, which sought more effective pedagogy and curricula for poor, minority children.

Through the Syracuse study, Fantini, his successor (Gerald Weinstein), and their team of researchers, helped to shift the blame for educational failure from the purported behavioral pathology of poor black students and their parents to the system that had demeaned these pupils and suppressed their culture. Nevertheless, Fantini remained committed to a psychological solution, a "curriculum of affect" in which "the personal and interpersonal" and students' real-life "concerns" were privileged over cognitive learning as the key to educational success.[75] This priority reflected affective education's first aim: "the development of human beings with a sense of self-worth and an ability to function affirmatively and humanely with their fellow men."[76] While a humanistic reform intended to restore the "psychological health and racial integrity" of black children, affective education also clearly had the fundamentally assimilationist aim of social adjustment in providing the psychological tools to "reverse the spiral of futility and break out of the poverty-stricken ghettos."[77] Equipping students with "a richer range of responses . . . in dealing with their concerns" would introduce them to behaviors that would help them participate in "reconstructing negative aspects of the environment so that it can affect human development positively."[78]

Fantini and Gittell believed strongly that this behavioral adjustment could only happen in all-black neighborhood schools. In doing so, they subscribed to the cutting-edge research of sociologists Andrew M. Greeley and Peter H. Rossi, who had recently begun to overturn the conventional wisdom of the *Brown* era that school segregation would destroy students' self-esteem. Instead, they attributed the success of the parochial school students they studied to "the security generated by the ghetto atmosphere of Catholic schools," a finding deeply consonant with developmental separatism.[79] Marilyn Gittell suggested that "community control of schools in black urban ghettos" might "promote exactly those qualities of security, identity and purpose" for black children and their communities that Greeley and Rossi found among Catholic school students, because, as she, Fantini, and Magat put it, "the educational environment is far less likely to be hostile or intimidating to the minority child."[80]

Significantly, for Fantini, Gittell, and Magat, the idea of the ghetto community and its schools as providing an assimilative training ground offering security and self-esteem to students and their communities in general stemmed largely from the scholarship and experience of white ethnics like themselves, including the Irish American Andrew Greeley and Italian American Peter H. Rossi. These scholars and their Ford Foundation counterparts represented the liberal wing of the white ethnic revival of the late 1960s and 1970s. They were "Ellis Island" Americans seeking to replicate for the black ghetto the strength of immigrant cultures and communities that they believed was responsible for their remarkable upward mobility, as well as that of countless other Catholics and Jews in U.S. society.[81] To do so through the schools, Fantini and Gittell borrowed heavily from the pioneering work of an Italian American principal named Leonard Covello, who in the 1930s innovated a "community-centered school" in the same East Harlem neighborhood in which I.S. 201 was located, which sought to bring that then-Italian immigrant community into the mainstream. He did so by providing the necessary subject-based skills for its children's elevation and by bolstering their self-esteem through recognition of their home culture in Italian history and language classes, so that they might "undergo the process of Americanization without experiencing ruthless assimilation."[82] Fantini identified personally with Covello's approach, given his own experience of "ruthless assimilation," when as the son of recent Italian immigrants he was humiliated by a teacher in elementary school as he struggled to master the American cultural idiom in the face of her preconceptions of his "cultural deprivation." He remembered how that experience effectively silenced him "for some time" at school.[83]

Thus, Fantini and his staff sought to find a current model that would view black children's "diversity and differences" as "assets."[84] However, in doing so, they did not reject assimilation as a primary goal in educating minority students. Inspired by Covello, they tapped into the cultural pluralism of the interwar period, particularly "melting pot" assimilation. This ideology posited that American culture was a hybrid and evolving one, constantly enriched by the infusion of new groups for whom the retention of ethnic trappings would facilitate their incorporation into the nation's life, through what the Foundation would call their "'negotiable position' in the American ethnic competition."[85] In Covello's mind, assimilation through pluralism could not be left to happenstance or individual enlightenment, but rather should be orchestrated through the deliberate reshaping of "traditional" ethnic culture to fit the modern context of the United States. Covello hoped to reinvent the Italian American identity into one that would instill the pride and confidence in such students to enter American civic life and encourage U.S. society to support them as full citizens. He did so by teaching, celebrating, and making public the greatness of Italian culture and history through multicultural education. In other words, Covello schooled immigrant children in their own heritage, teaching them a public version of it—ancient Rome, Renaissance art, Verdi opera, and so on—that they would never have learned from their peasant parents, in order to facilitate their assimilation according to his model of cultural pluralism. Significantly, when the East Harlem neighborhood in which he taught became predominantly Puerto Rican in the 1950s, Covello applied exactly the same approach to his new students, demonstrating that it could be applied to any newcomer group.[86]

Like Covello, the Ford Foundation's reformers believed schools could become an essential bridge to assimilation by refashioning students' identity through teaching and affirming a celebratory rendering of their home culture. In fact, Covello's findings dovetailed with Fantini's Syracuse research, which placed "identity education" at the center of its affective curriculum.[87] Thus, while black cultural nationalists' request for the teaching of Swahili to black students was often denigrated as being irrelevant in the American context and having little connection to the regions in Africa from which most black Americans originated, Covello had shown that the preservation or teaching of heritage languages was actually a key factor in creating a secure minority identity that would ultimately lead to assimilation. Hence, Fantini, Gittell, and Magat believed that such invention of tradition for African Americans would result in cultural respect and pride that would open students and their parents to the skills and values that schools could teach them about becoming part of the wider world. Thus, the schools would function "as an acculturation tool, an educational instrument, and a community center attempting to make viable connections between different homes and different cultures in a climate that respects and cherishes creative differences."[88]

This confidence that a new cultural pride and psychological robustness would lead to behavior modification and significant amelioration of the condition and achievement of African Americans corresponded to school reformers' understandings of "control," "opportunity," "black values," and most notably "power." For Ford's experts, these concepts seemed to reside purely in the affective or political realms with which Fantini and Gittell's research dealt. While rarely explicitly defining these keywords in the community-control lexicon, they repeatedly spoke or wrote of increasing black commu-

nities' and students' "*sense* of self-worth" to combat their "*feelings* of powerlessness or alienation"[89] in order to "develop *strength, self-confidence,* and
a *feeling* of control over their destiny."[90] Never pinpointing specific "black
values" that might help ghetto communities in this quest, Fantini, Gittell,
and Magat instead suggested that the spirit of black power affirmations like
"black is beautiful"[91] or "I am somebody"[92] would help students build self-
esteem within community schools. When they wrote of turning the community into an "opportunity setting" through participatory democracy, they did
so in psychological terms of fostering "personal development, growth, and
fulfillment"[93] for its residents.

Notably absent from these therapeutic prescriptions were any promises
of material power. In fact, the school reformers implicitly admitted that economics did not figure into their definition of power, which was confined
to the formal political realm. Today, they wrote, "[t]here is a strong, open
conflict between ethnic groups and the dominant society, between the affluent and the poor, and between generations." While this conflict "concerns
wealth and other material resources . . . the basic issue is the division of political power."[94] Denying a link between politics and economy, and focusing
their objectives on the former, power for black parents would remain largely
within the perceptual, psychological, or symbolic spheres.

In the end, both the idea of systems reform and a narrow definition
of power led the Foundation's school reformers and MAP to the hopeful
conclusion of community control's potential for universal empowerment.
As one document regarding the panel's report put it, echoing Gittell's presumption that power was an "expandable" resource: "We must emphatically
reject the notion that granting power to one group . . . means taking it away
from others. We want a stronger district superintendent, not a weaker one;
we want stronger and more secure principals, we want teachers set free to
do their jobs, and we want a community which takes an active part in the
educational process." In short, the panel hoped to "reverse a tightening spiral of suspicion and fear and replace it with a gradually growing process of
mutual confidence in which all concerned can be liberated—most of all the
student."[95]

Such a vision of universal empowerment was consistent with the Foundation's ultimate objective for school decentralization and community control. It was motivated first and foremost, as it was in much of its postwar
grant making, by the objective of conflict resolution. Opening the system
through decentralization would transform the school into an "organic, uni-

fying institution in the community,"[96] binding the urban poor, teachers, and the "system" into an unbroken social whole. Furthermore, community control's rearrangement of power relationships in the schools would create a dynamism in the system in which all voices could be heard, particularly those of parents and teachers in individual schools, thus providing constructive collaboration. "Commonality of interest would be strengthened" between parent and teacher as "each agent realizes that the other possesses power to affect the process in which they are both interested."[97] So, for example, black parents, by having a role in the running of the schools, would learn a "new respect for the complexity for the professional problems in urban education" and would no longer "oversimplify and lay the blame for failures solely on the professional."[98] Similarly, teachers would no longer be focused upward, on the Board of Education, but rather on students and their parents. As Marilyn Gittell put it, "No harmony between teacher and parent, teacher and pupil, can begin to exist when both are isolated from each other by a bureaucratic system designed as a barrier." However, "[w]hen teachers work together with parents, under accountable school boards, then, their attitudes will be shaped more by the realities of the needs of the school's clients."[99] Such a vertical coalition, uniquely possible in a decentralized system according to Gittell's pluralist ideal, would be extended even further as community "paraprofessionals," working as "foster teachers," bridged the cultural and social gap between teachers and the community in which they worked and as more African Americans were hired as teachers and administrators, thus completing the links in the chain from community to Board of Education. The Ford Foundation worked to fund and facilitate all of these developments to create a school system based on "coordination, cooperation, and mutual respect."[100]

Reconnection for Learning constituted a bald statement of Ford's school reformers' almost unquestioned faith in the ability of consensus building through systems reform and community action to solve the problems of the ghetto. While the report admitted that decentralization would not "wipe out the generations of deprivation" affecting thousands of students, "meet the great deficits in health and welfare services that beset many families" or "wipe out the poverty and physical squalor" in which many students lived, it claimed that it would nevertheless "help to make these developments possible in time . . . by reversing the spiral of fear, suspicion, recrimination, and tension; by strengthening the ability of all participants to turn their talents and energies toward making things happen, instead of devoting their lives to holding one another in check."[101] Such was the strength of the MAP authors' liberal faith in systems reform and community action.

The Black Public Sphere and the Call
for Community Control

Black community-control advocates had no interest or faith in the new social consensus or assimilative "reconnection" imagined by MAP. In fact, their call for community control signaled the countless betrayals that had resulted in their utter loss of faith in the liberal "system's" promise of integration and equality of opportunity. Instead, black school activists sought to go it alone. They hoped such autonomy would allow the further mobilization of black New Yorkers for self-determination beyond the schools and ultimately the transformation of the nation through genuine racial equality. In short, the "reconnection" sought by black advocates of community control was of a black community torn asunder by migration to and ghettoization in the urban North, so that it could achieve its own liberation. Ultimately, unlike their assimilationist white allies, black community-control activists sought black liberation that would result in the radical transformation or overthrow of the "system."

The Rev. Milton Galamison, the prominent black schools activist, explained in his unpublished memoir how he and the black freedom struggle in New York City ended up abandoning desegregation and coalescing around the call for community control. Galamison began his school activism in the 1950s as a radical integrationist, but the ugly lesson of institutional and white citizen resistance to this possibility, and that of racial equality more generally, led him to believe that African Americans could no longer "pay the price good relationships with white people cost." As a result, he transferred his efforts from integration to community control, following countless others before him who had "withdrawn to their own world and to their own strategy."[102] This group had experienced an estrangement from the system and the society that produced it as profound as whites' demonstrated desire to dissociate themselves from blacks. As Galamison put it, the "emerging Black consciousness" was "inevitably anti-white to the degree that whites are anti-Black."[103]

Given their bitter experience, black New Yorkers rejected whites' liberal

Figure 5. Although the Foundation funded SCOPE, his community-control venture, the veteran schools activist Milton Galamison had an uneasy relationship with Ford. Photographs and Prints Division, Schomburg Center for Research in Black Culture, The New York Public Library, Astor, Lenox and Tilden Foundations.

faith in the nation's egalitarian promise; instead they developed their own explanatory framework for understanding their subordination and exploitation, based largely on colonialism and Jim Crow. For Galamison, for example, "the colonialist school system" showed its true colors in the I.S. 201 controversy when, after refusing to integrate the school, the school board assigned it a white principal. It was clear to him from this struggle "that white people not only wanted segregated schools, [but] they wanted to continue to dominate the lives of Black children in those segregated schools."[104] For Preston Wilcox—a longtime leader in the antipoverty movement in East Harlem who was a prolific theoretician of community control—such examples of white perfidy demonstrated the "master-servant relationship—Northern style."[105] The African-American Teachers Association, a prominent voice for black cultural and political autonomy during the schools crisis, called for the end to this form of "colonialism," adding that "[a] school is not segregated because it is all Black." Instead, "[a] school is segregated when it is controlled by outsiders whose only interest is exploitation."[106]

Inverting the dominant understanding of black underachievement as having roots in African American culture, black school activists believed that this system of racial subordination had resulted in *white* cultural pathology, manifested as racism, "the twistedness and sickness [of] which distorts so many minds," including those of black children infected by their bigoted teachers.[107] So intractable was this mental illness that Galamison believed that if community control were to happen, certain "teachers and principals, reared in the swamp of the colonialist structure . . . could never adjust to community control and work shoulder-to-shoulder with people whom they regard as inferior and whose very existence they inherently despise."[108]

This kind of rhetoric was so ubiquitous among black school activists that, after hearing it one too many times, a flippant MAP staffer encapsulated the public testimony of a community-control activist simply as the "need for a Bastille Day, Disturbed Teachers and Deprived Principals, etc."[109] While the Foundation's school reformers dismissed such talk as emotional hyperbole, the consistency of these formulations revealed an extraordinary consensus among African Americans about the need for the radical reform of community control and the reasons behind it. That concurrence meant that black school integrationists and civil rights activists, emerging black power organizations, parents' groups, and high-profile black establishment figures would all work, and often work together, in the struggle for community control. Such unity was a potent example of the alternative African American social vision of the twentieth century's "long" civil rights movement. While black people in the United States may have shifted tactics and differed over strategies for liberation, they developed and unified around an alternative vision of freedom and equality that rejected the national democratic myth and individualist prescriptions for social reform. Instead, African Americans chose collective action and group-based solutions to overcome their shared racial exploitation. Further, blacks of all ideological stripes advocated for racial self-determination so that African Americans could emerge as potent political actors to transform the United States according to their alternative vision.[110]

How did this black public sphere operate in the case of the struggle for community control? Again, Milton Galamison's path from integrationism to community control is instructive, this time in demonstrating the oppositional social vision that drove black school activists of all stripes as well as the unity that diverse black actors achieved in their call for community control. Galamison was a Presbyterian minister from Brooklyn with many associations with black and white leftists with whom he united in the postwar period over their shared racial integrationism. He had been at the forefront of community organizing for what he called "full equality desegregation" since the 1950s, primarily through the Parents' Workshop and his leadership in organizing the mass school boycott in 1964.[111]

Galamison's commitment to integration extended far beyond the assimilation or simple desegregation this term often implies to the institutional transformation of the United States. In a 1963 televised debate with Malcolm X he declared that there was nothing in America that did not belong to him; his struggle was to claim that patrimony. Eschewing any kind of assimilation into the racist culture that had created exclusionary institutions, Galamison argued instead that they had to be reconstructed on an egalitarian basis in order for true integration to occur. In this process, American society would be fundamentally transformed. Consequently, he was opposed to the separatist ideology of the "new nationalists," as he called them, and even the perspective of many black parents who would rather focus on improving ghetto schools than achieving the integration of a relatively few individual students. He believed that both groups had abandoned African Americans' right for total inclusion in American society and had been infected by the "race arrogance" of whites by advocating black separatism and supremacy.[112]

Nevertheless, Galamison shared many perspectives and goals of his nationalist and community-focused counterparts. An anticolonialist ever since an extended trip to Africa, he respected Malcolm X—who, unlike white teachers, had been a vital ally in his school boycott movement—and admired his efforts "to undo three-hundred years of racial lies and distortions" by describing "the oppression and the oppressor and the techniques of oppression" and by working "to help his Black brothers and sisters understand that black Americans were worth infinitely more than white America characterized Blacks to be."[113] Galamison's appreciation derived in part from the failure of his direct-action efforts to achieve school desegregation, despite the extraordinary organizing talent and energy demonstrated by him and the thousands of black New Yorkers involved in this campaign.

Galamison's dedication to the empowerment of minority communities through grassroots organizing was equal to his commitment to radical integration, and so his strategic move to community control was a consistent one. Furthermore, he did not find the separatism implicit in community control to be incompatible with his vision of an integrated society. In fact, for many years he had contemplated "that it might be necessary for Black people to abandon the integration offensive." In a logic that paralleled the Foundation's developmental separatism, he believed that by "escaping the pull of racial gravity, ascending in spirit, self-image and power[,]" African Americans would then be ready to challenge and transform American society by "making a re-entry on the national scene at the proper moment in history."[114]

Galamison's critique of a racist education system bent on black subjugation, his focus on black self-determination and community organization, and his ideologically diverse circle of associates and allies in pursuing this goal, along with the fluidity of his strategic thinking, were matched by the black nationalists who worked with him in the battle for community control. This alliance belied the notion of fractious conflict between "integrationists" and "separatists" or "civil rights" and "black power" advocates. Instead, at least in the case of the schools, all of these groups shared an oppositional social vision that rejected the dominant liberal mythos about a color-blind America of equal opportunity and which they believed could materialize through collective black autonomy.

However, despite this radical commitment to self-determination, black community-control activists still worked with the Ford Foundation, a bastion of racial liberalism committed to bringing African Americans into the national fold. The key to this paradox is to understand that, notwithstanding the radical transformations they sought through black self-determination, many black power activists' thinking was still shaped by a mainstream liberal conception of pluralism, race, and social change, particularly as it pertained to their theorization of the black "community" and how it might best be mobilized for black freedom. Thus, while the Ford Foundation and the leaders of the community-control movement had very different goals and social visions, they believed in taking the same pathway to achieve them. Both groups believed that a "sick" school system had harmed black children. Both presumed that the negligence of ghetto schools to educate children was a betrayal of the American city's erstwhile promise of opportunity and upward mobility. Both understood that these failings perpetuated black poverty and alienation, which they interpreted largely through the lenses of community disorganization, behavioral pathology, and cultural insecurity. Finally, both had faith in a model of developmental separatism to overcome black community and individual deficiencies. This shared framework demonstrated the hegemonic power of the dominant forms of liberal postwar poverty knowledge to explain the urban crisis—a framework for which the Foundation had been a powerful proponent and promoter.[115] These points of intersection and the Foundation's willingness to act on them would make Ford seem, despite its antithetical aims, an acceptable, even essential, powerful white ally to black activists in the uphill fight for community control.

Understanding how these partners in community control first came together over the I.S. 201 controversy, despite working at cross-purposes, helps to explain their connection and its legacy. The I.S. 201 activists whom Bundy and Fantini encountered in their mediating efforts had a fully developed and articulated vision of what they wanted from community control. They had worked for many years on school reform and were closely allied with Preston Wilcox, who wrote extensively on the concept of community control. An instructor at the Columbia School of Social Work in the 1960s, Wilcox had also been working in East Harlem since the 1950s as a community organizer, most recently for the antipoverty group East Harlem MEND, where he began working with local parents on the I.S. 201 issue. Another admirer of Malcolm X, Wilcox was strongly committed to black self-determination and racial pride, both of which figured prominently in the dozens of papers and articles he wrote advocating and fleshing out his conception of community control.

The most fundamental link between Ford's school reformers and the I.S. 201 activists, including Wilcox, was their shared belief that ghetto schools must become opportunity institutions. The call for community control began as an effort to reverse the long and astounding record of student underachievement and failure in ghetto neighborhoods. Student learning, as

Figure 6. Preston Wilcox, pictured here in a suit behind schoolchildren, was the chief theoretician of community control. His vision of racial revitalization for radical social transformation presented a fundamental contradiction to the assimilationist reformism of Ford's school decentralization advocates. Photographs and Prints Division, Schomburg Center for Research in Black Culture, The New York Public Library, Astor, Lenox and Tilden Foundations.

traditionally defined by the three "Rs," was the first goal of community control. Black school activists knew that the stakes of student success or failure were especially high for ghetto dwellers in the postindustrial economy, in which the erstwhile opportunities for poor and uneducated migrants had inexorably disappeared. In this context, the miseducation of inner-city children virtually ensured the perpetuation of poverty and economic ghettoization by failing to prepare students for the job market or higher education, one of the Board of Education's stated goals for educating its students.

This failure felt like even more of a betrayal, given that black New Yorkers, like their white counterparts, subscribed to the popular understanding that the city's public school system had in past generations played a key role in the upward mobility of European immigrants and their white ethnic descendants. David Spencer, a black parent leader in the struggle over I.S. 201, told white New Yorkers, "I love my kids and I know that I want the best for them." He wanted them to recognize this feeling in themselves and he asked them to look back into their history to "find Italian gangsters, Irish gangsters, Jewish numbers bankers—who didn't want their kids to be numbers bankers [or] gangsters . . . !" Spencer reminded the respectable white ethnic middle class that their shady ancestors had wanted "the best" for their kids and had struggled successfully to "separate" the next generation from the underworld. Spencer said, "[M]y community feels the same way! We want to separate our kids from what is bad or wrong in our community—and we want a chance to do it! That is all we want! And education is the key!"[116]

The fight for community control was animated by the refusal of white parents and the school board to answer Spencer's entreaty "to deliver" what Preston Wilcox called "a piece of [the] dream to youth in the ghetto."[117] In response, black school activists advocated the separatism of community control, claiming that they "would be better off to upgrade the educational offerings in our own community" by "hiring superior Negro and Puerto Rican teachers" who would understand and respect students and parents, and their needs.[118] These community schools would bring out, in the words of Preston Wilcox, the "latent potential that an alien society has encouraged black youth to hide under a bushel."[119]

Recognizing such potential would require a "relevant" education that acknowledged the realities faced by black youth, so black school reformers placed enormous importance on the implementation of a curriculum that members of East Harlem MEND believed would "take into account the real needs of the students to understand and successfully deal with the world in which they live."[120] Wilcox elaborated that "the content of the curriculum should enable students and their families to understand not only the conventional meaning of democracy, American idealism and the like but the realities of the kind of world they reside in: racism, police corruption and oppression, slumlordism, the illegal activities—narcotics addiction, numbers, etc.—controlled by outsiders, consumer exploitation, residential segregation, etc." He concluded that "attention should be given to the transmission of life skills as well as information."[121] Such a curriculum would make schooling pertinent to inner-city youth, setting them on a path toward scholarly success. Furthermore, this education, by relating to their experience and expertise, would excite black students' desire to learn and increase their self-esteem; by making education applicable to their particular circumstances, black youth might, according to Preston Wilcox, "begin to rely on themselves" and thus "rid themselves of the need to deny their own identities in order to feel 'important.'" Community-run boards, by advocating for local students and insisting on high standards, could "help the youth believe that they can be black *and* successful."[122]

This "relevant" curriculum with its stated goal of improving black students' self-image and confidence had clear connections to Fantini's affective education and its focus on students' self-esteem. However, while Ford's reformers sought individual accomplishment and assimilation through this approach, black activists intended to mobilize students' new confidence and academic success to contribute to the community. As Preston Wilcox put it, the objective of the independent school boards would be to prompt "youth to adopt a positive stance toward their own communities and to stimulate them to employ their own intellectual resources outside of the classroom, as well as within."[123] Indeed to some, this was "the measure of success of public school education."[124] East Harlem MEND asked rhetorically, "Why can't we organize a school that would turn out outstanding graduates—boys and girls who could go to the best colleges and universities, excel in their fields, and serve the country and East Harlem?"[125]

Making community versus individual uplift a priority in school reform had been an important value for New York's black school activists since the beginning of their campaign in the 1950s, but after the I.S. 201 controversy it became their predominant goal.[126] In acting on this objective, they plugged into a tradition of independent educational efforts aimed at black liberation. For example, they sometimes compared their aims for the schools to those of SNCC's Mississippi Freedom Schools of the civil rights movement.[127] Along with supplementing a substandard Jim Crow education to black children, the Freedom Schools were most important to SNCC in terms of preparing black community members, whatever their ages, for self-determination through exposure to the critical, alternative social vision of the black public sphere. According to Charles Cobb, one of the Freedom Schools' originators, they provided "an educational experience for students which will make it possible for them to challenge the myths of our society, to perceive more clearly its realities and to find alternatives and ultimately, new directions for action."[128] In New York City, Malcolm X's OAAU had adopted the Freedom School curriculum to its own ends, as had the participants in the 1964 school boycott, along with HARYOU-ACT, Harlem's largest antipoverty agency.[129]

Similarly, black community-control advocates hoped to use the public schools to promote black liberation. They envisioned a community-centered school, which could become the "focal point" of community life, as an institution that would be most responsible for "dispensing or promulgating those values which identify a group's consciousness of itself."[130] Thus, all of the black community-control schemes saw community outreach as one of their most important objectives in achieving the goal of making black ghettoes into "viable, effective social units" for self-determination.[131]

Creating community-centered schools that actively involved as many adults as possible sounded very similar to the Foundation reformers' developmental objectives for community participation in the schools. So did the black school activists' focus on black pathology as an essential reason why this development had to happen in the first place. Like the Ford Foundation's white liberals, black school activists adopted the conventional wisdom of a black "culture of poverty" as a devastating barrier to African American social development. Preston Wilcox, for example, was an adherent of white public intellectual Michael Harrington, whose 1962 book, *The Other America: Poverty in the United States*, had become part of the mainstream framework for understanding the nation's poor. As Wilcox quoted Harrington, the American poor were "those who do not belong to anybody or anything." Their deracination led to deprivation beyond the material, which in turn led to alienation: "They are no longer participants in an ethnic culture from the old country; they are less and less religious. . . . They are not seen, and because of that they themselves cannot see. Their horizon has become more and more restricted; they see one another, and that means that they see little reason to hope."[132]

In order to overcome this hopelessness, black New Yorkers needed the chance to see that they could shape their own destiny, especially as it was clear that no one else was committed to improving their lot. As Preston Wilcox defined the problem: "The professional caste system in the ghettos has so effectively intervened" in the community's social welfare agencies and the schools, "that the key decisions are often made by [the professionals] rather than the families they come to serve." However, "[t]he art of decision-making cannot be learned if the opportunity to learn how to do so is not afforded." Invoking the therapeutic peer-support model of twelve-step programs to address this dilemma, Wilcox insisted that the poor could not be helped but must help themselves, by defining their own problems, issues, and strategies for change through mutual support.[133] Thus community control was a healing and developmentalist prescription for the black poor. As the I.S. 201 group of community controllers put it, "We intend to prove that increased responsibility by ghetto parents in their children's education will result in higher educational achievement by the children as well as a greater sense of self-esteem on the part of the parents."[134]

Providing such opportunities for self-help, Wilcox believed, would help the black poor "exercise their own latent power," which he, like the Ford Foundation reformers, defined as purely psychological and political, not material. He insisted that "[d]espite the rhetoric of the sociologists and the politicians, the black poor are not powerless." Instead they were impotent "only because they have come to accept this view of themselves and others have enabled them to do so."[135] If power were psychological and experience-based, as Wilcox posited, community control of the schools would provide the perfect opportunity to demonstrate to the black poor their own capacity to bring about positive change in their own lives. In fact, he had found that in his own involvement with I.S. 201, the "biggest job was to convince the usually-absent parents that they had a right to have their ideas heard."[136] Community control would provide just such an opportunity to develop that sense of citizen entitlement. As East Harlem MEND put it, "By taking positive action to provide better education for their children through the operation of a community-run school," black parents would "uplift the community and stimulate greater participation in forming educational policy by disadvantaged groups."[137]

Thus, while black advocates for community control might have subscribed to many of the tenets of mainstream behavioral science as a framework to understand the lot and mind-set of ghetto dwellers, their version of developmental separatism and community action was very different from that of the white liberals who made this strategy a hallmark of their efforts to combat the urban crisis. The Foundation focused outward on the social development of poor minorities so that they could assimilate into American institutional life. By contrast, the black community-control movement looked inward by calling for the development and mobilization of a community of purpose in the ghetto so that poor African Americans could help themselves collectively to determine their own destiny.

That fundamental difference was clearest when contrasting what both Ford's reformers and community-control activists envisioned as the culmination of their respective visions for community control. So, for example, the power dynamics in the community-centered schools envisioned by black activists were antithetical to what the Ford Foundation imagined in its dream of consensus building of all players through universal empowerment in the schools. In the black community-control model, parents and other community members, rather than teachers, would be the unquestionable experts and leaders when it came to determining their children's educational needs. Teachers would need to work with the community on its own terms, becoming its instrument, and submitting to its assessment of their effectiveness in this role.[138] In short, community control for black activists meant the subordination of the school system to the community's aims; this model contained none of the power sharing envisioned by the Foundation in its vision for school reform. It also took for granted a level of black grassroots initiative and capacity that Ford's reformers could not imagine from their developmentalist perspective.[139]

Similarly, this black power perspective presumed an essential value for black culture that upended white liberalism's pathologizing and assimilationist assumptions. Preston Wilcox was influenced by Leonard Covello's model for community-based schooling and cultural pluralism and in fact he introduced Covello's work to Fantini during the I.S. 201 negotiations. However, the autonomous cultural development Wilcox promoted had very different aims than white ethnics' "melting-pot" cultural pluralism, which posited an American creed of acceptance and openness toward ethnic difference and minority culture that African Americans had never experienced. In a racist society where blacks had been judged solely by white standards, which they could never achieve by virtue of being black, community control was part of the "black agenda" of the late 1960s for African Americans "to expunge from themselves the need to be validated as being 'human' solely by whites." Such "internal self-recognition" was both "self-liberating," and "soul-cleansing," according to Wilcox, and would "make blacks black and not white."[140] Celebrating blackness as a positive racial identity entirely separate and antithetical from whiteness thus was a mark both of healthy black psychology and of black defiance against hegemonic culture. "Behaving black is . . . based on the recognition of the . . . indestructibility of Black men by a society set up to protect the interests of whites." African Americans' desire "to humanize" their survival in a white world "is the intrinsic meaning to Black Americans of the black power thrust," which sought to overcome blacks' conditioning "to view 'whiteness' as a humanitarian goal" and to reject the possibility of black humanity.[141] In this sense, blacks were only "disadvantaged" if judged by white "values and practices which have historically required that those of color give up a big piece of themselves in order to achieve the desired standard."[142]

This racial revitalization necessarily required a period of separation from whites, but ultimately many community-control advocates hoped that these efforts toward self-determination would transform the United States according to their radical egalitarian social vision. In their minds, African Americans were the only ones who could humanize a nation whose Constitution and Bill of Rights, Preston Wilcox reminded his readers, "were molded while Black Americans were considered to be inhuman."[143] In fostering "human values," the black movement for community control had a role to play for the nation as a whole. If blacks were assumed to be "qualified for full membership in the human race" and to be a "part of this society," they had a "dual responsibility" deriving from their "unique social history to participate fully in avoiding further exploitation and in helping to shape society so as to incorporate [their] own concerns."[144] In other words, by participating in their own deghettoization, poor African Americans might not only help in their own community's development but also bring about the egalitarian transformation of the nation as a whole.

Establishing Allies and Enemies

While the Foundation's school reformers might have envisioned a key role for ghetto dwellers in prompting systems reform in public education, they never considered that African Americans' initiatives for self-determination might stimulate the transformation of American society. Such an idea contradicted the Foundation's developmental separatism and its racial liberalism more generally, which could not conceive of African Americans taking the lead in national renewal without their assimilation first into the existing mainstream of American society.

Nevertheless, despite their fundamental differences, black school activists welcomed the Ford Foundation's recognition and support, seeing it as a victory in their struggle to take the community-control campaign "from protest to program,"[145] as Preston Wilcox put it. Like other black power activists, Wilcox surely understood the inescapable paradox that, short of revolution, the implementation of his scheme for black self-determination would require the permission and financial support of agents of white power. However, Bundy and Fantini's rhetoric and resolve on fundamental reform of the schools and their invaluable support on the I.S. 201 issue gave Wilcox and his fellow community-control activists reason to believe that the Foundation was a different kind of white ally, ready to stake its reputation and money on support for the fight for community control.

Furthermore, black activists accepted the Foundation's help because of where they placed the blame for black deprivation and marginalization. In their conception, the urban crisis was rooted in local institutions and politics and not in structural issues or the corporate capitalism that was responsible for both the Ford Foundation and urban deindustrialization. Most notably, in targeting the schools, black community-control advocates pragmatically chose a most visible source of exploitation over the intangible and seemingly indefatigable forces of a racialized economy that had led to the dead end of the postindustrial, inner-city ghetto. It was no wonder that one group went so far as to claim that the city's schools were "the primary cause of poverty in this city!" given how battleworn they had become from the ongoing hostility and stonewalling they had faced from the Board of Education, teachers' union, and white parents in the schools war.[146] Thus, East Harlem MEND's proposed school curriculum, "The Sources and Uses of Power," prioritized state and political power, consigning economic power to the last place on its list, after the sources of "physical or natural power," like electricity.[147]

Placing the blame for the crisis in the schools on urban politics and municipal authorities made black activists' alliance with the Foundation and other elite institutions an unproblematic one at first. In an early community-control document in which Preston Wilcox came down hard on white teachers and their reported denigration of black children's culture and humanity as the root of the schools crisis, he praised a program that he had helped spearhead, in which inner-city high school "underachievers" from New Jersey attended a summer program at Princeton University. Supported by teachers at the Ivy League school who were ready to meet the students more than halfway, encouraged inductive and intuitive reasoning, and sought to develop critical thinking, Wilcox believed that "the legitimate concerns and available skills of the students [were] . . . called into social usefulness" and validated by an elite institution that transcended the parochial racism that plagued the New York City Board of Education.[148] He hoped that the Princeton program would be the beginning of universities' positive intervention in turning around failing school systems and their putatively incompetent teachers. Similarly, while black activists might not have seen the Foundation as "anti-establishment," as the Foundation saw itself, nevertheless they did not see it as part of the system that had failed their children, and it was clearly an ally in their desire to overturn the status quo in the public schools and its apparent support of community control.

However, despite the points of agreement on which they forged their alliance, fundamental differences remained between black school activists and Ford's school reformers, which would become increasingly clear as activists faced the internal and external challenges of establishing the three community-control demonstration districts that would become the next battleground in the schools crisis. In the end, while black activists initiated the community-control model, the vast power differential between them and the Foundation as the moneyed agent of the American liberal establishment meant that the Ford Foundation controlled both the shape and the ultimate outcome of the community-control experiment as much as or more than the demonstrations' antagonists. Such an understanding reveals much about the post-civil rights "turn" in racial liberalism and the ongoing force of white power in the black power era.

Chapter 4

Black Power and the End of
Community Action

In the first months of 1968, the newly elected governing board for the I.S. 201 community-control demonstration district and its recently hired administrator, Charles E. Wilson, sent the Ford Foundation's Mario Fantini their proposal for the schools in East Harlem, along with a request for the Ford Foundation to fund and otherwise support the plan. The board, which was dominated by activists from East Harlem MEND who had been involved in the schools fight at least since the I.S. 201 controversy, was more than ready, as Wilson put it, for "the forces in favor of community control" to "take the offensive." They wrote Fantini because, although the Board of Education was the official sponsor of the I.S. 201 "unit," the Foundation had been the district's de facto benefactor, providing it with the financial and technical support for its planning and election phases. Wilson and the board also believed that Fantini and the Foundation were their allies, based on their words and actions ever since McGeorge Bundy's 1966 intervention in the I.S. 201 crisis. Wilson and the board wanted four things from Ford: first, a "lump sum grant" to put their community-control plans into place; second, "expertise, as and when [they] request [it]"; third, "a forum and a platform from which [they] can get [their] message across," and fourth, "access to other financial sources and institutions." In short, they desired the Foundation to be the servant of the unit—to bankroll and advocate for it, while respecting the district's authority and autonomy as an experiment in community control. In no way did they seek a "dependency relationship" with or "counterfeit nurturance" from the Ford Foundation, both of which they knew would threaten the black self-determination that for them was this experiment's raison d'être.[1] To these ends, the governing board requested that the Foundation compel Columbia University to release the ghetto development portion of its recent $10 million grant from Ford to the I.S. 201 unit. Thus, according to Spencer and the board, the Foundation would undo the presumption of white supremacy underlying its controversial gift by giving the people of East Harlem the resources to dictate their own destiny.[2]

The Foundation's inaction on any of these requests demonstrated that perhaps it had not moved as far from the paternalism of its Columbia University grant as it was widely credited with or condemned for at the time. The I.S. 201 demonstration district was one of three chosen and funded by the Ford Foundation in the summer of 1967 in anticipation of the school decentralization plan created by the Mayor's Advisory Panel (MAP); the others were located in Manhattan's impoverished Lower East Side (the "Two Bridges" unit), and in Ocean Hill–Brownsville, a neighborhood in the midst of central Brooklyn's enormous ghetto. The Foundation established these experimental districts to demonstrate the model of systems reform through community action that McGeorge Bundy and Mario Fantini were certain would peacefully distribute a proportionate amount of political power to black New Yorkers and bring inner-city communities into the American educational mainstream. Thus, while the Foundation might have supported community control in the demonstration districts, it did so from the therapeutic and assimilationist context of the community-action paradigm and developmental separatism. This meant that the Foundation was first and foremost interested in overcoming the problem of black alienation from the status quo, a fundamentally reformist preoccupation that did not include ceding complete control of the operation of the schools to black New Yorkers as Wilson and the I.S. 201 board envisioned.

In fact, while the Foundation was widely portrayed by opponents in this period as underwriting an antiwhite black power project in the schools, the Foundation, as much as or more than community activists, was responsible for the initiation and shape of the projects. In other words, what may have looked from the outside like radical grassroots experiments in participatory democracy were actually initiated by the Foundation from above in order to achieve its assimilationist ends, not those of black self-determination. Furthermore, the Foundation resisted funding the projects directly and instead continued to depend upon Marilyn Gittell, its white, university-based intermediary, to vet and hold the purse strings of the community-control demonstrations. Finally, the Foundation never funded the experiments with an amount more than a tiny fraction of the Columbia University grant and abandoned them when they failed. In short, Wilson and his board learned soon enough the depth of their "dependency relationship" with Ford.

Bundy and Fantini's effort to reconnect inner-city communities peacefully to the school system backfired completely. The demonstrations aroused
enormous controversy based on the fact that they were each run by an
elected community board of parents and local citizens who acted on the belief that they now ruled the schools, including having control over curriculum and personnel decisions. These actions prompted an outraged reaction
by the white-majority United Federation of Teachers (UFT), which saw its
members' hard-won job protection and professional authority undermined.
The teachers' strikes that ensued from this unrest shut down the city's classrooms for weeks in the fall of 1968, making front-page news nationwide.
Since then, historians have recognized the schools crisis as an emblematic
turning point in the history of American racial liberalism, marking the beginning of the end of the postwar civil rights consensus and the victory of
a white, conservative backlash against the claims of the African American
freedom struggle.[3]

The enormous political turmoil that resulted from the efforts of the demonstration districts laid bare the misconceptions on which the Ford Foundation had created, funded, and managed this experiment. Instead of creating
a new consensus as the Foundation desired, the districts became the touchstone for the New York City schools crisis, caused by the vociferous power
struggle between black activists and the UFT. Meanwhile, the inner workings
of the demonstrations exposed the fallacy of social development through
participatory democracy within extremely impoverished black communities in postindustrial New York. Finally, the inherent contradictions between
Ford and its black allies' respective vision for community control quickly became clear once the demonstrations were up and running. The districts' black
leadership experienced none of the assimilationist social development that
the Foundation had intended for them through their new responsibilities;
instead of becoming agents of peaceful reform through their incorporation
into the system, they stuck both to their plan for autonomous community
control and to their strategy of inflammatory protest politics. In short, the
Foundation's school reformers expected too much and had gained the wrong
outcomes from these experiments; this failure led ultimately to the search
by the Foundation's leadership for new approaches to deal with the social
development of inner-city communities in order to allow for more control
over this process. In the end, Bundy and his officers would eschew the inevitable conflicts and power struggles of participatory democracy. Instead,
they began to focus on choosing and developing black leaders who fit their

acculturative vision for the black community rather than relying on black activists whose transformative social vision was antithetical to the Foundation's liberalism.

The Ford Foundation in Charge

McGeorge Bundy and Mario Fantini had no inkling of the difficult lessons ahead for the Foundation as they worked on the Mayor's Advisory Panel to flesh out their plan to operationalize systems reform and community action by decentralizing New York City's schools. They were blindsided by the political turmoil created by the demonstrations, in large part because of how sheltered they had been from hearing or acknowledging dissenting voices while working on MAP. This insulation began with the panel's composition. In order to avoid the political problems of representing the various groups involved in the schools, MAP included no teachers or parents; instead it consisted of a "blue ribbon" group of mayoral appointees. Bundy and Mitchell Sviridoff, a Bundy ally, were by far the most influential panel members. They were buttressed by the only nonwhite members of the panel or its staff, Antonia Pantoja and Benetta Washington. Pantoja was the founder of the Puerto Rican Forum, a self-help-oriented community-development organization, while Washington was director of the Women's Job Corps and the wife of Walter Washington, the former Lindsay-appointed chair of the New York City Housing Authority and future mayor of Washington, D.C. They both supported decentralization and community control but played a limited role within the panel.[4] The Board of Education president Lloyd Garrison and then his successor, Alfred Giardino, presented a consistently skeptical and critical perspective on the panel's majority views, culminating in Giardino's lone vote against MAP's final report. Garrison and Giardino were sometimes, but not ultimately, joined in their minority position by Francis Keppel, a former U.S. Education Commissioner, who in the end signed on to MAP's recommendations.

The panel's pro-Bundy composition resulted in one of many paradoxes of the schools crisis—that of an elitist and top-down body, MAP, working to develop a model of participatory democracy through decentralization and community control. This contradiction between the panel's operation and its objectives was only reinforced by the similarly top-down workings of its staff, who were responsible for all of MAP's empirical, conceptual, and political legwork, including writing the final report and recommendations. Fantini's vastly disproportionate influence on the panel's workings was due at least in part to the fact that he was the only one of four staff members who had more than an avocational interest in issues of public school administration or politics. Further reinforcing this staff inexperience and the tokenism of Pantoja's and Washington's appointments to the panel, none of the staffers and practically none of the consultants to the panel were black or Puerto Rican, despite the fact that the body was intended to solve the crisis in minority education.[5]

Bundy, Fantini, and the Foundation's disproportionate influence on MAP's operation reinforced what MAP staffer Richard Magat retrospectively believed to be "a kind of institutional, or [egocentric] or messianic overlay." He elaborated that the Foundation's officers' attitude in this endeavor was "that we deliver the truth and others will be wise enough to follow." But, he concluded, this attitude betrayed "a certain parochialism." "When," he asked, "did Bundy ever go into a New York City public school?"[6]

This omniscient posture belied the panel's work, which was far from comprehensive. Created at the end of April 1967, MAP's initial deadline for the first draft of a decentralization plan was June 30. In the end that version was not complete until September, a delay resulting from an overworked, inexperienced staff working under enormous pressure to deal with the "innumerable complex and difficult questions" of decentralization and community control for the nation's largest school system. Adding to this burden, the panel was expected to meet and consult the countless constituencies connected to the public schools.[7] Magat noted that, given the staff size and time constraints, "any effective liaison at the same time the study was going on just wasn't possible." Further, he noted that the staff lacked the "right people" who "knew the city . . . in a very deep political way."[8] Such naiveté was marked by staff reports like the one that optimistically predicted MAP's ability to mobilize white support for decentralization against the opposition of "Brooklyn-Jewish-civil service types" at the Board of Education and in the UFT.[9] This projection represented a fantasy of true believers; even a cursory study of New York City's demographics and politics would demonstrate that instead of representing a minority position, the predominantly Jewish UFT membership personified New York City's white-ethnic and emerging white-collar majority, which is why UFT president Albert Shanker and his teachers could ultimately scuttle the Ford Foundation's decentralization dreams.[10]

Although the panel and its staff met with more than one hundred local "organizations and institutions" connected to the schools, these were skewed heavily, although not exclusively, to pro-decentralization groups.[11] Moreover, even when they were told that they might be wrong in their thinking, the singlemindedness of the staff and panel majority did not waver, even when the skepticism came from their own consultants or allied groups and individuals. Staff and panel members heard from a number of experts who raised serious questions about the legal authority of community boards to control personnel and curricula. They also heard concerns about the technical ability of lay boards in very poor communities to run the schools. They themselves echoed the questions of consultants who wondered both how "community" should be defined when a majority of poor black and Puerto Rican New Yorkers were unsettled recent migrants. They also wondered whether the movement for community control might backfire by being more potently employed by the city's large white middle class in a backlash against the city's growing minority population.[12] Despite these questions, the panel and its staff remained steadfast in promoting Bundy's vision. However, this faith would not prevent any of these fears from coming to fruition as a result of the three demonstration districts.

Given their ongoing desire to create a meaningful Foundation role in solving the urban crisis, Bundy and Fantini would never have been satisfied simply to publish their recommendations so that others could act upon them. Thus, even prior to their participation in MAP, they looked for ways in which to achieve their vision for decentralization and community control. They succeeded when in April 1967 the Board of Education called for proposals from community groups for experimental decentralized school districts, and in July the board gave the go-ahead to three plans.

Bundy and Fantini were more than ready to act on this opportunity. As early as January 1967—when Bundy first articulated his vision of decentralized, local control of the schools—the Ford Foundation started working with its MAP ally, Mayor Lindsay's Human Resources Administration, to initiate the competitive subdistrict model that Sviridoff and Fantini had envisioned as an alternative to the autocratic Board of Education. Undoubtedly these men would have preferred a more wholesale reform of the school system, like the thirty to sixty independent districts proposed by MAP, or the genuinely independent schools that Sviridoff and Fantini wanted to create rather than the small-scale decentralization experiments that were all to which the recalcitrant Board of Education would agree. Nevertheless, the demonstrations were undoubtedly a step in the right direction according to the Foundation's framework of social change. For one, demonstration-based social science was the tried-and-true basis of the community-action approach. Second, in its intermediary role in the I.S. 201 controversy, the Foundation felt extraordinary pride in how it had forged what it hoped would be a consensus model of community control to be shared by bitterly divided school activists, teachers and the Board of Education. It hoped that through the demonstration districts it could extend this success to other "alienated community groups" and thus show once again that it had the right strategy to extinguish the fire of the schools controversy.[13]

When the Board of Education called for proposals from nonprofit neighborhood groups that wished to create decentralized districts in their communities, it was with the understanding that the Foundation would provide the successful applicants with planning grants to begin working on the nitty-gritty groundwork for the new districts as well as to hold elections for the governing boards that would run the new districts. The Foundation boasted that this move represented the "culmination of the Foundation's efforts to reconnect the opposing forces," since it meant "official Board of Education recognition of the several neighborhood groups as legitimate bargaining units," as well as the board's "agreement to the formation of new experimental school units supervised by locally elected governing councils responsible directly to the central Board."[14]

Sviridoff—who became the Foundation's vice president of National Affairs, and hence in charge of the demonstrations, shortly after serving on MAP—was technically right when he was later reported to have insisted that the "planning councils" were "creatures of the Board of Education" and that the Foundation simply "supplied funds for their support at the direct request of the Board."[15] However, this initiative did not really originate with the board, and it was not one in which, under different circumstances, it would have participated voluntarily. Instead, the mayor, New York State's decentralization legislation, black school activism, and the threat of summer rioting pressured the Board of Education into collaborating with this Foundation-led initiative.[16]

After negotiations among the mayor's office, the board, the UFT, and black community-control activists, the schools superintendent, Bernard Donovan, announced that the board would consider applications for community-control districts that could be funded by private sources, a decision made specifically to enable the Foundation's experiment. Anticipating this action, the Foundation had already identified the three districts where it wanted to locate the demonstrations along with the local organizations it would support to spearhead community control in those areas: the Community Association of the East Harlem Triangle, Our Lady of Presentation Church in Ocean Hill-Brownsville, and the Parents Development Program (PDP) of the Two Bridges Neighborhood Council on the Lower East Side. The Foundation provided all three with technical support for their applications to the board. In the end, these three Ford-chosen and -supported organizations were the only ones that the board put forward for Foundation planning grants.[17]

The Foundation deliberately chose to fund groups to plan the demonstrations that it saw as being "representative of the most militant, the most alienated, the most mistrustful, the most volatile grassroots people challenging the educational system in New York City," according to the internal Foundation document that formalized the request for the planning grants. These activists were not "'do-gooders,'" the request continued, "and they are not compromisers." Instead, they were "suspicious of any establishment ideas and associations and even raise questions about [the Foundation's] interest in their problems."[18] Acknowledging and funding these difficult groups was precisely the point, according to the assimilationist rationale for the grants. Elevated in funding and prestige by the Foundation's patronage, these groups could become levers to systems reform, according to the Foundation's model of community action. Through this process, their alienation might be overcome by giving them "the sense of identity and self-confidence they [were] striving for"—reasoning that betrayed the Foundation's faith in behavioralist explanations for black power. If all went as planned, according to this mind-set, these newly self-actualized and empowered activists would engage in what the grant request anticipated would be a "process of cooperative planning" with teachers in their respective demonstrations, which would "bring about a stronger partnership" or consensus among these erstwhile antagonists—or the kind of peacemaking that was always the Foundation's objective. Nevertheless, the grant request recognized that the path to this outcome would be rough and that funding these activists presented enormous risks and challenges. "The coordinating and planning experience . . . for the local groups [would be] a new and untried process," and the groups had "never before worked together, nor have they knowledge in professional education." Even more dangerous, the volatility of the grantees meant "the slightest setback could demolish all the progress wrought" since Bundy's mediation began, and the one-time militants "could very well revert to the intense alienation out of which they [had] been coaxed."[19] However, for the Foundation, the demonstrations' potential for constructive community action and social development were clearly worth the risk.

While the Foundation might have framed its choice of planning grantees as "representative" of the most militant black activists on the ground in New York, the truth was that its choices were dictated more by personal contacts than any systematic study of the crowded field of marginalized ghettoes and black activists in the late 1960s, as demonstrated by its choice of the PDP for the Lower East Side demonstration project. While supportive of the concept, community control had not been a focus of the PDP, which had originally approached Ford to fund one of its existing programs; instead the Foundation requested that the PDP submit a decentralization plan for the Two Bridges neighborhood.[20]

Similarly, the Community Association of the East Harlem Triangle was dominated by members of East Harlem MEND, a federally funded antipoverty group, many of whose members had been privileged by the Ford Foundation as black community spokespeople in its negotiated settlement of the earlier I.S. 201 controversy. The Foundation chose Our Lady of Presentation Church for the demonstration in Ocean Hill–Brownsville because of Father John Powis, an activist white priest heavily influenced by the New Left who quickly became close to Mario Fantini. Powis was a leader of the Independent School Board of Ocean Hill–Brownsville, a grassroots organization created to protest the domination of white Brooklynites' interests in policy decisions concerning school construction, upkeep, and integration, all to the detriment of the city's growing black neighborhoods. For the Foundation there was "no question about the depth of [Powis's] commitment and his frustration with and distrust of the Board of Education."[21] The Foundation's promotion of these three agencies would have significant implications in terms of the shape of community control, not least because all three faced significant, ongoing opposition over their leadership and vision from within the communities they claimed to represent. This tension came about because the Foundation's patronage had catapulted the agencies to a level of power and influence they would not otherwise have enjoyed.

The Ford Foundation's mediated settlement in the I.S. 201 controversy became the basis for the planning proposals of all three demonstrations.[22] Negotiated amid heated controversy over the appointment of a white principal, Stanley Lisser, Fantini noted that the agreement that resulted at I.S. 201 "was not exactly a 'partnership' . . . with each party trustworthy of the other." "Rather," he noted, "it was a very pragmatic relationship based on a mutual need to try to resolve a real problem."[23] Hammered out between black community-control activists and representatives of the UFT who were brought to the table by the Ford Foundation, the settlement proposed that a coalition of parents, community members, and teachers would rule the schools in East Harlem. Premised like the MAP report on the greater empowerment of both parents and teachers in the education of ghetto children, in part through their representation on local governing boards and in part by including the pet programs of both groups, it certainly did not achieve a true collaboration between the stakeholders but instead encapsulated the conflicts that would become sparks for the schools crisis without acknowledging or attempting to resolve them. For example, the settlement promoted the expansion of More Effective Schools (MES), the compensatory education program in which the UFT was heavily invested, even though black schools activists objected to this approach as pathologizing black children, rather than the true villain in their view, the school system, including many of its teachers. Meantime, the 201 proposal effectively gave the local governing board, to be dominated by parents and community representatives, enormous powers, including terminating teachers, an action that would lead to the schools crisis because of its contravention of the teachers' hard-won contractual rights and its threat to their union's equally hard-won role as "co-manager" of New York City's public education system.[24] In short, despite the Foundation's sense of achievement in negotiating this settlement, it represented nothing more than a paper consensus and was one that would crumple as soon as it was put into practice in the three demonstration districts.[25]

A major roadblock to conflict resolution was that while Ford's school reformers talked about consensus and reconnection in bringing school activists, teachers, and board officials together, their primary agenda was decidedly nonconsensual—to leverage their own vision for systems reform by using the community-control activists they funded as the catalyst. This Foundation willfulness revealed itself when the board first approved the planning projects, giving the three groups permission to go ahead with planning their demonstrations, but only "subject to [the board's] final approval" as Bernard Donovan wrote to Fantini "after the projects had been presented in their final form."[26] The board's refusal to grant anything but a vague agreement in principle for the planning districts smacked of the kind of foot dragging in which it had engaged in for years over any meaningful reform, including school integration. Undaunted, the Foundation moved full speed ahead on its plans for community control in the experimental districts, perhaps deliberately misinterpreting the Board of Education's willingness to participate in a process into which it had been forced and which Foundation officers intended to use to usurp its centralized authority.[27]

In a July 1967 press release that accompanied the announcement of the planning grants, the Ford Foundation publicly misconstrued a number of points pertaining to the board members' theoretical endorsement of the demonstrations. First, it implied the board's approval of the key "concepts embodied" in the grant proposals, including elected governing boards of local parents, leaders, and teachers that would have the autonomous power to select administrators, set curricula, control their budget allotments from the central board, and create contracts with private educational consultants. Furthermore, the board and the UFT believed that these grants marked only the beginning of a long administrative process that they would ultimately control, through which a new decentralized school system might be devised. Conceived at the start of the schools' summer break, they certainly did not expect much action on the plans before September. Nevertheless, in the same press release, the Foundation announced Donovan and the Board of Education's assurance "of speedy review of detailed plans," and it predicted that "some of the experimental districts could be in actual operation within the year."[28] On this basis, the Foundation announced its planning grants to the three projects at the beginning of July, which required that by the end of the summer all of the units "must have their proposals for experimental school units ready for implementation, the local governing boards organized and prepared for their responsibilities, and basic administrative staff for the projects functioning."[29]

Each of the districts' planning councils fulfilled these terms in a relatively timely manner. The quickest was Ocean Hill–Brownsville, where on 29 July, after a deliberate twenty-six-day planning period led by the new unit administrator, Rhody McCoy, the interim planning council devised a blueprint for the district's operation and scheduled elections for the governing board, which were held on the third of August. The other two projects, which were slowed down by conflicts within the districts over the planning councils' legitimacy in representing the community and, in the case of Two Bridges, over the neighborhood residents' very desire for community control, would complete the planning process, including board elections, by the end of 1967.[30]

The Foundation's own evaluation admitted that the delayed and difficult planning and election processes in the demonstrations "dealt severe blows" to its aims to carry out "the demonstration projects through cooperation and coalition."[31] In truth, putting the demonstrations into place merely exposed the tensions and contradictions embedded in the Foundation's objectives for consensual power transfer and sharing in the schools. In all three projects, for example, the latent conflict between teachers and community activists quickly became painfully obvious. Despite teacher representation on the planning councils, all of the finalized plans for the projects eliminated MES, the teachers' pet project. Ocean Hill-Brownsville's teacher representatives reported an "extremely hostile and negative" atmosphere in planning meetings in which teachers were characterized as "bigoted, incompetent, disinterested, and obstructive."[32] Meanwhile, in the Two Bridges project, teachers, opposed to the way that they believed that community-control activists had disrupted teachers' positive relationships with parents, held up governing board elections for months with their opposition to members of the PDP running for the elections that the antipoverty group itself had organized.[33]

The election eventually happened in Two Bridges but only because, as the teachers contended, the process was rigged by the Ford Foundation's sponsorship of the PDP, which catapulted this organization into an unfamiliar position of authority. Quite simply, the Foundation had chosen Two Bridges as one of the planning districts, and it had granted the PDP the money to hold an election for the governing board, and so it did, even though community control was a minority position in the area. In a very different context, the members of the I.S. 201 Planning Council faced intense criticism and questions from the myriad other antipoverty and community-control groups and activists in Harlem, including from HARYOU-ACT, the nation's largest and best-known antipoverty agency, over its legitimacy to spearhead this high-profile initiative. After all, Harlemites had not chosen the Harlem MEND-dominated Association of the East Harlem Triangle to lead the demonstration district plan; the Ford Foundation had handpicked it out of a crowded field.[34]

The elections themselves reinforced the Ford grantees' power in relation to other community interests, organized and otherwise. In all three of the elections, members or individuals closely affiliated with the planning councils made up the vast majority of the parent and community representatives on the new governing councils. For example, in Ocean Hill-Brownsville, election canvassers paid by the unit's planning council won all seven of the governing board seats reserved for parents in the same election on which they were hired to work; these elected parent representatives in turn selected five community members for the board, all of whom had belonged to the planning council that had hired the canvassers in the first place. Similarly, in the Two Bridges project, community opponents joined the teachers in complaining about the apparent conflict of interest when the PDP ran a full slate of candidates for the governing board even though it was also the agency designated by Ford's grant to run the election. Furthermore, the PDP's access to antipoverty funds meant that it had more resources than any other community organization to campaign for its nominees against a significant group (organized around the local schools' parent associations) that was opposed to the community-control experiment as laid out by the PDP. These controversial practices called into question whether the governing boards were truly representative of their communities and hence whether they could carry out "community" control legitimately. Such doubts only escalated after the elections; for example, in Two Bridges only five of ten board members were active, and of these only one was not associated with the PDP after all teacher representatives resigned. In addition, the elections in all three districts only attracted about a quarter of the eligible electorate, a percentage no greater in any of the districts than for other municipal elections.[35]

The central Board of Education's utter passivity in the projects' operation beyond its agreement in principle with their creation was a major reason for these conflicts of interest, the governing boards' predetermined composition, and the low voter turnout. The board had provided no guidelines or technical support for planning the projects, defining their powers, or for holding elections, leaving the initiative to the Ford Foundation grantees, none of which had experience in these matters. During the elections, the board refused to supply lists of eligible voters to the planning councils, which necessitated hiring the canvassers. After the elections, while the board paid for "the basic costs of education" in the three districts and "dealt with them de facto," it refused to define their rights and responsibilities formally or to give them any authority. Whatever the central Board of Education's reasoning for this inaction, its inertia reinforced the fact that it had not volunteered but had been conscripted to participate in the demonstrations. In short, the elections and the projects as a whole only really represented the initiative of the closed circle represented by the Ford Foundation and its grantees, with uncertain support from above or below.[36]

Faced with widespread criticism for its oversight of these undemocratic practices, the Foundation prepared its defense against its detractors; the board's recalcitrance had made fair elections impossible, and besides,

in other community-action initiatives, including most notably those sponsored through the Johnson administration's War on Poverty, it was "an accepted practice," although admittedly an "unorthodox" one, to allow paid
staff members to seek elected board positions for the agencies that employed
them. Quitting their federal or demonstration district jobs in order to run
for office was a scruple that residents could ill afford in the employment des-
ert of the postindustrial ghetto. As Ford's justification for the practice went,
unless he could keep his job, "the poor man cannot afford to make . . . a
contribution to his community."[37] Unspoken in this defense of bending the
rules of democracy was the Ford Foundation's deep commitment to its belief
that it could reform the public school system through community action,
buttressed by its long-standing elitism and mistrust of popular rule. Now
that a few "poor men" and women had shown themselves to be indigenous
allies in the quest for systems reform, they needed to be supported against
the forces of reaction, however strong, within their communities. Indeed, the
Foundation viewed these figures as forming an advance guard whose formal
recognition through the elections would snowball to further community mobilization. This group had "spearheaded local concern" about the schools, so
it was "natural that they were in the forefront of the planning councils, and
were dominant among the candidates for election." According to the Foundation, it followed in theory, if not in fact, that these community figures' ongoing leadership meant "that more parents are more thoroughly involved in
school affairs than ever before."[38]

The Demonstration Leaders' Quest for Community Control

After the governing board election in Ocean Hill-Brownsville, Marilyn Gittell cautioned unit administrator Rhody McCoy that keeping three staff
members on his payroll while they simultaneously sat on the community
board was "unsound." McCoy did not heed her warning and she did not press
further. McCoy would have had a number of reasons not to follow Gittell's
advice, most of them distinct from but parallel to the Ford Foundation's justification for the demonstrations' election and governing practices. Among
them was his feeling that the tight-knit group of community-control activists
in the district, among them the poor single mothers on his staff, needed to be
supported and nurtured by the project if its larger objectives for community
control were to succeed.

For McCoy, grassroots activism, like that of the women on his staff who were elected to the governing board, was essential to the process of the poor "coming together to overcome their invisibility." In fact, McCoy believed that it was through "the course of political struggle" of their ongoing schools activism that the Ocean Hill-Brownsville community had finally "defined itself."[39] From the very first calls for community control, the "local leaders and parents" of the People's Board of Education, who later dominated the demonstrations in East Harlem and Ocean Hill-Brownsville, called themselves authentic "'inside' experts who should be given a real say in the policy-making and administration of the . . . schools." They intended to use their expertise "to encourage people in local communities to exercise power on their own behalf" and to "help them to take control of their public schools and to direct their children's education."[40] Members of the Two Bridges PDP expressed a similar vanguardism in its original mandate "'to activate large numbers of uninvolved parents" in local schools. [41]

These activists interpreted their election to the demonstrations' governing boards—along with the Board of Education's own initiation of the projects and the Ford Foundation's funding for their planning efforts—as a clear victory for the forces of educational self-determination. The I.S. 201 project's celebration of the governing board election—complete with an elaborate installation ceremony, which included a speech by Manhattan Borough President Percy Sutton and a documentary film about the five schools in the district—symbolized the proponents' understanding that there was no question that they were on the way to gaining community control.[42]

Acting on this presumption of autonomy and authority, and having been given as little regulatory guidance or support by the Board of Education as they had been for the district board elections, the demonstrations began their work. The Ocean Hill-Brownsville unit, in particular, wasted no time in asserting authority over the district's schools. Rhody McCoy's plan for community control, which he developed with the district's planning group prior to its board election, claimed local control over the schools' budget, personnel decisions, and curriculum. One of his first acts once the new board was elected was to appoint new principals in the district without consulting the Board of Education or using its examination process for appointing school administrators, but instead hiring candidates on the basis of their support for and compatibility with the community and the community-control idea. Similarly, McCoy charted an independent course when it came to district teachers. His plan for Ocean Hill-Brownsville was conceived over the sum-

Figure 7. A 1968 confrontation between UFT teachers and supporters of the community-control school board in the Ocean Hill-Brownsville demonstration district. Instead of the social "reconnection" that the Foundation hoped to create through decentralization and community control, open conflict prevailed throughout the New York City schools crisis. Sam Reiss Photographs Collection—Part III, Tamiment Library/ Robert Wagner Labor Archives, New York University. Photograph by Sam Reiss.

mer of 1967, when the teacher members of the district's planning council were on vacation; once September arrived, Ocean Hill-Brownsville, like the other two community-control demonstrations, defied the UFT by keeping their districts' schools open during a one-week teachers' strike in September 1967. In May 1968 McCoy "terminated" nineteen teachers and assistant principals in the district, an action that sparked the school strikes and crisis of 1968–1969.[43]

Other equally oppositional actions marked the demonstrations' determination to forge an independent path to self-determination. For example, one of McCoy's choices for principal was Herman Ferguson, a founding member of both the radical Revolutionary Action Movement (RAM) and Malcolm X's nationalist Organization of Afro-American Unity (OAAU). At the time of his appointment in Ocean Hill-Brownsville, Ferguson was under indictment for a purported RAM conspiracy to kill Roy Wilkins and Whitney Young, the respective leaders of the NAACP and Urban League. For McCoy, these controversial charges, which may have been the result of an FBI setup, were beside the point. Ferguson was an ideal candidate for principal in his school district. Ferguson had been a teacher and assistant principal in New York public schools, but he also had impeccable credentials as a black nationalist and had developed a groundbreaking black liberation school curriculum for the OAAU. While the Board of Education did not agree with McCoy about this contentious figure, the supporters of the I.S. 201 demonstration did. After the board refused to approve Ferguson's appointment, the East Harlem district used Foundation money to hire him as a paid consultant.[44]

Ferguson's involvement in the demonstrations contributed to growing white unease about the schools' activities. In February 1968 Ferguson helped organize an I.S. 201-sponsored Malcolm X memorial at which he spoke at length about the necessity of African Americans' preparation for armed self-defense against whites. In another case, Leslie Campbell, who taught at I.S. 271, Ocean Hill-Brownsville's most explicitly "black power" school, read a student's blatantly anti-Semitic poem on a community radio show after he was asked how his pupils had responded to the teachers' strikes. Such rhetoric fanned the flame of white paranoia, especially as teachers in the Ocean Hill and I.S. 201 projects faced physical and verbal attacks in the classrooms and hallways of their schools and were left undefended by school administrators or the governing boards.[45]

These events, combined with the Ocean Hill-Brownsville district's personnel decisions, generated an enormous amount of white outrage and media commentary about the vengeful and violent potential of black power. Antiteacher violence and bigotry, along with the rhetoric of racial retribution, fueled white fear about black power. These actions thus grievously undercut the possibility of widespread white sympathy for or understanding of community control's larger objective—schools with the autonomy to become crucibles of black self-determination and community regeneration—without which any pragmatic, reformist possibility of achieving this aim through the demonstrations was impossible. For example, while I.S. 201's Malcolm X me-

morial garnered an enormous amount of white media attention because of
Ferguson's pronouncements and the antiwhite rhetoric of the black-nationalist
playwright Amiri Baraka's Spirit House Movers and Players, the larger point
of both the gathering and these men's contributions to it was lost on most of
the white public. As a reporter from the black *New York Amsterdam News*
who attended the all-black memorial summed it up, "taken in sequence and
context [it] was not an anti-white rally." If anything, she continued, "[I]n addition to shaming Afro-Americans into 'waking up' it was a black pride festival dedicated to the slain man, whom [those in attendance] worship."[46] The
New York City Commission on Human Rights concurred, reporting that the
memorial demonstrated "the distinct merit of the idea of community control," which was "the school being used as a community institution," in this
case to "[honor] the community's own heroes."[47] Other "moderate" black
leaders agreed with this characterization: James Baldwin, a mainstream-
sanctioned spokesman for black America, traveled from Europe to participate in the memorial, a testament both to the significance of Malcolm and to
the widespread excitement among African Americans about the potential of
the community-control experiment to achieve the assassinated black nationalist's dream of genuine black self-determination.[48]

Nevertheless, controversies like the one brewed by the memorial raised
the hackles of Board of Education members, on whom the transformation of
the demonstrations into anchors of black community regeneration depended.
Despite the fact that all three districts met the stipulations of the Foundation's
original grant in terms of planning, electing a governing board, appointing a
unit administrator, and developing fleshed-out programs for the schools, the
Board of Education never recognized them beyond its original agreement
in principle. What this meant was that while the demonstration districts received the same basic operating budget as every school in the city, they ob-
tained no supplement to support special programming, leaving them to find
their own funding. This inaction soon made it clear to the demonstrations'
leaders that the Board of Education did not intend to recognize or support
them in any way. For example, when the Two Bridges governing board asked
the central board to renew funding for a paraprofessional reading assistant
program for which the schools in the demonstration had received a budget in
the years leading up to the experiment, it reported being told that "now [that]
we are decentralized, we can go handle our problems." The demonstration's
board members felt that "this is probably the general attitude at the Board
of Education" and bitterly concluded that "we are floating on our own with

probably less negotiating power and informal authority than before we were 'decentralized.'"[49] The demonstrations' leaders understood all too well that this laissez-faire approach indicated the Board of Education's ongoing power. After Bernard Donovan washed his hands of the controversy over the Malcolm X memorial by stating publicly that he had no authority over the I.S. 201 district or what happened in its schools, the governing board in East Harlem exploded in frustration over this widely held misapprehension "that 201 is being operated by the Harlem community." In fact, it stated, "201 has always been completely under the control of the Board of Education."[50]

Hamstrung by the board's refusal to support the demonstrations, and without any other immediate source of funding, the demonstrations' leaders unsurprisingly turned to the Ford Foundation, as the initiator of the projects, to make their vision a reality. While the African Americans involved in the demonstrations were not as guileless about the Foundation's politics as John Powis—he had told Fantini that he saw Ford as part of "the 'revolution' that we are all involved in," while urging him to read Frantz Fanon's anticolonial tract *The Wretched of the Earth*—they nevertheless approached the Ford Foundation both with an understanding that they had no other moneyed ally to which to turn and with wary hope that the Foundation might help them resolve the paradox of their dependence on white institutions without having to compromise their vision of black self-determination.[51]

The district representatives had reason to be optimistic. After all, there was no way that community control would have gotten as far as it had without the Foundation's support, and Ford had actively defended the vision of black community-control advocates over those of the teachers union, the central board, or even other community figures. For example, even though many black teachers and leaders actually protested the ouster of I.S. 201's white principal, Stanley Lisser, because of his successful track record in building school community and fostering student success in Harlem, the Foundation decided to appease the more militant black activists who vehemently opposed anyone but a community-chosen black man to lead the school. Similarly, Marilyn Gittell met with the community-control advocates on the Two Bridges governing council to strategize with this group about how to work to counter their duly elected opponents on the district's governing board, as well as those in the community.[52] The Foundation also funded School and Community Organized for Partnership in Education (SCOPE), Milton Galamison's community-control organization, with a grant to spread the gospel of self-determination among black parents, and it chose Marilyn Gittell's

Institute for Community Studies (ICS) as its subcontractor for its New York City grants, which further confirmed Ford's commitment to its demonstration district grantees and to community control.

Thus the demonstrations' leadership continued to look to the Ford Foundation to realize their ambitious schemes for community mobilization, control, and development through the schools. For example, in September 1967 Rhody McCoy presented the Foundation with a request for $768,000 to fund an adult education and paraprofessional program that he hoped would initiate his plans to turn the school into the crucible of community regeneration.[53] Similarly, Charles Wilson and the I.S. 201 governing board made its ambitious proposal that the Foundation siphon off part of the Columbia grant so that I.S. 201 could begin the hard and costly work of bringing about genuine community control. Additionally, they asked that McGeorge Bundy provide "direct and public support" for the projects by lobbying "to the national news media" and all levels of government for the demonstrations' official recognition and funding, as well as for Ford to create and lead a consortium of foundations to fund programs in the districts.[54] The Foundation's grant assessor reported that Wilson wanted the Foundation "to hold the establishment (Board of Education, Donovan, UFT, State Legislature, etc.) off, while the IS 201 Demonstration District 'did its own thing.'"[55] Such subsidized self-determination was absolutely essential to the demonstrations so that they could "prove," in the words of the Ocean Hill-Brownsville board, "how community participation in the schools could improve the education of . . . children."[56] Otherwise, as the I.S. 201 board put it, "[T]he question can be raised as to just what it is that we are demonstrating."[57]

The Foundation did not share this view of its responsibilities to the demonstrations. Despite repeated meetings and copious correspondence, including increasingly desperate and angry entreaties for additional funding, it took a full year after the planning grants until the Foundation opened its purse strings to the demonstrations, except for a paltry $30,000 in "supplementary" emergency funding split between the three utterly bankrupt demonstrations in November 1967. Disabused of his previous faith in the Foundation by this miserly contribution, John Powis apologized to a Ford staffer for being "so abrupt" with him over the phone but nevertheless complained bitterly about the "entirely insufficient" supplementary grant, which for him demonstrated "unwillingness on the part of the Ford Foundation to go all out in any meaningful real change in public education."[58] The mix of apology and anger in this exchange demonstrated the profound depth of the demonstrations' dependence on the Foundation.

The Foundation was hesitant to provide anything but planning funds to the demonstrations because it considered them a failure of systems reform and consensual power sharing as long as the Board of Education did not support them, and hence recognize and legitimate them. That is why, before making the supplemental grants, F. Champion Ward, the vice president of the Foundation's education division, had to reassure Bundy that they "do not in any way interfere with the Board of Education's commitment to future fiscal support of these demonstration projects" but simply reflected "unexpected developments during the planning phases of the project."[59] Charles Wilson bitterly concluded from Ford's miserliness that while "[t]he foundations may support you in principle," they "do not seem to want to provide the necessary leverage that will support you in fact."[60] In reality, though, the "principle" on which the Foundation supported the demonstrations was fundamentally different than that of Wilson or its other community-control grantees.

Furthermore, the failed goal of systems reform gave the Foundation an excuse to begin disentangling itself from the demonstrations once the controversies over its actions began. After the Malcolm X memorial and mounting criticism over its instrumental role in the demonstration districts, the Foundation issued a press release that minimized the memorial as "peripheral" to the "difficult effort to solve educational problems in the cities"; nevertheless the release worked to distance Ford from the project and its "racially inflammatory activities" by strictly delineating its connection and responsibility to the demonstrations. Encapsulating what would become the Foundation's official line, the communiqué tossed the hot potato of the demonstrations to the Board of Education, characterizing them as the board's effort "toward decentralization of the public schools," emphasizing that Ford's involvement was "limited" to the planning grants. Detaching itself even further from the units by obscuring its central role in the effort for their official recognition and reversing its former disdain for the Board of Education, the document went on to state that "we [at the Foundation] understand that a proposal for administration of the project will be presented to the Board of Education to determine whether it will recognize the governing board of the I.S. 201 complex as the official agency for governing the cluster of schools under the Board of Education's supervision" and that the Foundation's "further support" would depend first "on the Board of Education's approval and commitment to decentralization experiments."[61]

Hogtied by the board's stonewalling and the Foundation's unwillingness to fill the breach, the demonstrations' governing boards and unit administrators found themselves in a vacuum and not "a successful educational experiment," let alone "a transfer of power to the community." The "lie that the Governing Board is living" in the I.S. 201 district, according to Charles Wilson, was the "fraud" perpetuated by the demonstrations' creation: "society" was not "willing to permit black and Puerto Rican people to have a voice in their own destiny."[62] While the media regularly portrayed the demonstrations as dangerously radical black power experiments, the truth was that white institutions refused to share their power so that black school reformers could create anything approximating community control.

The Institute for Community Studies as Foundation Proxy

The Board of Education's recalcitrance to recognize the demonstrations placed the Foundation in a bind regarding its commitment to them as "the model" to "demonstrate the feasibility of using a sub-system as a lever for total system reform."[63] The board—"the body that should be helping them," according to Sviridoff—had to fund the projects in order for them to succeed in the Foundation's mind. Ford's officers were unclear about how long they should "fill the gap" to keep the districts alive as they waited to see whether state legislation would bring about decentralization and reforms to school governance that might automatically force public funding for the demonstrations. However, in the meantime the limbo in which the demonstrations had been placed made their governing boards and unit administrators understandably restless, especially given the Foundation's inaction on their behalf, despite what Sviridoff acknowledged internally to be its "tacit commitment to the three demonstration projects." [64]

Finally, in April 1968, almost a year after the planning grants and months since the unit administrators had begun asking the Foundation for program funds, the Foundation took action. Believing it needed "an intermediary institute which has the staff, time, and resources necessary" to deal with the projects, the Foundation created Marilyn Gittell's ICS by granting her $905,000 to be Ford's subcontractor and proxy in serving the demonstrations. Only $400,000 of Gittell's Ford grant was earmarked for direct program grants to the three demonstrations—$275,000 to Ocean Hill–Brownsville, $75,000 to I.S. 201, and $50,000 to Two Bridges. These were hardly adequate sums for

independent school districts, especially given that the Foundation was virtually their only source of funds. Instead, the bulk of the ICS grant was meant
to assist, assess, and research the demonstrations and other independent or
yet-to-be created community-control experiments in the city. By focusing on
technical assistance, the Foundation saw itself as simply facilitating through
ICS the transfer of power to community residents that it hoped would come
with decentralization legislation, instead of taking on the program funding that had to be publicly bankrolled in order for the demonstrations to be
a success in terms of systems reform. Not incidentally, the ICS grant also
allowed the Foundation to remove itself from direct involvement with the
demonstrations and the politically explosive schools crisis.[65]

ICS was not the only contender to take on this role as Foundation dele-
gate. Milton Galamison, New York's most venerable black school reformer
and an expert and experienced community organizer, may have introduced
the idea of subcontracting the technical assistance and assessment aspects of
the demonstrations in August 1967 when he discussed his new organization,
SCOPE, with the Foundation. SCOPE, like ICS, was purpose-built for taking
on this role. Edward Meade, the Foundation's vice president of education, initially enthused about Galamison's proposal to provide "technical assistance . . .
to neighborhood groups to enable them to organize . . . and to effectively relate themselves to schools in their communities," praising him for "put[ting]
his finger on a gap that exists in urban educational affairs, particularly if decentralization is to become a reality in this city or any other," and calling Galamison "the person most able to carry this [project] off."[66] However, after he
submitted a proposal that Meade accused of being "loaded down with fat,"
Foundation officers abruptly changed their mind about Galamison, deciding
they could not provide him with the $750,000 he had originally requested for
a citywide program or even with the pared-down $380,000 from a modified
proposal that he had produced at Meade's request. Furthermore, the Foundation was worried that Galamison would not confine his work to a technical service and that SCOPE would become a political lobby for community
control.[67] Meade pointed to SCOPE's supporting role in founding the United
Federation of Parents, an organization whose name alone suggested its opposition to the UFT. "If SCOPE is to organize community-school groups,"
Meade pointedly asked Fantini, "what is it organizing them for?"[68] In the end,
SCOPE received a grant of $160,000, paired with smaller ones to the estab-
lished and moderate United Parents and Public Education Associations for a
supporting, communications role "to advance parent-teacher collaboration

and to increase public understanding of issues in the New York City public schools."[69]

In contrast to its fears about Milton Galamison's and SCOPE's partisanship, Bundy's Ford Foundation had no such reservations about giving Marilyn Gittell's ICS a grant even larger than the one Galamison had originally proposed. ICS was the ideal proxy for the Foundation's systems-reform efforts. Because Gittell was a preeminent researcher in the field of decentralization to foster community participation in education, her advocacy of this concept could be couched within the respectable confines of scholarly inquiry. In addition, Gittell had already proven herself as Fantini's collaborator on MAP and as a consultant to the three demonstrations through a $38,000 Ford grant in 1967 to support and evaluate them during their planning phase. Finally, like Fantini, Gittell was an action-oriented academic, and she perfectly fit the ethos of the Foundation.[70]

Furthermore, the choice of a white college professor over a black community organizer was perfectly consistent with an ongoing commitment to community action to effect the intertwined goals of systems reform and the social development of the black community, both of which were indelibly shaped by the Foundation's ethos of expert-led social engineering. The Foundation framed the "complex and difficult process" of "effective community participation and control of public education" as one dependent on effective "technical assistance" and "a new orientation and adjustment in their outlook" for "parents and community people" who could not otherwise "take on the responsibilities outlined under any of the decentralization plans."[71] Accordingly, Gittell promised to produce a "cadre of specialists" from the ranks of the community, who would "eventually," according to Sviridoff and Ward, "offer the expertise [ICS] now provides."[72] This fledgling group would be developed through careful supervision by ICS faculty, as well as undergoing training in specialized academic programs tailored specifically to their background and needs. Such diligent oversight and mentoring also extended to the demonstrations' workings. In fact, the Foundation based its grant to ICS based on the urgent need for an "intermediary . . . which has the staff, time, and resources necessary to . . . the delicate task of working with and developing emerging community groups and deciding at what point and to what extent they require funds."[73] Thus, in the top-down tradition of its form of community action, the Foundation intended that ICS would orchestrate black New Yorkers' assumption of control over their children's education through developmental separatism.

When announcing the ICS grant, Bundy highlighted Gittell's role as an objective researcher by emphasizing that she and her staff would provide technical assistance and evaluate the demonstrations "in a responsible and dispassionate way."[74] In fact, Gittell was the passionate standard bearer of a hypothesis about school reform to which her Foundation partners also adhered. Gittell's primary goal was to demonstrate that public education could be revamped in New York City by opening up the closed political system of the schools from below through the community participation possible through decentralization. As a liberal systems reformer, Gittell's objective was to effect change through the political incorporation of erstwhile excluded groups. Likewise, her notion of community involvement and participatory democracy represented an adjustment to rather than a rejection of the elitism of postwar American democratic theory. While Gittell believed all New Yorkers should have a voice in the system, she thought that in order to be organized and represented effectively, every group in every level of society, high or low, had to develop a "status and authority hierarchy" with its own leaders at the top who would then provide effective representation by competing within the existing political system, thereby turning it from a "horizontal" to a "vertical elite structure." Increasing the range of elite representation in the system through decentralization would increase the "probability of change" through a more democratic political system.[75]

This model of using decentralization to effect school reform through the development of community leaders and their political incorporation propelled Gittell's actions in the demonstrations. In Two Bridges this first meant shoring up the forces of community control. Gittell worked actively with the PDP members against adversaries who may actually have represented the majority position in the district. Further, she neglected to invite those Two Bridges board members opposed to the PDP's dominance to a number of important meetings, including one with Bundy. In the Ocean Hill-Brownsville and I.S. 201 districts, where support for community control was solid but where the demonstrations' leaders struggled with establishing their legitimacy among those they purportedly represented, Gittell hired the individuals and organizations who would receive leadership training through the Foundation's grant—including Rhody McCoy's daughter, numerous governing board members, and organizations connected to the demonstrations' leadership—providing them with jobs, university education, or funding.[76] For Gittell and her Foundation backers, these efforts on behalf of demonstration proponents amounted to valuable capacity building to make the districts successful and was not biased patronage, as her critics would charge. Meanwhile, in an update to Sviridoff, she dismissed opponents to the governing boards as having "been organized by [the] UFT and/or [the Board of Education-sanctioned parent's group] UPA," and she explained the governing boards' loss "of community contact and/or support" as a product of their "internal struggles and . . . conflict with the Board of Ed[ucation]," both of which reinforced the Foundation's rationale for her oversight and involvement in the demonstrations' affairs, were they to result in successful systems reform. [77]

At the same time that Gittell worked to protect the demonstrations from their outside opponents, she also inadvertently contributed to their internal strife in her quest to develop leaders within them. To this end, she privileged the districts' unit administrators and not their elected governing boards, much to the chagrin of the local representatives who made up these bodies and who had been the ones to hire these men to run their districts.[78] Gittell told the Foundation's grant assessor that rather than dealing with a "lay," community-elected board "that is not always available," she found it "much easier to provide technical services" to and "buil[d] up relations" with professional administrators who, at least in Ocean Hill-Brownsville and Two Bridges, were not residents of the communities they served.[79] ICS channeled the grant money through these men, who controlled the purse strings and often did not divulge the amounts they were receiving from board members. She sought to increase the number of professionals in the demonstrations by influencing the districts' hiring practices and in at least one case she put her and Rhody McCoy's favored job candidate on the ICS payroll to work in Ocean Hill-Brownsville so that he could do the job for which the local governing board had refused to hire him.[80]

Gittell was particularly concerned about the vocal members of the "professional poor" who had been elected to seats on the governing boards, including people like Ocean Hill-Brownsville's John Powis and the I.S. 201 Board Chair David Spencer. These men, who had continued to engage in confrontational techniques and inflammatory rhetoric after taking their seats, suggested to Gittell the communities' immaturity. "[W]e must anticipate that some community groups must go through this kind of process" of development, she wrote Sviridoff, "in order to recognize the advantage of compromise and private negotiation." She hoped that the demonstrations could "survive the next year or so" while waiting for them to develop out of the "militant phase."[81] Meanwhile, Gittell told Sviridoff that ultimately in order for the demonstrations to succeed the Foundation "must guarantee broader involvement and a mobility of leadership" through "building . . . structuring mechanisms for feeding in new community leadership."[82] In another memo, she made clear her objectives for such a course. Gittell believed that one way to deal with the "militants" on the I.S. 201 governing board who were clamoring to control the Ford grant money that Gittell was channelling through the unit administrator was "to convince the Governing Board of the need for its own training so that the inactive Board members (a majority) can be activated to cope with this faction."[83] Hence, Gittell's commitment to creating indigenous experts in the schools was not simply to empower local people to run their own affairs but rather to engineer a more moderate and ostensibly rational community leadership. This group of "participants from the community" would have the essential "new orientation and adjustment in their outlook" that was key to the political incorporation that Gittell hoped to generate for the communities represented by the demonstrations.[84]

Gittell had great influence over the shape of the demonstration projects. While organized opposition to the projects may have been manipulated from above as Gittell claimed, ICS, on which the demonstrations were utterly dependent for funding, was also a powerful outsider institution interfering in the demonstrations. As the Foundation's own assessment of the demonstrations pointed out, Gittell's intervention contravened a cardinal principle of school decentralization, and one that she shared in theory—"that different areas have different needs, and local people would be more sensitive to what their own community needs," and therefore were needed as authorities in their own schools.[85] Clearly, Gittell's involvement in the demonstrations far exceeded the straight technical support of the Ford Foundation's rationale for the grant to ICS over SCOPE, but her actions were consistent with the reformist and therapeutic notions of participation and social development that both she and the Foundation shared. From this perspective, both the refusal of the governing board "militants" to compromise or negotiate and the organized opposition to the demonstration in Two Bridges represented barriers to the demonstrations' success in reaching the ultimate goal of systems reform to bring about the assimilation of inner-city communities into schools governance. The Foundation needed to find a way to bypass these roadblocks were it to achieve its aims, either by empowering the professional unit administrators or by promoting and developing indigenous community leaders who shared the Foundation's goals.

The Problem of Community

While the Foundation struggled to get the districts to catalyze systems reform from above and to bring forth black social development from below, the even more fundamental problem of defining community revealed itself as Fantini and his colleagues sought to put their ideas about decentralization and community control into action. The problem first became clear for MAP's staff, which spent an enormous amount of time discussing district boundaries for the decentralization plan. Along with considering the complex bureaucratic and political implications of its choices, the panel also soon realized the problems of both delineating the ideal school community and promoting it as the instrument of decentralization's assimilationist aims. Was community racial or spatial? Who were the members of school "communities"? Parents? Teachers? Activists? The community at large? If district boundaries promoted separate social development for beleaguered and ghettoized racial minorities, what about for the privileged and exclusionary white middle class? How was community to be defined or developed in poor neighborhoods characterized by enormous transience or in those that had a mix of classes and races with diverse wants and needs? As the staff painstakingly outlined for the panel, each one of these questions and others had multiple possible answers, all with myriad potential costs and benefits.[86]

Despite, or perhaps because of, the enormous complexity uncovered by the panel over the question of community and how best to engineer it, the Foundation proceeded with the three demonstration districts as experiments deeply rooted in its firmly held convictions about race, social development, and systems reform and without consideration of the thorny issues raised by MAP's staff. When put into place, all three districts confounded these convictions, ultimately forcing the Foundation to shift its strategy in the inner city, if not the ideology underlying it.

Despite their differences, the Ford Foundation and black school activists' visions for community control were premised upon a notion of consensus and unity of purpose within inner-city neighborhoods. However, such unity did not exist, and both groups found it virtually impossible to create any sense of solidarity due to the pluralism they found in even racially homogeneous neighborhoods. This problem of community building was most acute in the Two Bridges demonstration district. In 1969, about 85 percent of its public school students were either Chinese or Puerto Rican, with the rest about equally split between black and white native-born English speakers. However, this population profile was a mere snapshot; a large influx of Chinese immigrants from Hong Kong and the departure of other groups from the area meant a dynamic and shifting demographic situation. However, the Two Bridges planning council had no Puerto Rican members and only one Chinese American representative, Goldie Chu, who spoke very little Cantonese and had few connections with the new Hong Kong immigrants. The fractious ten-member governing board that was elected as the culmination of the planning process had three Chinese members and two Puerto Ricans. Two of the Chinese members joined a number of Chinese neighborhood leaders who were opposed to the community-control experiment and the dominance of the PDP—which included Chu, the third Chinese board member—on the planning council and governing board.[87]

The Ford Foundation's official assessment of the demonstration districts blamed the opposition to the experiment in Two Bridges largely on the Chinese. The authors repeatedly described this opposition as racial and cultural; according to them, the Chinese belonged to a group that was "generally apathetic, very conservative, and [has] great deference for authority." Furthermore, the report continued, "[T]he recent migration from Hong Kong has brought in large numbers of Chinese who have had great difficulty in adjusting to Western society." "As one black mother said," the assessment concluded, quoting her, "'We have been working together for the school, but most of the Chinese are a drag; they are coolies.'"[88] The Ford Foundation's unquestioning adherence to such racial typologies explained away Chinese resistance to or indifference toward community control through centuries-old stereotypes of Chinese cultural pathology that positioned this group as alien and passive and in opposition to both blacks and whites in the American racial scene.

Such stereotyping also showed how the Foundation understood New York's urban crisis purely in terms of black and white. Community control began as a call from black activists and was supported by the Foundation and other powerful white liberals as a measure to forestall rioting and more broadly to deal with the age-old "Negro problem," now refigured as the "urban crisis." While the Foundation did regularly use the term "minority groups," it did so almost always as a euphemism for African Americans, and not as a term that reflected an understanding of the diversity of interests among the nation's people of color. As with the Chinese, nonwhite and nonblack groups had yet to emerge for establishment liberals as publics with which they had to deal in the way that black people had through their freedom struggle. Therefore, even though the Foundation based its assimilationist model for African

Americans on the experience of the earlier, "Ellis Island" generation of immigrants, it had little interest in the particular claims of these more recent offshore newcomers because they did not present the "problem" that African Americans did in the black power era.

Thus African Americans and their particular claims remained the universal minority issue as far as the Foundation was concerned; if Ford's officers or the black activists it supported thought of other nonwhite people at all, they did not consider that these groups might not back the community-control initiative or would feel threatened by it.[89] For example, while Foundation staffers paid lip service to the needs of the Puerto Rican community in the community-control struggle, and despite Ford's long-standing concern over Puerto Rican assimilation stretching back to the 1950s, they never truly responded to this very large minority group's distinct interests during the schools crisis. Puerto Ricans had different linguistic and cultural issues than African Americans had, and they also legitimately feared that their concerns would be ignored in community control by virtue of the fact that African Americans dominated them politically, even in neighborhoods where Puerto Ricans dwarfed blacks numerically, including in I.S. 201's East Harlem.[90] However, like the Chinese, this non-English-speaking group did not figure into the Foundation's preoccupations, beyond noting the ostensible cultural lag that meant, according to one Foundation document, that Puerto Ricans had "yet to reach the level of involvement of the black population" in the demonstration districts.[91] In fact, the Foundation did not consider these two groups in any significant way in the schools question until it was ready to close out the planning grants, and after Chinese and Puerto Rican parents had mounted anything-but-passive opposition against the Two Bridges and I.S. 201 projects, respectively; at that time, Fantini proposed one small grant for each group as tokens to show "the Foundation's intent to 'balance' its interest with minorities."[92] Based on the Puerto Rican community's growing activism, in 1972 the Foundation would also underwrite the founding of the Puerto Rican Legal Defense and Education Fund whose major early victory—coming at the heels of a landmark bilingual-education Supreme Court case, *Lau v. Nichols* (1974), launched by Chinese American activists in California—concerned the rights of non-English-speaking students to receive bilingual education in the city's public schools.[93]

The Foundation's preoccupation in the community-control era with the black-white dyad also made it very difficult for it to deal with any kind of more complicated pluralism and the myriad publics and perspectives involved in the school experiment. So, for example, according to the grant assessment Marilyn Gittell saw the Two Bridges neighborhood's "strange mix" and consequent "lack of ethnic identification" in the neighborhood and on the governing board as "the biggest problem plaguing [the] District."[94] As an example of this supposedly impossible "fragmentation," the assessment elaborated that "there are not only demands for Afro-American history, but there are also demands for Spanish-American and Chinese-American history," suggesting a potentially insurmountable curricular complexity.[95]

Seeing such diversity as a problem corresponded to the Foundation's developmental separatism to understand and deal with black rebellion. African Americans, in its staffers' minds, required time alone to build community and catch up socially, culturally, and politically with whites. That is why MAP concluded that district boundaries needed to be delineated by race, "particularly in the ghettoes" where African Americans needed "to develop strength, self-confidence, and a feeling of control of their destiny." "Requiring interaction with other groups at this time," MAP's reasoning went, "would not only make this difficult, but might generate strife and factionalism."[96] Such developmentalist reasoning also explains why all three demonstration districts were located in ghetto neighborhoods. While in retrospect figures like MAP staffer Richard Magat joined the Foundation's critics in questioning the political wisdom of not funding a demonstration in a majority or all-white district, the fact was that this possibility never occurred to the Foundation given that the districts were first and foremost meant to spur social development and assimilation.[97]

In reality, while this purely racial view of community might have applied to virtually all-black places like Ocean Hill-Brownsville, it did not to either East Harlem or the Lower East Side, areas whose racial pluralism was typical of many areas of New York City. An attempt to develop a decentralization district in one such neighborhood on Manhattan's Upper West Side foundered on the shoals of racial and class conflicts about whose interests represented "community" in this mixed area comprising a majority of working-class black and Puerto Rican residents and a significant minority of middle-class whites.[98] The Foundation had nothing to do with this aborted plan, and in fact the developmental separatism that helped drive Ford's strategy for the schools emerged in part from a desire to avoid the kind of interracial "strife and factionalism" that plagued the West Side effort, a fact lost in the political uproar that nevertheless resulted from the Foundation's demonstrations. Having rejected the possibility of integration or any wholesale subversion of racial categories in its search for a way to manage the racial crisis in the city, the Foundation had instead settled on a strategy that reified existing divisions in order to avoid conflict. However, this balkanizing approach meant that the Foundation did not wrestle with the pluralist reality of many of New York's neighborhoods or of the city as a whole. As the West Side Committee for Decentralization pointed out, while "[l]ocal control in Harlem will give minority parents power" since they represented the majority in that district, "local control in the integrated West Side community may or may not give power to Negro, Puerto Rican and poor parents," considering the disproportionate resources, both material and political, held by the large white middle class in the neighborhood.[99] By defining community so narrowly according to its ideological and political goals the Foundation avoided dealing with complex social realities in New York City, including very real issues of power. The Foundation's commitment to developmental separatism also helped to contribute to cementing the identity politics and racial essentialism of post-civil rights America.

Furthermore, while many "ghetto" neighborhoods in New York may have been racially homogeneous, in other fundamental ways they least conformed to the static notion of community implicitly presumed by the Foundation's separatist formula for uplift. For example, despite having an almost totally black population, it was nearly impossible for most students to develop a group or individual sense of strength and control as the Foundation intended in Ocean Hill-Brownsville's schools, where, as the *New Republic*'s Joseph Featherstone put it, a "human river" of students meant that "it was not extraordinary for half of those who started in the fall to be gone by spring."[100] These students had often attended a half dozen schools before their tenth birthday. More often than not their rootlessness was even more profound, because less than half of Ocean Hill-Brownsville's residents had lived in the area for more than five years or had been born in New York City, most of them having joined the even greater flow of black migration out of the South that had grown broader and deeper in the decades since World War II.[101]

This pluralism and transience caused serious difficulties in creating and using participatory democracy to create consensus in the demonstration districts. For instance, in 1969 Milton Galamison proposed creating a cadre of paraprofessional "school aides" to visit parents in their homes after having experienced the frustrations of mobilizing the "community" when none cohered in the demonstration neighborhoods. He had found in Ocean Hill-Brownsville, for example, that "[p]arents with few exceptions appeared to

know very few if any other parents in their child's room" and often "didn't
know others in their apartment building" because of their reluctance to leave
their children at home to attend meetings due to their isolation and the area's
high crime rates.[102]

Such efforts expressed the frustrations of Galamison and other school
reformers in getting parents involved in the projects. While fear of crime,
lack of community ties, and political inexperience may have been part of the
problem, there is also evidence beyond the vocal opposition in Two Bridges
that parents did not necessarily see the projects as representing their interests. The demonstrations' pedagogical experiments were a particular point of
disagreement between the units' leadership and the parents they represented.
For example, the Ocean Hill-Brownsville governing board contracted the Behavioral Research Laboratories of Palo Alto, California, to implement its self-
directed, ungraded, programmed learning programs called Project READ
and Project LEARN, in which students essentially taught themselves at their
own pace. The laboratories' offer of free programming was undoubtedly attractive to the cash-strapped demonstration, but it also appealed to Fantini
and Gittell's notions of affective education, and it attracted Rhody McCoy
by providing a pedagogical model in which minimally trained paraprofessionals could effectively act as teachers' aides. While district leaders worked
hard to sell the educational effectiveness of this effort—in one lavish claim,
the demonstration's newsletter boasted that it could "look admiringly at one
[elementary school] student presently engrossed in the pages of *Ulysses* by
James Joyce," thanks to this "radically new approach to . . . education"—there
is no evidence that it produced any overall improvement in black students'
achievement, and many black parents never bought this approach. [103] An
arm's-length survey of six hundred parents conducted for the central board,
as well as informal polls and anecdotal evidence provided by both opponents
and supporters of the demonstrations showed that while district parents
supported some of the curricular innovations in the demonstrations, like
the emphasis on African American studies, they believed that less crowded
classrooms in which teachers taught by maintaining order and discipline in
a traditional classroom setting, rather than self-directed, affective education
were essential for children to develop their cognitive skills. Such pedagogical
inconsistencies over children's schooling were particularly glaring given that
black school activism had been predicated first and foremost on improving
black students' scholastic achievement based on the wishes of their parents.[104]

Part of the demonstrations' disconnect from community wishes had to do with their governance. In all three demonstrations community members appointed to the governing boards, and not the duly elected parent members, controlled those bodies' workings. This influential cadre consisted of the community-control activists who had planned the districts and run the elections. In turn, the boards had less influence than the unit administrators whose power was bolstered by Gittell's support. Furthermore, aside from the elections, when funds were available for voter education, very few parents involved themselves in the workings of the districts. Their poverty and the districts' lack of money for mobilization meant that a small minority of administrators and largely nonparent school activists called the shots in the demonstrations. In essence, the demonstration districts were to a greater or lesser degree minority projects that had neither the resources nor the inclination to reckon with the pluralism that existed within all of their boundaries and to build genuine community.[105]

Lessons Learned

The external challenges facing the districts proved to be even more problematic than the internal ones. A battle raged in the city between the community-control advocates and their white elite supporters (including Bundy, Lindsay, and their allies in the media, including the *New York Times*) and the city's white ethnic middle-class majority (ably represented by the UFT and Albert Shanker, and the populist promoters of the teachers' cause). In a dogged public relations campaign, Shanker effectively condemned and attacked the demonstrations, an easy task considering some of the actions of their leadership and supporters, including the teacher terminations, anti-teacher violence, anti-Jewish speech, and advocacy of armed self-defense. The Ford Foundation proved an equally vulnerable target. Shanker attacked its elitist and unaccountable intervention in the city's schools, charging it with political interference and calling for the end of its tax-exempt status for its efforts "to influence the educational policies of the city."[106] In insisting that the Foundation be considered a political lobby, Shanker noted its inordinate influence over MAP and its planning grants to the demonstrations. Furthermore, he pointed to the fact that three of the Lindsay appointees to an interim Board of Education established during the schools crisis— including chair John Doar, president of Brooklyn's Development and Services community-development corporation (described in Chapter 5); SCOPE's

Milton Galamison; and member Hector Vasquez from the Puerto Rican Forum—were recipients of Foundation grants on which their organizations depended.[107]

The decentralization bill passed by the state legislature in 1969 was the measure of Shanker's success in squelching community control. It effectively destroyed the Foundation's experiment by establishing thirty districts with much more limited powers and much larger boundaries and enrollments than those that made up the demonstration or were recommended by MAP. It also entirely reconstituted the Board of Education—effectively removing the majority of community-control supporters that Lindsay had been able to name during the schools crisis—leaving the mayor with only two appointees, with the rest to be appointed by borough presidents. Meanwhile, Shanker defanged the Ford Foundation by taking his charges about it to Washington, D.C., aiding in the conservative campaign to bring about the 1969 tax-code revisions that prohibited philanthropy's direct, partisan involvement in politics or public affairs.[108]

The Foundation defended itself against this criticism and the tax-code revisions, but in doing so, it demonstrated its readiness to abandon the experiment. Distancing itself from any political advocacy of community control, in 1968 it refused to re-fund Milton Galamison's SCOPE, after he was charged with using $5,000 of his $160,000 grant for lobbying Albany on behalf of an alternative decentralization bill. Further, Ford began a wholesale public relations campaign emphasizing to the media and its critics that it had merely "cooperated" in the demonstrations, noting that they were officially a Board of Education project to which Ford had only "provided some initial financial support." In addition, the Foundation insisted that it had been "scrupulous in its policy of non-interference" in the demonstrations and that, in fact, "if Ford were to be held responsible for all actions of the individuals and parties involved in the demonstrations, then their purposes would be corrupted." Finally, it emphasized that the demonstrations were "experiments," which by their nature "may produce controversy" but would ultimately have to be "judged" for their effectiveness, suggesting that they might very well fail and be abandoned.[109]

Fantini repeated the claims of noninterference in an interview where he was asked to respond to criticisms that the Foundation left the communities high and dry after mobilizing them for confrontation. Denying any Foundation "control" over the units, he explained that they had received grants with "no-strings attached" in order not to "defeat the very purpose of a movement aimed at self determination."[110] However, the Foundation's black grantees felt enormously betrayed by their abandonment by the Foundation as a powerful white ally whose resources and support—financial, technical, and ideological—they saw as the linchpin to the success of their fight for community control. Milton Galamison accused the Foundation of cowardice in the face of the UFT's threats. "I feel cheated," he wrote, "when an agency like the Ford Foundation with three and a half billion dollars is intimidated by Shanker, chickens out and leaves the struggle to me." [111] Rhody McCoy concluded that this struggle would never be the Ford Foundation's or any white institution's, however liberal, because of all whites' ultimate commitment to "protect the social and economic benefits of racism." He concluded from his experience in Brooklyn that "no white community is about to educate its black population" without compulsion; "[l]acking an economic and political power base to bargain from, the [black] community is forced not to bargain at all," Mc-Coy continued, and thus had to resort to its "only power," the "futile and self-defeating weaponry . . . of violence and disruption."[112]

Nevertheless, while the Foundation distanced itself from the districts and the black project for community control, McGeorge Bundy continued to see the urban crisis as the critical issue of his presidency. He responded to an irate former principal who blamed the Foundation for the schools mess, that the "crisis" of racial inequality in public education, and by extension the city, "was already acute before anyone at the Ford Foundation was involved in it" and that "my own belief is that . . . we were too slow to see how important and urgent it was to have action here—not too fast."[113] Hence, while the Foundation might have abandoned the fight for decentralization based on community action, the Foundation continued to seek the right solution for the ghetto, based on the lessons it had learned from the demonstrations.

Primary among these was how the Foundation had made a mistake in extending authority to black communities in the hopes that a participatory form of community action, motivated in part by the threat of black power insurgency, would jump-start social development and its assimilationist outcome. Instead, the leadership of the demonstrations began to work toward the oppositional and liberationist social vision of the black public sphere. While Fantini continued to be a stalwart advocate of poor people's participation in their own schools after his departure from the Foundation in 1970, he now predicated that involvement on communities having reached "a certain stage of development," rather than their involvement being the instrument of their development. Bundy also conceded to the *New York Times*'s Fred Hechinger that the Foundation "should have" taken the time to establish "a better developed plan for the demonstration district."[114] These admissions pointed to what would soon become a much more top-down and directive orientation for social development.

Key to this new thrust was finding black leadership sympathetic to the Foundation's vision in an era when white stewardship of black people and communities was no longer tenable. The Ford Foundation had found the grassroots leaders of the community-control movement to be sorely lacking; Bundy rued the Foundation's failure to "find men of goodwill and competence who can reach across the conflicts" and lead the districts. [115] Galamison's ongoing political activism; the reports of unchecked chaos, violent conflict, and black power rhetoric in McCoy's and Wilson's districts; and the inability of the Two Bridges' leadership to assert control over its opponents all pointed to these figures' deficiencies from Bundy's perspective. In the midst of the crisis, a sympathetic staff presentation to the Foundation's trustees defending the community-control experiment rationalized that the demonstration leader who "from our vantage point" looks "like a radical is often seen as a moderating influence in the community" and " is . . . fighting on his left flank while trying to protect his right."[116] However, in the meantime, this same staff had begun to pay attention to identifying and training black leaders whom they thought could guide the black community toward its social development objectives, rather than working with grassroots torchbearers of black self-determination.

While their experience in the schools crisis led Bundy and his officers to eschew the participatory democracy of community action, they nevertheless continued to foster the spirit of the demonstrations' pedagogical experiments in affective education to build a positive racial identity among African Americans. As Fantini put it, the units' key, concrete accomplishment was in establishing "diversity as a value, not as an obstacle" to learning.[117] Indeed, while the scholastic achievement of the students in the demonstrations stagnated or fell rather than rose, a trajectory that would continue for decades to come overall for the city's nonwhite students, affective and multicultural education would continue to flourish as the most obvious legacy of the experiment. The Foundation would continue to support the building of a strong black cultural identity in the schools and beyond as the second prong, after leadership development, of its alternative approach to social development through developmental separatism. The two chapters that follow examine the results of this revised strategy to reconfigure racial liberalism in the wake of the black freedom struggle.

PART III

Cultivating Leadership

Chapter 5

Multiculturalism from Above

On August 14, 1966, the *New York Times* published a guest editorial by Douglas Turner Ward, the African American playwright, director, and actor who had recently become a darling of the New York theater world. Ward's breakthrough had come thanks not only to his undisputed talent but also to his race in a period when white audiences and critics were hungry for realistic theatrical expression of the "black experience" as a way to understand African Americans' claims and actions in the black power era. He capitalized on this moment of white attention and the *Times*'s bully pulpit to make the case for the immediate creation of what he called "a permanent Negro repertory company of at least off-Broadway size and dimension," which he promised his readers would revitalize the American stage. "[J]ust as the intrusion of lower middle-class and working-class voices reinvigorated polite, effete English drama," Ward claimed, "so might the Negro, a most potential agent of vitality, infuse life into the moribund corpus of American theater." However, Ward insisted that this lifegiving force could only succeed through the creation of a separate, all-black company that would play to mixed but majority black audiences; otherwise, Ward felt the refreshing possibilities of black drama would be lost, with the "Negro playwright" doomed as always "to be witnessed and assessed by a majority least equipped to understand his intentions, woefully apathetic or anesthetized to his experience, [and] often prone to distort his purpose." By contrast, "with Negroes responding all around," Ward claimed that "white spectators, congenitally uneasy in the presence of Negro satire," among other genres, "at least can't fail to get the message."[1]

Thus, Ward outlined his claim for black theater based on what African Americans could do for a white-dominated national culture if they were allowed to intervene and join in it on their own terms. Despite framing his argument to appeal to the interests of the white theatrical cognoscenti, Ward's multicultural vision was a radical one that posited genuine, equitable cultural and social integration as a precondition to material black equality. Ward was careful to distinguish his "Negro" theater from black power's dominant strain of cultural separatism. While, Ward hoped, as black nationalists did, for "an all-embracing, all-encompassing theater of Negro identity, organized as an adjunct of some Negro community" as the solution to the "Negro dramatist's dilemma," he insisted that such efforts were doomed to "exotic isolation" as "[s]mall-scale cultural islands in the midst of the ghettoes," unless they arose "as part of a massive effort to reconstruct the urban ghetto" through a "committed program of social and economic revitalization." Until then, Ward believed that a theater based on his model would be a first step toward this urban transformation through the effective communication of black life and social vision to mixed audiences. In the meantime, Ward promised, American theater would be transformed.[2]

The Ford Foundation's Vice President of Humanities and the Arts, W. McNeil Lowry, received Ward's article very warmly; within months of its publication, Lowry asked Ward to head up the Negro Ensemble Company (NEC). This was the first foray into a new program to establish and fund nonwhite theater as part of McGeorge Bundy's Foundation-wide social development initiative. As with the case of the Foundation's school reformers, Lowry found points of intersection with his black theater grantees without having to share their liberationist goals. Lowry loved Ward's idea of a theater developing and showcasing black artists in the midst of the erstwhile white cultural mainstream, but he did so for its assimilative potential, not to help achieve Ward's transformative ends. Meanwhile, the Foundation funded director Robert Macbeth's New Lafayette Theatre (NLT) in Harlem, an all-black cultural nationalist project of exactly the kind that Ward had warned against. In this case, Lowry's support of this effort simply reflected the dominant belief at the Foundation that black poverty was a function of culture and psychology, not the structures of American society, as Ward would argue. Likewise, while Robert Macbeth, like many cultural nationalists, shared a psychological conception of black powerlessness with the Foundation, Lowry was not interested in cleansing black minds of a corrupt white culture as Macbeth intended; instead he wished to build the self-esteem of the black poor as the essential, behavioral element of an assimilationist developmental separatism.

Despite his differences with them, Lowry was receptive to Ward and Macbeth in his quest to respond to the Black Arts movement, a central element of black power, particularly in New York City. In this era, black artists left the interracial bohemian scene of the Lower East Side, returning "home" to Harlem to organize the black community for cultural self-determination, predominantly through theater and performance. They imagined that a black cultural revival, serving black communities and resurrecting or inventing new indigenous themes and genres, could revitalize African American society and thereby mobilize the black masses to spark the creation of the black nation, however it would be defined. This project was one of the most fully realized of the black power era, and the sometimes antiwhite and vengeful message of the artists, as well as the movement's real and imagined connection to revolutionary nationalism, caused outrage and fear among many whites.[3]

Like many black nationalists, white liberals who wanted to domesticate black power and neutralize its threat to the status quo also saw black culture as a starting point. For Ford's liberals in particular, the promotion of black culture was at the fulcrum of their efforts toward the separate social development of the black poor, as demonstrated by Mario Fantini's focus on affective education to foster a positive black identity among ghetto schoolchildren. Meanwhile, the assimilation of African American voices into the existing national culture was a relatively easy step to take in dealing with the demands of the black public without having to tackle entrenched structural issues. In the case of black theater, these goals meant that McNeil Lowry intended that the NEC, located in the East Village and in the heart of New York's burgeoning off-Broadway scene, would become an incubator and showcase for black talent. As such, Ward's theater advanced the Foundation's larger pluralist strategy to develop and incorporate black elites into the American mainstream. Foundation officers saw this diversification of American institutional life as restoring social equilibrium in the face of the demands of the black freedom struggle. In the case of the NLT, the Foundation had encouraged a black theater in the ghetto to pursue its developmentalist aims for poor African Americans within their own community. For the Foundation, the NLT's cultural and racial identity-building approach provided an opportunity to achieve the therapeutic uplift of the black poor within a controlled environment of strong, top-down black leadership and outside of the volatility and unpredictable consequences of the community-action approach.

Lowry was clear from the beginning that he pursued the development of black theater for its instrumental, "sociological result," rather than for its artistic accomplishment.[4] Commentators often compared the NEC and NLT to Yiddish theater in earlier decades of the twentieth century, with the NLT echoing the identity- and community-building role of ethnic performance in the tenement enclaves of the early 1900s, and with the NEC reproducing the culmination of that earlier movement in the success of black counterparts to figures like Oscar Hammerstein who had risen from the "ghetto" to the top ranks of the American stage.[5] From this perspective, black theater's sociological role was the contribution it could make to the replication of the script of white ethnic succession for African Americans. In the end, what resulted was a model for mainstream artistic multiculturalism that did not transform American theater through the collective intervention of black artists, as Ward had hoped. Nor did it foment a vanguardist cultural revitalization movement among black Americans as Macbeth intended. Instead, it expanded the dominant model of cultural pluralism in order to include African American performers and repertoire within its ideological confines. Meanwhile, the black poor were left in the ghetto with only exhortations for cultural pride to build self-esteem, untouched by the socioeconomic renewal that Ward saw as the political culmination of his artistic vision.

These disparities between what the Foundation and its grantees wanted from a relationship would, as in the case of community control, prove problematic for both, despite the fact that in this case, unlike during the schools crisis, Ford had the luxury of carefully choosing its black proxies. In doing so, Lowry selected men whom he believed fit the bill of strong, top-down black leadership that Ford's own leaders more and more believed to be essential to successful black social development. Unfortunately for the Foundation, while both Ward and Macbeth ruled from the top in their companies, they did so to fulfill their own ends, not the Foundation's. In the end, it would be the force of the Foundation's financial discipline that would steer the NEC to the Foundation's goals, not Ward's. Meanwhile Macbeth's theater failed utterly in achieving any element of the developmental separatism for which the Foundation had created it. Thus, finding appropriate leadership to shepherd African Americans to their assimilation remained a confounding roadblock for the Foundation's social development program.

W. McNeil Lowry and the Revolution in American Theater

The black theatrical renaissance of which the NEC and NLT played a part was itself located within a larger national flowering of noncommercial theater during the 1960s. What resulted was an utterly transformed American theater scene exploring new forms and themes often connected to the social change and political events of the decade. While the most experimental and innovative elements of this movement for socially relevant theater clearly had roots in countercultural ferment from below, the Ford Foundation was almost singlehandedly responsible for institutionalizing and mainstreaming this movement. Through its ambitious program of developing nonprofit, repertory companies, which began in earnest in 1962, the Foundation could legitimately claim that it had instigated what it called a "revolution of perception of what theatre is in the United States": American theater had gone from being a commercial cultural commodity almost entirely confined to Broadway to a "serious" performing art that no city should be without.[6]

Between the late 1950s and the early 1970s, the number of nonprofit, professional repertory theaters in the United States rose from barely a handful to around forty, and by 1969 they employed more actors than Broadway did. The Foundation could take most of the credit for this florescence. Between 1962 and 1976 Ford spent almost $20 million to establish or exponentially expand seventeen theaters, including what would become such nationally respected companies as the Arena Stage in Washington, D.C.; the Guthrie Theater in Minneapolis; the American Conservatory Theater in San Francisco, and the Alley Theatre in Houston. Nonprofit companies outside of this charmed group still lived in the Foundation's shadow; the era's only other national arts funders, the Rockefeller Foundation and the National Endowment for the Arts (established in 1965), modeled their theatrical grantsmanship on Ford's and often made their funding contingent on matching financial support from the Foundation. No other funder for the performing arts came close to Ford's resources until the National Endowment for the Arts (NEA) finally caught up in the 1970s.[7]

By moving into arts funding, the Foundation extended the reach of American industrial philanthropy into a virtually new field. It did so spurred both by the windfall created by its divestment from Ford Motor stock in the late 1950s and because of a widespread cultural anxiety that the postwar onslaught of mass media and its crass commercialism posed a threat to democracy and the moral fabric of American life. The Foundation's 1962 *Directives and Terms of Reference for the 1960s* outlined the trustees' goals in funding the arts as a way to strengthen the "moral and ethical quality of American life," serving as a counterweight to the explosion of commercial entertainment in the television age.[8]

The man responsible for turning the trustees' cultural mission into domestic Foundation programming was W. McNeil Lowry. In his years at Ford, he transformed the American cultural scene to such an extent that Lincoln Kirstein, a founder of the New York City Ballet, only exaggerated a little when he called Lowry "the single most influential patron of the performing arts that the American democratic system has produced."[9] Following successful careers as an academic and a journalist Lowry joined the Foundation's education program in 1953 before being tapped in 1957 to start up Humanities and the Arts. In his seventeen-year tenure as the Foundation's Medici, Lowry's efforts were responsible for promoting not only theater but also the symphony, ballet, and opera across the country, institutionalizing these noncommercial high-art forms by supporting and bringing tiny, struggling groups to unimagined heights of professionalism and stability.

Lowry chose the development of noncommercial, regional theater as the demonstration project for this new program area, reflecting both his personal cultural preferences and the Foundation's larger motivations in funding the arts. His goal was to institutionalize what he and others at the Foundation called "serious American drama," or theater "as an artistic rather than a commercial resource," thereby providing a "community service" in cities throughout America that "not only entertains but also comments on and interprets society."[10] In this, he looked with admiration at the great, state-subsidized theaters of Europe like the Berliner Ensemble, the Comédie Française, and Ireland's Abbey Theatre as bedrock repositories and creators of national high culture. He hoped to use Foundation funding to create private versions of these European state theaters throughout the American hinterland that would perform edifying theatrical classics and develop a new mainstream American repertoire, all the while leveraging the Foundation's risk capital into self-sufficiency through audience development and local philanthropy.[11]

As the 1960s unfolded, Lowry's commitment to building the moral and ethical role of the performing arts took on added valence in terms of its role in society's "value-making process," providing a potent opportunity for the "discovery or . . . rediscovery of values or an opportunity to relate one's values to the challenge of others." In that turbulent decade, according to the Foundation, "young artists and young audiences" innovated "new outlets and forms for artistic expression" that not only resulted in an innovative repertoire but also reflected an "intense drive toward new ways of communication and participation."[12]

Many of these artists, including Douglas Turner Ward and Robert Macbeth, hoped that their creative efforts might initiate social change through the artists' direct contact with audiences, sharing the Foundation's claim that the arts "comprised the most immediate and the most intense means of communication."[13] However, the fact was that no matter how avant-garde or revolutionary in intent, the relationship between theater performers and their audiences was bounded and mediated, not direct, as the Foundation claimed. In fact, it was precisely this distance that made cultural patronage even more attractive to the Foundation's officers and trustees during the dissent-ridden late 1960s, given the premium they placed on peaceful, nonradical conflict resolution or "value making" within the nation's existing institutional framework. In short, Foundation officials hoped to channel social conflict into its dramatization, allowing at least some of the challenge and turmoil of the 1960s to be diverted into the safe waters of cultural expression.

However, it is doubtful whether Lowry and his officers in Humanities and the Arts, for whom the struggle for racial equality was of decidedly secondary importance, would have championed the NEC and NLT as they did without Bundy's Foundation-wide imperative of fostering minority social development.[14] This was the driving impetus behind funding both theaters, among other black cultural institutions funded by the Foundation, like the Dance Theatre of Harlem and the Symphony of the New World, along with a variety of Latino, Native American, and Asian American endeavors in the Southwest.[15] These cultural institutions would allow minorities to develop professionally before they entered the cultural mainstream. They would also help to develop distinctively "racial" cultural expression within existing high-art forms. "Ethnic identity," stated one 1968 document regarding social development, was "once minimized in the hope of national unity." However, Foundation officers now believed that such identities were "a fact of American life and one of the principal means by which diverse immigrant groups negotiate their entry into the mainstream." In fact, these revisionists believed, as Fantini did about minority education, that it was only through "the development of legitimate pride in the history, culture and individual achievements of the group . . . shared by members of that group and by the majority" that minorities had ever been able to overcome the internalization of the "crushing weight of majority opinion in America," which created "profound psychological barriers from full entry" into American society and citizenship.[16]

Thus the social development program worked with Lowry and his officers to use "ethnically oriented art" to repair "some of the results of prejudice, discrimination, and poverty . . . primarily in the lives of black people." In doing so, they hoped to use the arts to achieve both black "self-realization that counteracts the destructive opportunities and effects of ghetto life," and a "'negotiable' ethnic identity through public and private practice of the . . . culture of a particular minority group."[17] This reasoning would impel the Foundation to fund the NEC's Off Broadway offerings as the "public" and NLT's ghetto arts as the "private" practitioners of a robust and separate cultural identity for African Americans through which they could overcome their psychological damage and negotiate their assimilation into the American mainstream.

The Negro Ensemble Company

Since 1963 Lowry had been searching for the right people to lead a Foundation-funded black theater effort. He first engaged in three years of conflict-ridden planning with an ideologically diverse group hoping to revive the American Negro Theatre, a successful Harlem-based nonprofit company in the 1940s. Lowry grew frustrated, especially with the intractable debates among the group's principal advocates over whether a radically integrationist or separatist theater would provide the best vehicle for cultural liberation. Lowry complained privately that the members had "strained themselves through conflicting socio-cultural deliberations."[18] He neither understood nor cared about their larger objectives or the stakes involved for them in choosing a direction for their theater. As a result, he was happy to abandon this effort and shift gears in 1966 when Douglas Turner Ward appeared on the scene. Along with the *Times* article calling for a black theater, Lowry was impressed by Ward's collaborator, actor Robert Hooks, who had already shown the potential of Ward's vision through his Group Theatre Workshop (GTW), a training program for inner-city youth run out of Hooks's Chelsea loft. The GTW had recently become a cause célèbre in New York's theatrical mainstream with its critically acclaimed production of Ward's satirical plays *Days of Absence* and *Happy Ending*.

In November 1966, Lowry invited Ward and Hooks to meet with him, along with Gerald Krone, a white producer with whom they had worked, to talk about their theatrical vision. The meeting exceeded Lowry's expectations; he noted approvingly that the three men articulated a pragmatic plan "without . . . talk about integration, segregation, or multi-racial [*sic*]."[19] Instead, according to Lowry, they had established through the GTW some "small but tested foundations for an American Negro Theatre . . . and an apprenticeship training program" to "fill a part of the vacuum in opportunities for producing Negro craftsmen."[20] Impressed by this apparently nonideological, action-oriented approach, Lowry worked to convince Hooks and Ward, both of whose individual careers were taking off, to embark on the creation of a "Negro theater." Ward and Krone accepted the challenge, with long-distance and largely moral support from Robert Hooks who decided to pursue television opportunities in Los Angeles. With Lowry's invitation, the Negro Ensemble Company was born as the only theater conceived by the Ford Foundation.

Lowry's interest in Ward and Hooks was undoubtedly piqued when he went to see Hooks's production of Ward's plays. Like the white critical establishment in New York City, Lowry had responded with relief to Ward's playful, satirical bent as a playwright, comparing his work favorably to the condemnatory invective of the "black anger" plays, most notably those of LeRoi Jones (soon to be Amiri Baraka), that had taken Off Broadway theater by storm in the early and mid-1960s. By contrast, as Howard Taubman of the *Times* put it, Ward had shown that "laughter can be as effective as anger in telling white America what the Negro has on his mind." Jerry Tallmer of the *New York Post* praised Ward in a positive comparison to the "dramatic malevolence of a LeRoi Jones or James Baldwin." This preference for the GTW actors' comedic efforts and *The New Yorker*'s characterization of Ward and his fellow black cast members as "superb entertainers" were typical responses from white critics.[21] By contrast, Jones's and Baldwin's recent plays made such assessments impossible; neither Jones's *The Dutchman*, the prizewinning 1964 dramatic allegory about the endemic and ultimately murderous racism of white liberals, nor Baldwin's *Blues for Mr. Charlie*, a 1964 play about the miscarriage of justice after the 1955 lynching of Emmett Till, could be construed as "entertainment."

The Foundation also welcomed Ward because he promised to achieve the developmental separatism that it looked for in all of its "minority" efforts. The grant proposal that Ward, Krone, and Hooks prepared at the Foundation's invitation and with its guidance reinforced these points. They sought to establish a dramatic incubator "to stimulate and foster the participation of Negroes in all phases of the theatrical profession." To this end, they envisioned a professional repertory theater, a permanent company of fifteen actors, a theatrical training program for adults, a youth workshop modeled on the GTW, and a directors' and playwrights' unit, all under one roof and all interconnected and mutually reinforcing. In this way, the NEC promised to "make its unique contribution to the arts through the productivity of the playwrights, artists, and craftsmen whom it trains for the theatre." It also hoped "to provide the place for some of those Negroes who may not previously have seen any hope for a professional career in theatre."[22]

While their proposal began from an understanding that the NEC would be an "ethnic" theater, Ward, Hooks, and Krone insisted that their productions "be attended by as broad a range of the community as possible." Thus, the three men hoped to locate the theater somewhere easily accessible both to New York's dispersed "Negro communities" and to "a cross-section of regular New York theatre-goers." In order to appeal to a broad, interracial audience, they proposed to develop and produce plays "of sufficient general interest to attract paying audiences," promising to finance production costs through ticket sales. By providing a popular showcase for black theatrical talent, the NEC promised to provide "a model opportunity for the Negro to be a self-recognized 'giver' in the American arts."[23]

The Foundation accepted this proposal in May 1967, pledging $434,000 to launch the NEC, following up with $750,000 in 1968 for two additional years of support. Ward became the theater's artistic director and driving force, and he set up shop at the St. Mark's Playhouse in the East Village, in the heart of a flourishing, noncommercial, Off Broadway scene. Many black critics complained bitterly about the NEC, as Peter Bailey did in *Negro Digest*, saying that the ensemble was not "black" theater.[24] The fact that it was "slavishly dependent" on the Ford Foundation, as Clayton Riley, another black critic, put it, disqualified it for that title and instead made it "white art in black face."[25] Other black detractors also censured its East Village location, interracial audiences and personnel, and problematic favor from white critics. They were no doubt concerned that the NEC's wealth and prominence threatened to overshadow the emergent cultural nationalism of the Black Arts era, which sought to emancipate black cultural expression from white influence and patronage.

Ward did not care about this criticism, deliberately distancing himself from *black* power dogma by defiantly naming his theater the *Negro* Ensemble Company, a gesture that linked the NEC back to the roots of Ward's own political and artistic awakening in the postwar black Left. While McNeil Lowry approvingly identified Ward as "one of those theater persons who has no politics," Ward was actually an intensely political artist who had renamed himself "Douglas Turner" after radical abolitionist Frederick Douglass and slave rebel Nat Turner.[26] After having grown up on a Louisiana plantation and in the bustling, working-class black community of wartime New Orleans, Roosevelt Ward, as he was then named, went north in 1949, where he began his political radicalization. In New York City he wrote for the Communist *Daily Worker* and headed up the New York Labor Youth League. Through these activities, he was drawn into the political performance practices of the black Left, writing a number of pieces including a twenty-five-minute cantata, *The Star of Liberty* (1950), about the life of Turner, which was well received at a large Communist rally. Inspired by this experience to become a playwright, he eventually joined the influential leftist and nationalist Harlem Writers Guild where he and his roommate and fellow dramatist, Lonne Elder III, met and worked with Lorraine Hansberry, soon to be the playwright of the landmark *A Raisin in the Sun*. Subsequent to this period of intense activism, culminating in his politically motivated arrest, jail time, and house arrest in Louisiana for draft evasion during the Korean War, Ward returned to New York City. There he focused on writing and acting in the bohemian milieu of the downtown Off Broadway scene before being cast in 1959, with Hansberry's direct intervention, as Sidney Poitier's understudy in the Broadway production of *Raisin*. He would go on to replace Poitier as the play's hero, Walter Lee Younger, during its blockbuster national tour. This success allowed Ward to return to New York to focus on his playwriting and acting and to begin his collaboration with Robert Hooks.[27]

During Ward's political and cultural education in postwar Harlem, he would have been in dialogue with or inspired by a group of black leftists that included such luminaries as Hansberry, preeminent black intellectual W. E. B. Du Bois, novelist Julian Mayfield, and sociologist E. Franklin Frazier. These figures saw African American cultural autonomy from U.S. national interests as critical to their fight for the radical socioeconomic integration that they believed was essential to black freedom and the social democracy to which they were committed. For them, cultural integration could only happen on the terms of absolute racial equality that would necessarily result in a radical transformation of American society, based on the entry and intervention of an autonomous, oppositional African American culture onto the national scene.[28]

Echoes of this program pervaded Ward's 1960s vision for black theater and radical conception of cultural integration. He hesitantly characterized himself as an integrationist because he did not "think the U.S. is going to give us Utah," or sovereignty over any other territory; he believed that "whether we like it or not, whether it's hard or not," whites and blacks "have to sit down together, after all the shouting's over and work out policy." However, he believed that such negotiations had to happen from a position of black strength, and so he sought to work for African Americans' "political and economic control of their own institutions" and thus control over their "relations to white power."[29]

Given his emphasis on black autonomy, Ward disliked "those Black plays," like *The Dutchman*, which to him seemed "to be so clenched-fist-and-teeth, almost shrill, in their attack against Whitey," believing that they emerged from the playwright's "knowledge that he's talking to white people who don't hear him, don't understand him. He's got to rage and clamor to get through to them."[30] By contrast, the NEC was not alienated from its target audience, African Americans, due to what Ward held was an inherent racial "solidarity, a feeling of togetherness, a feeling of wanting to celebrate oneness with one's people."[31] In other words, Ward's definition of "ensemble" was an expansive one that included not only NEC members but also their black patrons. Such a positive mission to present diverse portraits of African American life in ways that were familiar and appealing to other black people reinforced the NEC's autonomy in Ward's mind. Presenting such plays and directing them *first* toward black people in an integrated setting implicitly helped put African Americans collectively in a position of cultural strength and self-confidence in which they could revitalize the theatrical mainstream on their own terms. In short, as Ward exulted after the NEC was created, "Until now, the theater has more or less defined, created and controlled the possibilities of Negro stage activity." However, with the NEC's creation, "Negroes" would be "controlling their own possibilities."[32]

Ward had another, more direct response to his critics about the Foundation's underwriting support of his theater. He believed that his pre-NEC experiences of creative autonomy, which he and Hooks had already put "into practice on a small scale" and "without support from anybody" through the GTW, had invalidated any notion that white patronage or support could dilute his independence and potential to achieve his integrationist vision. Instead, patronage on the scale offered by the Foundation was simply the next, imperative "larger scale" step required to achieve his objectives. In Ward's view, the Foundation had created and funded the NEC as "an artistic venture that is worthy of . . . support," thanks to the success of his earlier, autonomous efforts and not for some "crude" effort to control content, which Ward would never abide.[33] Furthermore, the Ford Foundation's largesse meant that for the first time a black theater could thrive because it would be underwritten by "an organization which could finance it."[34]

The NEC's Ambiguous Legacy

The NEC project more than paid off in achieving the Foundation's goals for black theater. In 1978, the company could legitimately claim in a fund-raising brochure that it was a "National Treasure of Black Theatre." Since its founding in 1967, it had "produced or workshopped" about one hundred plays by living, African American playwrights, most of whom had never before seen their work performed. The NEC had played a significant, even preeminent, role in opening regional theater, Broadway, and Hollywood to positive portrayals of the "black experience." And through its development and employment of black theater workers, it had created a "Black generation" whose members grew up "thinking they could be playwrights, actors, directors, [and] technicians."[35] Indisputably, the NEC had become America's marquee black theater.

The NEC's most visible achievement was in its development and showcasing of black actors. Indeed, the NEC's alumni made up a "Who's Who" of black talent in commercial theater, television, and film; as Steve Carter, head of the company's playwriting workshop, put it, the NEC "peopled Broadway and Hollywood."[36] One of the founding members of the company's acting ensemble, Hattie Winston, who herself went on to become a successful television actor, described the NEC as such an important and prestigious "portal" for black actors to mainstream success that "even people who didn't pass through . . . claim that they did."[37] Movie and television stars like Denzel Washington, Angela Bassett, Laurence Fishburne, Samuel Jackson, and Phylicia Rashad appeared in NEC productions early in their careers. Meanwhile, the NEC offered veterans like Esther Rolle (who later starred in television's *Good Times* and *Maude*) their big break after long careers struggling to survive as black artists, and, through its training program, it discovered neophytes like Richard Roundtree (the star of the blaxploitation film *Shaft*). While these actors became celebrities, the NEC's larger legacy was the dozens of journeyman performers whose faces, if not names, were familiar to stage, television, and film audiences from the late 1960s to today. These artists found steady, remunerative work in their chosen field thanks to the opportunities afforded by the NEC's training program and its professional productions.

Figure 8. The Negro Ensemble Company in 1969 after the opening night of Lonne Elder III's successful family melodrama, *Ceremonies in Dark Old Men*. Elder and NEC founders Robert Hooks, Douglas Turner Ward, and Gerald Krone appear, left to right, in the front row. © Bettmann/CORBIS.

The rags-to-riches experiences of a number of NEC playwrights also demonstrate the ensemble's unique and instrumental role in creating individual opportunity and success. In the company's first years, it was inundated by hundreds of scripts by black playwrights who burned to see their work produced. One of these writers, Joseph Walker, languished for years as a cab-driver, a junior high school English teacher, and, in what he called the "the graveyard of black intellectuals," at the U.S. Postal Service before the NEC produced his plays, including its first Broadway hit, *The River Niger*, which won the Tony Award for Best Play in 1974.[38] Judi Ann Mason, who became a successful television writer for the 1990s *Cosby Show* spinoff *A Different World*, and who wrote the screenplay for the 1993 Whoopi Goldberg vehicle *Sister Act 2*, had been a Louisiana orphan and factory worker putting herself through Grambling State University when the NEC produced her first play, *Livin' Fat*, in 1976.[39] Lonne Elder III, who had begun writing plays in the early

1950s with Ward and Hansberry, had waited for years for his chance to see his work produced professionally by biding his time as a "hustler," as he put it, working as a numbers runner, dockworker, waiter, and actor. Finally, in its second season, the NEC produced his *Ceremonies in Dark Old Men* to enormous critical acclaim. The play went on to be adapted as a made-for-television film by ABC in 1975, while in the meantime, and no doubt due to the success of his NEC debut, Elder moved to Hollywood. In 1972, he was one of the two first African American screenwriters to be nominated for an Academy Award for his adaptation of the children's book *Sounder*.[40] While most of the artists who worked with or were trained by the NEC did not experience this kind of material success or recognition, by the mid-1970s, Ward could boast that the NEC had launched the careers of 3,500 black professionals through its interlocking training, apprenticeship, workshop, and performance programs.[41]

Given the success of its playwrights, the NEC could also claim an essential role in developing a new black repertoire for American theater. Performance schedules were composed almost entirely of new work by writers such as Walker, Elder, Mason, Samm-Art Williams, Leslie Lee, and Charles Fuller, whose *A Soldier's Play* won the Pulitzer Prize for best play in 1982 and went on to be adapted into an award-winning film, *A Soldier's Story*, in 1984. Meanwhile, in its early seasons, the NEC provided a venue for renowned playwrights from around the African diaspora; in the late 1960s, Ward staged the first full-scale U.S. productions of the work of future Nobel laureates Derek Wolcott and Wole Soyinka.

These accomplishments led to the NEC's recognition as "a black national theater" by Clive Barnes, the *New York Times*'s venerable theater critic.[42] The company's numerous Obie and Tony nominations and awards, including a special Tony in 1969 for distinguished achievement in the theater, along with invitations to the World Theatre Season in London in 1969 and the 1972 Olympic Festival in Munich, national and regional tours underwritten by the NEA and other funding agencies, the success of Fuller's *A Soldier's Play*, and prestige national television productions of Elder's *Ceremonies*, Philip Hayes Dean's *Sty of the Blind Pig*, and Leslie Lee's *The First Breeze of Summer*, were all clear indications of the ensemble's mainstream recognition.

Also essential to Ward, the NEC could also claim the mantle of "national" theater among African Americans. Throughout its first decade, and most often by invitation and to full houses, it repeatedly toured black communities, colleges, and arts festivals throughout the country. After its first season, when mainly white patrons filled the seats of its home at the St. Mark's Playhouse, NEC audiences then became predominantly black—always at least 60 percent African American by Ward's reckoning—thus fulfilling one of his most important objectives. While members of the black middle class fervently supported the ensemble, including through a "Friends of the NEC" group, Ward attracted a new, black working-class, Off Broadway audience with bargain-priced, nonsubscription tickets and publicity that specifically targeted black patrons through radio ads, beauty salons, barber shops, and churches, as well as predominantly black unions and schools.[43]

However, despite these successes Ward learned soon enough that the NEC's achievements most often came at the cost of some element of his vision for the theater while fulfilling the Ford Foundation's parallel mandate. Ward's commitment to black cultural autonomy was undermined by one inescapable fact: the NEC was, as W. McNeil Lowry put it, "an activity we [at the Ford Foundation] . . . ourselves established" and not an institution founded or funded by Ward and his ensemble.[44] While, as Ward had surmised, the Foundation would never be so hamfisted as to try to control the NEC's repertoire, its power over the ensemble's fortunes ultimately had an enormous impact in undermining Ward's objectives that conflicted with its own.

From the beginning, Lowry knew the NEC would necessarily require "a higher mix of subsidy than most theater projects the Foundation would ever consider."[45] He recognized that, unlike the Foundation's other theater grantees, the NEC was starting from scratch, and it served a relatively poor audience in a 145-seat theater that was, despite Ward's promises otherwise, too small for its box-office support to ever come near to financing the NEC's performance season, let alone the costs for its free training program or resident acting ensemble.[46] Nevertheless, after the Foundation underwrote the NEC entirely for its first three years, Lowry began pushing Ward inexorably toward financial independence. After 1970, all future Ford grants were largely conditional upon matching funds, first at double and then triple the amounts the Foundation would provide.

This move suggested Lowry's priority for the NEC as a temporary instrument of social development and assimilation, rather than as a permanent and autonomous arts institution, as Ward envisioned it. Lowry sold the first NEC grant to McGeorge Bundy in 1966 by assuring him that the NEC's "[d]ramatic materials reflecting the Negro's own identity do not have to be finished masterpieces" but that even "unpolished" materials would "still make better vehicles" than any other "for a minority audience" and for "classes . . .

designed for the training of Negro actors, directors, and technicians."[47] These low expectations differed dramatically from Lowry's lofty artistic goals for Ford's white regional theater grantees. So too did his laissez-faire attitude toward the NEC's institutional survival and growth. From the beginning of the NEC's funding in 1967 Lowry believed that "even three years of existence for this particular project would be an important achievement."[48] He made this point even more strongly in 1970 when he recommended that the Foundation move to matching grants for the NEC. He wrote that while "there is no question that the Negro Ensemble Company has been a success," both in terms of training and performance, "there is a question [of] how long the continuing needs of black theater will require the NEC's existence."[49] This candid comment gave credence to Gerald Krone's bitter suspicion, expressed to Rockefeller Foundation officials as he scrounged for matching funds, that McNeil Lowry was "ready to write . . . off" Ward's theater "as a noble and successful but short-lived experiment."[50]

As the 1970s proceeded, Lowry's pressure on the NEC became even greater, especially as the Foundation began cutting its own budget. Despite the fact that the Foundation and not Douglas Turner Ward had created the NEC, and created it fully aware of its need for a subsidy, Lowry and his officers became increasingly preoccupied with the "avoidance of dependency" in the Foundation's relationship with the NEC and their other social development grantees.[51] Thus, the Foundation's move to matching grants represented Lowry's compromise effort to deal with this albatross. If the NEC could raise funds and survive on its own, the Foundation's developmentalist and assimilationist goals would be fulfilled by creating a mainstream black theater. However, if the NEC failed to be weaned off of the Foundation's subsidy, Ford's officers could still take credit for having jump-started black theatrical expression and opportunity in the United States without being guilty of capricious grant making, as it might have been had it abruptly withdrawn its support.

Ward complained, sometimes publicly, about the financial regimen the Foundation had imposed upon him. He insisted to *Playbill* in 1970 that the NEC must always be a "deficit operation," at least as long as it had a training program and sought to develop a black audience, key elements of his vision.[52] Furthermore, he told NEC alumnus Roscoe Lee Browne in a CBS television interview in 1972 that he had no compunctions about ongoing dependency upon the Foundation; given all that African Americans had contributed to the "great white fortunes," such funding was actually their due.[53]

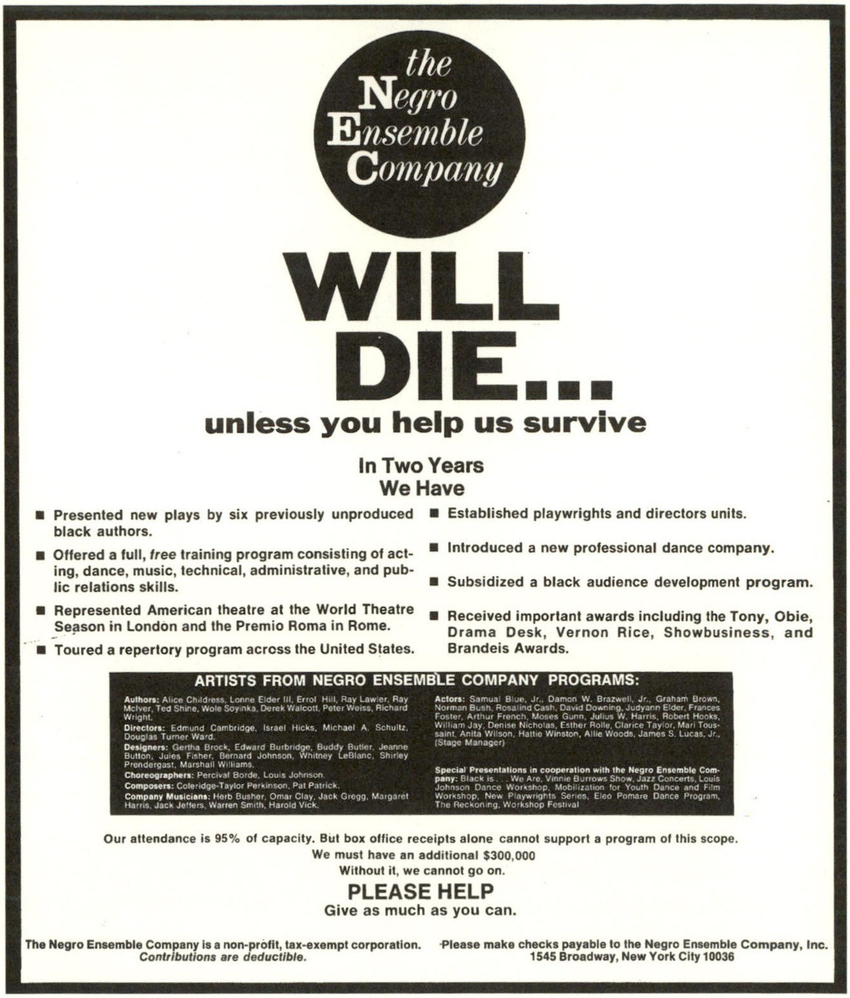
the Negro Ensemble Company

WILL DIE...

unless you help us survive

In Two Years
We Have

- Presented new plays by six previously unproduced black authors.
- Offered a full, *free* training program consisting of acting, dance, music, technical, administrative, and public relations skills.
- Represented American theatre at the World Theatre Season in London and the Premio Roma in Rome.
- Toured a repertory program across the United States.
- Established playwrights and directors units.
- Introduced a new professional dance company.
- Subsidized a black audience development program.
- Received important awards including the Tony, Obie, Drama Desk, Vernon Rice, Showbusiness, and Brandeis Awards.

ARTISTS FROM NEGRO ENSEMBLE COMPANY PROGRAMS:

Authors: Alice Childress, Lonne Elder III, Errol Hill, Ray Lawler, Ray McIver, Ted Shine, Wole Soyinka, Derek Walcott, Peter Weiss, Richard Wright.

Directors: Edmund Cambridge, Israel Hicks, Michael A. Schultz, Douglas Turner Ward.

Designers: Gertha Brock, Edward Burbridge, Buddy Butler, Jeanne Button, Jules Fisher, Bernard Johnson, Whitney LeBlanc, Shirley Prendergast, Marshall Williams.

Choreographers: Percival Borde, Louis Johnson.

Composers: Coleridge-Taylor Perkinson, Pat Patrick.

Company Musicians: Herb Busher, Omar Clay, Jack Gregg, Margaret Harris, Jack Jeffers, Warren Smith, Harold Vick.

Actors: Samual Blue, Jr., Damon W. Brazwell, Jr., Graham Brown, Norman Bush, Rosalind Cash, David Downing, Judyann Elder, Frances Foster, Arthur French, Moses Gunn, Julius W. Harris, Robert Hooks, William Jay, Denise Nicholas, Esther Rolle, Clarice Taylor, Mari Toussaint, Anita Wilson, Hattie Winston, Allie Woods, James S. Lucas, Jr., (Stage Manager)

Special Presentations in cooperation with the Negro Ensemble Company: Black is . . . We Are, Vinnie Burrows Show, Jazz Concerts, Louis Johnson Dance Workshop, Mobilization for Youth Dance and Film Workshop, New Playwrights Series, Eleo Pomare Dance Program, The Reckoning, Workshop Festival

Our attendance is 95% of capacity. But box office receipts alone cannot support a program of this scope.
We must have an additional $300,000
Without it, we cannot go on.

PLEASE HELP
Give as much as you can.

The Negro Ensemble Company is a non-profit, tax-exempt corporation.
Contributions are deductible.

Please make checks payable to the Negro Ensemble Company, Inc.
1545 Broadway, New York City 10036

Figure 9. A Negro Ensemble Company fund-raising flyer circa 1970. It encapsulates both the NEC's achievements and Douglas Turner Ward's struggle to perpetuate them in the face of Ford Foundation funding discipline. Manuscripts, Archives, and Rare Books Division, Schomburg Center for Research in Black Culture, The New York Public Library, Astor, Lenox and Tilden Foundations.

Meanwhile, he refused to accept the Foundation's apparent willingness to see the NEC fold. As he defiantly wrote in the revised and whittled-down grant proposal that the Foundation had required of him in 1971, the NEC had shown that "Black-oriented cultural projects" were no mere "temporary necessities." Instead, his ensemble was "an ongoing venture" of "magnitude and importance."[54]

Nevertheless, Ward had to submit to the Foundation's discipline if he were to keep the NEC alive at all, forcing him to compromise on his vision. The first casualty was the resident acting ensemble, which Ward had to cut in 1970 because of the expense and the theater's much reduced production schedule. Similarly, the free training program, for which Ward sacrificed the acting ensemble, suffered from steady shrinkage as well, until, by 1979, he had had to shut it down completely. Both of these forfeitures pointed to the diminishment of Ward's expansive vision of "ensemble"—of black students, artists, craftspeople, and audiences celebrating their culture together, and, through that holistic collectivity, creating opportunities for an autonomous and progressive intervention in American culture. Instead of hiring a group of actors, Ward had to job in particular ones for single productions; instead of hiring graduate trainees for the NEC's professional productions, he and his staff had to encourage their students to "make their mark outside," after graduation or even before; and instead of holding on to the craftspeople and administrators the NEC had trained on the job, he had to let them go when they invariably found better-paying work.[55] These actions contributed enormously to the NEC's well-deserved reputation for creating the conditions for the numerous individual successes that its alumni achieved after they left. However, these discrete opportunities happened almost entirely in the context of white-controlled cultural production and were emblematic of the ways in which the Foundation's funding discipline promoted its own objectives for black theater over Ward's.[56]

Furthermore, tighter budgets affected the NEC's productions and the repertoire it could develop. After 1970, the NEC presented fewer and fewer full productions, and those it did were more and more predicated on production costs and box-office potential than artistic considerations. Thus Ward abandoned his ambitious plans to revitalize the musical genre and to encourage forays into the theatrical avant-garde.[57] Instead, he relied more and more on family melodramas to keep the company afloat. The NEC had first experienced critical and financial success with naturalistic domestic plays, such as its 1969 production of Lonne Elder's *Ceremonies in Dark Old Men*. How-

ever, this initial stage triumph was dwarfed in 1973 when, struggling finan-
cially and subject to the Foundation's edict that it stage only one full-fledged
production per season, the NEC hit paydirt with another such play, Joseph
Walker's *The River Niger*. After more than one hundred Off Broadway performances, this production moved to the 1,060-seat Brooks Atkinson Theatre
on Broadway, where it had a successful eight-month run.

While these domestic melodramas were box-office successes, cheap to
produce, and contained rich material for actors, what first attracted Ward
to them was that their content created the kind of unity between performers
and audiences that was his first goal; these plays were singularly appealing to
black audiences unused to seeing themselves portrayed realistically on stage.
The sociological and political "messages" of Elder's and Walker's plays were
also unsurprising, given Ward's politics. He and his cohort were part of a
leftist tradition in American theater, going back to the 1930s and the work
of playwrights like Clifford Odets for the Group Theatre (after which Robert
Hooks's GTW was named) as well as the postwar black cultural Left of which
Ward had been a part, that had used naturalistic melodrama to achieve political ends. *Ceremonies* and *The River Niger* dealt critically and at length with
the personal and social consequences of postwar ghettoization for African
American families, with Walker's work also considering the heritage of black
activism born from these structural conditions. Black Arts playwright and
critic Larry Neal summed up the significance of these plays in a commentary
about *The River Niger*. He praised Walker's work as having achieved "a . . .
kind of greatness with a conventional play."[58] Neal further commended the
work's success in achieving what so many cultural nationalists had failed to
do through their genre experiments: it had connected current black struggles
with the revolutionary past and had invoked memories of African origins in
an accessible dramatic form that appealed to ordinary black New Yorkers.[59]

While black critics like Neal saw the inherent political content in Walker's domestic melodrama, white critics ignored the social commentary of
the play, focusing instead, as Clive Barnes did, on the "true and soul-like"
dialogue that "derives from black gospel sermons" and "snake[s] out dangerously in a way no white man would use the language."[60] It was this distinctively black speech and essentialized and ephemeral "soul," and not the play's
political content, to which these critics responded positively as "bringing an
infusion of plasma to the American drama," according to the *Chicago Tri-
bune*.[61] Critics missed or neglected politics completely and instead praised
the play's "universality," which, as the critic for *Chicago Today* put it, "tran-

scends color, vocabulary, and victimization by a social malaise predating the Declaration of Independence."[62] Such responses were typical of white critical interpretation of the NEC's offerings. Ward sought to intervene against this misreading of the NEC's work in 1972 by extending his black "ensemble" through the creation of what he called a "unit" that would develop a cadre of black theater critics, and by buying newspaper ad space to publish black-authored reviews, positive or not, of NEC productions.[63] However, both efforts were short-lived, and did little to combat white critics' embrace of the NEC's offerings, not as challenging interventions in the cultural status quo but as welcome supplements to it, an outcome entirely in keeping with the Ford Foundation's goals, not Ward's.

While Lowry had aimed for a crossover success like *The River Niger* from the NEC's founding, Ward was enormously ambivalent about the move to Broadway, given what he saw as the artistic sterility of the profit-driven commercial theater scene. However, as he told the *New York Post*, "survival dictates that we . . . consider just about anything . . . includ[ing] Broadway."[64] More compromises were to follow. After *The River Niger*'s success the NEC made an unmistakable shift in its melodramatic offerings to more commercial fare that would confirm white critics' view of the ensemble's work. These works included Leslie Lee's *The First Breeze of Summer* (1975), which had a short Broadway run in the summer of 1975 and which Hollywood producers also considered seriously as the basis for a commercial TV series, and Judi Ann Mason's *Livin' Fat* (1976), which she herself characterized as a "sentimental domestic comedy accented by colorful black slang."[65] Seeking "to share" her racial pride "with everyone," Mason told an interviewer that "the play was not written for blacks only," so its "universality was illuminated" for all audiences.[66] Similarly, Lee sought to improve the "image" of blacks in his plays and television scripts through a proud embrace of "sentimentality" and a desire for the "black experience" to be "shared rather than isolated." He wanted to be the "spokesman for everyone" and not just blacks through his plays' global appeal.[67] Both plays achieved this universality by focusing not on situations borne of ghetto exploitation but on ubiquitous human experiences and "positive" portrayals of African Americans, middle-class characters, or, in Mason's case as she described it, a romanticized black community "with no particular social level distinctions."[68]

White critics responded to this work's anodyne appeal, with the *Times*'s Walter Kerr, in a typical comment characterizing *First Breeze* as "a play at which someone who is not black can feel . . . completely at home."[69]

These self-consciously positive, sentimental, and universal portrayals of black life reflected a more commercial direction for the NEC's repertoire, from which we can see echoes in later popular television offerings from the 1980s and 1990s like *The Cosby Show* or *A Different World*, to which NEC alumni contributed both on- and offscreen. Ward made this shift in the mid-1970s because he had to. Stagflation, combined with a marked decline in philanthropic and government interest in black arts once the urban crisis of the 1960s had been pacified, made the expansion into commercial theater, television, and film necessary if the NEC were to be one of the few black theaters left standing after the movement's heyday in the 1960s. However, Ward understood well what compromises to his vision would accompany these moves. He struggled to keep the NEC alive by searching for "possibilities for additional earned income" in film, television, and on Broadway, knowing that these efforts, if successful, could "result in the demise of the very program which they so urgently are designed to support."[70]

The New Lafayette Theatre

Despite Ward's radical politics, the NEC owed its success to fitting comfortably within the confines of racial liberalism. By contrast, for many outside white observers the New Lafayette Theatre stretched far beyond the cultural mainstream. Supported by the Foundation from 1967 to 1972 with similar funding to what the NEC received, the NLT was explicitly nationalist and separatist in its orientation. Located in Harlem, this "uptown" theater followed the trajectory of many Black Arts organizations in the late 1960s by producing black theater only for black people in their own communities for the purpose of racial revitalization and cultural mobilization in the ghetto. The NLT's mission rejected any form of cultural integration; like many of New York City's community-control activists and other black power advocates, Robert Macbeth and his colleagues believed that white culture was at the root of African Americans' problems, and thus it was something from which black people had to separate themselves completely.

Nevertheless, funding the NLT was perfectly consistent with the Foundation's two-pronged strategy for the social development of African Americans. While in underwriting the downtown NEC the Foundation hoped to further its pluralist strategy to identify and incorporate exceptional African American individuals and repertoire into the American mainstream, with

the New Lafayette Theatre the Foundation intended to pursue its developmentalist aims for poor African Americans within their own communities.
For Ford, Robert Macbeth's vision of cultural revitalization in the ghetto provided an opportunity to work toward the social development of the black
poor through identity-building behavioral methods and not the unpredictable political means that had contributed to the schools crisis. Furthermore,
this transformation would occur not on the volatile streets but within the
controlled and bounded environment of the theater and under Macbeth's
single-minded, explicitly top-down leadership, thus avoiding the participatory democracy that had fueled black power demands like the one for community control of schools. Thus the NLT appealed to the Foundation, not
because of its nationalist vision but for its therapeutic potential to develop
the black masses psychologically without any of the nationalist consequences
envisioned by Robert Macbeth.

Macbeth's background was significantly different from Ward's. Most notably, his experience was almost only confined to acting in white venues and
he had none of Ward's connections to the black Left and literary scene. After
arriving in New York City in the mid-1950s, Macbeth became a member of
the Living Theatre, an experimental Off Broadway company. Meanwhile, he
paid his bills by acting on Broadway where he was the understudy to Billy
Dee Williams in *A Taste of Honey* in 1958; in 1962 he appeared in *Tiger, Tiger
Burning Bright* with Diana Sands. Thus, by the early 1960s, he had participated in the full spectrum of New York's white theatrical scene as an actor,
but he had no experience in black theater or more generally with playwriting
or directing. His first theatrical experience in black New York came after he
was named to run the theater lab at HARYOU-ACT, Harlem's largest antipoverty program. He spent one year at the lab, leaving it in 1966 to set up a
small acting workshop in Harlem for black youth, which he called the New
Lafayette Theatre and Workshop.[71]

Robert Macbeth first contacted McNeil Lowry in 1966 with a plan to expand his workshop. Lowry turned down the idea because he was still preoccupied by the project to expand professional opportunities to African
Americans in theater that would culminate in the NEC. Macbeth received
an entirely different reception when he wrote Lowry again the following year,
at the suggestion of Iris Siff of Houston's Alley Theatre, one of Ford's most
favored regional theater grantees. This time, Macbeth goaded Lowry, telling
him that for the months since Ford's rejection letter, he had been "stifling
the urge to write back a long tirade" about why the Foundation's approach to

black theater was all wrong, and he hoped that Lowry would agree to meet to "discuss these differences."[72] Readily taking the bait, Lowry invited Macbeth to his office. According to Macbeth, Lowry greeted him with an unexpected "interest and understanding." In fact, this "enjoyable and encouraging talk" culminated in the Ford Foundation's first grant to the New Lafayette in 1967.[73]

Lowry's turnaround was testament to Macbeth's persistent and pitch-perfect fund-raising campaign, in which he moved swiftly from being an unknown and untested cultural nationalist who had never before directed a play to being the recipient of more than a million dollars, largely from the Ford Foundation, for his theater. Building a buzz about his project among influential white as well as black contacts in American nonprofit theater, including Siff, no doubt helped his cause.[74] However, none of this networking would have worked with Ford if Macbeth's cultural nationalism and theatrical vision had not resonated so deeply with Lowry's notions of the ethical and culture-building role of nonprofit theater and the ghetto-development aspects of the Foundation's separatist vision for African Americans. Macbeth began from the shared premise of cultural nationalists and American racial liberals that African Americans had been fundamentally damaged by the destruction of their African heritage. This deracination, combined with the mainstream culture's refusal to acknowledge the history or contribution of African Americans, led to what Macbeth called a cultural "death," in which black people lacked any of the sense of national belonging that was required in order "to face the present and the future." Therefore, Macbeth sought, in terms that intersected with the Foundation's ghetto-development strategy, "the realization of [a] true cultural and historic lineage" through an indigenous theater "in the Ghetto." This theater would create the necessary foundation of "a true historical perspective, a mythology, a background," from which black people could understand and face the crises confronting their community and build a common future.[75]

Macbeth engaged the crisis of American theater by defining his project as a quest for "real theatre" in contrast to Broadway's aridity, which he believed stemmed from its lowest-common-denominator attempts to maximize profits through a bland universality that could entertain anyone. Like Ward, and to the delight of the Foundation, Macbeth also repudiated the trap of downtown theater for playwrights like Jones/Baraka who appeared to be caught in a "self conscious obsession" with exposing the "immediate racial conflict or confrontation" to their white audiences.[76] Instead, "real theaters" for Macbeth were "always indigenous to the communities in which they exist." These "community theaters" achieved this meaningful "universality" by reflecting the communities' "own special national or ethnic experience." In terms that echoed Lowry's own goals for repertory theater, Macbeth claimed that his community theater would play the same cultural role as the great national stages of Europe by creating a "theatre of a particular people, in a particular place, which spoke of human destinies that were of interest to its audience, and tried to pass on a heritage of perception."[77]

Given such lofty high-art precedents, Macbeth's nationalist model required "the reinvolvement of . . . Negro intellectuals and artists" as leaders in the life of the ghetto as they "take on this task" of community theater.[78] While he wrote of black artists and audiences, "organically related by blood as well as by experience, attitude, history and geography," coming together as "equal participants in the theatrical event," his was not a collaborative vision.[79] While artists were necessarily inspired by ghetto life, their transcendent creative visions of that life meant that they inevitably led, while the audience, from whom the artists drew inspiration, followed. Or, in Robert Macbeth's words, "The community in which we exist must participate in the theatre's work" but only "by being its audience."[80]

Such a top-down model touched the very heart of the Foundation's social development project for the ghetto. No doubt Macbeth's personal magnetism and ostensible leadership potential reinforced this point for Lowry. He must have been even more pleased if Macbeth had shared with him what he told others about his desire to build what he called a "director's theater" modeled on Orson Welles's and John Houseman's singular creative vision at the Lafayette Theatre, Harlem's 1930s Federal Theatre Project venture after which Macbeth named the New Lafayette and in whose building the NLT was originally housed.[81] All of this would have been deeply compelling to a Foundation that made not only "professional leadership" but also "preferably leadership with evident charisma," its first prerequisite for "the arts as social development of minorities," in order to convince "the community at large that the project is worth supporting."[82]

Unsurprisingly, then, Lowry became Macbeth's greatest white champion, and the Ford Foundation took the lead in funding the New Lafayette Theatre. In 1967, it authorized an $18,500 demonstration grant to Macbeth, matched by the Rockefeller Foundation, to put the theater in working order and to set in motion an inaugural season. In justifying the grant, Lowry emphasized, like he had for the NEC, the professionalizing opportunities that the NLT would provide for African Americans interested in the theater. However, he agreed with Macbeth that the NLT's most significant impact would be its potential for community uplift. Lowry liked that Macbeth's project was "more intimately fixed in the Negro community" and "closer to the street than the concept motivating Ward and Hooks."[83] Interpreting the NLT in terms of the culture-building potential that had driven his ongoing regional theater initiative, Lowry seemed to see the "ghetto" as another American region for which the benefits of noncommercial culture had heretofore been missing. Lowry was delighted with what the NLT achieved with the first grant, and especially with what he saw as its "real success in involving an audience right off the street in Harlem," most of whose members "had little exposure to professional theater work." Lowry believed that Macbeth was on his way to building "an important symbolic center for the Harlem community and the personal sense of identity of the Harlem resident," and he told his Rockefeller Foundation counterpart, Norman Lloyd, that he placed "great faith in Robert Macbeth both as a director and a finder of new plays."[84]

In the spring of 1968 this faith led Lowry to encourage Macbeth to tell other prospective funders that the Foundation "was interested" in the New Lafayette "in a major way."[85] Lowry hoped that this leverage would help Macbeth to relocate the theater and dramatically expand its activities after its original facility burned down in January 1968. Macbeth planned to hire and pay a resident ensemble of twelve actors to perform in an ambitious, forty-week season. He also intended to develop a playwrights' workshop and children's theater program. He hoped that a "patronage" group of prominent black New Yorkers would help the NLT buy its own space and that a publicity and fund-raising campaign among ordinary Harlemites would build support for the theater in the community. On this basis, the Foundation announced a second one-year grant to the New Lafayette of $167,000 in May 1968, to contribute to a total projected budget of just over $400,000. The Rockefeller Foundation followed with $150,000 several months later.[86]

Lowry was very pleased with the addition of the New Lafayette to his stable of social development grantees. He told McGeorge Bundy at the time of the NLT's second grant that Ford's initiatives had contributed to "a significant change for the Negro professional and for the young Negro seeking exposure and professional apprenticeship." Furthermore, with grants to the NEC, the NLT, the American Place Theatre (an Off Broadway theater that had presented the first professional productions of many black playwrights), and the Arena Stage (located in Washington, D.C., and which had an integrated acting company) "[a]lmost every separate intellectual or racial concept about theater in the black community is represented in the Ford Foundation program."[87] In the case of cultural nationalism, the thorniest of these "racial concepts" for liberals, the Foundation boasted in its annual report about discovering and funding the New Lafayette Theatre, one "ghetto-based artistic group" that promised to "serve artistic purposes at least as much as social goals" and that showed "promise of achieving permanence" and could "draw support from other sources."[88]

The NLT's Ambiguous Legacy

Macbeth's first achievement was to attract funding. In Lowry's words, the NLT enjoyed "having it all ways" by pursuing its goal of cultural self-determination on white philanthropy's dime.[89] Between 1967 and 1969, a wide range of national and regional white funders, including media mogul Carter Burden, bankrolled the NLT with grants in the $5,000 to $25,000 range, as did a variety of New York funding agencies and the NEA. No doubt the ongoing urban rebellions, including the one in Harlem following Martin Luther King's assassination in 1968, had something to do with this depth of support. However, the Ford Foundation and Rockefeller Foundation had combined pledges of more than $300,000 in this period, and this probably signaled to smaller funders, including other Rockefeller family foundations, that the NLT was the right place in which to put their money for arts projects in the ghetto. After 1969, the Foundation began to chart its own path with the NLT, based on Lowry's enthusiastic assessment of its achievements and promise. Ford upped the ante and gave the NLT a two-year grant of $529,000, which was to provide the theater with more than half of its projected budget, with no requirement for matching funds. In doing so, the Foundation began to break away from the Rockefeller Foundation, which until this point had nearly equaled the Foundation's contributions. Instead, Rockefeller contributed only $150,000 to the NLT for its 1970–1971 season, which would be the last year in which it supported the theater. Significantly, the NLT's other institutional funders, other than the Rockefeller Brothers Fund, declined to continue their support after 1970.[90]

Macbeth took the money while it lasted and ran with it. He understood that the bounty he had received would allow him to achieve what no other Black Arts theater had the money to do—he would have the full fruition of his vision for a nationalist (and national), noncommercial community theater. Paradoxically, white philanthropy allowed Macbeth and his NLT colleagues to reject any other white participation in their theater, including white critics, who were banned from the productions from 1968 to 1970; it also enabled the NLT to eschew all conventions of Western theater and commercial culture as oppressive, corrupt, and totally antithetical to its liberationist objectives. As Macbeth put it to the Rockefeller Foundation, he and his colleagues found it "very hard to resist accepting what was called 'Theatre'" and presenting it as something they "should 'sell' in the community" by "charm[ing] a paying audience with colorful costumes, hip jazz, and Black Power rah rah rah." White largesse was the force that allowed them the luxury to resist the pressure to commercialize and instead to search for "an art form," which would make the NLT an "organic part of the creative urge of our people" and not simply, in a likely jab at the NEC, "a Black Lincoln Center."[91]

The intensity of Macbeth's ambition to reach these objectives and the flurry of activity that followed the NLT's funding demonstrated the urgency of his mission and ultimately the depth of his hubris. "This theatre has perhaps more to do than any other theatre in the world," he wrote. "It should have come into existence a hundred years ago," but since it did not, he continued, "it has a hundred years to make up for."[92] Accordingly, Macbeth used the money to create a nexus of cultural activity at the NLT, all aimed at creating an autonomous theatrical aesthetic that would advance his cultural nationalism. First, he created a tight-knit company. At its core was a group of twelve actors whom he could pay enough so that they could devote themselves entirely to his vision without having to pursue any outside work. These performers were the envy of New York's other black artists; the $200 weekly salary for each was a "princely sum for a single person living in Harlem at the time," according to Roscoe Orman, one of the actors, and was significantly more than the Off Broadway rates that members of the NEC's acting ensemble received. For Orman, this money gave Macbeth's actors "the sense of security [they] needed in order to focus on [the] creative mission," including the financial independence to remain in Harlem, unsullied by the corruption of white-controlled commercial "entertainment."[93] Instead, Macbeth's company could be dedicated solely to the creation of the autonomous theatrical aesthetic that Macbeth intended to lead to black cultural liberation.

The NLT's deep pockets also meant that the acting ensemble worked and performed in a state-of-the-art facility, supported by production values that rivaled the best-funded Off Broadway theaters and of which other Harlem nonprofit theaters could only dream. Such professionalism was essential to Macbeth's goal to create not only an aesthetically autonomous theater but also one that was "artistically superior to anything our community has ever seen."[94] So, while another Black Arts theater director, Barbara Ann Teer, was holding deviled egg sales to scrape together the $20 she needed to rent chairs for her National Black Theatre's performances, Macbeth was working with Hugh Hardy, a nationally known and cutting-edge white theater architect, to design a maximally flexible space for the NLT that could be reconfigured in any number of ways to suit the ensemble's innovative experiments.[95] Macbeth also forged a relationship with some of the leading visual artists of the Black Arts movement, all members of the celebrated Weusi Collective. The NLT worked with and could pay Weusi artists, including the collective's founder Ademola Olugebefola, along with Bill Howell, Abdul Rahman, and Otto Neals to create its striking logo and gorgeous sets, tickets, and promotional posters, thus demonstrating the potential of a distinctive visual aesthetic for black theater. Similarly, a number of musicians like percussionists Chief Bey and Sonny Morgan, African instrumentalist Nadi Qamar, and saxophonist Pat Patrick, who among them had performed and recorded with such leading jazz innovators as Sun Ra, Pharaoh Sanders, Art Blakey, John Coltrane, Charles Mingus, and McCoy Tyner, were paid participants in the NLT's activities, providing the very best afrocentric musical accompaniment possible. As Orman remembered, these artists transformed the theater "into a stunningly evocative environment" that perfectly complemented the "new and highly stylized form of expression" of the NLT's performances; together, Orman concluded, these black performers and artists "transported" the audience "to a higher collective consciousness."[96]

Macbeth made a crucial addition to this impressive group of artists when he lured playwright Ed Bullins from California to join him as creative leader of the NLT. Bullins, whom black theater historians Errol Hill and James Hatch have called the second-most important "militant" playwright (after LeRoi Jones/Amiri Baraka) of the Black Arts era, had the background in black theater that Macbeth lacked. Even more important to the NLT's reputation, Bullins had the political and artistic experience within black nationalism to give the NLT the credibility in Harlem's cultural and intellectual circles that Macbeth had not earned.[97] Bullins was a founder of two important Black Arts institutions, San Francisco's Black Arts West, and Black House, which was the de facto Black Panther headquarters in that city. While Bullins was a committed cultural nationalist—and had a personal link to that movement's preeminent figure, his former college roommate Maulana Karenga (né Ronald Everett)—he also had strong links to revolutionary nationalists through

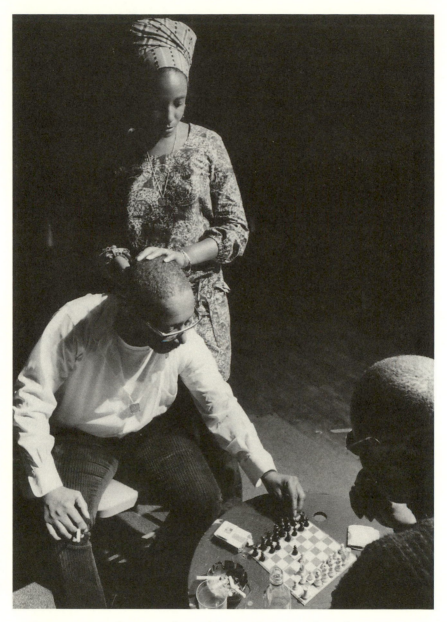

Figure 10. A performance photo of the New Lafayette Theatre's production of Ed Bullins's *Goin' a Buffalo*. Bullins's naturalistic "Twentieth-Century Cycle" plays were the NLT's most popular offerings. Photographs and Prints Division, Schomburg Center for Research in Black Culture, The New York Public Library, Astor, Lenox and Tilden Foundations. Photograph by Doug Harris.

his connection to the Panthers, for whom he acted briefly as Minister of Culture, and his mentorship by Amiri Baraka during a California sojourn by the more established playwright.[98]

Bullins was indispensable to the NLT's creative vision. He wrote or had a hand in writing the entire NLT repertoire, including six plays included in his social realist "Twentieth-Century Cycle," which comprised the theater's most popular offerings by presenting deliberately nondidactic material to black audiences with which, like the NEC's family melodramas, they could readily identify. Also white critics and theatergoers enjoyed what they saw as these plays' apolitical universality and sympathetic portrayal of black life—the Rockefeller Foundation's Norman Lloyd praised Bullins's "unerring ear for urban Negro speech rhythms" and plays "of compassion, concerned with the human condition"[99]—when they saw them in their multiple downtown productions at high-profile Off Broadway theaters, like the Public and American Place theaters, as well as at Lincoln Center. While at the NLT, Bullins received substantial recognition, including Obie awards, a Drama Desk Award, and fellowships from the NEA and the Rockefeller and Guggenheim foundations.[100]

Although Bullins's Twentieth-Century plays undoubtedly built mainstream credibility for the NLT, Macbeth's first objective was to develop a new cultural form for African Americans in collaboration with Bullins and the rest of the NLT company. What they settled on to achieve this aim was the "community ritual," which employed the spiritual aspects of African and African American culture, as Macbeth put it, to "clarify for black people their ultimate strengths and powers."[101] The titles of the New Lafayette rituals—*A Ritual to Bind Together and Strengthen Black People So That They Can Survive the Struggle That Is to Come*, *To Raise the Dead and Foretell the Future*, and *A Black Time for Black Folk*—made their revitalizing intentions clear. These nonnarrative pieces—*A Black Time* did not even use the spoken word—were developed by the NLT's community of artists to uplift and unify audience members by involving them directly in the pieces' music, drumming, dancing, and chanting. After 1969, rituals dominated the NLT's repertoire, along with Ed Bullins's closely related "mystic dramas" *The Devil Catchers* (1970) and *The Psychic Pretenders* (1972), deeply symbolic allegories about black people's spiritual corruption by white culture and how they could overcome it through racial unity. Macbeth called the NLT's rituals a "deadly serious effort" by black people "to use their spiritual forces toward one . . . object, which is the togetherness, the nation, the nationhood, the Being, the realization, the recognition of Self!"[102]

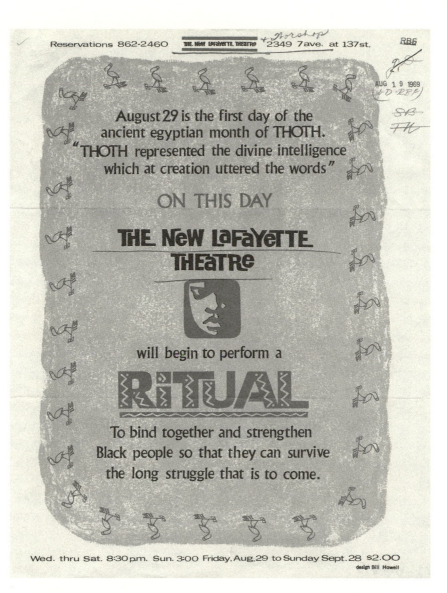

Figure 11. A flyer designed by Bill Howell of the Weusi Collective for one of the New Lafayette Theatre's ritual performances. Rockefeller Brothers Fund Archives. Courtesy Rockefeller Archive Center.

Along with forging new, distinctively black theatrical forms, the NLT also used its resources to reach beyond the stage to create autonomous community among black artists at home and nationwide. In its first two years, the theater served as a community center for cultural nationalists, holding high-profile events like a symposium about Harold Cruse's book *The Crisis of the Negro Intellectual*, in which Harlem's black power luminaries participated. The NLT also sponsored a public debate between Amiri Baraka, Larry Neal, and Askia M. Touré about Ed Bullins's play *We Righteous Bombers* in which they discussed the connections and antipathies between revolutionary and cultural nationalism and the role and responsibility of the artist in black liberation.[103] The artists, activists, and intellectuals who attended these events also celebrated the NLT's opening as a landmark event; those present at the inauguration of the Hardy-designed theater included Baraka, SNCC leader H. Rap Brown, Black Arts novelist and Harlem Writers Guild leader John O. Killens, and CORE's national chairman, Floyd McKissick. Others, like jazz pianist and singer Nina Simone, were NLT regulars.[104]

Like the NEC, the NLT also had a successful playwrights' workshop run by Ed Bullins, which launched the careers of Richard Wesley, OyamO, J. E. Gaines, and Martie Charles, who all went on to create works Off Broadway. The NLT workshop's barebones performances of its participants' plays were often better attended than the NLT's full productions. Further, Whitman Mayo, a founding member of the acting ensemble, ran the NLT's Playservice, which for a time became the largest repository of plays by black authors in the United States by publishing and distributing throughout the nation the work of dozens of affiliated black playwrights, including Bullins, Marvin X, Richard Wesley, and Sonia Sanchez.[105] Finally, and most significantly, from 1968 to 1972 the NLT published *Black Theatre* magazine, an important Black Arts mouthpiece that helped to fuse the dozens of experiments in black theater throughout the nation into a movement by reporting on artists' activities and by publishing the criticism of a wide spectrum of the most prominent cultural nationalists. At least sixty-five of the approximately one hundred black theaters in the country received *Black Theatre*, which, at its peak, had more than two thousand subscribers.[106]

Consequently, in significant ways the NLT, like the NEC, became a national black theater and a beacon to aspiring black artists. Letters flooded into the theater from playwrights and directors from places as diverse as Minneapolis, Minnesota; Knoxville, Tennessee; Tacoma, Washington; Little Rock, Arkansas; Louisville, Kentucky; and West Chester, Pennsylvania, all requesting material from the Playservice, expressing their appreciation for the NLT's work, and asking for advice about their own theatrical projects.[107]

Lowry boasted of the Foundation's daring and foresight in funding the NLT. He believed that "one can only guess at the time that will pass before separatism is lost in integration" and that, given "what is apparent in the whole urban culture," African Americans "for many years may still be 'telling it' in their own terms through their own writers and performers." Given this situation, Lowry supported "Macbeth and the New Lafayette" as the "toughest, purest, and most committed of the separatists."[108]

However, this tough separatism was of a very particular kind that appealed to the Foundation's developmentalism. In Lowry's mind, the NLT's form of cultural nationalism was enormously positive, first because it avoided the racial confrontations threatened by revolutionary nationalists. So, for example, while he mischaracterized Ed Bullins in 1969 as a playwright who "styles himself Minister of Culture for the Black Panthers," Lowry nevertheless got the story right when he wrote that, despite these roots, "Bullins' plays deal with the steamy daily lives of the blacks in Harlem rather than with black or white hatreds in the style of the LeRoi Jones repertoire." These "cultural materials intensifying the black's sense of identity" were exactly the kind of separatist ghetto arts the Foundation hoped to promote.[109] Lowry liked Bullins's social realism and the NLT's rituals because they described ghetto life and sought to ameliorate African Americans' condition therapeutically from within, without directly confronting outside agents or structures of oppression.

Furthermore, the theater provided a mediated environment for the expression of African Americans' discontent. Lowry wrote approvingly that NLT audiences remained silent, while the artists on the stage or screen "speak not only to the black but for the black." Lowry's presumption of the NLT's channeling and command of its audience reflected his broader faith in Robert Macbeth as a kind of superman who could steer the Black Arts movement at will. Lowry wrote Bundy that the NLT was "the creation of a man who can relate at once to almost all elements of the urban structure and can gather sufficient tokens of power and influence in his own hands." He wrote also of Macbeth's "ability to attract—and apparently also to control—talented writers of radical views," namely Bullins, thus giving "Macbeth a special position and special opportunity," presumably to shape black cultural production.[110] Such a misguided reading of Macbeth's relationship with Bullins demonstrated both Lowry's ignorance of what was happening at the

NLT and his wishful projection onto Macbeth the image of the omnipotent black leader the Foundation hoped to attract and develop: someone who was strong, autonomous, charismatic, and thus able to shepherd or control other black people, guiding them to the safe shores of developmental separatism.

Lowry's perception of Macbeth's leadership potential and the developmental possibilities of the NLT was at odds with virtually all of his fellow philanthropists. At the very point in 1969 when the Ford Foundation ramped up its support for the NLT, Macbeth lost or began to lose his other white patrons, most notably the Rockefeller Foundation. While Lowry's "only criticism" of the NLT, according to Rockefeller's Norman Lloyd, was that Macbeth had not yet had time to mobilize Harlemites to build community support for the theater, either through audience development or fund-raising, Lloyd himself was beginning to see this as a major shortcoming that Macbeth might never overcome.[111] Consequently, Lloyd reluctantly but resolutely began to taper off the Rockefeller Foundation's funding, with one of his subordinates commenting that the NLT's failures had taught both their foundation's program officers and Macbeth "important lessons about imposing culture" on communities; the Ford Foundation was left to pick up more and more of the tab for the NLT after 1970.[112]

Despite the fact that it was the reason he lost Rockefeller funding, Macbeth made no apologies for the NLT's lack of engagement with Harlem residents. In one annual report after another to Ford, Macbeth reported dismal statistics; despite free or nearly free tickets, the NLT's productions almost never filled more than 30 percent of his theater's three hundred seats, and often much less. Macbeth explained this failing in terms of the New Lafayette's vanguardism. Macbeth believed that the NLT, in its quest for a new aesthetic, would have to "face the critical eyes of some of our less perceptive fellows" and wait patiently to see the theater's "effect on the artistic and aesthetic climate of the Black community."[113] The delay might be a long one, since it had become clear to Macbeth by 1970 that a "paying audience of any size and/or consistency is impossible in the Black world at this time unless we are to develop a 'following,' or design a more 'marketable product.'" He refused either of these options, because for him in "neither case would we be serving the needs of Black art or black people." Instead, the NLT's artists "must follow the demands of our creative impulse and make theatre as theatre must be made in our place and condition."[114]

As long as the Ford money kept coming Macbeth could continue to disdain the Harlem community by requiring its members to catch up culturally to the NLT's enlightened aesthetic, rather than the NLT developing theater that responded to the tastes and needs of its intended audience. This disconnect between the theater and the community was most glaringly obvious with its ritual productions, the NLT's worst attended offerings. Even critics within the Black Arts movement lambasted these performances, as afrocentric playwright and black theater scholar Paul Carter Harrison did, as "self-righteously indulgent," filled with "esoteric bombast," and "in isolation from the realities of [the] daily struggle" of its intended audience.[115] Furthermore, as a number of other black critics have since pointed out, the NLT's vanguard theatrical aesthetic paradoxically did not connect to any theatrical genre or cultural tradition, black or white, with which black audiences were familiar.[116] Larry Neal remembered the NLT's offerings as being almost unwatchable "failures of energy . . . slow, plodding, and done with a very solemn air."[117] Neal condemned Macbeth and his company for not tapping into what he called all of the "handy," familiar rituals available from African Americans' existing cultural and spiritual heritage, instead creating ersatz ceremonies from a "vague memory of Africa." The result, concluded Neal, was "tedious and pompous," and it left Neal with the distinct impression that Macbeth was telling his audience, "I know it all, I'm God."[118]

The NLT's insularity from the black community and the larger black theatrical world was reinforced by its rigid and actively enforced racial and aesthetic orthodoxies. Macbeth fired actors who dared to take work outside of Harlem, even at black-run Off Broadway theaters, like Ellen Stewart's La MaMa ETC. *Black Theatre* also regularly denounced the work of black theater artists, like those at the NEC, who presented their work outside of Harlem or who did not share its editors' cultural nationalism. In one memorable article, for example, Ed Bullins called a production of Clifford Mason's *Sister Sadie* at the New Dramatists' Workshop "that tremendous Mason turd"; he then went on to describe how he and other NLT participants loudly voiced their criticism while the play was being performed one night, with one of them also letting out a "full scream" in front of the stage during intermission. Similarly, NLT members heckled the speakers at a forum on black theater at the Eugene O'Neill Foundation Theatre in Hartford, Connecticut, after Macbeth was not invited to participate.[119]

Even within the community of cultural nationalists the NLT isolated itself. At the same time that *Black Theatre* and the playwrights' service bound together the black nationalist theater community nationwide, NLT members regularly rejected the work of ostensible allies. For example, they sought to disrupt a 1970 conference on black theater brought together by the like-minded Hazel Bryant of the Afro-American Total Theatre. Similarly, Macbeth rejected an invitation to join the newly formed Black Theater Alliance, and he refused to rent the NLT's unsurpassed facilities to any other black cultural groups in Harlem, contravening his promise, to the Rockefeller Foundation at least, that the NLT would raise its profile as a community theater by opening its doors to other groups and art forms. This self-imposed estrangement from other members of the black theater movement severed the NLT from its most likely sympathizers, thus making further African American community support even less likely.[120]

What allowed Macbeth to alienate both his erstwhile and potential black allies was the continuing and even increasing support from the Ford Foundation. Between 1969, when it gave the NLT its first significant grant of $529,350 over two years, and 1972, when the NLT received its one-year terminal grant of $333,725, the Foundation had given the NLT more than a million dollars. While this grant already represented about 60 percent of the NLT's total income for the 1969–1970 fiscal year, by 1972, the NLT was virtually totally dependent on the Foundation, with no other even nominally significant source of funds, either from box-office receipts or individual and philanthropic contributions.

Lowry's ongoing support of the NLT pointed to the Foundation's vision of its relationship with the New Lafayette. As a social development program, the Foundation was interested in using the NLT to build community involvement in the therapeutic benefits of theater as well as to create opportunities for black artists. With respect to these expedient aims, it treated the New Lafayette as a special case among its theater grantees, including the NEC, only not in the way that Macbeth wanted. This difference in perspective became obvious in February 1971 when Macbeth submitted a far-fetched request for a terminal three-year grant from the Foundation of over $1,000,000, at the end of which Macbeth promised that the NLT would be entirely self-supporting. In his proposal, Macbeth articulated his beliefs about what white philanthropy owed the black community and added another argument about the artistic excellence of the NLT, putting it in the same league in this respect as the Foundation's "regular" regional theater grantees to whom, according to Macbeth, Lowry had shown "patience and understanding . . . in allowing most of them five to ten years of developing time." Macbeth insisted that the NLT deserved at least the same indulgence from Ford, given that the New Lafayette had reached what he called an "artistic standard" that was "high enough to be compared with the world's best," all the while remaining "organic to the Black aesthetic" and facing the challenge of "building [an] audience for theatre in a 'disadvantaged/deprived' community," without a "prosperous location" or "prosperous audiences." The uniqueness of the NLT project in terms of delivering both artistic excellence and social development, Macbeth concluded, meant that "there [were] few theatres *in the world* that [could] compare."[121]

Lowry, as it turned out, saw the NLT very differently by this time. He bridled at Macbeth's "comparison of [the Foundation's] financial support of The New Lafayette" with that of Ford's marquee repertory theater grantees, "the Alley, Arena and the American Conservatory," reminding Macbeth that Ford's support for these companies was "not only . . . mixed with other large contributed funds" but also combined "with even larger sums from the box office," both forms of income that Macbeth had failed to obtain. Lowry warned Macbeth against continuing with his comparison. "In other conversations," Lowry reminded Macbeth, "you have not likened The New Lafayette to the resident companies that have had large support from us, and I think you were more nearly right then." In fact, he told Macbeth, if Ford had compared the NLT in that way, "we would have tapered off our support before now."[122]

Significantly, Lowry did not address Macbeth's claim to the NLT's artistic greatness. In fact, the Foundation had never been very interested in the quality of the NLT's productions; unlike the Rockefeller Foundation, it rarely sent monitors to the shows. Instead, Lowry had depended on Macbeth's leadership to achieve Ford's social development objectives for black theater, and the NLT had failed in every respect from this perspective; Macbeth had not found an audience or community support for nonprofit theater in Harlem and, beyond the insularity of his relatively small ensemble, he had not maximized the NLT's potential to increase opportunities for black artists and to control them as Lowry had wished. In 1972, the Foundation hastily granted the NLT the terminal grant to phase out its activities and then closed the book on Macbeth's project.[123]

The sexism and homophobia that increasingly characterized the NLT's cultural nationalism may have been the last straw for the Foundation.[124] By 1971, an explicitly patriarchal, all-male council governed the NLT. The women who had participated in the NLT's ensemble, sometimes from its beginning, had come to have no say in any decisions. A sheepish *Black Theatre* coeditor and playwright, Richard Wesley, explained this "ticklish" issue to a black feminist interviewer in 1972 "as an outgrowth of . . . traditional African society which was male dominated," before referring her to Macbeth and Bullins who "are proficient in this field."[125] What may have made these prejudices truly problematic for the Foundation was that they were publicized in the *New York Times*. In April 1972, white theater critic Eric Bentley, who had recently come out as gay, renounced his positive review of the New Lafayette and its then current production, *The Psychic Pretenders*. Bentley's denunciation came after the NLT, which used his review in its publicity, sent him material outlining the theater's philosophy. In it, the NLT called into question the blackness of celebrities like Diahann Carroll, who "wears a wig," and Sidney Poitier, "who goes with a white girl," and it condemned French playwright and "pervert" Jean Genet's "faggoty ideas about Black Art, Revolution, and people." Black people could not allow "white perversion to enter their communities and consciousness, even if it rides on the back of a Panther," a thinly veiled reference to Genet who, although white, had close associations with the Black Panthers and whose play *The Blacks* was often credited with launching the black theater movement in New York.[126] The NLT's crude antihumanism, as Bentley characterized it, exposed by a major white critic would have damaged the relationship that the NLT had with the Ford Foundation. As demonstrated by the NEC's trajectory, the Foundation was moving inexorably toward an expansive mainstream multiculturalism that would eventually grow beyond race to include recognition, tolerance, and equal opportunity for all racial, gender, and sexual identities.[127]

While the NLT and Macbeth disappeared from the American theater scene, the New Lafayette's ethos and repertoire lived on, incorporated into the black studies departments that American universities began in the 1970s, often funded by the Ford Foundation. The NLT's rituals, for example, became standard offerings from black theater groups at largely white-majority and -controlled colleges, but they were rarely performed outside an academic setting to the black poor of the inner city they were originally intended to liberate. In fact, a number of the NLT's most stalwart participants ultimately found work in major research universities. Ed Bullins and his playwright workshop protégés Richard Wesley and OyamO became tenured theater faculty at Northeastern University, New York University, and the University of Michigan, respectively.[128]

More surprising were the number of NLT alumni who found success in venues that Macbeth had explicitly eschewed or attempted to escape, like downtown theater or even Hollywood, the crucible of commercial entertainment, sometimes with specific institutions or individuals who had been once been particular targets of Macbeth's ensemble's wrath. Ed Bullins, for example, ended up as playwright in residence at the American Place Theatre, the Off Broadway company that had often presented his work during the NLT days, despite Macbeth's disapproval. Joseph Papp's Public Theatre presented the first full production of *The Black Terror*, a play written by *Black Theatre* coeditor and playwright workshop participant Richard Wesley, while his workshop colleague OyamO saw his plays produced by the NLT's most inveterate target, the NEC, and performed at the National Playwrights conference, sponsored by the NLT's erstwhile adversary, the Eugene O'Neill Foundation. OyamO also served as a site monitor to the NEA, whose funding Macbeth had refused to pursue after his Rockefeller funding dried up. Richard Wesley went on to Hollywood after he was approached by none other than Sidney Poitier, who had been the reviled object of the NLT's anticommercialism agitprop, to write *Downtown Saturday Night*, the 1974 Poitier and Bill Cosby vehicle, and its 1975 sequel *Let's Do It Again*. Actor and Playservice director Whitman Mayo played Grady Wilson from 1973 to 1977 on television's *Sanford and Son*, and since 1974, NLT founding member and *Black Theatre* coeditor Roscoe Orman has been Gordon on *Sesame Street*, as well as a guest star on many popular TV series. In short, the NLT alumni moved on to success in mainstream American culture, both nonprofit and commercial, helped along by the new openings in mainstream culture and media facilitated by the multicultural model sponsored by the Foundation.

An Equivocal Performance of Social Development

Both the Negro Ensemble Company and the New Lafayette Theatre weathered many attacks from cultural nationalists regarding their acceptance of the Ford Foundation's patronage. McNeil Lowry was vehement in his response to these broadsides when they came within his radar. As he responded to black theater critic Clayton Riley, who had written in the *New York Times* about the NEC's dependency upon the Foundation, "The Ford Foundation does not influence or dictate repertoire of any artistic group, and that repertoire varies greatly."[129] From a narrow perspective Lowry was right, but he ignored the fundamentally distorting impact of the Foundation's funding and institution building. In an important sense, Lowry, not Ward or Macbeth, was the true genitor of the Negro Ensemble Company and the New Lafayette Theatre, neither of which had been conceived fully before the Foundation offered funding. Ward and Macbeth, both bent on black cultural autonomy, learned the truth of their dependence the hard way. The Foundation's attempts to force the NEC to achieve financial self-sufficiency after Ford's initial generosity meant that the ensemble was forced to choose a repertoire that would accommodate rather than transform the theatrical mainstream as Ward had initially intended. Meanwhile, the Foundation's largesse meant that the NLT never felt compelled to reconcile its avant-garde didacticism with the tastes of the "ghetto" audience it hoped to cultivate, resulting in the theater's demise and the failure of its dream to create an authentic, indigenous black theater to serve and uplift the community at large. In both cases, the Foundation called the shots, despite Ward's and Macbeth's valiant efforts to maintain their cultural independence and advance their liberationist aims. Their protests notwithstanding, the Foundation effectively disciplined both men, its handpicked black leaders, through its funding regimen.

From the Foundation's perspective, its actions to create and shape both companies led to resounding success. First and foremost, its "sociological" arts philanthropy created two hothouses for cultivating African American artists, producing hundreds who joined and enriched the American cultural mainstream. In doing so, both theaters flawlessly performed the script of assimilation through developmental separatism. Meanwhile, these successful artists contributed to the Foundation's second objective: to promote a positive racial identity for black people in order to facilitate their acculturation. However, because even the NEC did not cultivate a mass black audience, and given both theaters' success in cultivating black talent for Broadway, Hollywood, and television, this message was delivered most effectively not through autonomous institutions to achieve liberationist ends, as Ward and Macbeth had hoped, but rather through the ideological framework of mass media or the rarified confines of black studies programs. This kind of mainstream multiculturalism served both the Foundation's assimilationist goals for African Americans as well as its desire to elevate the ethical and moral content of commercial culture. It did so through a sentimental message of superficial cultural difference that nevertheless revealed a humanistic universalism, thus obscuring and smoothing over the racial conflict and inequality that persisted in the United States, despite American liberalism's best efforts to resolve them.

Meanwhile, the New Lafayette's sideways turn showed the Foundation that despite choosing Macbeth for his putative leadership qualities and therapeutic conception of black theater, it still was making mistakes in choosing the right individuals or instruments to establish successful social development in the ghetto. This tenacious barrier to the full fruition of the Foundation's solution to the urban crisis would lead it to tackle economic issues in the inner city and, ultimately even more important, to find a way to develop its own black leaders whose worldview and ambitions would not simply intersect but actually fit with Ford's own.

Chapter 6

The Best and the Brightest

In January 1979, the Ford Foundation announced that Franklin Thomas would replace the retiring McGeorge Bundy as the president of the Foundation, which was still the nation's largest and most powerful philanthropy. In making this appointment, the trustees made a monumental gesture that symbolized the culmination of Ford's long-standing commitment to racial assimilation. Thomas was not only black but also a Foundation protégé, having spent ten years from 1967 to 1977 as the handpicked, founding president of Brooklyn's Bedford-Stuyvesant Restoration Corporation (BSRC), a demonstration by Senator Robert F. Kennedy and the Ford Foundation to institutionalize establishment liberalism's attack on the urban crisis through the creation and support of community-development corporations (CDCs).

Unlike most of the other African American grantees with whom the Foundation had dealt in the late 1960s, Thomas had not disappointed Ford's officers and trustees, and the CDC model had cultivated his talents and those of the dozens of black leaders he had helped to develop at BSRC. Thomas's appointment as the Foundation's president was tangible proof that social development's strategy of black leadership development and individual upward mobility had worked and that Ford's own scheme for community development had fostered that success. Thomas's move was also widely interpreted both inside and outside the Foundation as a portent of further racial progress and perhaps even a postracial future. As the *New York Times* editorialized, "When corporate America can hand such power to a black citizen, there is truly hope that race will one day be irrelevant."[1]

The Foundation's announcement of Thomas's appointment was a long way off in 1967, when he took the helm at BSRC. It was also after what Paul Ylvisaker called the Foundation's "beautiful running time" during the first half of the 1960s, when his enormously influential strategy of systems reform and assimilation through community action shaped the cutting edge of the era's activist federal social policy. By 1967, Ford's social-engineering approach to the urban crisis faced intense scrutiny and criticism.[2] Black insurgency and rebellion, along with the white backlash against it, suggested that the Foundation's strategy had done nothing to quell the urban crisis and, as a growing number of critics charged, may have even abetted it.

The Ford Foundation found itself at the center of this political maelstrom thanks to actions like its involvement in the schools crisis, which prompted both vocal and nationwide criticism, along with institutional review from within. After the failure of initiatives like the community-control experiment and the punitive federal tax reforms that followed it, the Foundation beat a retreat from the political arena. Nevertheless, Bundy and his officers stuck by their conviction that "the fact that large numbers of . . . minority group citizens live in poverty and isolation in depressed central city . . . areas," as Vice President of National Affairs Mitchell Sviridoff put it, represented "the nation's most serious democratic problem."[3] Solving that problem remained the Foundation's key domestic mission. However, in the wake of the controversy surrounding its own recent community-action activities and the ones they inspired through the War on Poverty, the Foundation altered its strategy for social development in the ghetto to one that followed the national political mood and its own ideological roots by shifting right. It moved toward individual versus group-based initiatives; local rather than national programs; capitalist economic development over social welfare programs; less government and more private-sector involvement in the ghetto; the rejection of grassroots participatory democracy for the top-down leadership of the elite theory of democracy; and the values and practices of corporate America, all the while retaining the assimilation-through-segregation strategy of developmental separatism.

The instrument that the Foundation settled on to achieve this reorientation was the CDC, an institution that it did not originate but that it had been shaping through funding since community development's first incarnations in the early 1960s. The CDC offered a new place-based, public-private model for the economic and social development of the nonwhite poor, once again putting the Foundation at the forefront of American social policy, this time by anticipating the nationwide trend toward localism and privatization that eschewed the grandiose, statist solutions of the dying New Deal order. Also in keeping with the national mood, the CDC retained the Foundation's ongoing focus on race- and ghetto-based solutions, rejecting any whiff of integrationism sure to arouse controversy among blacks and whites alike in the post–civil rights 1960s and 1970s.

By the time that the Foundation joined Kennedy in building a CDC from the ground up, it could take what it liked from existing community-development initiatives around the country. It then molded those elements to its ends of finding a liberal solution to the ongoing "problem" of directing African Americans, after their hard-won entrance into public life, onto the path of assimilation that would leave the structures of the American political economy intact. The Bedford-Stuyvesant project, and ultimately other Ford-funded CDCs, worked to accomplish that goal by combining the systems-reform effort of Gray Areas along with a strong emphasis on individual indigenous leadership that the Foundation first toyed with out of necessity in school decentralization and community control. After that earlier effort had failed from the Foundation's perspective, Ford's officers sought to find a way to develop black leadership through a framework outside of the volatility, compromises, and coalition building required by the democratic political process, and that allowed more careful selection, development, and monitoring of handpicked, "grassroots" leaders. These black and brown "public entrepreneurs," as the Foundation liked to call them, ran their CDCs according to the management philosophy of their white counterparts at the Foundation and corporate America. They also replicated the elite theory of democracy in the ghetto through a top-down approach to the black community and thus earned the trust of the white establishment. At last the Foundation had found the right instrument for its assimilationist goals and faith in meritocracy by helping to develop through the CDC model a tiny, incipient black establishment to manage the remaining black majority and to define and represent the interests of the African American community at large. The symbolic culmination of this success in developing black leadership through the CDC was the rise of Franklin Thomas to the Foundation's presidency.

New Politics and the Road to Community Development

While the community-development corporation's name and genesis in the late 1960s might suggest origins in a black power effort toward self-determination, like community action this "community" initiative often came about from outside intervention to solve the urban crisis and the political and social conflict it engendered. Understanding these roots, as well as the CDC's ongoing attraction for the American political, corporate, and philanthropic elite, liberal and conservative alike, helps to explain why this model has persisted, bridging the establishment liberalism of the 1960s to the neoliberalism of the 1980s and beyond. In fact, the CDC story from above suggests an alternative founding story, this one about the roots of the late 1960s conservative transition that resulted in the diminution, privatization, and localization of social-welfare policy and delivery. The inception of this shift is usually ascribed to Richard Nixon and the dictates of his New Federalism. However, in the years before his presidency, Nixon's supposed archrivals, "limousine liberals" like Robert Kennedy, McGeorge Bundy, and the Foundation's domestic program officers—whom conservatives blamed for the statism and welfare dependency that necessitated their right-wing revolution—had begun to conceptualize this transition. They did so largely through the CDC.

These liberals found inspiration in the nation's initial community-development efforts, which had their origins in early 1960s liberal civil rights activism but moved away from protest toward pragmatic and "positive" programs to institutionalize the movement and deal with the complex urban crisis of ghettoization and black poverty. These were initiatives like the Watts Labor Action Council, the United Auto Workers' (UAW) "community union" in South-Central Los Angeles; the Rev. Leon Sullivan's job-training and cooperative community investment efforts in Philadelphia; or Chicago's Woodlawn Organization, which by the 1970s had transformed itself into an agency that engaged in a variety of neighborhood rehabilitation and job-creation schemes. These endeavors sought ghetto-based solutions to end the economic isolation and soaring joblessness of their communities while calling for the separate uplift of the poor on their home turf before their successful assimilation into the mainstream. Founded through private initiative and funding and focused on economic development, these organizations worked largely parallel to the political and social-service orientation of the community-action agencies of the War on Poverty.[4]

Democrats and Republicans flocked to these projects, as did philanthropic and government funders, all based on community development's promise to solve ghetto problems without any fundamental social, economic, or political disruption. This potential was so attractive that it formed a centerpiece of Robert Kennedy's effort, culminating with his 1968 presidential bid, to reshape Democratic politics and repair a postwar liberal consensus torn asunder by the black freedom struggle, urban rebellions, the Vietnam War, and the resulting New Left and Right. Kennedy was an intensely ambitious politician who had the supreme confidence of McGeorge Bundy and other fellow New Frontiersmen to perfect American society through the means of liberalism and capitalism. He sought policy alternatives to LBJ's Great Society that not only would more effectively respond to the ghetto conditions that sparked black rioting but also would simultaneously stanch the growing defection to the Republican Party of white Democrats who blamed the War on Poverty for ongoing urban unrest and growing black welfare dependency. As Kennedy acted on his presidential aspirations he sought to find policy interventions that he could effect from his Senate seat that would both demonstrate this new political alternative and work without the involvement of a federal social-welfare bureaucracy under President Johnson's control and underfunded by war appropriations.[5]

Community development provided Kennedy with the perfect demonstration of his new political and policy approach, distinct from Johnson's Model Cities program, also announced in 1966. First, Kennedy emphasized that community development was based on the notion of African Americans helping themselves in what he called the "critical" task of "building . . . self-sufficiency and self-determination within communities of poverty." Bolstering this American ethos of self-reliance, the public money for CDCs was not to be distributed through one-size-fits-all welfare programs that Kennedy claimed had "stripped" the poor "of their dignity and treated them as a nation apart" but via block grants in which independent nonprofit agencies in each "single community" competed for and administered funds on their own "in direct response to the needs and wishes of the people themselves." Finally, Kennedy saw the free enterprise of the private sector, or what he called "the sinew and strength of America," as playing an instrumental role in community development, providing technical and managerial know-how, spurring business and capital investment in the inner city, and building capacity among indigenous black leaders who would be schooled in corporate management through the experience of running community corporations in their own neighborhoods. He intended that this private-sector involvement would "end the isolation of these areas," by bringing "not just individual residents, but the entire community, into the mainstream of American life."[6]

Kennedy's distillation of community development's promise was a brilliant demonstration of his genius for coalition building. By offering a ghetto-based solution to the urban crisis centered on job and business creation, the CDC responded to black power's call for both self-determination and an end to a colonial relationship with the state and capital. Concurrently, this approach rejected the racial integration that was anathema to wavering white

Democrats, while simultaneously appealing to their widely and deeply held conviction that hard work and self-reliance were a universal path to upward mobility and assimilation. Similarly, Kennedy could promote the program's focus on transferring to ghetto dwellers the means to achieve what he called "the same entrepreneurial vision that has brought the rest of us to our present state of comfort and strength" by comparing it favorably to Johnson's Community Action Program, criticized by black activists for not providing the material resources to effect change and by white conservatives for fomenting unrest and encouraging black welfare dependency.[7] Furthermore, it would replace the Community Action Program's controversial emphasis on participatory political processes with pragmatic and concrete programs run without political interference from above or below. Most immediately, Kennedy's CDC scheme seized on a moment of tremendous, riot-fueled anxiety on the part of the corporate establishment that it must intervene before cities were burned to the ground.

Kennedy and his staff spent most of 1966 using his clout and connections in putting the political pieces together to create the sine qua non of CDCs—one that would demonstrate how the liberal establishment writ large supported and could effect ghetto revitalization. Early in the year, he worked with his fellow New York senator, liberal Republican Jacob Javits, to amend the Equal Opportunity Act to include the Special Impact Program (SIP), which would provide the block-grant funds that would underwrite funding CDCs, and particularly Kennedy's brainchild, what would become the Bedford-Stuyvesant Restoration Corporation. In the spring, he again joined forces with Javits by playing a prominent role in the Ribicoff Hearings (also known as the City Hearings), a months-long bipartisan congressional attack on Model Cities, in which Kennedy could showcase his CDC alternative.[8]

Meanwhile, Kennedy used his exemplary connections with the liberal establishment to bring about the capital transfer to the ghetto that was a linchpin of his scheme for community development. He collected an all-star cast of American corporate and financial power in active support of his scheme. This group was led by André Meyer, the head of the investment bank Lazard-Frères, who was also the financial trustee to the Kennedy family and one of Lyndon Johnson's confidants. Meyer's involvement, along with Kennedy's personal and family charisma and his bipartisan efforts with Javits, helped attract the active support of other blue-chip leaders like International Business Machines (IBM) president Thomas Watson, Jr.; Columbia Broadcasting System (CBS) CEO William Paley; former Treasury Secretary and diplomat

C. Douglas Dillon; pioneering venture capitalist Benno Schmidt; First National City Bank (later Citigroup) chairman George S. Moore; corporate lawyer and once Deputy Secretary of Defense Roswell Gilpatric; and former director of the Tennessee Valley Administration and past chair of the Atomic Energy Commission David Lilienthal.[9]

For RFK biographer Evan Thomas, the energy behind Kennedy's relentless push to activate the CDC model was fueled by his family's "elite and anti-establishment" spirit, born out of their Catholic, arriviste roots in Boston, the crucible of America's WASP upper class. Thomas elaborated, characterizing Kennedy's idea of the CDC as "small, anti-bureaucratic, seemingly democratic but in fact tightly controlled, [and] operating outside the mainstream and proud of it."[10] His family had imbued him with these values and characteristics, but they were not the Kennedys' alone: this ethos was shared by a large subset of their establishment liberal contemporaries, including the corporate types who supported the CDC effort. Furthermore, that bona fide Boston Brahmin McGeorge Bundy and his Ford Foundation officers also imagined themselves decentralizing American institutional life from the top down, as in the case of New York's public school system.

In fact, as early as September 1965 Paul Ylvisaker had begun to consider community development as the Foundation's next policy innovation, now that the Great Society had adopted his community-action approach. Foundation trustees were primed to support such a move. Reassured by their elevator meeting with Leon Sullivan in 1964, they had agreed to support the minister's work in Philadelphia, which by all accounts had been vastly more effective than that of the city's dysfunctional Gray Areas agency. They also joined the Rockefeller Foundation in helping to support the UAW's efforts in Watts. Now it was time for the activist Foundation to create its own version of these efforts: "a new type of non-profit organization, deeply identified with the physical area which it is to serve, to bring substantial amounts of capital, know-how, and indigenous control to bear on the area's own needs" (in other words, a scheme very similar to Kennedy's).[11] These plans picked up steam in the first half of 1966 as Bundy and his staff worked on the Foundation's new social development approach and were well under way in the fall that year when Robert Kennedy's staff first met with Ylvisaker (on the brink of resigning from the Foundation), along with Louis Winnick, the program officer in charge of the Foundation's Urban and Metropolitan Development program. Winnick continued to work with Kennedy's men in shaping the program, especially as it came to fruition in Bedford-Stuyvesant.[12]

What, beyond its political appeal, committed Kennedy and the Foundation's leaders to the CDC model? Foremost, they saw it as restoring the assumptions and objectives of establishment liberalism that they felt the Great Society had betrayed. Although both Ford's officers, through Gray Areas and the Mobilization For Youth community-action program, and Kennedy, through his leadership of the President's Committee on Juvenile Delinquency, had contributed to some of the most significant ideas and demonstrations undergirding Lyndon Johnson's program, they saw that in implementation it had fallen far short of their expectations as a solution to the urban crisis. In fact, by 1967, prevailing liberal opinion saw LBJ's behemoth domestic agenda as a fiasco. Public assistance programs, and particularly the predominant "welfare" program, Aid to Families with Dependent Children, had, according to Kennedy, "stripped the poor of their dignity and treated them as a nation apart," and the federal manpower program, intended to address welfare dependency, instead "trained people for jobs that did not exist," in marked contrast to efforts like Leon Sullivan's privately initiated job training and creation efforts in Philadelphia. Meanwhile, the Community Action Program, the initiative at the center of the War on Poverty that was supposed to offer black people a voice in their own affairs, instead only gave them the power to protest instead of the power to "act" on or "decide" their own affairs.[13]

These failings could be blamed on what Paul Ylvisaker called the "obsolete," and even "medieval," "hierarchically organized public bureaucracy" of the welfare state. Ylvisaker held that such hidebound institutions guaranteed silo thinking, one-size-fits-all solutions, and needless red tape, even in the face of urgent social distress. Instead, Kennedy and the Foundation were moving toward comprehensive programs to suit local needs made possible through the "public philanthropy" of block grants, like the ones available through Kennedy's SIP amendment. Even better for Kennedy and his Foundation counterparts, such programs, as early community-development efforts had shown, could mobilize private as well as public means to achieve their ends. The failure of the "bureaucratic tradition," as Ylvisaker put it, as well as public spending on Vietnam, may have spurred the shift to finding private monetary and technical assistance for public projects.[14] However, the evolving notion of what would come to be known as the public-private partnership also appealed to establishment liberals, because, unlike traditional welfare-state programs, it reflected their belief in the corporate capitalist system and its ability to serve all Americans.

Therefore, despite their support of expanded federal programs and spending on the urban crisis, these liberals believed, as Ylvisaker did as early as 1966, that this move should coincide with "energizing the vast resources of the private sector to fulfill a public purpose" through "private mechanisms" like nonprofit and even for-profit corporations.[15] Furthermore, according to the Foundation, private-sector involvement in public policy would energize government bureaucracies through "the drive of talented businessmen and their readiness to solve problems through research and development."[16] These "public entrepreneurs," as Ylvisaker and others called them, would know, unlike their civil-service counterparts, how to "create jobs, get performance, cut through red tape, and do a job."[17] Of course, public entrepreneurship of this type was the Foundation's stock-in-trade, and the CDC's public-private model offered it a role at the cutting edge of public policy that it had been missing since the Gray Areas program.

The community-development corporation concept got to the heart of what Kennedy, Bundy, and their peers believed was at the root of the urban crisis. Kennedy defined community development as a matter of economics, in which a "foundation of individual and community self-support" would allow black communities to escape "degrading and imprisoning dependency." This dependency had been created because, like third world nations, "the ghettos of poverty" were "outside the great chain of investment, production, and consumption." This chain "must be extended to include the inner city," spurring "investment to create productive jobs, which will afford the jobholders the income they need to consume."[18] Such economic integration, as the Foundation's National Affairs division summarized its argument for the creation of its kind of CDC, was the most potent tool of assimilation: "a closer working relationship with downtown business leadership" would lift the ghetto from a "public welfare fief" to "the mainstream of the City's economic and social life."[19] Thus, a fundamental and distinguishing element of Kennedy and Ford's concept of the CDC was an active partnership with corporate sponsors who were essential to the economic de-ghettoization of the inner city. This focus reflected their confidence in the liberal establishment and the tenets of postwar liberalism.

Such a model had added valence for Kennedy and Foundation officials in terms of their mutual commitment to developmental separatism. They all presumed that urban African American communities effectively existed outside of the national community. Kennedy counsel and speechwriter

Edgar Cahn even summed up the CDC's "massive infusion of private resources, governmental programs, and expertise" as a form of "'foreign aid'
to the underdeveloped country of the ghetto," a view very much shared by
Ford staffers and one that animated other liberals in the CDC field.[20] Such
a formulation of the ghetto precluded any notion that it could or should be
integrated at present into the American mainstream, even if the assimilation of black people remained the ultimate goal. Kennedy made this key
point of developmental separatism explicitly clear in his 1967 essay on the
CDC model, where he, like his Ford Foundation allies, rejected racial integration outright as a solution to the urban crisis because he insisted that
economic and community development could only happen successfully
within the ghetto itself. Kennedy claimed that "many in the slums are un-
equipped to seek jobs away from the areas in which they live," psychologically conditioned as they were by "a century of insecurity." He also believed
that the "fundamental pathology of the ghetto" meant that African Americans and other minorities required "community achievement" in order
to overcome their marginalization and alienation, and to establish "basic
financial and social security" that would lead ultimately to their full and
equal participation in the "great creative enterprise in the life of this nation." Black power, then, for Kennedy as for the Ford Foundation, was at its
root a behavioral issue; it boiled down to "a sense of Negro self-reliance and
solidarity . . . which has been the base on which earlier minorities [eventu-
ally] achieved full integration in American life."[21] In the meantime, though,
African Americans had to stay put, if only so that Kennedy could sell this
program to recalcitrant whites, a political imperative that reinforced his
and the Foundation's developmental separatism.

Finally, the CDC offered a pathway to conflict resolution in the ghetto,
the Foundation's fundamental objective since the 1940s in its work with
African Americans. It avoided the political pitfalls of citizen participation
that had made the community-action approach so conflict-ridden and unpredictable for both the federal government in its antipoverty program and
the Ford Foundation in its foray into community control. By contrast, and
in the spirit of the elite theory of democracy, RFK's and the Ford Foundation's kind of CDC was outside of politics and run on corporate principles
by managerial and technocratic experts. However, it would take the implementation of the Bedford-Stuyvesant CDC for Kennedy and the Ford Foundation to understand that those experts could be black as well as white.

Franklin Thomas, the BSRC, and the Evolution
of the Black Public Entrepreneur

Finding a place to demonstrate the CDC plan was an afterthought for Kennedy and his Foundation allies whose first priority was to develop their idea and then to assemble political support for it in Congress, in New York City, and among the nation's corporate leadership. This top-down approach gave little or no consideration to the desires, talent, or leadership potential of the local place or people where the corporation was to be located, despite Kennedy's avowal that specific community needs were at the heart of his vision. Establishment liberals like Kennedy, who most often labeled all inner-city black communities with the universal and undifferentiated descriptor "the ghetto," had little sense of these neighborhoods' diversity and understood them only in terms of their residents' assumed behavioral disabilities. This expectation of pathology made it unthinkable to elite whites that local African Americans could effectively run their own affairs, especially according to the establishment's notions of expertise and leadership.

Unsurprisingly, then, broader political considerations, not locally expressed needs, put Kennedy's CDC in Bedford-Stuyvesant. He had wished to locate it in Harlem, the nation's most iconic black community, but he also had wanted free rein with which to implement his idea, which Harlem's own powerful political machine would not allow. As a consolation, his staffers came up with the idea of Bedford-Stuyvesant, the biggest area in the conglomeration of black neighborhoods in north and central Brooklyn—including Ocean Hill and Brownsville—that together made up the largest ghetto in New York City. While Bedford-Stuyvesant would have been little known or understood by the likes of Kennedy, it had the virtues of being sizable, in New York, and known locally as emblematic of the urban crisis, especially after a 1964 riot had occurred in the area.

In the late 1960s, Bedford-Stuyvesant had about 400,000 residents, mostly migrant families from the American South or the Caribbean, including Puerto Rico. While the community had a relatively large rate of homeownership—at least 15 percent of its residential buildings were owner-occupied, compared to only 2 percent in Harlem and about 20 percent for New York City overall—it had been hit hard by deindustrialization. As the captains of finance and industry whom Kennedy had recruited for his effort oversaw New York's transformation into what historian Joshua Freeman has called "the headquarters for world capitalism," the black working class of Bedford-

Stuyvesant found itself disproportionately shut out of the postindustrial labor market.[22] Brooklyn's black workers had been displaced by automation, laid off when major industrial employers like the Brooklyn Navy Yard shut their doors, and excluded by lack of education or by de facto Jim Crow prejudice from most opportunities for upward mobility in the city's new white-collar economy. Meanwhile, the neighborhood's population growth was a function of not only postwar black urban migration but also deliberate ghettoization. Since the New Deal, the city's real estate industry and banks had exploited white flight to the suburbs and employed a pernicious combination of urban renewal, public housing development, and federal redlining to reshape Brooklyn's racial geography, forcing both old and new black Brooklynites into the center of the borough's northern half, thus "saving" South Brooklyn for white development. In 1930 no neighborhood in the borough could be accurately described as African American and, in fact, black Brooklynites were less spatially segregated than the city's white ethnics. However, by the time Kennedy chose the neighborhood for his community-development efforts, black people in Brooklyn lived in New York City's largest ghetto thanks to the deliberate efforts of powerful white economic interests.[23]

No one in Kennedy's office or at the Ford Foundation ever acknowledged the roots of racial segregation and impoverishment of Bedford-Stuyvesant residents in a racialized economy that profited from African Americans' exploitation and exclusion. Instead, they hewed to the orthodox explanation that the ghetto was a "natural" product of black urban migration in which African American cultural pathology had driven prejudiced whites out of their homes and into the suburbs. Kennedy had little opportunity to disabuse himself of this interpretation; unlike the care he had taken in assembling what was often modestly called his "businessmen's committee" of establishment heavy hitters, he left the community consultations in Bedford-Stuyvesant to his staff after a brief high-profile tour of the area in February 1966. These staffers took a desultory approach to this duty, only making sporadic stops in the neighborhood during the spring and summer of that year, meaning that the senator's office never gained more than a superficial notion of the social and political workings of Bedford-Stuyvesant.

Kennedy's team quickly cemented a relationship with the most obvious social-service agency in Bedford-Stuyvesant, the Central Brooklyn Coordinating Committee (CBCC), an umbrella group of churches, civic groups, and social workers. The CBCC had originated the area's federally funded antipoverty agency, Youth in Action, whose most active adjunct, the Renewal and

Rehabilitation subcommittee, had been working for a few years with private and academic urban planners to put together a redevelopment scheme for the area. The senator's office's other main community contact was Thomas Jones, a civil court judge and former state assemblyman who was leader of one of black Brooklyn's many rival Democratic factions. Without seeking to understand the area's complex political landscape, Kennedy had fallen under Jones's influence during his February visit when the judge openly challenged the senator to put his community-development plans into action. Trusting Jones as an advisor within this highly partisan local scene led to a number of gaffes that demonstrated the superficiality of Kennedy's efforts to understand the area. These included the exclusion of the judge's bitterest political rival, Shirley Chisholm—who was the area's state assembly representative and a soon-to-be nationally known congresswoman and presidential candidate— from any consultations about the CDC project.[24]

After these preliminaries in the neighborhood, Kennedy publicly announced the creation of his Bedford-Stuyvesant community-development project at the CBCC annual housing conference in December 1966. Surrounded by Javits, Meyer, and Mayor John Lindsay, he announced the formation of two corporations: Renewal and Rehabilitation (R&R), whose board would comprise the members of the CBCC committee of the same name and be chaired by Judge Jones; and the Development and Services Corporation (D&S), chaired by C. Douglas Dillon and comprising members of Kennedy's businessmen's group. In his statement, Kennedy declared that R&R would devise programs and priorities for Bedford-Stuyvesant's social, physical, and economic redevelopment, while D&S would provide managerial advice to R&R and work to attract capital to Bedford-Stuyvesant. Demonstrating that the private sector had already begun to answer his call for funding, he also announced that the Vincent Astor Foundation had committed $1 million for planning projects in the area and for two park and playground "superblocks" to be designed by I. M. Pei, the cutting-edge architect who had designed the Kennedy presidential library. Furthermore, the Foundation had committed $750,000 for administrative support to get the corporations off the ground so that they could attract the public and private funds required for community development.[25]

The dual corporation was the scheme of Ford's Louis Winnick and RFK staffer Thomas Johnston. They assumed that the CDC's power would rest with D&S and not R&R, acting on the presumption that the community board was not ready to take on such responsibility. Therefore Ford insisted that all of its funding be funneled through the "white" corporation, and not to its community counterpart. In an unspoken comparison between the two groups, a project monitor explained this choice by claiming that Ford "had confidence in the caliber of the men who were on [the D&S] Board."[26] Furthermore, the Foundation hoped that by making D&S the key partner, the project could take full advantage of the elite group that Kennedy had assembled. Kennedy and his Foundation allies believed that the high profile D&S board could harness the "drive of talented businessmen and their . . . readiness to solve problems through research and development" to find a solution to the urban crisis. In addition, they imagined it would be in these white leaders' interest to provide "opportunities for profitable private investment" in the "underdeveloped economic region" of the ghetto and to foster the economic "integration" of the "ghetto" with the rest of "downtown."[27] In short they believed that D&S would deliver on the promise of a massive capital transfer to the ghetto.

Conversely, Kennedy and the Foundation expected that, for the time being at least, R&R would remain a largely token body. Kennedy's staff had chosen the "indigenous" leaders for R&R who would broker for Bedford-Stuyvesant without any broad consultation with or participation by the community at large. Meanwhile, R&R had little power in the dual corporation model. While Kennedy wrote of the CDC precipitating "community achievement," giving communities the "power to act" and creating a "participating democracy," these promises proved to be little more than expedient rhetoric in the age of the call for black self-determination.[28] Kennedy and the Foundation, despite the fact that they had begun to focus on fostering minority leadership by the time they were involved with Bedford-Stuyvesant, shared a developmental mind-set that meant that for them the innovation of their project was not that it would be black-led but that, unlike any other CDC in the country, it would connect the ghetto with the very top rank of the nation's white leadership and expertise.

Nowhere were these intentions for Bedford-Stuyvesant more evident than in the courtship of the nationally prominent white talent that quickly began to stream into D&S's Manhattan headquarters to plan the community's future. The list of high-profile recruits began with Edward Logue, the national leader in top-down, if socially progressive, urban renewal, who Kennedy hoped would eventually lead the white corporation and who drew up the initial, ambitious redevelopment plans for the neighborhood.[29] Eli Jacobs, a young, well-connected investment banker who was appointed as the corporation's acting executive director, also brought in some of the nation's top modernist architects and urban designers, including Pei, Philip Johnson, and David Crane, to put into practice Logue's "macroscale" ambitions for the neighborhood. These included a network of superblocks, or landscaped walkways closed to traffic, and the redevelopment of a two-block-wide corridor between Fulton Street and Atlantic Avenue that would run like a spine through the length of the area's major commercial corridor, with nodes of retail, community, government, cultural, and recreational services along its length. Jacobs used his business contacts to consult with legendary residential property developers William Levitt and Samuel Lefrak about this large-scale redevelopment, and he worked with the groundbreaking shopping-center developer James Rouse and renowned architect James Polchek to draw up plans for what Jacobs dreamed would be the nation's largest shopping mall, to be built over the Long Island Railroad at the eastern end of Logue's corridor. Jacobs hoped that "Broadway Junction" would ultimately draw two to three million customers yearly, especially from suburban Long Island. Other white consultants developed equally ambitious and quickly conceived plans to found a private-school system and a college in Bedford-Stuyvesant and to transform the neighborhood into New York City's next garment district, creating jobs in what had become a postindustrial wasteland.[30]

While Jacobs and Logue developed their grandiose plans at D&S headquarters, the R&R Corporation foundered. Reflecting its subsidiary role in its white sponsors' minds, the community corporation remained unfunded and unstaffed, and hence it was utterly incapable to withstand the onslaught of experience and ambition emanating from Manhattan. R&R had no chance to perform its putative role as the initiator of programs that D&S would then help it operationalize. Always an afterthought for Kennedy and the Foundation, R&R remained without an executive director for months after Jacobs and Logue had drawn up their plans for the neighborhood. To compound this gap, a latent power struggle between Judge Jones and the CBCC members on the R&R board intensified and erupted into open conflict when the leadership search finally began.

From the beginning, Jones acted as Kennedy's agent in the R&R Corporation. Kennedy staffers imposed him on the CBCC members who made up the core of the board of the CDC's community arm. This majority, resentful of the manipulations that resulted in Jones's being the board chair, fought his efforts to control them, most notably during the contentious search for the corporation's president. Upon the recommendation of U.S. Attorney Robert Morgenthau, Kennedy selected Franklin Thomas, who was a New York City deputy police commissioner, former assistant U.S. attorney, and trusted deputy to Mayor Lindsay, as his handpicked candidate for the post. Jones's task was to promote Thomas in the face of the board majority, which supported the CBCC's executive director, Donald Benjamin, a seasoned veteran of the social-welfare field within Bedford-Stuyvesant. After a bruising interview with the R&R board, Thomas told Kennedy that he would accept the job only if the dominant and hostile CBCC faction could be neutralized and if he could be assured free rein in running the corporation. Kennedy and Jones, intent on hiring Thomas, cooked up a plan to expand R&R's board from twenty to fifty members, diluting CBCC's power.[31] If that scheme did not work, they intended to bypass the CBCC group altogether by establishing a new community corporation behind which Kennedy would throw his weight and which Thomas would run and Jones would chair.[32]

These machinations resulted in a flagrant coup. As expected, the CBCC group refused to countenance Jones's board-expansion scheme, and he lost a confidence vote. No sooner had Jones activated the backup plan by announcing his resignation from R&R and the creation of a new community corporation—with Franklin Thomas as its executive director—than he received prearranged telegrams of support for his action from Jacob Javits, John Lindsay, and Kennedy, who also announced that this new organization would replace R&R as the community arm of the CDC. These manipulations spurred the brouhaha that ensued in which everyone from the CBCC group to the *New York Times* noted the obvious political machinations that had transpired.[33]

In drumming up political support for the new corporation in the face of the CBCC's many community allies, Kennedy enlisted the support of Sonny Carson, the controversial and confrontational black power figure who led Brooklyn's nationalist Congress of Racial Equality (CORE) chapter. While this move did not silence Carson's anticolonial criticisms of Kennedy's work in the community, Carson and other Brooklyn CORE leaders began to inveigh against the middle-aged women who made up the CBCC group for "emasculating the community and denying [them] models of black manhood." Carson threw his support behind Jones by accepting a board position for the new corporation.[34]

Carson's gendered critique echoed those of both the Kennedy and Ford Foundation staffs, who justified the new entity on the basis of the period's conventional wisdom that black women had blocked opportunities for strong, male leadership in the black community and hence had blocked African American progress. In fact, these "middle-aged women" were almost always criticized as the source of the problems at R&R, even though Judge Jones could just have easily occupied the hot seat. As "one well-informed official" said to the *New York Times*, "The situation really confirms all that's been written about the power of the matriarchy in Negro communities."[35] Two assumptions shaped this expedient and effective deployment of a presumptive "matriarchy" operating at the CBCC. The first was that the committee's female leadership lacked the experience, talent, and confidence to put Kennedy's ambitious, "hard" plans for community economic development into practice. As one of Kennedy's staffers put it, "A new ballgame came to town," in the form of the CDC model, "and the women were only good at the old one," which was a traditional form of "soft" social welfare.[36] Such gendered assumptions saturated the masculinist imagination of postwar establishment liberals, and particularly their vision of effective leadership, black or white. Second, and by extension for the Ford Foundation and the Kennedy team in the black power era, the authentic black subject was not only male but also young, representing both the iconic rioter and the leader who could bring him back from the brink. Thus, the board at R&R needed to be expanded because, as Louis Winnick said to McGeorge Bundy, the CBCC group of middle-aged women was simply "unrepresentative" of the community, despite its long history and umbrella leadership of multiple local agencies. By contrast, Foundation officers applauded the involvement of Sonny Carson and other young male figures in the new corporation. They interpreted this participation as a significant step forward to the creation of a bona fide community agency, despite the fact that these young men represented Bedford-Stuyvesant no more than did the CBCC reformers.[37]

While the CBCC group was vilified by received wisdom that unquestioningly elevated both men and youth as the true representatives of black America, in truth none of the African Americans involved in the Bedford-Stuyvesant CDC could claim to be "community" leaders for another reason—Robert Kennedy's blatant presumption in anointing them to and, in the case of the CBCC, rejecting them from this role. As CBCC ally Walter P. Offutt put it, the question left hanging in the air after this episode was whether "an outside force" could "enter into a community and dictate to it whom its leaders should be."[38] For "elite, anti-establishmentarians" like Kennedy and Bundy the answer was "yes," given that they already thought that they knew the black community and what ailed it. Furthermore, the Foundation—despite its early, positive experience with "indigenous" black leadership through Leon Sullivan in the Ylvisaker era—was in the process of being badly burned by its community-control experiment. Officers would be more careful in the future to partner with and choose only those African Americans whom they knew and trusted to carry out their vision. Even then, they only rarely treated these leaders as anything more than tokens or figureheads, even when the Foundation or its allies handpicked them. At least that was the case until Franklin Thomas demonstrated to the liberal establishment that there were black men like him, "ready" for power.

Thomas exactly fit the Foundation's bill for black leadership. Born and raised in Bedford-Stuyvesant by a widowed, immigrant mother from Barbados, the thirty-three-year-old Thomas was a local boy who had most decidedly made good. While he still lived in the neighborhood in 1967, his considerable professional energy was focused in Manhattan, New York's power center. He had attended Columbia, choosing it for its prestige over several other schools that offered him basketball scholarships, and graduated from the university's law school in 1963. He then worked in the U.S. attorney and mayor's offices, gaining the attention of powerful superiors, including Robert Morgenthau and John Lindsay, who were impressed by his intelligence, resolve, and loyalty in the difficult and ultimately frustrated effort to create a civilian police review board. Nevertheless, on the surface, Thomas's job experience hardly seemed equal to that of Donald Benjamin, his main rival for the CDC leadership, who had years of experience in the social welfare field serving Bedford-Stuyvesant. However, Thomas was surely more qualified to direct a CDC than had been the thirty-four-year-old McGeorge Bundy when, without holding a Ph.D., he became the dean of arts and sciences at Harvard, or indeed when, fresh from the National Security Council, new to the Ford Foundation, and totally without experience in dealing with domestic social issues, he decided to tackle the "Negro Problem," writ large.[39]

Indeed, in choosing Franklin Thomas, Kennedy and the Foundation were implicitly choosing a black leader whose gender, education, and even outward appearance mirrored the liberal establishment's own self-perception as the natural born leaders of America, up to any task. Like them, Thomas's style was tough, top-down, and activist; his education was Ivy League; even his dress tended toward dark, narrow Kennedyesque suits. Thomas's appeal to the liberal establishment might be understood through the lens of Roger Wilkins, one of the few black New Frontiersman in the Kennedy administration, who assessed his success in Washington—and presumably his

Figure 12. Franklin Thomas directing a tour by U.S. Senators Edward
Kennedy and Jacob Javits, as well as Robert Kennedy's widow, Ethel,
through Brooklyn's Bedford-Stuyvesant. Thomas's model of "public
entrepreneurship" became the Foundation's ideal for post–civil rights
black leadership. Photographs and Prints Division, Schomburg Center for
Research in Black Culture, The New York Public Library, Astor, Lenox and
Tilden Foundations.

appointment to run the Foundation's social development program—this
way: "what white people saw [in me] was a well-educated, well-bred, sen-
sible Negro who, but for the unfortunate color of his skin, was very much
like them." "I was just the kind of person they wanted," Wilkins continued,
"because I was 'ready'—ready to face white people."[40] Meanwhile, Thomas's
youth and masculinity, best represented by his impressive physical stature,
suggested to his white supporters that he was ready to lead black people as
well. Thomas Jones claimed that in Kennedy's mind, Thomas's height and size
were among his most important qualifications. The Ford Foundation grant
assessor and future grant officer R. B. Goldmann concurred; in his appraisal,
he commented that Thomas's "towering, attractive figure was ideal for a
ghetto community starved for male images that reflect strength and leadership."[41] In short, Thomas literally embodied the goals of the project as defined

by its liberal establishment founders, as a figure whose gender, youth, size, clothes, and résumé could appeal to both his white patrons and the black people he was to lead.

Unlike Leon Sullivan, the Foundation's first towering and trusted black leader, who had come to Ylvisaker and the trustees' attention after he had already created a successful program on his own in Philadelphia, Kennedy and Ford officials at first chose only to exploit Thomas's symbolic strengths and not his managerial smarts. Thomas quickly assumed "complete authority" over BSRC and its board, which he had insisted upon before taking the job. However, he struggled to assume any power, let alone rough equality in relation to his white brethren at D&S, despite having the foresight of negotiating preconditions like a salary equal to Eli Jacobs's. Neither Jacobs nor Logue relinquished any of their control to Thomas, and they faced no pressure from the Foundation to do so. The two men continued with their grandiose planning for Bedford-Stuyvesant's redevelopment, cutting BSRC out of a visioning process that the community corporation was to have led from the beginning. More generally, they insisted that D&S continue to have absolute financial control over both corporations. BSRC was very much the subsidiary partner in this respect; for example, it had to apply for any resources it needed through elaborately detailed proposals that D&S was free to reject.[42]

Thomas bridled at this paternalism. Even before he accepted his position he began a shrewd and unrelenting almost seven-year campaign to reverse these practices so that BSRC would eventually subsume D&S while retaining the support of its white, corporate proponents. His approach was an astute one that showed his white patrons that he was no mere puppet but that, beyond his appearance, his actions reflected their values and worldview and also fulfilled their notion of leadership. His first victory was over Logue and Jacobs. He asserted BSRC's role as the originator of the CDC's program by rejecting their ambitious redevelopment schemes, and he reminded Logue that BSRC was, in effect, D&S's client. Soon after this encounter, Logue left D&S to run for mayor of Boston. That left Thomas to develop his own program, which he described as "very simple," "manageable," and focused on "tangible results," aimed at community support for the CDC.[43]

Thomas's initial move was to put into place an exterior renovation scheme (CHIP) in which blocks of homeowners applied as a group to have the outsides of their brownstones cleaned, repaired, and painted. In exchange they paid $25 each and pledged to maintain their properties and keep their streets clean by collecting and storing trash in metal garbage cans emblazoned with

the BSRC insignia. This kind of "simplest of programs," as Thomas characterized CHIP, fulfilled the goals of jobs and housing for the neighborhood, and
it put the incremental self-help and self-esteem objectives of developmental separatism into action. Thomas told an interviewer that CHIP took "guys
on the street corner, who are unemployed and who have no commitment to
this community, and whom everybody felt were the logical people to burn
the place down" and got "them to work on the buildings right in their own
blocks, owned by people, who look like they do, and who live here." Thomas
hoped that this experience would make these men "feel . . . that this is their
community and a place to be preserved," while the homeowner beneficiaries,
who Thomas believed were the neighborhood's essential "anchor on which to
build," would resist the urge to abandon the community when they "start to
see in those faces of guys on the corner not the enemy but their friend, because they're at work improving neighborhoods in which everybody lives."[44]

Thomas extended this pragmatic localism to his proposal for $7 million in
grants from the SIP program, which would largely underwrite BSRC's work.
Along with expanding CHIP, he outlined plans in line with other CDC efforts
around the country for job training and creation connected to the physical
and economic revitalization of the neighborhood. He intended to create jobs
and spur entrepreneurship through manpower training and small-business
loans. He also put forward a scheme for local contractors and construction-
work trainees to rehabilitate the Sheffield Dairy building, located on a central
commercial strip, into a community center to house the offices of BSRC and
other social, financial, and community services. Meanwhile, Thomas worked
with the D&S board to use its members' banking connections to put a community mortgage pool in place and with the IBM president and D&S board
member Thomas Watson, Jr., to locate a plant in the neighborhood. Future
projects included manpower programs, the creation of subsidiary companies to manage local properties for the federal Department of Housing and
Urban Development, and to build low-cost housing and a small community shopping center. All of these already tested and relatively small projects
conformed to the SIP priorities of jobs and housing for community people,
thereby lacking any element of Logue's master plan.[45]

Thomas won kudos for what Kennedy staffer Adam Walinsky called his
"doable" program of the modest and pragmatic goals that the Ford Foundation had urged Kennedy to consider from the beginning.[46] While Logue's
and Jacobs's plans had the enormous scope that, if achieved, might actually
have brought about the extraordinary economic revitalization and job crea-

tion intended by Kennedy and that would have set his project apart, the age of wholesale, top-down urban renewal was over. These plans were too rich for the federal government, and their logistics were also overly complex and risky for the private-sector investors Logue and Jacobs courted but had not convinced. Furthermore, Logue's master plan's political repercussions were untenable, especially in terms of the inevitably lengthy and contentious community consultations that would have been required. By contrast, without fanfare but with community support, Franklin Thomas got two hundred local men working on exterior renovation in the summer of 1967, even before the SIP funds came in. However, these miniaturized and pragmatic efforts, starting with CHIP, with an emphasis on community self-help through support for jobs, entrepreneurship, housing development, and homeownership, did not pioneer anything new in community development, despite BSRC's auspicious origins and Kennedy's ambitions. Instead, the programs replicated other pioneering CDCs' more modest efforts and would in turn become the model for other CDC activities nationwide in the years to come, when the conservative turn would necessitate the scaling down of ambitions for community development to local and "doable" projects focused on individual uplift.[47]

Meanwhile, despite CHIP's achievements and his successful grant application to SIP, Thomas still had to contend with BSRC's subordinate role in relation to D&S. As he recalled his struggle for a "transfer of power" to BSRC, "[n]othing evolved naturally"; every concession from D&S "was very grudging, very difficult."[48] While Thomas made sure that the SIP proposal went out under both corporations' names, and he achieved a joint check-signing protocol with D&S, the white corporation's staff and board refused Thomas's many attempts to get D&S to act upon its March 1967 commitment to the merger of the corporations' operations, meaning that until 1974 D&S had effective oversight over BSRC's day-to-day management and the final say over its program. Thomas chafed under what he called this "master-slave" relationship, but he understood its causes.[49] He believed that his white patrons in government, the Foundation, and D&S saw him as a kind of superman anomaly among African Americans. As he put it, "I think . . . what they believed way down deep was that, 'Okay, we may be lucky and get Frank and his background, but the odds are that we won't be able to get ten Franks in that corporation, because there just aren't that many black guys around." Indeed, D&S board member Benno Schmidt confirmed these suspicions when he made the histrionic claim that Thomas "may be the best black administrator in existence."[50]

Thomas worked hard at disproving his white patrons' ignorant assumptions: he attracted a staff of highly accomplished, competent, and likeminded black men with education and experience comparable to his. These were figures like BSRC's counsel, Ronald Huntley, a former staff lawyer for CBS who had, like Thomas, been an assistant U.S. attorney; Owen Hague, the director of finance and administration, a retired Air Force lieutenant colonel and former Tuskegee airman who held a faculty position in accounting at Brooklyn College and had experience managing two antipoverty programs (HARYOU-ACT in Harlem and Brooklyn's Youth in Action); and Alvin Puryear, the director of economic development who held a Ph.D. from Columbia and was an associate professor in Rutgers University's business school.[51]

These overqualified men's impatience to assume the authority they deserved was compounded by their legitimate contempt for a D&S administration that was decidedly amateur in comparison, even though it oversaw BSRC's operations. Between 1968 and 1973, D&S was run by a former Kennedy staffer, John Doar, the acclaimed assistant attorney general for civil rights during the height of the Southern black freedom struggle. While a highly accomplished lawyer and negotiator, Doar had virtually no experience and little knowledge about the Northern urban crisis, and in fact he took the job in Brooklyn as a crash course to attain both. Furthermore, he was decidedly distracted at the beginning of his tenure at D&S when, amid the school decentralization crisis, John Lindsay tapped him for the presidency of the New York City Board of Education. Minding the store at D&S while Doar was preoccupied by this task was a uniformly young and inexperienced white staff. Unsurprisingly, of sixteen program contracts that had been approved by D&S by December 1968, BSRC had put all but one forward, despite Doar's group's ostensible responsibility for economic development. No wonder then, that Thomas asked this "basic question" of D&S: "Will the white power structure deal directly with competent representatives of the black community or does there still have to be a layer of whites in between?"[52] Despite repeatedly asking this pointed question, neither Doar nor the D&S board would budge on a move that would eliminate their jobs. The merger finally happened in 1974, in the months after Doar left D&S, with Thomas in charge of a consolidated staff.[53]

While Doar's departure provided a belated opening to the amalgamation of BSRC and D&S, Thomas's efforts to make BSRC's operations irreproachable and its program peerless in the eyes of its benefactors doubtless finally led to his victory. Beyond anything else, Thomas worked to distinguish BSRC from the poverty programs of the Great Society, especially by eschewing the Community Action Program and its mandate for "maximum feasible participation," by what one BSRC manager called "unsophisticated" and "inexperienced" community members. Instead Thomas was guided, as one report summarized, "by the principles that serve to make large industrial firms effective, mobilize resources, and generate substantial returns."[54] This guiding ethos pleased BSRC's white supporters who blamed community action for the poverty program's reputation as cumbersome, ineffective, and corrupt. As one Foundation discussion paper put it, "a major reason, if not the basic cause of the trouble" with the federal approach, "has been inadequate capability in the depressed areas to give substance to the kind of participation and leadership they were called upon to exercise," resulting in the tendency of federal antipoverty groups' tendency "to consume themselves in process with little product to show for it."[55] Indeed, participatory democracy's apparent shortcomings, not only with the Community Action Program but also in the community-control demonstrations, prompted the Foundation's transition from community action to the CDC model.

In contrast to the poverty programs, and indeed most other CDCs, while Thomas and his staff very much believed they served the people of Bedford-Stuyvesant, they did not even pretend to work with them or follow their lead. As a precondition for taking the job, Thomas insisted that he must be a strong executive who, rather than community members or even his board, determined the corporation's mandate. He depended on the expertise of his staff to put programs in place quickly and effectively, without having to train them or to explain and justify technical details to uneducated laypeople. Meanwhile, BSRC used its power in the community as a provider of jobs and affordable housing to practice a kind of internal paternalism in the community that harkened back to an older era of black uplift and respectability. It retained the right of inspection of brownstones renovated by CHIP to ensure that homeowners lived up to their pledge to maintain the exteriors and restore the interiors of their properties once BSRC's work was complete. Similarly, BSRC used the desirability of its own rental properties to exercise strict control over tenant selection, investigate residents' housekeeping, require tenants to take home economics classes, and enforce an eviction policy so strict that it rivaled any other landlord in the community. Reinforcing this distance from participatory democracy, BSRC's offices were housed outside of Bedford-Stuyvesant, at the Granada Hotel in downtown Brooklyn until its headquarters at the newly renovated Sheffield Farms complex was complete in 1971. Thomas's management style was deeply appealing for "elite, anti-establishment" liberals like Kennedy and Bundy, true believers in the elite theory of democracy and particularly for the supposedly rudderless black community.[56]

In seeking an appropriately professional headquarters, Thomas signaled his intention to run his CDC according to the standards of corporate America, earning him yet further kudos from the Foundation. While he hated the oversight of the D&S staff, he very much saw the value of its board in terms of the economic doors its members could open to Bedford-Stuyvesant. As he explained to an interviewer, "If you start with the premise that we're a capitalist country" and "if you can tie in the sources of capital and the controls of capital in what you're doing," then "you're going to find a tremendous variety of ways, most of which may well be beyond your imagination when you start out, to involve them [corporate leaders] in the process" of community regeneration.[57] So Thomas worked hard to earn the D&S board's trust by emulating their values and practices at BSRC. He made sure that BSRC "realize[d] the efficiencies of a business structure as opposed to an 'anti-poverty' structure," and he exercised extreme probity in its financial dealings, including his requirement that every check bear his signature or initials.[58] "The whole notion," Thomas explained, was "to really work like hell to make programs . . . that were good, solid, and substantial, so that when somebody lifted the lid, what they saw just kept getting better and better and better."[59] Clearly BSRC's white patrons liked Thomas's modeling of their corporate values and practices; by 1971 he had been named to the boards of First National City Bank, CBS, Lincoln Center, and Columbia University, largely thanks to his links to the D&S board.[60]

Finally, Thomas and his staff came much closer to the Foundation's vision of ultimate black assimilation into the American mainstream through developmental separatism than the activists of the black freedom struggle with their radical visions of collective racial self-determination or even the cooperative capitalism espoused by other CDCs. As one interviewer described an unnamed BSRC executive's vision for the community, while he hoped that neighborhood residents would be "be more concerned with less fortunate people, those having drug, alcohol, or other social or psychological problems" and "to work to help their less lucky brothers," his larger vision was one of independent bourgeois success. He hoped to create a "prosperous middle-income community, with a variety of significant business ventures owned by local residents, increased opportunity for individual action in the private sector, rewards consistent with those gained for similar efforts elsewhere, and a quality of life commensurate with such gains."[61] In short, through BSRC programs like CHIP's exterior renovations and incentives for small business, this respondent wanted to engineer Bedford-Stuyvesant's transformation into a black Brooklyn Heights, another brownstone neighborhood that had, through a transfusion of white professionals attracted to the area's housing stock, become a thriving postindustrial, middle-class outpost in an otherwise declining outer borough.[62]

Mitchell Sviridoff and the Shift from Community Action to Community Development

Franklin Thomas's achievements in Bedford-Stuyvesant cemented the Ford Foundation's commitment to the CDC as the ultimate instrument for social development. After Robert Kennedy's assassination, the Foundation became the standard-bearer for what would become the dominant, corporate model of community development, patterned closely on BSRC. Furthermore, these local and private nonprofits, competing for funding from private and public sources, with their pragmatic, self-help focus on developing affordable housing, minority enterprises, and productive workers, would become a primary conduit for serving the needs of impoverished, inner-city communities in the new political and policy era brought in on the wake of the collapse of the state-centered New Deal order. They would become so dominant in large part because of the work of Mitchell Sviridoff, Bundy's vice president of National Affairs, whose success at fostering and molding the community-development approach was a central achievement of his time at the Foundation, earning him widespread and ongoing credit for spreading and institutionalizing CDCs nationwide. As a marker of the increasing focus and prestige that the community-development approach gained within the Foundation's domestic agenda under Sviridoff, by 1971 the CDC program supplanted all others within the social development office and it had become the predominant Ford approach to resolving racial inequality.[63]

Part of the reason for Sviridoff's focus on CDCs had to do with two external factors. The first concerned changes in federal law regarding philanthropy that were contained in the Tax Reform Act of 1969. This legislation was the result largely of a populist, right-wing campaign against the Foundation as the emblem of a purported giant conspiracy by the liberal establishment, in which it used enormously wealthy, unaccountable, and tax-exempt foundations to underwrite partisan social-engineering efforts that favored liberal causes, particularly racial ones. As evidence of these allegations, Foundation critics pointed to its partisan involvement in political issues like school decentralization, a voter-registration campaign in Cleveland to elect Carl Stokes as the first black mayor of a major American city, and study grants given to aides to Robert Kennedy in the months after his assassination. The new law's "McGeorge Bundy" amendments—as they were called after his defiant performance in front of the House Ways and Means Committee caused him to be blamed for pushing its members over the brink in their quest to shut down liberal foundations' activism—put strict new controls on philanthropies' political involvement. Many of Bundy's peers in the philanthropic community also blamed him for a new, and for them, punitive, 4 percent tax placed on their income. Tax reform took the wind out of liberal philanthropies' reformist sails; all of them, including Ford, beat a retreat—as the Foundation had done during the conservative 1950s congressional attacks against its integrationism—away from any grant making that might attract negative publicity, especially those activities tainted by civil rights activism.[64]

Furthermore, budget cuts at the Foundation, starting in 1971 and caused by inflation and market instability, meant that the social development program could no longer sustain a comprehensive approach of many different demonstrations. Instead the Foundation chose to collapse these efforts into a focus on community development as a strategy that could keep the multifaceted approach alive, albeit in miniature and at the local level. Throughout the 1970s, the Foundation shrank or eliminated many of its programs, marking the end of the heady period of the 1950s and 1960s in which it actually had to expand into new areas, like the humanities and the arts, in order to disburse enough of the enormous investment income generated by its behemoth endowment. Both of these external factors marked the end of the salad days in which its coffers were full and when activist Democratic presidents solicited its help as a progressive "change agent" in forging both the New Frontier and Great Society.

However, even without this outside pressure, Sviridoff's arrival at the Foundation would probably have marked the social development program's growing concentration on community development, based on the new vice president's outlook and prior experience. Another white beneficiary of the Foundation's meritocracy, Sviridoff was a former sheet-metal worker without a college degree but was very much imbued with the values of establishment liberalism. A quintessential "new man of power" within the postwar American labor movement, by the age of twenty-seven Sviridoff had risen in 1946 to lead Connecticut's branch of the Congress of Industrial Organizations, newly purged of its popular-front, left-wing union affiliates.[65] A New Deal Democrat who had become a New Frontiersman, he first came to the Foundation's attention in the early 1960s when reformist New Haven, Connecticut, Mayor Richard Lee called him back from a stint as a special assistant for the Alliance for Progress, JFK's modernization effort in Latin America, to engage in domestic development by running what Ford considered the most successful, and by any measure the most hierarchical, iteration of Gray Areas.

Associates variously described Sviridoff as a "genius at organization" and "a born leader with a tremendous conceptional [sic] mind."[66] These qualities no doubt attracted Mayor John Lindsay, who in January 1966 poached Sviridoff from Gray Areas in New Haven to head a Ford Foundation–funded systems-reform study to reorganize New York City's mismanaged and ineffective poverty and social-service programs. Sviridoff based his plan on the Gray Areas precedent of an umbrella agency meant to achieve an effective and coordinated antipoverty thrust by cutting through bureaucratic firewalls that had heretofore prevented such a comprehensive approach. With great fanfare and pride at nabbing one of the nation's most celebrated antipoverty administrators, Lindsay appointed Sviridoff in August 1966 as the first head of the new entity, called the Human Resources Agency (HRA). Sviridoff's experience in planning, if not implementing, this systemwide overhaul, as well as his past presidency of the New Haven Board of Education, no doubt also led to his appointment by Lindsay to Bundy's school decentralization panel where he promoted systems reform and private-sector involvement as a lever for public school reform. Already a strong proponent of community development and manpower programs in New Haven and at the HRA, Sviridoff also played a crucial role in ensuring the Bedford-Stuyvesant CDC's survival after its rocky start; as one of Lindsay's most trusted advisors, Sviridoff overcame the mayor's political rivalry with Robert Kennedy, and he secured the city's support of the Brooklyn experiment, including the coup that brought Franklin Thomas to power.[67]

When Sviridoff accepted the Foundation's offer to lead National Affairs, just under a year after assuming his HRA post, his move was widely interpreted as an escape from what the New York Times called the "irate poor people and recalcitrant civil servants" he had encountered in his effort, not to mention the enormity of the poverty problem in postindustrial New York,

Figure 13. National Affairs Vice President Mitchell Sviridoff would successfully navigate the Ford Foundation's social development programs through the post-1968 conservative turn in American politics by focusing on black leadership and community development. Ford Foundation Archives. Courtesy Rockefeller Archives Center.

all of which had and would continue to challenge his belief that his master plan for system overhaul would reduce poverty.[68] This failure would soon be followed by the school decentralization fiasco with its similarly disillusioning political obstacles. Personally unscathed but no doubt chastened by these debacles of systems reform, at Ford Sviridoff turned to the CDC model, a manageable, surrogate approach to the enormity of bureaucratic overhaul, and without its myriad and inevitable political pitfalls.

Like Robert Kennedy and Bundy, Sviridoff was preoccupied with finding a post–civil rights and post–Great Society solution for the ruptures in American liberalism caused in part by the urban crisis. For example, he understood that, after the debacle of Lyndon Johnson's failed and underfunded domestic policy, the federal solutions that had undergirded American social policy since the 1930s were no longer politically or fiscally feasible; he looked to local government and the private sector to step into the breach. Similarly, despite or perhaps because of his participation on the mayor's decentralization panel, he abjured the community-action approach for privileging process over product and for fomenting the racial division that led to Nixon's victory and the end of the New Deal Democratic coalition. Instead, he looked to universal, apolitical, and technical solutions to the issue of racial inequality in the United States that would impact both blacks and whites and resonate deeply with mainstream American notions of individual self-help. Sviridoff believed that such an approach would lead to the reforging of American liberalism, or the reconstitution of what he called "a nonrevolutionary yet dynamic approach to social change" akin to the New Deal.[69]

In putting his beliefs into action, Sviridoff pulled the Foundation back from an earlier strain of social development, exemplified by its schools activism, that would have extended civil rights racial liberalism by promoting capacity building and political participation by the poor as the center of community development. Roger Wilkins, who served as the first program officer in charge of social development under Sviridoff, chafed under the vice president's regime. As a former assistant attorney general in the Lyndon Johnson administration and the nephew of Roy Wilkins, the executive director of the NAACP, Roger Wilkins was no radical, but he was an inveterate civil rights liberal. His racial consciousness had grown during his time at the Ford Foundation, as had his conviction that the social development program should be "a continuation" of the "thrust for equal rights . . . for minority people" that demonstrated a "sustained moral commitment to equal justice" against growing white backlash and apathy that either repudiated or marginalized this recent driver of the nation's domestic agenda.[70] During Wilkins's tenure, he promoted an earlier version of community development that put group uplift at the forefront. For example, under his watch the Foundation spent $3.5 million to establish the Center for Community Change, an antipoverty organization with roots in the explicitly community-action-oriented and Foundation-funded Citizens Crusade against Poverty. Continuing that tradition, the center was unequivocally committed to the political empowerment of the poor.[71] Given his objectives for social development generally, and community development in particular, it was no wonder that Wilkins fought furiously against Sviridoff's announcement in 1970 of plans to cut the social development budget by $1 million in order to fund new National Affairs programs for the environment and police training. These were efforts that engaged Sviridoff's strategy to create more "universal" domestic programs that would appeal to white middle-class Americans so that they would swallow the pill of minority social development, made yet more palatable to them by Sviridoff's definition of the program as leading to individual, not group, gains. Fighting a losing battle, Wilkins left the Foundation in 1971 after delivering an impassioned memo to the trustees about their "very tight and homogenous vision of American society and the world." He urged them to fulfill their duty to extend the philanthropy's civil rights legacy by bringing in "minority" voices, including women, youth, people of color, and representatives from the so-called third world, as Foundation decision makers.[72]

Significantly, Sviridoff did not hire another African American or a civil rights lawyer to replace Wilkins to run the social development office; instead he chose the white economists and international development experts Eamon Kelly and Sol Chafkin as successors. They shared Sviridoff's vision for a "domestic development process" in which the CDC on the BSRC model would be the pivot.[73] Instead of advocacy for the poor or participatory democracy, they were committed to jobs and income creation to end the urban crisis and poverty in the ghetto, a process that they imagined would happen not by addressing deindustrialization or other structural factors, or even necessarily by focusing on working-class employment, but rather by capital transfer from government and the private sector into the inner city for business development and job creation. However, in order for this transfer to be effective, institutions had to be in place that could successfully forge what the Foundation called a "coalition" between the "leaders of the deprived community and of the established civic and business interests in its city" so as to attract outside funds to the ghetto.[74] Such fund-raising abilities had to

Figure 14. Roger Wilkins, the Ford Foundation's first program officer in charge of social development, objected strenuously to Mitchell Sviridoff's move away from the group empowerment of the minority poor as a primary Foundation objective. Ford Foundation Archives. Courtesy Rockefeller Archives Center.

be partnered with these instruments' capacity to absorb resources by "successfully running programs that increase jobs and income, improve housing, and secure better services." If successful, Sviridoff and his officers predicted that CDCs following this model would become self-sufficient engines of economic growth, leading ultimately to black community enterprises' "ability to penetrate the economy of the mainstream," and the consequent upward mobility of individual African Americans.[75] Sviridoff and his staff focused their efforts not on advocacy for the poor but on retaining and attracting the middle class in the black community as an essential "anchor" for community development. In the end the middle class would remain living in its own improved neighborhoods, not because ghettoized, but by choice and as a matter of racial pride deepened by the prosperity fostered by the CDC. In short, the CDC changed "the mood of the community" from "apathy and despair to expectation and hope," but it also had to "play its part" in the Foundation's ultimate assimilationist aim for developmental separatism, "a single though pluralistic national community," largely based on an expanded middle class and elite that would share the economic, if not cultural, interests of the white majority.[76]

This model, with its vision of black community uplift without community control or participatory democracy, ghetto prosperity without structural reform, race and class coalition and capital transfer without conflict between the corporate "establishment" and the ghetto, and black economic assimilation without social integration, encapsulated the Foundation's longstanding and elusive objectives for African Americans' social development. The Foundation's version of the CDC also differed from many earlier community-development efforts, which promoted participatory democracy and measured the project's success based on a conception of community capitalism that privileged collective versus individual capacity building and wealth creation. Nevertheless, those CDCs that wished to receive funding in the Sviridoff era would have to fall in line with the Foundation's ethos. In short, the CDC had become a potential cure-all for Sviridoff and his officers—one in which community development could be facilitated through the funding of corporate capitalism and the state channeled through a politically immune entity run by black professionals with the technical skills and charisma to solve the urban crisis by directing Foundation-defined development objectives on a local level.

In the 1960s and 1970s, the Foundation would fund up to fourteen CDCs at a time nationwide, both in cities and in the rural South, all of which were increasingly measured against this prototype and had ultimately conformed to it.[77] Of this group, the Foundation consistently named a handful as bona fide success stories, including the Watts Labor Action Committee in Los Angeles and Leon Sullivan's Zion Non-Profit Charitable Trust in Philadelphia. The Foundation rewarded these CDCs not only with grants and program-related investments—a new instrument designed specifically to prime the pump of CDC grantees through direct Foundation investment in their enterprises—but also with grant-writing assistance and introductions to the federal decision makers who would determine who would receive the federal support so crucial to CDC success.

Hovering above all of the Foundation's CDC grantees was Franklin Thomas's BSRC, Ford's "flagship" CDC, as Sviridoff called it, against which all other efforts were judged.[78] From 1966 to 1981, BSRC received more than $11 million from the Ford Foundation, leading any other grantee, CDC or not, receiving administrative support. In the same period, BSRC received almost one-third of all funding disbursed by SIP, the largest federal government program for community development.[79] The Foundation's institutionalization of the BSRC prototype culminated in the founding of the Local Initiatives Support Corporation (LISC) in 1979, which was Franklin Thomas's first major move as Ford Foundation president. First headed by Sviridoff, the Foundation underwrote LISC with $4.75 million matched by an equal amount from the corporate sector. It provided CDCs in the BSRC vein with loans, investments, corporate partners, and technical support so that they could scale up redevelopment efforts. LISC and its local subsidiaries remain the most important institutions supporting Ford's still dominant community-development model of public-private partnerships to fund local development projects.[80]

BSRC's influence in shaping the Foundation's version of community development extended to the growing importance Sviridoff and his staff placed on black leadership as both a precondition to and an outcome of CDC achievement. Thomas's success as what the Foundation privileged as a "dominant" leader of an institution outside the democratic political process and entrenched state bureaucracies demonstrated to the Foundation that a CDC with "indigenous" leadership could implement the top-down systems-reform model of Gray Areas without the volatility, compromises, and coalition building of the community-control experiment. Furthermore, Thomas's success proved that "grassroots" leaders did not have to be chosen by the black community but could be designated by outsiders. This "legerdemain of symbolic racial collectivism," as Adolph Reed has described this increasingly common phenomenon, meant that a black leader like Thomas, appointed by outsiders, could become a legitimate "community" representative for whites, and even most blacks, especially in a period of intense racial pride like the late 1960s and 1970s.[81]

In privileging this conception of tough, top-down individual black leadership and talent, the Foundation demonstrated that it finally fully understood that there was a "best and brightest" in the black community, as defined by the "best and brightest" of the white community. In fact, identifying these "public entrepreneurs" was inordinately important to the Ford Foundation, especially when it came to African Americans. In the wake of the failure of the War on Poverty, the social development division explained black poverty, not only as a problem of national programs and bureaucratic incompetence but also as a matter of "inadequate capability in the depressed areas to give substance to the kind of participation and leadership they were called upon to exercise."[82] According to Sviridoff, this "limited local capacity" to capitalize on the "relatively large amounts of available resources," which had been made available to ghetto communities, resulted in an inability for any program "to reverse the spiral of deterioration and despair."[83] Thus, it came as a relief to social development staff that effective black leadership (or capacity) could be found for an African American community that it implicitly defined as largely incompetent to run its own affairs. These successful leaders were "strongly individualistic executives who have demonstrated ability to devise programs, attract funds, inspire co-workers, earn the respect of people in the community, and harmonize conflicting forces." They would use these talents to bring disorganized and inarticulate communities out of the socioeconomic doldrums and prepare them for their incorporation into the American mainstream.[84] Accordingly, the fountainhead from which all community development should flow, as specified by one Foundation document after another, was the leadership of a "strong, enterprising personality" who, as some implied and others put explicitly, "cannot be trained." Rather, this individual "has to be discovered."[85]

Finding these black supermen might have been a matter of luck in the case of figures like Franklin Thomas or Leon Sullivan, but social development officers nevertheless also started an effort to discover and polish leaders within the black community; by the time of its budget proposal in 1968, minority "leadership development" commanded one-third of the subdivision's funds and comprised its largest proposed budget line. Foundation documents justified this thrust as an effort to develop "articulate, responsible" black leadership, the absence of which it interpreted largely as a matter of a lack of "managerial competence."[86] That year Sviridoff pointed out in his first National Affairs budget request that "the rise of black militancy and its counterparts in Puerto Rican, Mexican-American, and Indian communities" had finally disciplined the Foundation "to distinguish clearly for the first time between community action programs emphasizing program objectives and those designed to enhance community power in decision making."[87] His division worked to offer the former by delivering tangible results to ghetto communities through tough, top-down CDC leadership. These "performance"-oriented leaders were not "elected in formal elections." Rather, through "close and steady contact" with residents, they determined and acted upon "[c]ommunity attitudes and aspirations" without the intervention of the formal participatory processes. These, according to Sviridoff, "led to sterility and frustration for so many community organizations under the poverty program." Similarly, the Foundation highlighted the "dominant personality" of these leaders who "vastly prefer performance to rhetoric" and who became "impatien[t] when process becomes disproportionate to product." [88] They could also control ghetto residents' putatively unproductive and antisocial dissent, in the way that Franklin Thomas had been able to withstand the tempest in Bedford-Stuyvesant over the coup that put him in power. Thus the Foundation sought to channel black "militancy" into the CDC and the Hobbesian sovereign who led it. His ability to serve, control, and represent the black community signaled the political modernization of the ghetto, according to the elite theory of democracy, whose adherents could now countenance black leaders guiding the development of their own communities, thanks to pioneers like Thomas.[89]

Ultimately, one Foundation document admitted, it became "hard to separate 'leadership development' from community development."[90] Effective CDC leaders, characterized in part by their successful development of second-tier technocratic public entrepreneurs within their corporations, grew to be so important to the Foundation that by the 1970s this quality became among the most crucial variables that the Foundation used in measuring the success of its CDCs.[91] Furthermore, it put all of its social development eggs in the CDC basket, and it began more and more to elide the CDC and its leaders with the community it served, writing in various contexts that the corporation "embodied" the neighborhood and its potential for change.[92] Some Foundation documents even ascribed the success

or failure of entire inner-city communities to the presence or absence of
a CDC led by a "strong, enterprising personality," noting the "sharp contrast" of Bedford-Stuyvesant to the "continuing decay" of Brownsville, for
example, where the Foundation had ascribed the failure of its community-
control experiment in part to a lack of effective leadership.[93] In other words,
the success of the CDC in garnering grants, developing real estate, and
identifying and training technocrats to run its operations became a proxy
for uplift of the community as a whole.

This conflation was also reflected in the Foundation's growing assumption that the internal development of the CDC, including the upward mobility of its principals and staff, was the most effective strategy for community
development. The Foundation could justify this miniaturization of its focus
from the community to the CDC on the basis of its liberalism. Assimilation
through the ascension of individuals had been its objective from the start.
Thus, the fostering of public entrepreneurs in the CDC not only served
ghetto communities but also was an "income-elevating" objective for social
development, facilitating the upward mobility of individual African Americans.[94] As this concentration coalesced, Sviridoff and his staff also surmised
a connection between CDC prosperity and the ongoing focus on the middle
class as key to the health of the black community. So, for example, by the
early 1970s, the Foundation had deemphasized using CDCs to forge independent minority enterprises in ghetto communities and instead began to focus on fostering entrepreneurship within the CDCs themselves, particularly
"projects of scale," like housing developments, upon which no other entity in
the black community would be large enough to embark. These were the only
kinds of projects in their mind that brought "recognizable change," transforming "the tone and texture of the environment enough to retain or attract
middle-class residents."[95]

Furthermore, these large-scale endeavors would give entrepreneurial individuals working for the CDC the opportunity to be ambitious in
a way otherwise unlikely or impossible in the capital-poor ghetto. Thus,
the CDC's primary function became the incubation of individual entrepreneurs, whom the Foundation more and more saw as the essential precondition to community uplift. For Eamon Kelly, Roger Wilkins's replacement as
program officer in charge of social development, this objective was stymied
by the Great Society "mode of community corporate ownership—in which
individual gains are made dependent on group gains," limiting the salaries
of CDC managers and their ability to profit from their corporate entre-

preneurship. As a result, it was "difficult to build management incentives" into CDC "enterprises." Kelly called for "a new doctrine on the transfer of economic power" that would make legal "considerable personal enrichment for some of the principals." In short, he wished to use the CDCs to foster "a prorata share of millionaires and controllers of the sources of economic and hence political power" in the black community. Without this economic elite, "minorities cannot be deemed to be fully participating in the society."[96]

Thus, while one Foundation document had made the rare acknowledgment that the lives of inner-city residents had not "yet been materially improved" by its CDC grantees and had fretted that this program might have merely created a handful of "Potemkin villages," Ford's leaders continued to support its CDC blueprint.[97] They could point to the CDC program's fostering of a cadre of white-collar and professional African Americans as a tangible achievement of a long-standing ideal of individual assimilation through upward mobility. That was justification enough to make the CDC program the foundation of Ford's social development efforts.

The Business of Restoration

In May 1971, Franklin Thomas, John Doar, and their staffs finally moved their offices to Bedford-Stuyvesant and into a $3 million BSRC renovation of the old Sheffield Farms dairy building in the heart of the community's business district on Fulton Street. Including offices for government services and community nonprofits, a theater, and an ice-skating rink, the complex gave BSRC a visible anchor in the community. The renovation and move capped off three years of achievement for BSRC, including forty blocks of exterior renovations and dozens of scatter-site refurbishments of brownstones, all completed by local labor; the opening of an IBM plant that would grow to employ four hundred locals; and the completion of thirty-six loans to local entrepreneurs who opened businesses in the area.

Continuing federal, foundation, and private-sector support underwrote this flurry of activities in Bedford-Stuyvesant. Despite the Republican ascendancy in Washington, Thomas successfully negotiated a new $10 million SIP grant from the Nixon administration in 1970, demonstrating this Kennedy initiative's bipartisan staying power, given its strong emphasis on self-help and entrepreneurship. BSRC also won property-management contracts from the Federal Housing Administration, and it brokered with the agency on behalf of residents to make an exception of Bedford-Stuyvesant by loosening federal regulations for mortgage insurance in the area. The Ford Foundation both continued to bankroll BSRC's administration costs and offered a "working capital fund" to some of the business-loan recipients. Meanwhile, a consortium of New York banks led by George S. Moore, D&S board member and chair of the First National City Bank of New York, created a $65 million mortgage pool in order to combat the usurious lending practices that flourished in Bedford-Stuyvesant as a result of the FHA's and the real estate and financial industries' redlining practices in the neighborhood.[98]

These successes confirmed the liberal establishment's faith in the Bedford-Stuyvesant experiment, no doubt reinforced by the ongoing patronage of the Kennedy family. Robert Kennedy's widow, Ethel, joined the D&S board in 1969, and she and other family members hosted an annual ice-skating party on the BSRC rink, which had been built at the Kennedys' request, despite the fact that few of the neighborhood's Southern and West Indian residents were familiar with winter sports. The Kennedy influence also undoubtedly lent glamour to and shaped the program of the annual fundraiser, the Restore Ball, for BSRC's arts programming, inaugurated in 1971. That year, 1,300 guests paying $50 each joined co-chairs Ethel Kennedy, philanthropist and socialite Nancy Astor, Congresswoman Shirley Chisholm—now in the BSRC fold—and the wives of John Lindsay and Hollywood director Sidney Lumet in a star-studded affair. The evening boasted celebrity entertainers Lena Horne and Alan King as hosts who introduced performances by soul superstar Stevie Wonder, world-renowned opera singer Leontyne Price, and television comedians Jerry Stiller and Anne Meara, rounded out by a piano recital by a decidedly less accomplished artist, Edward Kennedy's wife, Joan. Given the array of talent drawn to this affair and the consequent publicity, concessions to the Kennedy family were doubtless a small price to pay for BSRC to perpetuate and benefit from its founder's legacy.[99]

However, despite BSRC's energetic economic development efforts, and its success at garnering federal and philanthropic support as well as the protective goodwill of a powerful patron, it did not come close to the comprehensive community development first envisioned by Robert Kennedy. It also did not achieve self-sufficiency or become the instrument of a middle-class transformation of Bedford-Stuyvesant, as imagined by Sviridoff, Thomas, and their staffs. Despite its exalted position, it did not even exceed the performance of other CDCs in the Foundation's stable, none of which reached Kennedy and Sviridoff's lofty goals, but some of which, particularly Leon Sullivan's projects in Philadelphia, brought in more capital investment, industrial development, and more and better jobs and job training for their communities than did BSRC.[100] Instead, what BSRC achieved in the long run was a "leadership institution" that fostered and developed black managers with little material payoff to the community at large. Stymied by a model of community development that did not acknowledge the engrained structural forces underlying black urban poverty, including those that prevented any kind of sustained "coalition" between capital and the ghetto, the best that BSRC could do was to make the physical rehabilitation of the community into an industry unto itself. In paring down its activities to staff and real estate development, BSRC once again forged the path that most of the nation's CDCs would follow. The result was a new model of public-private, nonprofit affordable housing that would grow to predominate a new, stripped-down national housing policy. As for alleviating the larger issues of economic underdevelopment, unemployment, and isolation from the mainstream economy, all efforts to address these problems resulted in failure.[101]

The first and foremost shortfall of community development in Bedford-Stuyvesant was the dual corporations' raison d'être: economic "coalition" between the corporate and financial establishment and the ghetto. D&S board minutes recorded numerous entreaties and prods to get members to do what they were appointed for in the first place, which was to spur outside capital investment in the ghetto. As John Doar reminded the board members, "[I]t was not enough to depend on black capitalism" for community economic development "but that American businesses would have to go into the ghetto, and provide job opportunities on a large scale."[102] Yet, aside from the IBM plant founded in 1968, during the crisis of the riots, nothing happened. Not even D&S board chair Benno Schmidt's vocal championing of this approach and a proposal to use $1.5 million of the CDC's budget to build a plant to a willing company's specifications resulted in any action on this front. Given the power and influence amassed on the D&S board, its collective combination of unwillingness and inability to attract industry to Bedford-Stuyvesant signified that American capital could not or would not turn back the clock on New York City's deindustrialization and transformation into a global financial and tourist center, particularly given the worsening local and national economy of the early 1970s.[103]

This truth became even clearer with BSRC's efforts to foster black capitalism. It hoped that supporting local entrepreneurship in Bedford-Stuyvesant would establish a manufacturing base and thus create jobs and wealth in the neighborhood. In the early 1970s, BSRC, the Ford Foundation, and financial institutions connected to D&S board members offered local businesspeople loans, direct investment, working-capital grants, and technical support for schemes to produce clothing, textiles, leather goods, and ultrasonic equipment in Bedford-Stuyvesant.[104] None of these inexperienced and undercapitalized newcomers succeeded. They were unable to penetrate a mainstream marketplace already crowded or dominated by a few big players. Even more modest niche market efforts fell flat, even when they had outside support and little competition. In late 1970, the white high-society textile designers D. D. and Leslie Tillett joined local black Brooklynites, artist Calister Thomas and jeweler Mark Bethel, to create Design Works, an upscale silk-screening operation that based its designs on African motifs. The Tilletts had been introduced to BSRC's work by their client, Jacqueline Onassis, and they came up with the idea of Design Works based on their international development experience in Africa, where they had worked on projects to foster indigenous textile design and manufacture. BSRC not only lent Design Works money but also invested directly in the firm. The Tilletts's business and social connections and Onassis's patronage led to exhibitions of the company's designs at the Metropolitan and Brooklyn museums, a *House Beautiful* spread of its work displayed in Onassis's New York apartment, contracts with Macy's department store, and production of its motifs on carpets, wallpaper, sheets, and towels, including those mass produced by textile giants Martex and West Point Pepperell. Nevertheless, Design Works folded in 1978, always operating at a loss except for one barely profitable year, and never getting close to its objective of training and employing 250 locals to run the company.[105]

BSRC's manpower and mortgage pool programs hit similar barriers. While BSRC had some notable success in placing local people in white-collar work inside and outside the community that might otherwise have been inaccessible to them, it could not make more than a tiny dent in the rampant unemployment of postindustrial, recession-era Bedford-Stuyvesant, especially among undereducated and inexperienced black men and young people who represented the core of Bedford-Stuyvesant's joblessness crisis.[106] Meanwhile, despite the fact that it offered the by far best terms available in

Bedford-Stuyvesant, by 1974 the neighborhood's residents had only used 30 percent of the mortgage pool to guarantee mortgages in the area, and 85 percent of those who had taken advantage of this opportunity were already property owners refinancing their mortgages, rather than first-time homebuyers. Worsening poverty in Bedford-Stuyvesant meant that the number of local people who had the wherewithal to buy property was shrinking, not growing, and so this instrument did little to achieve its major objective of expanding the area's homeowning middle class. Furthermore, real estate companies and mortgage lenders discouraged their clients from using the pool; these groups had a vested interest in the existing system in which minority mortgage holders were charged extra interest points typical in the tight housing market of ghetto neighborhoods redlined by banks and brokers. Again, even BSRC's high-profile efforts stood little chance against entrenched systems of black exclusion—this time America's deeply racialized property market.[107]

BSRC's Legacy

Despite these failures to revive Bedford-Stuyvesant, BSRC continued to thrive. Bipartisan support of the project, along with the Nixon administration's commitment to black capitalism and a decentralized welfare state, meant that BSRC was well positioned to continue to benefit from federal largesse, even during the program cutbacks of the second Nixon administration. Its reputation as an established, well-run organization with its eye on the bottom line made BSRC a prototype in the new regime in which local nonprofits competed for federal or federally funded loans, loan guarantees, and block grants in order to deliver social services to communities. However, this new arrangement with its narrowly focused programs abandoned any sense of the comprehensive community development imagined by Kennedy. In fact, the Nixon administration defined community development in purely economic terms, resulting in the shift of the SIP program to the Commerce Department after the dissolution of the federal Office of Economic Opportunity in 1974. This new iteration of SIP based its "community-development" program on a trickle-down philosophy that emphasized minority business, including profit-producing CDC enterprises that, if successful, could use their surplus earnings to fund local social programs and, more important to Washington, ultimately to become self-sufficient.[108]

That self-reliance never arrived. While everyone from federal officials to Mitchell Sviridoff to Franklin Thomas dreamt of BSRC showing the world that the CDC model could achieve independence for the ghetto from government and philanthropic support, all efforts failed. In 1982, the last year of the SIP program, one-third of BSRC's budget still came from federal funds. Consequently, when the Reagan administration cut off this lifeline, BSRC was eviscerated, reduced to a skeleton staff and program. Furthermore, even before these cuts, the residents of Bedford-Stuyvesant could see few tangible benefits from BSRC's work. Its efforts were no match for the structural forces of deindustrialization, stagflation, and neoliberalism that were inexorably shaping the city's and nation's economies. Significantly, BSRC's only visible achievements in the community, beyond housing, were the Sheffield Farms headquarters and a subsequent and adjacent shopping center development, completed in 1975; both were housed in industrial plants abandoned by deindustrialization. These businesses produced only professional and service-sector jobs reflective of a new urban labor market that offered employment either outside the qualifications of working-class black Brooklynites or without a living wage. Needless to say, joblessness and welfare dependency did not decrease with BSRC's work. In fact, neighborhood buying power fell 12 percent between 1970 and 1990, and while the poverty level in greater New York dropped from 14 to 12 percent in the same period, in Bedford-Stuyvesant, it rose from 27.5 to 34 percent, a trend that matched other inner-city neighborhoods around the country. [109]

Despite these failings, continued Foundation and federal funding suggested ongoing support for the BSRC model. With the diminished expectations that accompanied a realization of its limits, BSRC's leaders and funders focused on physical development, which they hoped could create the kind of community-generated benefits that undergirded developmental separatism. As Franklin Thomas declared optimistically, "[R]ebuilding the inner city is an industry in itself." [110] The precedent for this emphasis was BSRC's first and, according to the Foundation and BSRC, its "most impressive" and "most popular" activity, the exterior renovation program. [111] Certainly, it was a fast and cheap way to achieve "concrete, visible results" in the community. [112] It also provided job training and temporary work for unskilled local people, and its improvement of middle-class homeowners' brownstones suggested the possibility that, at least in the construction industry, the CDC could generate and perpetuate job creation and productive economic activity on its own. However, perhaps even more important, these limited physical development programs—which could never cure the community's economic and employment woes—helped anchor BSRC as a recognized community institution and as a "symbol of good and positive change" as Franklin Thomas put it, in a way that none of its other activities had done.[113]

Even though its efforts failed to achieve profits, good jobs in any appreciable number, outside investment in the community, black entrepreneurship, or a nonracialized private housing market, BSRC nevertheless persisted and lives on today. One major reason is its success at perpetuating itself as an institution by decoupling itself from the outside community. As efforts like attracting outside investment or generating black entrepreneurship failed, BSRC, encouraged both by its government and Foundation funders, confined its efforts more and more to activities it could control and direct within its own purview. So, for example, its for-profit construction and development units only ever worked on BSRC-initiated projects. Starting in the mid-1970s BSRC began to limit its commercial loans to local businesspeople who were tenants in the Sheffield commercial development or in operations like Design Works, in which it had a direct investment and whose president, Mark Bethel, served on the BSRC board. In this way, more and more, the reach of BSRC "community" development extended only within its own closed, self-perpetuating circle of employees, board members, and commercial and residential tenants. This group's ties to Bedford-Stuyvesant were even sometimes quite tenuous; in 1977, a majority of BSRC managers and almost half of its staff lived outside of the neighborhood.[114]

BSRC's persistence as a model for community development, despite its disappointing returns, is symbolic of the diminishing expectations of racial liberalism in the post–civil rights era. Bundy had begun his tenure at the Foundation seeking fundamental institutional reform to pursue his vision of social development for the ghetto. By the end of his presidency and the beginning of Thomas's in 1979, the Foundation had abandoned any notion of genuine transformation in the inner cities, where economic conditions and social marginalization had worsened, not improved. By that point, the Foundation had stripped down its objectives for CDCs to institution building only, largely to foster individual minority leaders and their meritocratic inclusion in the American elite. In doing so, the Foundation finally, if only implicitly, acknowledged the limitations of its racial liberalism, and its leadership's corresponding unwillingness and inability to confront the intractable structural problems facing the inner city. Nevertheless, the Foundation celebrated the CDC as its most successful work in social development, and it remains, despite its enormous limitations, a predominant instrument to achieve that still-elusive goal of the restoration of the city into a crucible of upward mobility and racial assimilation.

Epilogue:
The Diminishing Expectations
of Racial Liberalism

The diminution of the purview and program of the Bedford-Stuyvesant Restoration Corporation (BSRC) matched the Foundation's shrinking expectations for its community-development work overall. In the end, institution building and leadership development were the only concrete and lasting accomplishments of the Foundation's efforts to build and sustain community-development corporations (CDCs), which it nevertheless celebrated as the successful culmination of its work in social development. Ford readily conceded these shortcomings in assessments of its achievements on this front, both frankly admitting the impossibility of its earlier, lofty goals in solving the urban crisis and setting more modest and cautious goals for itself in achieving social change. A 1975 assessment of the model's limitations was typical, in that it concluded that while CDCs were "attempting to help overcome the severe adverse effects on the local community of the broader social, economic, and political forces at work," an individual corporation "should not be held responsible for adverse changes in such community-wide measures" nor "should it claim that its acts are solely responsible for any observed positive changes."[1]

The Foundation's recognition of and helplessness in the face of what it now acknowledged to be intractable structural issues represented a striking shift from the optimism of McGeorge Bundy's first years at the Foundation. Operational changes bore a major responsibility for this turn; after losing $1 billion of its $3 billion dollar endowment in the stock market downturn of 1974, Ford announced in December of that year that it intended to cut its annual grant giving by half, to around $100 million annually. This decline represented market realities as well as a new fiscal conservatism for Ford; despite scaling back giving at the beginning of his presidency, Bundy and the trustees had nevertheless persisted with the earlier practice of disbursing more than the Foundation earned, digging into its capital in the interests of aggressively pursuing program objectives during the affluence of the 1960s. Now, chastened by the market downturn, they would have to live within the Foundation's means.

These cuts came at a time when conditions were worsening for urban black America. Stagflation's pernicious mix of recession and inflation hastened American cities' postindustrial decline, leaving the working poor only with minimum-wage service jobs. Black unemployment rates skyrocketed in places like Bedford-Stuyvesant, once magnets for black migrants and immigrants who had found work in Brooklyn's robust postwar industrial economy. Meanwhile, cuts to social welfare programs, begun by Nixon in the late 1960s and marking the right's ideological rise, took on a new fiscal urgency in the 1970s. Furthermore, with the white workforce also reeling from the economic downturn, little political appetite remained among the racial majority and their political representatives for what they now largely perceived as costly 1960s-style social engineering and special pleading on behalf of the nation's nonwhite poor. In no time, the politically and economically expedient call for welfare reform would roll back the expansive idealism of the War on Poverty.[2]

Internally, Ford's leaders understood and acknowledged that the Foundation's cutbacks came at the worst possible time for the black poor in the context of these national realities.[3] Nevertheless, given its straitened circumstances, Foundation executives felt that they had no choice but to cut back on giving. Downsizing had a number of repercussions for the Foundation and its grantees. First and foremost, Ford no longer had the same capacity or will to intervene independently in social policy, as it had with Gray Areas or the community-control demonstrations, when it funded programs that deliberately sought to destabilize entrenched bureaucracies and government programs in order to spark change. Instead, the Foundation, which was also fearful of ongoing political attacks against its liberal activism, submitted and conformed to the discipline imposed by the conservative ascendancy. So, for example, it focused in this era on establishing technical support institutions, like the Local Initiatives Support Corporation (LISC), which served the downloading of social-service provision to the nonprofit sector by helping local organizations compete in the new market for government grants. It also set up think tanks like the Urban Institute, which acted as a contractor to fulfill government's social research priorities rather than spearheading its own. Finally, it continued its commitment to supporting the CDC program and to beginning new ones, like the Manpower Demonstration Research Corporation, that were thoroughly focused on narrow and quantifiable economic and labor-market development objectives.[4]

To be sure, these shifts marked the end of an era of ambitious, independent, and idealistic domestic program goals. However, it would be wrong to interpret these changes as representing a wholesale transformation of Ford's liberal vision or to think that these were entirely caused by the new funding discipline and political realities within and outside of the Foundation. In fact, the rightward turn complemented and served many of the long-standing interests at Ford. For example, Foundation officers had long advocated innovations in the free market that have since been attributed to conservatives, like "competitive subsystems" for public schools and the promotion of "public entrepreneurship" as key to successful community development. The Foundation's model of multiculturalism also presaged the Reagan era's television blockbuster *The Cosby Show*, which dominated the airwaves in the 1980s and starred Negro Ensemble Company alumna Phylicia Rashad. This TV show presented a reassuring fantasy of conflict-free American multiculturalism and equal opportunity palatable to white viewers in the same way that the NEC's family melodramas had been to white critics.[5]

Mitchell Sviridoff was a key figure in the Foundation's continuing political and policy vanguardism after the conservative turn. He remained at the helm of National Affairs throughout the 1970s, during which he shifted the Foundation's domestic programs away from an emphasis on a direct attack on racial inequality and ghetto poverty. Instead, he began to frame Ford's social development work by rejecting once again the controversy inherent in race-specific programs and promoting those that dealt more generally with behavioral issues as barriers to employment.[6] In doing so, he followed not only the national political mood but also the instinctive inclination of his bosses. Throughout its postwar history, the Foundation had only briefly, controversially—and from a programmatic and institutional point of view, unsuccessfully—focused explicitly on urban poverty as a product of entrenched racial inequality. Instead, its leaders had always preferred to interpret social problems as issues of individual behavior over structure. In fact, while the new political and economic environment could be seen as forcing Bundy and Sviridoff to modify the Foundation's domestic program and diminish its aspirations, it could also be interpreted as giving them the perfect opportunity to do so, especially given the conflict and negative attention that had ensued when they had been more ambitious in their aims. In any case, in the years following its 1974 budget retrenchment, the Foundation fundamentally scaled down ambitions for creating racial equality. By a 1984 retrospective summing up its past and current programs for black America, the Foundation would make a cautious promise that it would continue to "play a part—however small—in creating an American society that is color-blind and in which all members can participate freely and fully." At the same time it warned that the "resources that can be brought to bear" toward this goal "by the Ford Foundation and by other private funders, are limited."[7] Such modesty was remarkable, given the Foundation's overconfidence in earlier years.

Nowhere was this shift in attitude and action more evident than in the Foundation's ongoing support of community development. The BSRC survived the 1974 budget cuts and thrived as a hallmark of both Sviridoff's domestic-program priorities and the shrinking federal welfare state. It did so despite irrefutable and growing evidence that, on the aggregate and in the particular communities served by CDCs, the black, urban poor were worse off than they had been when community development or any subsequent Ford Foundation initiatives for African American communities had begun. In fact, journalists and scholars would soon begin to voice their fears that a significant minority of the black poor had dropped into a hyper-marginalized underclass.[8]

Two assessments from the 1980s were particularly revealing on this point. Despite worsening conditions in the ghetto, these reports concluded that the millions spent had all been worth it because of the indigenous black leaders who had come out of these programs and who were providing the kind of representation for minority communities advocated by the elite theory of democracy. Historian Kathleen McCarthy noted in an in-house history of the Foundation's Gray Areas programs that by developing minority professionals the Foundation had made a significant contribution in expanding the notion of who could be an expert and what constituted expertise in urban affairs, with significant implications for the Foundation's subsequent programs for minorities. She implicitly framed this "effort to cultivate new sources of expertise" and "to train and engage minorities in local and national decision-making processes" as a success story of individual upward mobility, making no mention of the foundering communities these supposed experts and leaders presumably both studied and represented.[9]

In their comprehensive 1989 assessment of all Foundation-funded CDCs, former Ford staffer David B. Carlson and Arabella Martinez, a founder of the Spanish Speaking Unity Council CDC in Oakland, made a more candid admission of this decoupling and privileging of leaders over the communities they served through the Ford CDC model. Carlson and Martinez fully acknowledged that none of the CDCs they studied would ever become self-sufficient. They also accepted that none had any significant economic impact on the communities in which they were located. Also, many of them did not have the kind of profile or involvement in the communities in which they were located in order to be truly representative of community interests. Nevertheless, the two authors celebrated the CDCs as "leadership institutions," acting as training grounds for minority "public entrepreneurs," as well as stepping-stones for these individuals whose CDC experience showcased their managerial and leadership capacity to the outside world. Underscoring the elitism of this system—of which Martinez had been a direct beneficiary herself—they conceded that these opportunities were available to only a small, closed, and self-perpetuating group in most communities where CDCs were located. Nevertheless they then went on to showcase the achievements of CDC "graduates": then mayors Wilson Goode of Philadelphia and Henry Cisneros of San Antonio, Congressman Esteban Torres of Los Angeles, and, of course, Ford Foundation President Franklin A. Thomas.[10]

McCarthy, Carlson, and Martinez were among the first, but certainly not the last, to celebrate the CDC program as an incubator for individual leadership development, even while often acknowledging the model's failure to achieve substantial community uplift.[11] However, their admission of the limitations of CDC success compares favorably to the discourse that continues to promote this model as a private-sector solution with what one skeptical political scientist, Kimberley Johnson, called "almost mystical powers" to regenerate poor places and their people.[12] While Robert Kennedy, McGeorge Bundy, and Mitchell Sviridoff could be excused for hoping this was the case when they helped originate their CDC model during the late 1960s, there has been no conclusive evidence in the model's forty-five-year history that validates this persistent claim.

In part, this faith endured because the CDC fit so perfectly with the "community capitalism" of grant-seeking local nonprofits at the center of the diminished and decentralized welfare state that has characterized the United States since the Nixon years. However, the CDC has served more than as an instrument of hollowed-out, neoliberal governance; Ford's community-development model has also functioned to support post–civil rights racial liberalism. Despite the ongoing devastation wrought in the ghetto by deindustrialization, by the late 1980s the conflict and disorder of the riots were long over, and so was the immediate need to deal with the Sisyphean task of dealing with structural ills facing inner-city communities. Therefore, the

Foundation could strip down its objectives for the CDC program to what it considered essential and doable: the fostering of individual minority experts and leaders, or "public entrepreneurs." This goal attended to a number of long-standing interests. It solved the political aspect of the urban crisis by ensuring that, notwithstanding their ruin, inner-city communities were nevertheless at least represented in the American body politic according to the expanded, post–civil rights pluralism of the elite theory of democracy. It also achieved a key objective of developmental separatism by establishing a ghetto institution that prepared CDC leaders for assimilation into mainstream public life. Meanwhile, CDCs' localism meant that the thorny issue of wholesale racial integration, anathema to the Foundation since the 1950s and no more palatable to white Americans today than in the 1960s, could continue to be avoided.[13]

What is striking about the ongoing legacy of the CDC into the neoliberal and post–civil rights era is that it was not a model cooked up by conservatives but rather by 1960s establishment liberals, and this same group pursued it in tandem with their right-wing counterparts. Sviridoff's LISC, for instance, became the model for the capacity-building institutions essential to the success of the decentralized, nonprofit-centered housing policy of the Reagan-Bush years.[14] Furthermore, while the paring down of the Foundation's objectives for CDCs in the 1980s and beyond might be interpreted as representing the evisceration of establishment liberalism during the conservative ascendancy, it could also be understood as a baring of this liberalism's essential features. Elitist, individualistic, and separationist solutions had always been at the heart of establishment liberals' solution to the urban crisis in the United States. However, after the 1970s this group expected that these fixes could not solve but would only manage the problem of racial inequality in the United States. Thus, liberals' differences with conservatives were a matter of degree, not kind.

Black Leadership in a New Era

To Foundation officers and other elite white liberals, effective post–civil rights black leaders had several characteristics in common, all reflecting Ford's social development objectives. First, like the members of the postwar establishment who opened the top echelons of institutional life to them, these African Americans succeeded in the interlocking elite network comprising Ivy League universities, multinational corporations, investment banks, corporate law firms, national media outlets, government agencies, and philanthropies. Despite success at the top, this black "overclass" retained and cherished a proud black cultural identity and a connection to the black "community," often expressed through a stint of public service or community-development work in the ghetto that served as a way station but not the ultimate destination. [15] Instead, this experience enhanced these leaders' racial identity and value in representing African Americans authentically in the highest echelons of the American meritocracy, which they had reached through their professionalization and socialization to elite praxis. This mix of experience resulted in what white commentators often perceived from outside and with approbation as these exceptional African Americans' putatively effortless double consciousness in being black in America.

White supporters and outside observers used the outlines of Franklin Thomas's life and what they believed they knew about his personality to develop a prototype for this new form of black leadership. When he was appointed president in 1979, the press marveled consistently about the journey that Thomas had made "with seeming smoothness" from "the macadam playgrounds of Bedford-Stuyvesant, where [he] learned to play basketball" to "the spectacular headquarters . . . of the nation's richest and most influential foundation."[16] These accounts almost always framed Thomas as essentially "a man of two worlds" who "still" lived in Bedford-Stuyvesant, albeit "in a tastefully restored brownstone," despite the fact that even before his appointment to Ford, as one account put it, he was already "resting securely in the bosom of the American Establishment."[17] He sat on the boards of several Fortune 500 companies, these accounts pointed out, and he had been Jimmy Carter's first choice to head the Department of Housing and Urban Development—an offer Thomas turned down. Socially, the press found his relationships with prominent whites notable. In particular, he had formed a close bond with Gloria Steinem, America's preeminent feminist and Thomas's peer in the nation's new, plural liberal elite. He also became close friends with John Jay Whitney, pioneering venture capitalist, diplomat, and scion of one of the WASP establishment's oldest and most socially prominent families.

Thomas's rise to the highest echelons of American society coincided with the fall of black New York writ large. The city's financial and business elite controlled the response to New York City's fiscal crisis in the 1970s, allowing them to roll back forty years of social-democratic municipal public policy wrought by the city's working-class majority and setting the stage for

Figure 15. Franklin Thomas was named president of the Ford Foundation in 1979. His appointment marked the culmination of the Foundation's social development efforts. Ford Foundation Archives. Courtesy Rockefeller Archives Center.

New York's neoliberal future. This powerful group was helped along in its task by new political alliances that united working-class, middle-class, and elite white New Yorkers against the demands and growing needs of inner-city communities of color. Shaped in part both by the memory of corrosive incidents like the schools crisis and by establishment aspirations of revitalizing New York by transforming it into a worldwide financial and tourist mecca, this white alliance was more than ready to accept that disproportionate and punitive cuts to welfare programs for the poor should be the first step toward reviving the city's economic health. Meanwhile, the disappearance of industrial work and massive cuts to public-sector employment, a corresponding evisceration of public services from transit to schools to free tuition at the City University of New York, drastic reductions in affordable housing caused by landlord abandonment and gentrification, and a skyrocketing cost of living all had a disproportionate impact on the lives and economic well-being of the city's nonwhite poor. Black New Yorkers found themselves without the power to join together and use a collective voice. They had lost their erstwhile white allies and had found themselves unprepared to fight back politically after a decade of mobilizing and organizing, not through mainstream electoral channels but through temporary, and now-defunct, measures like the antipoverty agencies or the community-control demonstrations.[18]

During this transition, white liberals abandoned the grand experiment, articulated by Paul Ylvisaker and put into place through the Great Society and John Lindsay's mayoralty, to deal with the urban crisis by engineering the modernization and assimilation of black and Puerto Rican migrants. For example, John Lindsay's housing commissioner, Roger Starr, voiced his loss of faith in this possibility in 1976 when, serving in a similar role for Lindsay's successor Abraham Beame, he advocated for a policy of "planned shrinkage" of the city's poor population. "Our urban system is based on the theory of taking the peasant and turning him into an industrial worker," Starr explained. Now that there were "no industrial jobs," he advocated instead a policy to discourage "the peasant" from migrating to the city by neglecting to replace abandoned housing stock in depopulating ghetto neighborhoods like Brownsville and the South Bronx. "Better a thriving city of five million than a Calcutta of seven million," he concluded.[19] Starr and other white liberals had essentially conceded that the city was no longer a place for the working poor except as an underclass, a far cry from the can-do optimism of the previous decade, in which experts thought they could return the city to its role as a crucible of upward mobility.

Nevertheless, a small minority of black New Yorkers beyond Franklin Thomas was able to adapt to this environment. In a 1979 *New York Magazine* article about the changing nature of black political power in New York City, black journalist Jacob Wortham chose to focus on the two highest-ranked African Americans in the administration of Mayor Ed Koch, whose election in 1977 demonstrated the power of the city's new political configuration. Wortham wrote his article in the wake of Koch's victory, which saw the collapse of the city's black political machine, including the Manhattan borough presidency, which had been held by an African American for twenty-five years. Searching for the most powerful black figures remaining in this apparent political wasteland, Wortham went behind the scenes to identify the new phenomenon of "apolitical black leaders—technocrats, foundation executives, and managers" who were "beginning to play a more significant role and [were] being increasingly wooed by white politicians," replacing elected officials and patronage appointees as the most influential African Americans in public life. [20] Wortham pointed to Haskell Ward, Koch's deputy mayor for human services, and Ronald Gault, the mayor's commissioner of employment, as embodying this phenomenon. According to Wortham, they represented "a new sort of leader . . . who believe[s] the best way for minorities to gain political and economic ascendancy is through the individual pursuit of excellence in policymaking jobs that lend themselves to constant public scrutiny." According to Ed Koch, neither Ward nor Gault had ties to the city's black political machine and both of them "won [their positions] on merit and not because they had friends who wanted them here."[21] Both men's most notable achievement prior to arriving at City Hall? They had cut their technocratic teeth as Ford Foundation officers.

Gault and Ward represented the fruit of a consistent Foundation strategy since the late 1960s. It sought the creation of a black "network" of experts, both within the Foundation and other elite institutions in America, in the belief that through this group's racial experience and technocratic expertise its members would both improve their own status within the American meritocracy and engineer equity for the nation's black population. Foundation officers, including Bundy and Thomas, assumed that, by helping to create the circumstances for the establishment of what one 1969 Foundation report called a "sophisticated, knowledgeable" web of "citizens devoted to rapid, orderly change in America," that they would "ensure minority group participation in the formulation of public policy" with "direct and important benefits to the disadvantaged," as another document claimed fifteen years later. [22] Thus, this strategy aimed not only to create equality within the highest ranks of American life through their racial diversification but also, through that pluralism, to improve what the Foundation called in 2004 the "quality and effectiveness" of policymaking and implementation, because the "people affected by social problems" would be "part of efforts to address those problems."[23]

This enduring assimilationist and trickle-down theory did not produce the intended effects, particularly after the conservative turn. For example, Haskell Ward came under particular criticism by black New Yorkers when he sought to clear the "corruption and waste" from the city's social-welfare Community Development Agency, a move widely interpreted by African Americans as an effort by the Koch administration to get rid of much-needed patronage in poor black communities. Ward responded with enormous regret to the political firestorm that followed. He argued in retrospect that his actions would not have been so controversial were he not the only black deputy mayor and if there had been more and more influential black public officials. It was instead for him a mark of growing "black powerlessness in this city" that he had come under such close, critical scrutiny from black New Yorkers for actions that he insisted he had meant, no matter Koch's potential ulterior motives, to deliver "efficient and compassionate service for the poor."[24]

Ward's lament encapsulated the position of a rising black, professional class, ascending individually within the nation's dominant institutions based on its members' experience, expertise, and diversity value in white America while leaving the masses of their brothers and sisters behind. Members of this group could make some changes from inside the belly of the beast, like both Thomas and former Foundation grantee Leon Sullivan did by leveraging their respective memberships on General Motors and banking giant Citicorp's board into a campaign of corporate responsibility against South African apartheid.[25] However, this group's actions were often interpreted to be extending elite interests and not those of the black community. Individuals like Ward were unable to transcend the forces that were both responsible for their exceptional assimilation and for the disempowerment of the race as a whole.

This was the dilemma of "serving two masters" that Harvard legal scholar Derrick A. Bell, Jr., identified in 1976 as confronting NAACP Legal Defense and Education Fund lawyers who were working on school desegregation. While they represented the interests of a "massive clientele" of African American students and parents through class-action lawsuits, Bell found that they really catered through a myriad of forces to the "miniscule constituency" of the NAACP and its benefactors who were committed to a strict interpretation of the *Brown* decision, whatever its costs to black children and their families' wishes. Bell's conclusions pertained even more to black professionals like Ward, hoping to serve poor African Americans within institutions in which power was arrayed against, not for, racial equality. In this context there was no easy double consciousness for Ward.[26]

The intraracial divergence of interest represented by Ward's actions or the NAACP fund's indefatigable battle for school desegregation had in part to do with the fact that the experiences, opportunities, and perspectives of the new black elite were less and less representative of those of the black public for which it stood in the highest echelons of U.S. society. While the Foundation, as well as other elite liberal institutions, continued to work toward a multiracial and multicultural professional workforce or university student body to "reflect the diversity . . . it represents or with which it works,"[27] these efforts actually bred real difference among African Americans. Thomas's, Ward's, and Gault's experiences encapsulated the growing wealth and opportunity gaps among African Americans in the post–civil rights era, as the explicit and systemic racial exclusion that had previously marked America was replaced by what Michael Katz, Mark Stern, and Jamie Fader have called "a subtler series of screens" that filter "African Americans into more or less promising statuses, progressively dividing them along lines full of implications for their economic futures."[28] The paradox of this internal differentiation has been the general persistence of inequality for African Americans, who have remained three times as likely as whites to be poor, while some individuals and subgroups among African Americans have prospered, experiencing substantial upward mobility in terms of income. Thus, between 1980 and 2008, the proportion of black families in the top quintile, or those earning $100,000 or more in constant dollars, rose by 9 points—to 13.4 percent— the largest percentage increase for African Americans in any of the 2008 U.S. Census family income categories. Nevertheless, in the same period, the share of black families at the bottom, defined by the Census as those who earned less than $15,000, fell by only 5 percent, remaining nearly a fifth of the total at 18 percent, while the distributions for the other Census income categories between the top and bottom earners remained comparatively fixed. Meanwhile, the median black income relative to that earned by whites has stubbornly stabilized over the last three decades, hovering around 60 percent.[29]

Katz, Stern, and Fader argued that this intraracial differentiation was a result of "the way American public policy usually works," which has been through "[s]olutions that promote individual social mobility without attending to the processes that reproduce inequality." Such an assumption would certainly apply to the Ford Foundation's philosophy in its cultivation of black leadership, as well as other of its programs, from internal affirmative action programs at the Foundation that only targeted professional staff, to its long-lasting fellowship program for minority doctoral education, which has supported a veritable who's who of postsecondary scholars of color in the United States since its origins in 1969.[30] These kinds of efforts have ensured that the top ranks of American life have diversified but have not helped those at the bottom to overcome the structural challenges that prevent them from reaching for the middle, let alone the top. Further, those rare individual African Americans who have ascended to the highest reaches of American society often have a tenuous hold on their status that makes its transfer to their children much less than a sure thing; while they might earn the same salary as their colleagues, most high-income black people lag far behind the intergenerational wealth of their white peer group, which is in part an inheritance of past racial privilege. In short, the social mobility produced by strategies like the Ford Foundation's has not erased economic inequality but has only made minor changes to its complexion in an era of growing polarization between rich and poor.[31]

Nevertheless, the Foundation's commitment to this strategy of elite cultivation only strengthened as the years went on. Bundy's only public foray into domestic social policy in the last decade of his presidency came in 1977, when he published a spirited defense of affirmative action in higher education in the *Atlantic Monthly* by weighing in on the landmark Supreme Court case to settle the dispute between Allan Bakke and the University of California over its minority set-aside policy for medical-school applicants. Bundy's lengthy article, subtitled "Who Gets Ahead in America?" upheld race as a "plus" in determining admissions for academically eligible applicants. He argued that such policies served as redress for racism—which he called the nation's "most destructive inheritance"—by making "room in the higher reaches of this world for those who have been held back so long," thus serving "constituencies . . . that have a right to an accounting."[32]

This rhetorical sleight of hand elided the fact that opening up the top reaches of American life would only ever let a very few get ahead. Even so, arguments like Bundy's for elite affirmative action have stood the test of time, even as other victories of the civil rights era have been grievously eroded in law or in practice. While the Court's 1978 decision in *Bakke* did not accept Bundy's argument about racial redress, Justice Lewis Powell's opinion concurred with him that university admissions committees should be able to consider race as one of many extra qualifications held by applicants, for the sake of creating a leadership class exposed through its training "to the ideas and mores of students as diverse as this Nation."[33] Twenty-five years later, in *Grutter v. Bollinger* (2003), regarding admissions practices at the University of Michigan law school, the justices upheld and bolstered Powell's argument by asserting that diversity at the top was essential to America's global marketplace competitiveness and national security. Further, the Court now echoed Bundy's earlier argument; writing for the majority, Justice Sandra Day O'Connor stated that "the path to leadership must be visibly open to talented and qualified individuals of every race and ethnicity" in order to "cultivate a set of leaders with legitimacy in the eyes of the citizenry."[34]

If Franklin Thomas paved the way on this path to a more representative leadership class, Barack Obama's election to the White House provided the crowning achievement of this strategy of elite pluralism. The broad sweep of Obama's life—his Ivy League education; his community organizing and corporate law experience; his privileged connections in the worlds of government, philanthropy, and business—provides a template for the pluralistic and meritocratic liberal establishment that the Foundation played a hand in creating in post–civil rights America.[35] However, unlike the white overachievers who preceded them in this rise, African Americans' ascension to the ruling class has not yet been accompanied by the mass upward mobility that made children and grandchildren of European immigrants unquestionably "white," with all the privilege that confers in American life, and placed most firmly in the middle class.

Nonetheless, Bundy would be proud. Forty years after first turning his attention to the "Negro problem," his promise that African Americans would take their rightful place among the nation's leadership had reached its ultimate fulfillment with Obama's election to the White House. Not only that, but the first black president owed his success in part to following a path within the American meritocracy that the Foundation had played a leading role in constructing. However, Obama's achievement is also emblematic of the fundamental failure of the Bundy-led Foundation's initial, expansive racial liberalism and its vision of equal opportunity for incorporation into and success in the American "system." That goal responded to the challenge of the urban crisis and black power, both of which reminded the American establishment that liberalism's egalitarian promise continued to betray African Americans, despite the apparent success of the postwar civil rights movement. While Obama's election is often interpreted as the ultimate sign of racial progress, the celebration of his individual ascension obscures that ongoing national breach of faith, which the black freedom struggle worked so hard to reveal to the nation.

Notes

Introduction

1. McGeorge Bundy, *Action for Equal Opportunity* (New York: Ford Foundation, 1966).

2. National Affairs, "Proposed Budget: Fiscal Year 1970," June 1968, Budget Papers, Box 8, Ford Foundation Archives (FF), Rockefeller Archive Center; Ford Foundation, *Management and Program Trends in the Fifties and Sixties* (New York: Ford Foundation, 1971), 47–48.

3. The extensive literature covering the Foundation's role in founding black studies programs indicates Ford's essential role in institutionalizing black power. I examine the other initiatives listed in the chapters to follow. See Fabio Rojas, *From Black Power to Black Studies: How a Radical Social Movement Became an Academic Discipline* (Baltimore: Johns Hopkins University Press, 2007); Noliwe Rooks, *White Money/Black Power: The Surprising History of African American Studies and the Crisis of Race in Higher Education* (Boston: Beacon Press, 2006); *Inclusive Scholarship: Developing Black Studies in the United States* (New York: Ford Foundation, 2007).

4. See, in particular, Devin Fergus, *Liberalism, Black Power, and the Making of American Politics, 1965–1980* (Athens: University of Georgia Press, 2009); Robert L. Allen, *Black Awakening in Capitalist America* (New York: Doubleday, 1969); Joan Roelofs, *Foundations and Public Policy: The Mask of Pluralism* (Albany: State University of New York Press, 2003); Rooks.

5. Allen J. Matusow, *The Unraveling of America: A History of Liberalism in the 1960s* (New York: Harper Torchbooks, 1986); Gareth Davies, *From Opportunity to Entitlement: The Transformation and Decline of Great Society Liberalism* (Lawrence: University Press of Kansas, 1996). For a New York–specific example of this argument, see Jim Sleeper, *The Closest of Strangers: Liberalism and the Politics of Race in New York* (New York: W. W. Norton, 1990). Devin Fergus's provocative book on liberalism and black power differs from these works in its more sympathetic treatment of liberals, whom he portrays as martyring their cause in order to save the nation in the face of the separatist threat of black nationalism. For other examples of prominent recent scholarship that internalize the trope of black power's prominent role in the death of postwar racial liberalism, see David Hollinger, *Postethnic America: Beyond Multiculturalism* (New York: Basic Books, 2000); Matthew Frye Jacobson, *Roots Too: White Ethnic Revival in Post–Civil Rights America* (Cambridge: Harvard University Press, 2006); Gary Gerstle, *American Crucible:*

Race and Nation in the Twentieth Century (Princeton: Princeton University Press, 2001); and Peter Schuck, *Diversity in America: Keeping Government at a Safe Distance* (Cambridge: Harvard University Press, 2003).

6. While some recent works have focused on the elite origins of today's post–civil rights racial liberalism, they focus almost exclusively on diversity in higher education and lack in-depth historical analysis. For two examples from very different perspectives, see Noliwe Rooks and Walter Benn Michaels, *The Trouble with Diversity: How We Learned to Love Identity and Ignore Inequality* (New York: Metropolitan, 2006).

7. Bundy.

8. There is a rich recent scholarship on black power that examines these processes. See Thomas J. Sugrue, *Sweet Land of Liberty: The Forgotten Struggle for Civil Rights in the North* (New York: Random House, 2008); Peniel E. Joseph, *Waiting 'til the Midnight Hour: A Narrative History of Black Power in America* (New York: Henry Holt, 2006); Matthew Countryman, *Up South: Civil Rights and Black Power in Philadelphia* (Philadelphia: University of Pennsylvania Press, 2005); Nikhil Pal Singh, *Black Is a Country: Race and the Unfinished Struggle for Democracy* (Cambridge: Harvard University Press, 2004); Robert Self, *American Babylon: Race and the Struggle for Postwar Oakland* (Princeton: Princeton University Press, 2003); and Jeanne Theoharis and Komozi Woodard, eds., *Freedom North: Black Freedom Struggles Outside the South, 1940–1980* (New York: Palgrave Macmillan, 2003).

9. Singh, 214. See also Nelson Lichtenstein, "Social Theory and Capitalist Reality in the American Century," in *American Capitalism: Social Thought and Political Economy in the Twentieth Century*, ed. Nelson Lichtenstein (Philadelphia: University of Pennsylvania Press, 2006), 13.

10. Jacquelyn Dowd Hall, "The Long Civil Rights Movement and the Political Uses of the Past," *Journal of American History* 91, no. 4 (2005): 1233-1263.

11. Martin Mayer, "Washington's Grant to the Ford Foundation," *New York Times Magazine*, 13 November 1966, 150.

12. Alan Brinkley, *Liberalism and Its Discontents* (Cambridge: Harvard University Press, 1998), 200.

13. Olivier Zunz, *Philanthropy in America: A History* (Princeton: Princeton University Press, 2012); Michael Latham, *Modernization as Ideology: American Social Science and "Nation Building" in the Kennedy Era* (Chapel Hill: University of North Carolina Press, 2000), 21, 40, 53-54; Alice O'Connor, *Poverty Knowledge: Social Science, Social Policy, and the Poor in Twentieth-Century U.S. History* (Princeton: Princeton University Press, 2001), 102-109, 130-132; Mark Dowie, *American Foundations: An Investigative History* (Cambridge: MIT Press, 2001), 105-140, 171-176; Richard Magat, *The Ford Foundation at Work: Philanthropic Choices, Methods, and Styles* (New York: Plenum, 1979), 93-97, 127-132; James Day, *The Vanishing Vision: The Inside Story of Public Television* (Berkeley: University of California Press, 1995).

14. Ford Foundation, *Directives and Terms of Reference for the 1960s* (New York: Ford Foundation, 1962), 6-7.

15. Alice O'Connor, "The Politics of Rich and Rich: Postwar Investigations of Foundations and the Rise of the Philanthropic Right," in Lichtenstein, *American Capitalism*, 228–248.

16. Nicholas Guyatt, "'The Outskirts of Our Happiness': Race and the Lure of Colonization in the Early Republic," *Journal of American History* 95, no. 4 (2009): 986–1011.

17. On industrial philanthropy's interest in African Americans' separate development, see James D. Anderson, *The Education of Blacks in the South, 1860-1935* (Chapel Hill: University of North Carolina Press, 1988), 79–109; Zunz, 30–40. For earlier examples of African Americans allying with whites on racial separatism, see Marie Tyler-McGraw, *An African Republic: Black and White Virginians in the Making of Liberia* (Chapel Hill: University of North Carolina Press, 2007); Kate Masur, "The African American Delegation to Abraham Lincoln: A Reappraisal," *Civil War History* 56, no. 2 (2010): 117–144; Robert J. Norrell, *Up from History: The Life of Booker T. Washington* (Cambridge, Mass.: Belknap Press, 2009).

18. On the Chicago school, see Alice O'Connor, "Swimming against the Tide: A Brief History of Federal Policy in Poor Communities," in *Urban Problems and Community Development*, ed. Ronald F. Ferguson and William T. Dickens (Washington, D.C.: Brookings Institution Press, 1999), 85–86. On Jim Crow "separate but equal" developmentalism, see Anderson, 79–109. On the myth of white-ethnic succession, see Jacobson, 177–205. On modernization theory, see Latham.

19. This dynamic corresponded with a more general effort to diversify the American elite through meritocratic reforms. See Nicholas Lemann, *The Big Test: The Secret History of the American Meritocracy* (New York: Farrar, Straus and Giroux, 1999).

20. Karen Ferguson, "Organizing the Ghetto: CORE, the Ford Foundation, and American Pluralism, 1967–1969," *Journal of Urban History* 34 (November 2007): 67–100.

21. Allen, 14; Fergus, 11.

22. Adolph Reed, *Stirrings in the Jug: Black Politics in the Post-Segregation Era* (Minneapolis: University of Minnesota Press, 1999), 17; Roelofs, 2.

23. Sugrue, 493–531; Hall.

24. Alice O'Connor, "The Privatized City: The Manhattan Institute, the Urban Crisis, and the Conservative Counterrevolution in New York," *Journal of Urban History* 34, no. 2 (January 2008): 333–353.

25. Daryl Michael Scott, *Contempt and Pity: Social Policy and the Image of the Damaged Black Psyche, 1990-1996* (Chapel Hill: University of North Carolina Press, 1997), 137–159.

26. The Ford Foundation began a major initiative to fund the doctoral education of minorities in 1969. See Ford Foundation, *Annual Report* (1970): 42–43. The Brookings Institution has recently demonstrated the failure of affective education to increase student achievement, especially in low-achieving schools, in Tom Loveless, *The Brown Center Report on American Education* 2, no. 1 (Washington, D.C.: Brookings Institution, 2006), 12–20.

27. In 2008, the Ford Foundation's relationship to the Bill and Melinda Gates Foun-

dation was approximately that of Ford to Rockefeller in 1966, with Ford's assets of $11 billion, or approximately one-third of Gates's $34 billion. See http://www.gatesfoundation .org/about/Pages/foundation-fact-sheet.aspx, accessed 29 January 2010, and http:// www.fordfound.org/about, accessed 29 January 2010. For the activities of the "new philanthropy," see Zunz, 264–293; a special issue of the *New York Times Magazine*, 9 March 2008; and Connie Brook, "Millions for Millions," *New Yorker*, 30 October 2006, http://www.newyorker.com/archive/2006/10/30/061030fa_fact1, accessed 16 June 2011. The Ford Foundation originated the microfinance strategy that plays a major role in today's philanthropic approach. Zunz, 279–281.

28. James Smethurst, *The Black Arts Movement: Literary Nationalism in the 1960s and 1970s* (Chapel Hill: University of North Carolina Press, 2005), 110, 111.

29. Craig Steven Wilder, *A Covenant with Color: Race and Social Power in Brooklyn* (New York: Columbia University Press, 2000); Wendell Pritchett, *Brownsville, Brooklyn: Blacks, Jews, and the Changing Face of the Ghetto* (Chicago: University of Chicago Press, 2002); Evelyn Diaz Gonzalez, *Bronx: A History* (New York: Columbia University Press, 2004).

30. Joshua B. Freeman, *Working-Class New York: Life and Labor since World War II* (New York: New Press, 2000); Saskia Sassen, *The Global City: New York, London, Tokyo* (Princeton: Princeton University Press, 2001); Vincent Cannato, *The Ungovernable City: John Lindsay and His Struggle to Save New York* (New York: Basic Books, 2001); John Mollenkopf, *Phoenix in the Ashes: The Rise and Fall of the Koch Coalition in New York City Politics* (Princeton: Princeton University Press, 1994); O'Connor, "The Privatized City"; David Harvey, *A Brief History of Neoliberalism* (New York: Oxford University Press, 2006).

31. "The Issue Before the Court: Who Gets Ahead in America," *Atlantic Monthly*, November 1977, http://www.theatlantic.com/past/politics/race/bundy.htm, accessed 4 April 2012. See also memo from John R. Coleman to McGeorge Bundy, 16 September 1966, Office of the President, Records of McGeorge Bundy, Series 2, Box 17, FF; Benjamin Marquez, "Mexican-American Political Organizations and Philanthropy: Bankrolling a Movement," *Social Service Review* 77, no. 3 (2003): 329–346.

Chapter 1

1. Ford Foundation, *Annual Report* (1967), 2, 4–6.

2. Olivier Zunz, *Philanthropy in America: A History* (Princeton: Princeton University Press, 2012), 173–174; Gregory K. Raynor, "Engineering Social Reform: The Rise of the Ford Foundation and Cold War Liberalism, 1908–1959" (Ph.D. dissertation, New York University, 2000), 71.

3. David Halberstam, *The Best and the Brightest* (New York: Ballantine, 1969), 226–239; C. Wright Mills, *The Power Elite* (New York: Oxford University Press, 1956); C. Wright Mills, *The New Men of Power: America's Labor Leaders* (New York: Harcourt Brace, 1948); Leonard Silk and Mark Silk, *The American Establishment* (New York: Basic Books, 1980), 126; Nelson Lichtenstein, *Labor's War at Home: The CIO in World War II* (New York: Cambridge University Press, 1982), 227; David R. Jardini, "Out of the

Blue Yonder: The Transfer of Systems Thinking from the Pentagon to the Great Society, 1961-1965," in *Systems, Experts and Computers*, ed. Agatha C. Hughes and Thomas P. Hughes (Cambridge: MIT Press, 2000), 321.

4. Mills, *The Power Elite*.

5. From the right, the identification of and attack against the liberal establishment began with William F. Buckley's *God and Man at Yale* (Chicago: Henry Regnery, 1951). From the left, C. Wright Mills was its first major critic, both in *New Men of Power* and *The Power Elite*. Although members of the establishment themselves used the term by the early 1950s, journalist Richard Rovere was the first to bring "the establishment" into popular usage in the United States in *The American Establishment and Other Reports, Opinions, and Speculations* (New York: Harcourt, Brace & World, 1962), 3-21. For earlier American usage, see Kai Bird, *The Color of Truth: McGeorge Bundy and William Bundy: Brothers in Arms* (New York: Touchstone, 1998), 120. With the debacle in Vietnam, the establishment came under enormous scrutiny, including extensive journalistic investigations like David Halberstam's *The Best and the Brightest* and more academic New Left treatments like William Domhoff's *Who Rules America?* (Englewood Cliffs, N.J.: Prentice-Hall, 1967). More recent scholarship on the postwar Establishment includes Alan Brinkley's *Liberalism and Its Discontents* (Cambridge: Harvard University Press, 1998), 164-209; essays in *Ruling America: A History of Wealth and Power in a Democracy*, ed. Steve Fraser and Gary Gerstle (Cambridge: Harvard University Press, 2005); and Geoffrey Kabaservice's *The Guardians: Kingman Brewster, His Circle, and the Rise of the Liberal Establishment* (New York: Henry Holt, 2004).

6. For the quintessential summary of this aspiration, see W. W. Rostow, *The Stages of Economic Growth: A Non-Communist Manifesto* (New York: Cambridge University Press, 1960).

7. Bird, *Color of Truth*, 102.

8. Alan Brinkley, *The End of Reform: New Deal Liberalism in Depression and War* (New York: Vintage, 1996); Godfrey Hodgson, "The Foreign Policy Establishment," in Fraser and Gerstle, *Ruling America*, 221-223; Lichtenstein, *Labor's War at Home*, 218-220, 233; Kabaservice, 63-64, 109-110, 132-139; Arthur M. Schlesinger, Jr., *The Vital Center: The Politics of Freedom* (Boston: Houghton Mifflin, 1949).

9. Halberstam, *Best and the Brightest*. On the postwar meritocracy, see Jackson Lears, "The Managerial Revitalization of the Rich," in Fraser and Gerstle, *Ruling America*, 181-214; Nicholas Lemann, *The Big Test: The Secret History of the American Meritocracy* (New York: Farrar, Straus and Giroux, 1999).

10. Zunz, 8-43; Brinkley, *Liberalism and Its Discontents*, 200.

11. Dwight Macdonald, *The Ford Foundation: The Men and the Millions* (New York: Reynal and Company, 1955), 8-10, 137-138, 140.

12. Rovere, 11. See also Macdonald, *The Ford Foundation*, 16; Kai Bird, *The Chairman: John J. McCloy and the Making of the American Establishment* (New York: Simon and Schuster, 1992); Alden Whitman, "Charles E. Wilson of G.E. Dies; Mobilized Industry in 2 Wars," *New York Times* (*NYT*), 4 January 1972.

13. On postwar Fordism, see David Harvey, *The Condition of Postmodernity* (New York: Oxford University Press, 1989), 125–140.

14. Macdonald, *The Ford Foundation*, 138. See also Raynor, xiii. On the ethos of the postwar establishment, see Brinkley, *Liberalism and Its Discontents*, 164–209; Mills, *The Power Elite*, 269–297.

15. Raynor, 98–110.

16. Dwight Macdonald, "Foundation: The French Just Don't Believe It," *New Yorker*, 26 November 1955, 57–95; Dwight Macdonald, "Foundation: How to Spend Henry's Money II," *New Yorker*, 3 December 1955, 55–109; Dwight Macdonald, "Foundation: Next Winter or by Plane IV," *New Yorker*, 17 December 1955, 40–77; Macdonald, *The Ford Foundation*.

17. H. Rowan Gaither, *Report of the Study for the Ford Foundation on Policy and Program* (Detroit: Ford Foundation, 1949), 22, 24, 9; Zunz, 2–8.

18. Gaither, 21–22.

19. Nils Gilman, *Mandarins of the Future: Modernization Theory in Cold War America* (Baltimore: Johns Hopkins University Press, 2003); Zunz, 185–186.

20. For modernization as an overarching postwar ideology, see Michael E. Latham, *Modernization as Ideology: American Social Science and "Nation Building" in the Kennedy Era* (Chapel Hill: University of North Carolina Press, 2000).

21. Gilman, 15–16, 55, 110–111.

22. Gaither, 14. See also Latham, 46–50.

23. Ronald L. Geiger, "American Foundations and Academic Social Science," *Minerva* 26, no. 3 (1988): 315–341; Gilman, 46, 77–78, 132–133, 158; Latham, 46–54; Raynor, 132–133; Bird, *Color of Truth*, 137–146.

24. Gaither, 45, 65. See also Raynor, 147–148.

25. Gaither, 28.

26. Ibid., 35, 70.

27. Ibid., 97.

28. Ibid., 46.

29. Ibid., 65. See also Mary L. Dudziak, *Cold War Civil Rights: Race and the Image of American Democracy* (Princeton: Princeton University Press, 2000).

30. Robert N. Bellah, *Beyond Belief: Essays on Religion in a Post-Traditional World* (Berkeley: University of California Press, 1991), xvi; Gilman, 250; Robert Booth Fowler, *Believing Skeptics: American Political Intellectuals, 1945–1964* (Westport, Conn.: Greenwood Press, 1978).

31. Howard Brick, *Transcending Capitalism: Visions of a New Society in Modern American Thought* (Ithaca, N.Y.: Cornell University Press, 2006), 151. For a concise elucidation of postcapitalist, postideological American social thought, see also Howard Brick, "The Postcapitalist Vision in Twentieth-Century American Social Thought," in *American Capitalism: Social Thought and Political Economy in the Twentieth Century*, ed. Nelson Lichtenstein (Philadelphia: University of Pennsylvania Press, 2006), 21–46.

32. Gaither, 35. For a good example of this presumption operating among labor economists, see Paddy Riley, "Clark Kerr: From Industrial to Knowledge Economy," in Lichtenstein, *American Capitalism*, 71-87.

33. Jardini.

34. Gaither, 28.

35. Peter Odegard quoted in Raynor, 103.

36. Gaither, 31-32.

37. Ibid., 81, 81-83.

38. Nils Gilman outlines the ubiquity of this "elite theory of democracy" among postwar American liberal intellectuals. Gilman, 47-56. See also Fowler, 149-175.

39. Gaither, 46.

40. Ibid., 46, 45, 44.

41. Ibid., 91.

42. Ibid., 97.

43. Ibid., 66, 97, 65.

44. Ibid., 97.

45. Ibid., 46.

46. Daryl Michael Scott, *Contempt and Pity: Social Policy and the Image of the Damaged Black Psyche, 1880-1996* (Chapel Hill: University of North Carolina Press, 1997), 97.

47. Gunnar Myrdal, *An American Dilemma: The Negro Problem and Modern Democracy* (New York: Harper & Row, 1944); Scott, 34-35.

48. Walter A. Jackson, *Gunnar Myrdal and America's Conscience: Social Engineering and Racial Liberalism, 1938-1987* (Chapel Hill: University of North Carolina Press, 1990), 271.

49. *To Secure These Rights: The Report of the President's Committee on Civil Rights* (New York: Simon and Schuster, 1947).

50. Scott, 115-116, 125-136; Dudziak, 79-114.

51. To get a sense of the FAE and education's importance to the Ford Foundation, between 1951 and 1953 the Foundation disbursed approximately $120 million in grants. Of this amount, $54 million went to the education program. In 1954, the FAE received $25 million of a total of about $68 million in grants made by the Foundation that year, making it Ford's largest grantee. See Raynor, 205-206; Macdonald, "Foundation," 57.

52. The Fund for the Republic, which was committed to civil liberties, had funded religious groups, the Southern Regional Council, and the NAACP to facilitate "intergroup relations" and school desegregation, especially in the South, as well as open housing, particularly in Northern cities. Thomas C. Reeves, *Freedom and the Foundation: The Fund for the Republic in the Era of McCarthyism* (New York: Alfred A. Knopf, 1969).

53. Raynor, 231-232, 237-261. See also John J. Scanlon, "Fund for the Advancement of Education," *AIBS Bulletin* 7, no. 3 (1957): 12-14.

54. Harry S. Ashmore, *The Negro and the Schools* (Chapel Hill: University of North Carolina Press, 1954), 48-49.

55. Ibid., 138.

56. For a modernization theorist's encapsulation of this argument, see W. W. Rostow, "The National Style," in *The American Style: Essays in Value and Performance* (New York: Harper and Brothers, 1957), 290.

57. Nelson Lichtenstein, "Social Theory and Capitalist Reality in the American Century," in Lichtenstein, *American Capitalism*, 12–13; Gilman, 38–39, 212; Dudziak, 215, 229–230.

58. Ashmore, 54.

59. Ibid., xiv.

60. Ibid., 126.

61. Ibid., xiv.

62. FAE document quoted in Raynor, 287.

63. Edgardo Meléndez Vélez, "*The Puerto Rican Journey* Revisited: Politics and the Study of Puerto Rican Migration," *Centro Journal* 17, no. 2 (2005): 192–221; Madeleine E. López, "Investigating the Investigators: An Analysis of *The Puerto Rican Study*," *Centro Journal* 19, no. 2 (2007): 60–85; Martha Biondi, *To Stand and Fight: The Struggle for Civil Rights in Postwar New York City* (Cambridge: Harvard University Press, 2003), 60.

64. New York City Board of Education, *The Future Is Now: The Puerto Rican Study: The Education and Adjustment of Puerto Ricans in New York City* (New York: Board of Education of the City of New York, 1958), 6.

65. Ibid., 31, 9, 21.

66. Ibid., 19, 23.

67. For a discussion of the impetus for and the impact of the Cox and Reece investigations, see Alice O'Connor, "The Politics of Rich and Rich: Postwar Investigations of Foundations and the Rise of the Philanthropic Right," in Lichtenstein, *American Capitalism*, 234–240; Zunz, 192–196.

68. Interview with Paul Ylvisaker by Charles T. Morrissey for the Ford Foundation Oral History Project, 27 September 1973, Ford Foundation Archives, Rockefeller Archive Center, 51–52; Latham, 214; Kabaservice, 134–139; Bird, *Color of Truth*, 122–133; Gilman, 214; Raynor, 291–301; Reeves; Alice O'Connor, "Community Action, Urban Reform, and the Fight against Poverty: The Ford Foundation's Gray Areas Program," *Journal of Urban History* 22, no. 5 (1996): 591–592.

Chapter 2

1. The Ford Foundation, *Directives and Terms of Reference for the 1960s* (New York: Ford Foundation, 1962), 4, 1. On Henry Heald, see Waldemar A. Nielsen, *The Big Foundations* (New York: Columbia University Press, 1972), 89–93.

2. Martin Mayer, "Washington's Grant to the Ford Foundation," *New York Times Magazine*, 13 November 1966, 150. The Foundation completed its divestment from Ford Motor in 1974. See Richard Magat, *The Ford Foundation at Work: Philanthropic Choices, Methods, and Styles* (New York: Plenum Press, 1979), 166, 176.

3. Ford Foundation, *Directives*, 6–7.

4. Ibid., 2.

5. Olivier Zunz, *Philanthropy in America: A History* (Princeton: Princeton University Press), 207-213; Nils Gilman, *Mandarins of the Future: Modernization Theory in Cold War America* (Baltimore: Johns Hopkins University Press, 2003), 225-226; Michael E. Latham, *Modernization as Ideology: American Social Science and "Nation Building" in the Kennedy Era* (Chapel Hill: University of North Carolina Press, 2000).

6. Paul N. Ylvisaker, "Blue Earth County, Minnesota: A Case Study in the Local Workings of American Government" (Ph.D. dissertation, Harvard University, 1948); Guian McKee, *The Problem of Jobs: Liberalism, Race, and Deindustrialization in Philadelphia* (Chicago: University of Chicago Press, 2008), 19-32; Kirk R. Petshek, *The Challenge of Urban Reform: Policies and Programs in Philadelphia* (Philadelphia: Temple University Press, 1973), 55-65; John F. Bauman, *Public Housing, Race, and Renewal: Urban Planning in Philadelphia, 1920-1974* (Philadelphia: Temple University Press, 1987), 118-143. The Fund for the Republic, the Ford Foundation subsidiary, even published a report in praise of Clark and his successor, Richardson Dilworth, a fellow municipal reformer. See James Reichley, *The Art of Government: Reform and Organization Politics in Philadelphia* (New York: The Fund for the Republic, 1959).

7. Bauman, 144-182.

8. Paul N. Ylvisaker, *Community Action: A Response to Some Unfinished Business* (New York: Ford Foundation, 1963), 3.

9. Ibid. Other poverty experts prescribed a laissez-faire approach to migrant assimilation, believing that the city's industrial modernity inevitably led to incorporation without considering the impact of postwar urban deindustrialization. Michael B. Katz, *The Undeserving Poor: From the War on Poverty to the War on Welfare* (New York: Pantheon, 1989), 32-34.

10. Ford Foundation, *Annual Report* (1957), 23; Suleiman Osman, *The Invention of Brownstone Brooklyn: Gentrification and the Search for Authenticity in Postwar New York* (New York: Oxford University Press, 2011), 69-75.

11. Ylvisaker, "Metropolitan Government—For What?" (1958), in *Conscience and Community: The Legacy of Paul Ylvisaker*, ed. Virginia Esposito (New York: Peter Lang, 1999), 86; Ylvisaker, "The Deserted City," *Journal of the American Planning Association* 25, no. 1 (1959): 3.

12. Ylvisaker, "Deserted City," 5.

13. Ylvisaker, "Metropolitan Government," 92, 91.

14. Ylvisaker, "Deserted City," 4-5. In the historical literature, Thomas Sugrue's *The Origins of the Urban Crisis: Race and Inequality in Postwar Detroit* (Princeton: Princeton University Press, 1996) would mark a return to Ylvisaker's original thinking on this phenomenon.

15. Ylvisaker, "Metropolitan Government," 93.

16. Paul Ylvisaker, "Diversity and the Public Interest: Two Cases in Metropolitan Decision-Making," *Journal of the American Planning Association* 27, no. 2 (1961): 107.

17. Ibid., 108.

18. Ibid., 115; Ylvisaker, *Community Action*, 3.

19. Interview with Paul Ylvisaker by Charles T. Morrissey, Ford Foundation Oral History Project, 27 September 1973, Ford Foundation Archives (FF), Rockefeller Archive Center, 19.

20. Ibid., 18-19. See also the interview with Paul Ylvisaker by Charles T. Morrissey, Ford Foundation Oral History Project, 27 October 1973, FF, 58.

21. Paul Ylvisaker interview, 27 September 1973, 20. Guian McKee has shown how white policymakers in Philadelphia during Ylvisaker's tenure there, along with other postwar liberals nationwide, remained silent on the issue of race in order to forge political consensus for their planning agendas. McKee, 6, 40, 77.

22. Daryl Michael Scott, *Contempt and Pity: Social Policy and the Image of the Damaged Black Psyche, 1880-1996* (Chapel Hill: University of North Carolina Press, 1997), 137-159, 184-185.

23. "Public Affairs Program Planning Budget Request for Fiscal 1967-1968-1969," June 1966, Budget Papers, Box 6, FF.

24. This was a classic strategy to legitimate expert intervention on behalf of the poor. Katz, 22-23.

25. Paul Ylvisaker interview, 27 October 1973, 60-61.

26. Ylvisaker, *Community Action*, 4.

27. Peter Marris and Martin Rein, *Dilemmas of Social Reform: Poverty and Community Action in the United States* (New York: Atherton Press, 1967), 53.

28. Ylvisaker, *Community Action*, 5.

29. Ibid., 6.

30. Ibid., 2.

31. Ibid., 10-15; Alice O'Connor, "Community Action, Urban Reform, and the Fight against Poverty: The Ford Foundation's Gray Areas Program," *Journal of Urban History* 22, no. 5 (July 1996): 607-613.

32. Paul Ylvisaker quoted in Alice O'Connor, *Poverty Knowledge: Social Science, Social Policy, and the Poor in Twentieth-Century U.S. History* (Princeton: Princeton University Press, 2001), 160. On the top-down management of the Gray Areas agencies, see ibid., 131-132.

33. Paul Ylvisaker quoted in Daniel Patrick Moynihan, *Maximum Feasible Misunderstanding* (New York: Free Press, 1969), 36.

34. Ylvisaker, *Community Action*, 5.

35. Scott, 139.

36. Ylvisaker, *Community Action*, 5.

37. Ibid., 7.

38. Ibid., 4.

39. Paul Ylvisaker, "What Is New in American Philanthropy" (1966), in Esposito, *Conscience and Community*, 275.

40. Paul Ylvisaker interview, 27 September 1973, 51-53; Richard Magat interviewed by Charles T. Morrissey and Ronald J. Grele, 24 January 1974, Ford Foundation Oral

History Project, FF, 15–16, 66–67, 71. On Robert Weaver's illustrious career, including at the Ford Foundation, see Wendell Pritchett, *Robert Clifton Weaver and the American City: The Life and Times of an Urban Reformer* (Chicago: University of Chicago Press, 2008).

41. Robert Booth Fowler, *Believing Skeptics: American Political Intellectuals, 1945–1964* (Westport, Conn.: Greenwood Press, 1978), 176–214. The classic text of political pluralism was Robert Dahl's *Who Governs? Democracy and Power in an American City* (New Haven: Yale University Press, 1961).

42. Paul Ylvisaker interview, 27 September 1973, 49–50. See also McKee, 135.

43. Ibid., 28.

44. O'Connor, *Poverty Knowledge*, 102–109, 130–132; Gilman, 46, 132–133; Latham, 53–54.

45. *Ford Foundation International Programs* (New York: Ford Foundation, 1979), 10; O'Connor, "Community Action," 606.

46. The Foundation's conservative antagonists used the farm team analogy. Alice O'Connor, "The Politics of Rich and Rich: Postwar Investigations of Foundations and the Rise of the Philanthropic Right," in *American Capitalism: Social Thought and Political Economy in the Twentieth Century*, ed. Nelson Lichtenstein (Philadelphia: University of Pennsylvania Press, 2006), 244. See also O'Connor, *Poverty Knowledge*, 128–129; O'Connor, "Community Action," 611–613; "Anti Poverty Expert: Mitchell Sviridoff," *New York Times* (*NYT*), 14 January 1966.

47. McGeorge Bundy, *Action for Equal Opportunity* (New York: Ford Foundation, 1966). Italics in original.

48. Bundy's path to the Foundation's presidency was a product of the tight network joining the establishment's various branches. For example, Bundy became president of the Foundation on the initiative of banker John J. McCloy, the unofficial establishment leader of his generation. McCloy asked Judge Charles E. Wyzanski, Jr., another Ford Foundation trustee and one of Bundy's Harvard mentors, to recruit him as president. Testifying to the power of the Foundation, Wyzanski told Bundy that he should think of the presidency as "a sort of ministry not only of education, but whatever may be important in the country." Wyzanski quoted in Kai Bird, *The Color of Truth: McGeorge Bundy and William Bundy: Brothers in Arms* (New York: Touchstone, 1998), 343. See also David Halberstam, *The Best and the Brightest* (New York: Ballantine, 1969), 50; David Halberstam, "The Very Expensive Education of McGeorge Bundy," *Harper's Magazine*, July 1969, 37; Paul Ylvisaker interview, 27 September 1973, 45–47.

49. Mayer, 58.

50. Bird, 63, 101–105, 117–153; Halberstam, *The Best and the Brightest*, 53–60. On the rise of elite "vital center" liberal intellectuals in public life, see Allen Matusow, *The Unraveling of America: A History of Liberalism in the 1960s* (New York: Harper Torchbooks, 1984), 3–13.

51. Halberstam, "The Very Expensive Education," 37.

52. On Bundy's Washington career, see Bird, 185–375. See also Halberstam, *The Best and the Brightest*, particularly 517–527, 625, 657.

53. Paul Ylvisaker interview, 27 September 1973, 40–42; memo from John R. Coleman to McGeorge Bundy, 27 September 1966, Office of the President, Records of McGeorge Bundy, Series 1, Box 3, FF; Mayer, 146; Roger Wilkins, *A Man's Life: An Autobiography* (New York: Simon and Schuster, 1982), 140–144, 174–183; National Affairs, "Budget Request, Fiscal Year 1968," June 1967, Budget Papers, Box 7, FF.

54. Bird, 316–320, 359–360, 367–370; Marilyn B. Young, *The Vietnam Wars, 1945–1990* (New York: HarperCollins, 1991), 228–230.

55. National Affairs, "Proposed Budget: Fiscal Year 1970," June 1968, Budget Papers, Box 8, FF, 24.

56. Eugene S. Staples to McGeorge Bundy, 27 September 1966, Records of McGeorge Bundy, Series 2, Box 17, FF. For a full discussion of liberals' response to the riots and black power, see Devin Fergus, *Liberalism, Black Power, and the Making of American Politics, 1965–1980* (Athens: University of Georgia Press, 2009).

57. Bird, 190; Halberstam, *The Best and the Brightest*, 519–520.

58. Ford Foundation, *Annual Report* (1967), 16.

59. *The Negro American*, ed. Talcott Parsons and Kenneth B. Clark (Boston: Houghton Mifflin, 1966); Ford Foundation, *Annual Report* (1967), 4; Bird, 380.

60. Halberstam, "The Very Expensive Education," 28. On Bundy's trip to Vietnam, see Bird, 305.

61. Steve Fraser and Gary Gerstle, "Introduction," in *Ruling America: A History of Wealth and Power in a Democracy*, ed. Steve Fraser and Gary Gerstle (Cambridge: Harvard University Press, 2005), 15.

62. Anonymous Ford Foundation official quoted in National Affairs, *Cleveland CORE–Target City: An Assessment of the Foundation's Grants to the CORE Special Purpose Fund* (New York: Ford Foundation, August 1969), 8.

63. Bundy quoted in Joseph C. Goulden, *The Money Givers* (New York: Random House, 1971), 275.

64. McGeorge Bundy quoted in Bird, 381.

65. Ford Foundation, *Annual Report* (1967), 5.

66. Halberstam, "The Very Expensive Education," 38.

67. McGeorge Bundy, *The Strength of Government* (Cambridge: Harvard University Press, 1968), 92.

68. Bundy, *Action for Equal Opportunity*.

69. Memo from John R. Coleman to McGeorge Bundy, 16 September 1966, Records of McGeorge Bundy, Series 2, Box 17, FF; Ford Foundation, *Annual Report* (1967), 16–17.

70. Mayer, 150.

71. Wilkins, 302.

72. Bundy, *The Strength of Government*, 10, 12, 13.

73. Christopher F. Edley to John R. Coleman, Attachment A, 18 January 1967, 67–152, R-1831, FF. Jeanne Theoharis points out that the pathologizing of northern blacks al-

lowed officials and journalists to discount African American self-assertion outside of the South. Jeanne Theoharis, "Introduction," in *Freedom North: Black Freedom Struggles Outside the South, 1940–1980*, ed. Jeanne Theoharis, Komozi Woodard, and Matthew Countryman (New York: Palgrave Macmillan, 2003), 7.

74. Matthew Frye Jacobson, *Roots Too: White Ethnic Revival in Post–Civil Rights America* (Cambridge: Harvard University Press, 2006), 178; Daniel J. Walkowitz, *Working with Class: Social Workers and the Politics of Middle-Class Identity* (Chapel Hill: University of North Carolina Press, 1999), 258–264.

75. The canonical work on black cultural pathology is Daniel Patrick Moynihan's "The Negro Family: The Case for National Action." See *The Moynihan Report and the Politics of Controversy*, ed. Lee Rainwater and William L. Yancey (Cambridge: MIT Press, 1967). For negative comparisons of African Americans to white ethnics, see Nathan Glazer and Daniel Patrick Moynihan, *Beyond the Melting Pot: The Negroes, Puerto Ricans, Jews, Italians, and Irish of New York City* (New York: MIT Press and Harvard University Press, 1964).

76. Scott, 150–156.

77. "Division of Education and Research Program Budget Request, Fiscal Year 1968," June 1967, Budget Papers, Box 6, FF, 6.

78. Edley to Coleman. On the policy implications of damage imagery, see Scott, 137–160.

79. "Division of Education and Research Program Budget Request," in *Management and Program Trends in the Fifties and Sixties* (New York: Ford Foundation, 1971), 22.

80. Latham, 146–149, 214–215. This concept about the nonwhite poor was a variation on a classic formulation of the poor as "strangers." See Katz, 5–7.

81. David E. Bell to McGeorge Bundy, 10 July 1967, David Bell Papers, Series VI, Box 36, FF; Latham, 189–190; Wilkins, 87, 91–92, 105–106, 140–143; Sol H. Chafkin staff biography, March 1980, FF; Eamon M. Kelly staff biography, March 1974, FF; Eamon M. Kelly curriculum vitae, www.payson.tulane.edu/peopledb/pdfs/Kelly,%20Eamon%20-%20PDF.pdf, accessed 21 February 2012.

82. "Summary of December 23rd [1965] Meeting of Domestic Program Directors," Attachment to Clarence Faust to McGeorge Bundy, 17 March 1966, Records of McGeorge Bundy, Series 2, Box 17, FF. See also Richard Magat interview, 101.

83. Staples to Bundy.

84. McGeorge Bundy, "The End of Either/Or," *Foreign Affairs* 45, no. 2 (1967): 194, 195, 196, 192.

85. Bird, 337.

86. Bundy, "End of Either/Or," 197. See also Bird, 315, 358, 365, 371–372; "Excerpt from the Address by Bundy on the Direction of US Policy in Vietnam," *NYT*, 18 October 1968.

87. Bundy, quoting Henry Stimson, in "End of Either/Or," 201. See also "Ford Fund to Aid Drive for Rights," *NYT*, 3 August 1966.

88. Robert L. Allen, *Black Awakening in Capitalist America: An Analytic History* (New York: Doubleday, 1969), 14.

89. Ford Foundation, *Annual Report* (1967), 3.

90. Division of National Affairs, "Proposed Budget: Fiscal Year 1970," 10.

91. *Ford Foundation International Programs*, 6-7.

92. Ibid., 7.

93. "Summary of December 23rd [1965] Meeting of Domestic Program Directors."

94. "Economic Development and Administration Planning Budget Request for Fiscal 1967-1968-1969," June 1966, Budget Papers, Box 6, FF.

95. "Public Affairs Program Planning Budget Request for Fiscal 1967-1968-1969."

96. Gareth Davies, *See Government Grow: Education Politics from Johnson to Reagan* (Lawrence: University Press of Kansas, 2007), 149-150, 155-157, 162-165; Benjamin Marquez, "Mexican-American Political Organizations and Philanthropy: Bankrolling a Movement," *Social Service Review* 77, no 3 (2003): 329-346; Ford Foundation, *Annual Report* (1970), 20; *Civil Rights, Social Justice, and Black America* (New York: Ford Foundation, 1984), 7-8.

97. Bundy, *The Strength of Government*, 82-83.

98. Ford Foundation, *Annual Report* (1967), 3-4.

99. Ada Louise Huxtable, "Ford Flies High," *NYT*, 26 November 1967.

100. Wilkins, 264-266.

Chapter 3

1. New York City Board of Education, *The Future Is Now: The Puerto Rican Study: The Education and Adjustment of Puerto Ricans in New York City* (New York: Board of Education of the City of New York, 1958), 9. For a full description of this study, see Chapter 1.

2. Howell S. Baum, *Brown in Baltimore: School Desegregation and the Limits of Liberalism* (Ithaca, N.Y.: Cornell University Press, 2010); Kevin M. Kruse, *White Flight: Atlanta and the Making of Modern Conservatism* (Princeton: Princeton University Press, 2005), 161-179; Jerald Podair, *The Strike That Changed New York: Blacks, Whites, and the Ocean Hill-Brownsville Crisis* (New Haven: Yale University Press, 2002).

3. Clarence Taylor, *Knocking at Our Own Door: Milton A. Galamison and the Struggle to Integrate New York City Schools* (New York: Columbia University Press, 1997), 47-175; Martha Biondi, *To Stand and Fight: The Struggle for Civil Rights in Postwar New York City* (Cambridge: Harvard University Press, 2003), 246-249; Podair, 22-32.

4. See, for example, John Kifner, "McGeorge Bundy Dies at 77; Top Adviser in Vietnam Era," *New York Times (NYT)*, 17 September 1996.

5. Fred M. Hechinger, "Columbia Starts 3-Year Campaign for $200 Million," *NYT*, 1 November 1966.

6. S. M. Miller to Fantini, Feldman, Pugh, and Riessman, 6 March 1967, Mayor's Ad-

visory Panel on the Decentralization of the New York City Schools (MAP), Box 14566, Ford Foundation Archives (FF), Rockefeller Archives Center.

7. Ada Louise Huxtable, "How Not to Build a Symbol," *NYT*, 14 March 1968.

8. Fred M. Hechinger, "Columbia Starts 3-Year Campaign."

9. Podair, 17.

10. For a full account of Galamison's leadership of the school integration campaign in New York City, see Taylor.

11. On PAT, see Podair, 27-30. New York City was not alone in its laissez-faire and open enrollment responses to desegregation. See Baum.

12. Taylor, 116-145, 147; Podair, 30-32.

13. Lisa Yvette Waller, "The Pressures of the People: Milton A. Galamison, the Parents' Workshop and Resistance to School Integration in New York City, 1960-1963," *Souls* 1, no. 2 (Spring 1999): 31-45.

14. Leonard Buder, "Showcase School Sets off Dispute," *NYT*, 2 September 1966; "City Won't Open Disputed School in Harlem Today," *NYT*, 12 September 1966; Thomas A. Johnson, "Militant Negro Groups Moving to Aid Parents in School Fight," *NYT*, 22 September 1966; Heather Lewis, "Protest, Place and Pedagogy: New York City's Community Control Movement and Its Aftermath, 1966-1996," (Ph.D. dissertation, New York University, 2006), 58-61.

15. Taylor, 180-191; Podair, 71-73.

16. Jerald Podair outlines how New York's postwar school bureaucracy had once been a source of opportunity and upward mobility for the city's working class (50-53). Suleiman Osman provides a brilliant examination of the shift in left/liberal thinking about cities and urban renewal in his *The Invention of Brownstone Brooklyn: Gentrification and the Search for Authenticity in Postwar New York* (New York: Oxford University Press, 2011).

17. New York City Board of Education, "Proposals for Improving Education in Schools in Disadvantaged Areas," 20 October 1966, MAP, Box 14566.

18. "There Are Three Committees Being Formed to Deal with the I.S. 201 Situation," 31 October 1966, MAP, Box 14566.

19. "Parent/Community Negotiating Committee for I.S. 201," 21 October 1966, MAP, Box 14566.

20. F. Champion Ward to McGeorge Bundy, 26 June 1967, 67-426, R-2372, FF.

21. "Points to Make on NYC Schools," MAP, Box 14567.

22. "Proposal for Academic Excellence: Community and Teachers Assume Responsibility for the Education of the Ghetto Child," 26 April 1967, 67-431, R-1863, FF.

23. Vincent J. Cannato, *The Ungovernable City: John Lindsay and His Struggle to Save New York* (New York: Basic Books, 2001), 108-112; Alex Abella, *The Rand Corporation and the Rise of the American Empire* (Orlando: Harcourt, 2008), 205-212.

24. Division of National Affairs, "'And Then, There Were the Children . . . ': An Assessment of Efforts to Test Decentralization in New York City's Public School System," May 1969, Report 002149, FF, 10-12.

25. F. Champion Ward to McGeorge Bundy.

26. "Points to Make on NYC Schools."

27. "More Brainpower for Every Buck," *Business Week*, 6 January 1968, 48.

28. Mario D. Fantini to McGeorge Bundy and Champion Ward, 11 October 1966, MAP, Box 14566.

29. Noel A. Cazenave, "Ironies of Urban Reform: Professional Turf Battles in the Planning of the Mobilization for Youth Program Precursor to the War on Poverty," *Journal of Urban History* 26, no. 1 (1999): 34-35.

30. Paul Ylvisaker, "What Is New in American Philanthropy" (1966), in *Conscience and Community: The Legacy of Paul Ylvisaker*, ed. Virginia Esposito (New York: Peter Lang, 1999), 275.

31. Ibid., 272.

32. "Points to Make on NYC Schools," 10. The view that the anger fueling black power was an unhealthy emotional response, rather than the result of rational analysis of social conditions was common among postwar racial liberals. See Daryl Michael Scott, *Contempt and Pity: Social Policy and the Image of the Damaged Black Psyche, 1880-1996* (Chapel Hill: University of North Carolina Press, 1997), 108-114.

33. National Affairs, "And Then There Were the Children," 13.

34. "Points to Make on NYC Schools," MAP, Box 14567, 6.

35. McGeorge Bundy, "Rough Outline," 22 December 1966, MAP, Box 14567.

36. "Background Points on Formal Agenda—Gracie Mansion Meeting," 3 May 1967, MAP, Box 14567; Panel on School Decentralization, "Agenda for Gracie Mansion Meeting," [May 1967], MAP, Box 14567.

37. S. M. Miller to Fantini, Feldman, Pugh, and Riessman.

38. "Points to Make on NYC Schools"; Sheila Gordon to Lew Feldstein, 17 October 1967, MAP, Box 14568; Mario D. Fantini to McGeorge Bundy, 22 November 1966, MAP, Box 14566. See also "Political Responsibility for Education," MAP, Box 14566.

39. Ellen Hoffman, "School Ideologist Is Good Listener," *Washington Post*, 8 December 1968.

40. "Points to Make on NYC Schools."

41. Mayor's Advisory Panel on Decentralization of the New York City Schools, *Reconnection for Learning: A Community School System for New York City* (New York: Praeger, 1969), xiii.

42. Ibid., 22.

43. Mario Fantini staff biography, January 1967, FF.

44. Richard Magat to Sims, Gordon, Fantini, and Gittell, 12 October 1967, MAP, Box 14567.

45. Marilyn Gittell, "A Typology of Power for Measuring Social Change," *American Behavioral Scientist* 9, no. 8 (1966): 25.

46. Ibid., 23-28; Ross Gittell and Kathe Newman, "Introduction," in *Scholar Activist: Selected Works of Marilyn Gittell*, ed. Ross Gittell and Kathe Newman (Thousand Oaks, Calif: Sage Publications, 2012), xvii; Maurice Berube and Ross Gittell, "Part I: Introduction," in Gittell and Newman, 3.

47. Marilyn Gittell, "Governing the Public Schools: Educational Decision-Making and Its Financial Implications in New York City," Staff Paper 9, Temporary Commission on City Finances, City of New York, August 1966, MAP, Box 14566.

48. Gittell and Newman, xi–xviii; Berube and Gittell, 3–4, 6. On Jane Jacobs's transformation, see Christopher Klemek, "From Political Outsider to Power Broker in Two 'Great American Cities': Jane Jacobs and the Fall of the Urban Renewal Order in New York and Toronto," *Journal of Urban History* 34, no. 2 (2008): 309–332.

49. "Education Planning Budget Request for Fiscal 1967-1968-1969," June 1966, Budget Papers, Box 6, FF. See also Fred M. Hechinger, "Decentralization: The Whys," *NYT*, 12 November 1967.

50. "Points to Make on NYC Schools."

51. Richard Magat, "Propositions on Quality Education and Decentralization," 8 June 1967, MAP, Box 14568, 6.

52. Ralph J. Cordiner, "Decentralization: A Managerial Philosophy," 26 April 1956, MAP, Box 14567. See also Nils Gilman, "The Prophet of Post-Fordism: Peter Drucker and the Legitimation of the Corporation," in *American Capitalism: Social Thought and Political Economy in the Twentieth Century*, ed. Nelson Lichtenstein (Philadelphia: University of Pennsylvania Press, 2006), 109–131; Kimberly Phillips-Fein, "American Counterrevolutionary: Lemuel Ricketts Boulware and General Electric, 1950-1960, in Lichtenstein, *American Capitalism*, 249–270; Gittell, "A Typology of Power."

53. Kai Bird, *The Color of Truth: McGeorge Bundy and William Bundy: Brothers in Arms* (New York: Simon and Schuster, 1998), 186.

54. "More Brainpower," 46.

55. Mario Fantini, Marilyn Gittell, and Richard Magat, *Community Control and the Urban School* (New York: Praeger, 1970), 44.

56. "Sviridoff Assails Schools as Rigid," *NYT*, 16 October 1967.

57. Mario D. Fantini to McGeorge Bundy and Champion Ward.

58. Christopher F. Edley to Mario Fantini, 13 November 1967, 67–431, R-1863, FF; "Meeting at Ford Foundation Luncheon Session," 14 July 1967, MAP, Box 14567.

59. Richard Magat to Mario Fantini, 18 November 1967, MAP, Box 14567; Fantini et al., 14.

60. Mayor's Advisory Panel, 15.

61. On suburban localism and school segregation, see Lizabeth Cohen, *A Consumers' Republic: The Politics of Mass Consumption in Postwar America* (New York: Vintage, 2003), 228–229, 240–251. On white resistance to integration in New York, see Podair, 25–30, 34–35.

62. Institute for Community Studies, "Educational Achievement and Community Control," *Community Issues* 1, no. 1 (November 1968): 9.

63. Mario D. Fantini to McGeorge Bundy, 22 November 1966.

64. Richard Magat interviewed by Charles T. Morrissey and Ronald J. Grele, 24 January 1974, Ford Foundation Oral History Project, 101, 75–76. See also Fantini et al., 36–38.

65. Alice O'Connor, "Community Action, Urban Reform, and the Fight against Poverty: The Ford Foundation's Gray Areas Program," *Journal of Urban History* 22, no. 5 (July 1996): 603–604.

66. Fantini et al., 42. Emphasis in original.

67. Ibid., 96.

68. "Local District Boundaries," ca. 3 August 1967, MAP, Box 14566.

69. Fantini et al., 41.

70. Cazenave, 34–35.

71. Fantini et al., 97, 96.

72. Ibid., 96.

73. Institute for Community Studies, "A Proposal for the Continuation of Facilitating Community Involvement in Education," [ca. 13 March 1969], 68–472, R-1094, FF, 19. See also Magat, "Propositions on Quality Education," 9; "Panel Agenda—Meeting of June 13," 23 May 1967, MAP, Box 14567.

74. Mario Fantini quoted in *Why Teachers Strike: Teachers Rights and Community Control*, ed. Melvin Urofsky (New York: Anchor, 1970), 92.

75. *Toward Humanistic Education: A Curriculum of Affect*, ed. Gerald Weinstein and Mario Fantini (New York: Praeger, 1970), 18.

76. Fantini et al., 183.

77. Ibid., 194.

78. Ibid., 197, 198.

79. Ibid., 192; Andrew M. Greeley and Peter H. Rossi, *The Education of Catholic Americans* (Chicago: Aldine, 1967).

80. Institute for Community Studies, "Educational Achievement," 11; Fantini et al., 193. On the *Brown* orthodoxy, see Scott, 124, and U.S. Department of Health Education and Welfare Office of Education, *Equality of Educational Opportunity* (Washington, D.C.: U.S. Government Printing Office, 1966).

81. Matthew Frye Jacobson, *Roots Too: White Ethnic Revival in Post-Civil Rights America* (Cambridge: Harvard University Press, 2006), 177–245.

82. Fantini et al., 81.

83. Hoffman.

84. Fantini et al., 41.

85. Division of National Affairs, "Proposed Budget, Fiscal Year 1969," June 1968, Budget Papers, Box 7, FF. See also Leonard Covello, *The Social Background of the Italo-American School Child: A Study of the Southern Italian Family Mores and Their Effect on the School Situation in Italy and America* (Leiden: E. J. Brill, 1967), 412; Peter H. Schuck, *Diversity in America: Keeping Government at a Safe Distance* (Cambridge: Belknap Press of Harvard University Press, 2003), 45.

86. Simone Cinotto, "Leonard Covello, the Covello Papers, and the History of Eating Habits among Italian Immigrants in New York," *Journal of American History* 91, no. 2 (2004): 503–507. On Covello's similar work with Puerto Rican students, see Madeleine

E. López, "Investigating the Investigators: An Analysis of *The Puerto Rican Study*," *Centro Journal* 19, no. 2 (2007): 67-69.

87. *Toward Humanistic Education*, 66-121.

88. Fantini et al., 81. See also Covello, 419.

89. Institute for Community Studies, "Educational Achievement," 4. Emphasis added.

90. "Local District Boundaries," 9. Emphasis added.

91. Institute for Community Studies, "Educational Achievement," 10.

92. Fantini et al., 184-185.

93. Magat, "Propositions on Quality Education," 5.

94. Fantini et al., 216-217.

95. Gittell, "A Typology of Power," 25; "Notes For Messrs. Magat and Fantini," 2 October 1967, MAP, Box 14567, FF.

96. "Panel Agenda."

97. Magat, "Propositions," 9-10.

98. Fantini et al., 96.

99. Institute for Community Studies, "Educational Achievement," 6-7.

100. Magat, "Propositions," 3. See also Gittell, "A Typology of Power," 26-27.

101. Mayor's Advisory Panel, 3.

102. Milton Galamison, "Period of the Pendulum," Milton A. Galamison Papers, Box 11, Schomburg Center for Research in Black Culture, 32.

103. Ibid., 41.

104. Ibid., 24.

105. Preston R. Wilcox, "A Proposal for the I.S. 201 Education Committee," n.d., MAP, Box 14566, 13.

106. African-American Teachers Association, "Mandate for Community Action in School Crisis," 67-426, R-2372, FF.

107. Milton A. Galamison, "Colloquy," Galamison Papers, Box 13.

108. Milton Galamison, "View from the Eleventh Floor," Galamison Papers, Box 11, 34.

109. Larry to Hilary and Sheila, 15 July 1967, MAP, Box 14566.

110. Nikhil Pal Singh, *Black Is a Country: Race and the Unfinished Struggle for Democracy* (Cambridge: Harvard University Press, 2004), 134-211. See also Biondi, 250-287; *Freedom North: Black Freedom Struggles Outside the South, 1940-1980*, ed. Jeanne Theoharis, Komozi Woodard, and Matthew Countryman (New York: Palgrave Macmillan, 2003); Robert Self, *American Babylon: Race and the Struggle for Postwar Oakland* (Princeton: Princeton University Press, 2003), 177-255.

111. Taylor, 99. For a discussion of this dynamic, see Daniel H. Perlstein, *Justice, Justice: School Politics and the Eclipse of Liberalism* (New York: Peter Lang, 2004), 97-113.

112. Galamison, "Period of the Pendulum," 11. See also Perlstein, 109-111; Waller, 39-41.

113. Galamison, "Period of the Pendulum," 1. On Galamison's relationship with Malcolm X, see also Taylor, 119, 158-160.

114. Galamison, "Period of the Pendulum," 13.

115. Alice O'Connor, *Poverty Knowledge: Social Science, Social Policy, and the Poor in Twentieth-Century U.S. History* (Princeton: Princeton University Press, 2001), 99–136.

116. David Spencer and Bernadine Klein, "I.S. 201: Community Action for City Schools," n.d., 67–431, R-1863, FF.

117. Wilcox, "A Proposal for the I.S. 201 Education Committee."

118. East Harlem MEND, "A Proposal for an East Harlem Community School," 67–431, R-1863, FF.

119. Wilcox, "A Proposal for the I.S. 201 Education Committee."

120. East Harlem MEND.

121. Preston R. Wilcox, "A Proposal for an IS 201 Complex Community Education Center," 28 February 1968, Preston Wilcox Papers, Box 1, Schomburg Center for Research in Black Culture..

122. Wilcox, "A Proposal for the I.S. 201 Education Committee." Emphasis in original.

123. Preston R. Wilcox, "A Summary Statement: To Be Black and to Be Successful," 21 February 1966, MAP, Box 14567.

124. East Harlem MEND.

125. Ibid.

126. Waller, 39.

127. See, for example, Preston Wilcox, "The School and the Community," MAP, Box 14567.

128. Charles Cobb quoted in Charles M. Payne, *I've Got the Light of Freedom: The Organizing Tradition and the Mississippi Freedom Struggle* (Berkeley: University of California Press, 1995), 302.

129. Black school activists around the country set up similar initiatives as part of their protests against the public schools. See Thomas J. Sugrue, *Sweet Land of Liberty: The Forgotten Struggle for Civil Rights in the North* (New York: Random House, 2008), 166, 297.

130. "Position Statement: Five State Organizing Committee for Community Control," 25 January 1968, 67–426, R-2372, FF. See also Wilcox, "The School and the Community"; Rhody McCoy to Mr. Fantini, 17 August 1967, 67–426, R-2372, FF.

131. Wilcox, "Proposal for an IS 201 Complex Community Education Center."

132. Michael Harrington quoted in Preston Wilcox, "Selected Principles for Involving the Poor," 25 May 1965, Preston Wilcox Papers, Box 1.

133. Wilcox, "The School and the Community." Daryl Michael Scott points out that such separatist and therapeutic notions of self-help were a key aspect of black power rhetoric. Scott, 164–166.

134. "Community Seminars in Education: A Proposal for a Leadership and Training Program for Parents and Residents of the Harlem–East Harlem Community," 67–431, R-1863, FF.

135. Preston Wilcox, "The Church and the War on Poverty," Preston Wilcox Papers, Box 1.

136. Preston Wilcox, "The 'Educated' and the 'Unlettered,'" ca. 7 April 1967, Preston Wilcox Papers, Box 1.

137. East Harlem MEND.

138. Perlstein, 132.

139. Wilcox, "The School and the Community"; "Training Opportunities for Board Members," 67-431, R-1863, FF.

140. Preston Wilcox, "Toward New Ideas in Urban Organizing: Promoting the Black Agenda," 15 November 1967, Preston Wilcox Papers, Box 1.

141. Preston Wilcox, "Behaving Black," 10 December 1967, Preston Wilcox Papers, Box 1.

142. Preston Wilcox, "Expanding Opportunities for Disadvantaged Youth?" 19 March 1965, MAP, Box 14567.

143. Wilcox, "Behaving Black."

144. Wilcox, "A Proposal for the I.S. 201 Education Committee."

145. Wilcox, "Proposal for an IS 201 Complex Community Education Center."

146. Edward Daniels to Gentlemen, 13 December 1966, MAP, Box 14566.

147. East Harlem MEND.

148. Wilcox, "Expanding Opportunities."

Chapter 4

1. Charles E. Wilson to Mario Fantini, 14 March 1968, 67-431, R-1863, Ford Foundation Archives (FF), Rockefeller Archives Center.

2. I.S. 201 Governing Board, "Presentation to the Ford Foundation," January 1968, R-1863, 67-431, FF; David Spencer to John Fischer, 11 August 1967, R-1863, 67-431, FF.

3. Jerald Podair, *The Strike That Changed New York: Blacks, Whites, and the Ocean Hill-Brownsville Crisis* (New Haven: Yale University Press, 2002); Vincent J. Cannato, *The Ungovernable City: John Lindsay and His Struggle to Save New York* (New York: Basic Books, 2001) 267-373; Diane Ravitch, *The Great School Wars: A History of the New York Public Schools* (New York: Basic Books, 1974), 251-398.

4. Leonard Buder, "Bundy Panel Asks Community Rule for City Schools," *New York Times (NYT)*, 8 November 1967; Division of National Affairs, "'And Then, There Were the Children . . .' An Assessment of Efforts to Test Decentralization in New York City's Public School System," May 1969, Report 002149, FF, 12. Pantoja and Washington were rarely mentioned in the MAP records, except when they were present for meetings for their respective communities. See, for example, "Summary of Meeting with Puerto Rican Leaders," 29 September 1967, Mayor's Advisory Panel on the Decentralization of the New York City Schools (MAP), Box 14567, FF. See also Richard Magat interviewed by Charles T. Morrissey and Ronald J. Grele, 24 January 1974, Ford Foundation Oral History Project, FF, 81.

5. V. Chen, "Draft Preface," 19 July 1967, MAP, Box 14566; the Staff to the Panel, 12 July 1967, MAP, Box 14568.

6. Magat interview, 90.

7. Sheila Gordon to Mario Fantini, 4 July 1967, MAP, Box 14568. On staff responsibilities and deadlines, see Panel on School Decentralization, "Agenda for Gracie Mansion Meeting," [May 1967], MAP, Box 14567.

8. Magat interview, 84.

9. Sheila Gordon to Lew Feldstein, 17 October 1967, MAP, Box 14568.

10. Podair, 50.

11. "Appendix D," MAP, Box 14567; the Staff to the Panel, 12 July 1967, MAP, Box 14568.

12. See, for example, H. Sims, "Suggestions Coming from the Panel in Reaction to the Materials Presented by the Staff," 14 June 1967, MAP, Box 14568; Harry N. Rivlin to Mario D. Fantini, 22 June 1967, MAP, Box 14567; S[heila] C. G[ordon], "School Decentralization: Positions and Concerns of Key Interest Groups—A Tentative Analysis," MAP, Box 14568; J. G. Simon to Mr. Magat, ca. 22 August 1967, MAP, Box 14566; "Meeting of Local School Boards and the Board of Education," 30 October 1967, MAP, Box 14566.

13. F. Champion Ward to McGeorge Bundy, 26 June 1967, 67-426, R-2372, FF.

14. Ibid.

15. "Addendum," MAP, Box 14568.

16. Division of National Affairs, 18-19; Podair, 71-79.

17. Division of National Affairs, 16-18.

18. Ward to Bundy, 26 June 1967.

19. Ibid.

20. Division of National Affairs, 27; "General Background," MAP, Box 14568, 16-17.

21. Richard Magat to Mr. Bundy, 7 September 1967, MAP, Box 14567.

22. "Proposal for Academic Excellence: Community and Teachers Assume Responsibility for the Education of the Ghetto Child," 26 April 1967, 67-431, R-1863, FF; "A Plan for an Experimental School District (in District 17, Brooklyn): An Ocean Hill–Brownsville Experiment," ca. 27 June 1967, 67-426, R-2372, FF; Two Bridges Neighborhood Council, "The Quest for a Child-Centered School System," 4 May 1967, MAP, Box 14567.

23. Mario D. Fantini to IR-4 Files, 12 February 1971, 67-431, R-1863, FF. See also Ravitch, 313.

24. Podair, 81.

25. "Proposal for Academic Excellence."

26. Bernard E. Donovan to Mario Fantini, 19 June 1967, 67-427, R-2368, FF.

27. "General Background," 18-19; Division of National Affairs, 25; Wendell Pritchett, *Brownsville, Brooklyn: Blacks, Jews and the Changing Face of the Ghetto* (Chicago: University of Chicago Press, 2002), 229-30; "A Plan for an Experimental School District."

28. "News from the Ford Foundation," 6 July 1967, 67-431, R-1863, FF.

29. Ward to Bundy, 26 June 1967.

30. Advisory and Evaluation Committee on Decentralization to the Board of Edu-

cation of the City of New York, "An Evaluative Study of the Process of School Decentralization in New York City," 30 July 1968, MAP, Box 14568, 68–81.

31. Division of National Affairs, 20.

32. Advisory and Evaluation Committee on Decentralization, 73.

33. Division of National Affairs, 27.

34. Ibid., 127.

35. Ibid., 22, 69–73, 84–85, 122–123; R[hody] A. McCoy to Mario Fantini, 22 August 1967, 67-426, R-2372, FF; "General Background," 19–20, 23; "Statistics on Ocean-Hill Canvassers," MAP, Box 14568; "Meeting with the Ford Foundation," 26 January 1968, 67-427, R-2368, FF; Advisory and Evaluation Committee on Decentralization, 79, 81.

36. "General Background," 24. See also Advisory and Evaluation Committee on Decentralization, 105–106; Marilyn Gittell to Mitchell Sviridoff, 7 March 1968, MAP, Box 14568.

37. Siobhan Oppenheimer to McGeorge Bundy, 2 September 1969, MAP, Box 14568.

38. "General Background," 23.

39. Daniel H. Perlstein, *Justice, Justice: School Politics and the Eclipse of Liberalism* (New York: Peter Lang, 2004), 131.

40. New York City People's Board of Education, "Brownsville Public Hearing," 3 January 1967, MAP, Box 14566.

41. Division of National Affairs, 73.

42. I.S. 201 Demonstration School, "Installation of Governing Board: 'An Educational Evening,'" 15 February 1968, 67-431, R-1863, FF.

43. Podair, 71–102.

44. C. Herman Oliver to Bernard Donovan, 1 September 1967, 67-426, R-2372, FF; "Governing Board: I.S. 201 Complex," 15 January 1970, 67-431, R-1863, FF. For Ferguson's political biography, see Thomas Sugrue, *Sweet Land of Liberty: The Forgotten Struggle for Civil Rights in the North* (New York: Random House, 2008), 313–314, 323, 351–353.

45. Cannato, 285–286; Podair, 143; Milton Galamison, "A Grand and Awful Time," Milton A. Galamison Papers, Box 11, Schomburg Center for Research in Black Culture, 17–18.

46. Sara Slack, "The Inside Story of the Malcolm X IS 201 Memorial," *New York Amsterdam News*, 2 March 1968.

47. New York Commission on Human Rights, "Report on Three Demonstration Projects in the City Schools," February–March 1968, MAP, Box 14568, 10–11.

48. IS 201 Governing Board, "Response to WINS Editorial of February 22, 1968," 29 February 1968, 67-431, R-1863, FF; Cannato, 285–287.

49. "Meeting with the Ford Foundation."

50. IS 201 Governing Board, "Response to WINS Editorial."

51. John Powis to Mario Fantini, 30 September 1967, 67-426, R-2372, FF.

52. I.S. 201 Planning Board, "A Brief Summary of the I.S. 201 Story," 67-431, R-1863, FF; "Meeting with the Ford Foundation."

53. Rhody A. McCoy to Mario Fantini, 22 September 1967, 67-426, R-2372, FF.

54. I.S. 201 Governing Board, "Presentation to the Ford Foundation."

55. Division of National Affairs, 133.

56. Ocean Hill–Brownsville Demonstration School District, "What Could Be—What the Truth Really Is! Telling It the Way It Is!" ca. March 1968, MAP, Box 14568.

57. I.S. 201 Governing Board, "Presentation to the Ford Foundation."

58. Rev. John Powis to Douglas Pugh, 6 November 1967, 67-426, R-2372, FF.

59. F. Champion Ward to McGeorge Bundy, 8 November 1967, 67-427, R-2368, FF.

60. "On Friday, February 16," 67-431, R-1863, FF.

61. "News from the Ford Foundation," 29 February 1968, 67-431, R-1863, FF.

62. "On Friday, February 16."

63. Sheila Gordon to Mike Sviridoff, 18 March 1968, MAP, Box 14568.

64. Mitchell Sviridoff and F. Champion Ward to McGeorge Bundy, 24 April 1968, 68-472, R-1094, FF.

65. Ibid.

66. Edward J. Meade, Jr., to Mario D. Fantini, 14 September 1967, 68-212, R-1248, FF.

67. Ed[ward J. Meade, Jr.,] to Mr. Fantini, 9 October 1967, 68-212, R-1248, FF. See also Milton A. Galamison to Mario Fantini, 3 August 1967, 68-212, R-1248, FF.

68. Edward J. Meade, Jr., to Mario D. Fantini, 16 October 1967, 68-212, R-1248, FF.

69. "News from the Ford Foundation," 30 May 1968, MAP, Box 14568.

70. Division of National Affairs, 58–61.

71. Sviridoff and Ward to Bundy.

72. Institute for Community Studies, "A Proposal for Facilitating Community Involvement in Education," 10 April 1968, 68-472, R-1094, FF; Sviridoff and Ward to Bundy.

73. Sviridoff and Ward to Bundy.

74. McGeorge Bundy quoted in "News from the Ford Foundation," 30 May 1968.

75. Gittell outlines her theory in "A Typology of Power for Measuring Social Change," *American Behavioral Scientist* 9, no. 8 (1966): 23–28.

76. Division of National Affairs, 61–62, 71–72, 75, 114–116, 118.

77. Marilyn Gittell to Mitchell Sviridoff, 29 June 1968, MAP, Box 14568.

78. Division of National Affairs, 133.

79. Ibid., 132. See also Marilyn Gittell to Mitchell Sviridoff, 20 May 1968, MAP, Box 14568.

80. Division of National Affairs, 59–60, 133, 188, 196.

81. Marilyn Gittell to Mitchell Sviridoff, 20 September 1968, MAP, Box 14568. See also Marilyn Gittell to Mitchell Sviridoff, 22 April 1968, MAP, Box 14568.

82. Gittell to Sviridoff, 29 June 1968.

83. Marilyn Gittell to Mitchell Sviridoff, 3 December 1968, MAP, Box 14568.

84. Sviridoff and Ward to Bundy.

85. Division of National Affairs, 116. See also 61–62, 71–72, 75, 114–116, 118; Gittell to Sviridoff, 29 June 1968.

86. Sims, "Suggestions Coming from the Panel"; "Discussion Paper—School District Boundaries," 3 August 1967, MAP, Box 14566; "Local District Boundaries," [ca. 3

August 1967], MAP, Box 14566; H[ilary] S[ims], "Points Which Must Be Made on District Lines," 23 September 1967, MAP, Box 14566.

87. Division of National Affairs, 67-68; Moses T. Y. Lee to Mario Fantini, 18 July 1967, 67-427, R-2368, FF; Pun Sun Soo to Mario Fantini, 12 June 1967, 67-427, R-2368, FF.

88. Division of National Affairs, 68. See also 37, 83.

89. For example, at a consultation meeting with "minority groups" arranged by Kenneth Clark for MAP and its staff, African Americans were the only "minority" represented. "Summary of Meeting with Minority Groups," 20 September 1967, MAP, Box 14567.

90. See, for example, "School Reform," *El Diario La Prensa*, 21 November 1967; "Summary of Meeting with Puerto Rican Leaders," 29 September 1967, MAP, Box 14567.

91. "General Background," 34.

92. Mario D. Fantini to Mitchell Sviridoff, 1 February 1968, 67-427, R-2368, FF.

93. Isaura Santiago Santiago, "*Aspira v. Board of Education* Revisited," *American Journal of Education* 95, no. 1 (1986): 157-161. Mark Brilliant has shown how issues of bilingual education for Chinese- and Spanish-speaking students prevented a coalition with desegregation-minded black civil rights reformers in California in the 1960s and 1970s. See *The Color of America Has Changed: How Racial Diversity Shaped Civil Rights Reform in California, 1941-1978* (New York: Oxford University Press, 2010), 227-256.

94. Division of National Affairs, 37.

95. Ibid., 68.

96. "Local District Boundaries."

97. Richard Magat interview, 78; Cannato, 277.

98. Carmen McIntyre to Bernard Donovan, 14 June 1967, MAP, Box 14567; Lois Winkler to McGeorge Bundy, 19 May 1968, 67-426, R-2372, FF.

99. "West Side Committee for Decentralization," 21 June 1967, MAP, Box 14567.

100. Joseph Featherstone, "Ocean Hill Is Alive, and, Well . . ." *New Republic*, 19 April 1969, 22.

101. Advisory and Evaluation Committee on Decentralization," 110,112; Podair, 18.

102. SCOPE, "Grant Proposal," 24 February 1969, 68-212, R-1248, FF.

103. "Project Learn at PS 144," *News from Ocean Hill Brownsville* [undated, unpaginated clipping], Box 1, Andrew Donaldson Collection, Schomburg Center for Research in Black Culture.

104. Advisory and Evaluation Committee on Decentralization, 110-133; Division of National Affairs, 177-178, 199; Charles E. Wilson, "Interim Report for the I.S. 201 Complex Demonstration District 33: The Beginnings of a Miracle," August 1969, 67-431, R-1863, FF, 49.

105. Division of National Affairs, 83-85, 138-139, 141-143, 177-178.

106. Richard Reeves, "Bundy Condemns Influence Charges by Shanker," *NYT*, 13 November 1968.

107. Leroy F. Aarons, "Ford Foundation Attacked in N.Y. Strike," *Washington Post*, 15 November 1968.

108. M. A. Farber, "Ford Fund Widens Reform Role and Draws Mounting Criticism," *NYT*, 23 December 1968. On the 1969 tax-code revisions, see Alice O'Connor, "The Politics of Rich and Rich: Postwar Investigations of Foundations and the Rise of the Philanthropic Right," in *American Capitalism: Social Thought and Political Economy in the Twentieth Century*, ed. Nelson Lichtenstein (Philadelphia: University of Pennsylvania Press, 2006), 244–246.

109. Siobhan Oppenheimer to Mr. Dressner, ca. 16 September 1968, MAP, Box 14568.

110. Mario Fantini quoted in *Why Teachers Strike: Teachers' Rights and Community Control*, ed. Melvin Urofsky (New York: Anchor Books, 1970), 104.

111. Galamison, "A Grand and Awful Time," 15–16.

112. Galamison quoted in Perlstein, 132–133.

113. McGeorge Bundy to Donald Joseph Ryan, 21 November 1968, 67-426, R-2372, FF.

114. Fred M. Hechinger, "Bundy Fears 'Sea' of School Hatred," *NYT*, 27 October 1968.

115. Ibid.

116. "School Decentralization," March 1969, MAP, Box 14568.

117. Fantini quoted in *Why Teachers Strike*, 105.

Chapter 5

1. Douglas Turner Ward, "American Theater: For Whites Only?" *New York Times* (*NYT*), 14 August 1966.

2. Ibid.

3. For a comprehensive survey of the Black Arts movement, its ideologies, and origins, see James Smethurst, *The Black Arts Movement: Literary Nationalism in the 1960s and 1970s* (Chapel Hill: University of North Carolina Press, 2005). See also the white reaction to Amiri Baraka's performance offerings at the I.S. 201 memorial to Malcolm X in Chapter 4.

4. W. McNeil Lowry to Henry T. Heald, 22 April 1964, 64-287, R-0948, Ford Foundation Archives (FF), Rockefeller Archives Center (RAC).

5. "Interviews: N[orman] L[loyd], Robert Macbeth," 10 November 1967, Rockefeller Foundation Papers (RF), Box 1335 (A77), RAC; Woodie King, Jr., "Black Theatre: Present Condition," *The Drama Review* 12, no. 4 (Summer 1968): 122; Arthur Sainer, "A New Look at the New Lafayette," *Village Voice*, 1 April 1971; Joel Dreyfuss, "'River Niger': Joy and Relief," *Washington Post*, 18 November 1973.

6. Humanities and the Arts, "Program Budget Request, Fiscal Year 1968," June 1967, Budget Papers, Box 6, FF, 15.

7. Joseph Wesley Zeigler, *Regional Theatre: The Revolutionary Stage* (Minneapolis: University of Minnesota Press, 1973), 63–65, 180–185; Paul J. DiMaggio, "Support for the Arts from Independent Foundations," in *Nonprofit Enterprise in the Arts: Studies in Mission and Constraint*, ed. Paul J. DiMaggio (New York: Oxford University Press,

1986), 113–119; Gary O. Larson, *The Reluctant Patron: The United States Government and the Arts, 1943–1965* (Philadelphia: University of Pennsylvania Press, 1983), 230; Richard Magat, *The Ford Foundation at Work: Philanthropic Choices, Methods and Styles* (New York: Plenum Press, 1979), 130; *Theatre Reawakening: A Report on Ford Foundation Assistance to American Drama* (New York: Ford Foundation, 1977), 5–8; Humanities and the Arts, "Proposed Budget, Fiscal Year 1969," June 1968, Budget Papers, Box 7, FF, 11; Humanities and the Arts, "Program Budget Request, Fiscal Year 1968," 10–12; Humanities and the Arts, "Proposed Budget: Fiscal Year 1970," June 1969, Budget Papers, Box 7, FF, 7.

8. The Ford Foundation, *Directives and Terms of Reference for the 1960s* (New York: Ford Foundation, June 1962), 15.

9. Jack Anderson, "W. McNeil Lowry Is Dead; Patron of the Arts Was 80," *NYT*, 7 June 1993.

10. *Theater Reawakening*, 7, 3.

11. Ibid., 5; Sheila McNerney Anderson, "The Founding of Theater Arts Philanthropy in America: W. McNeil Lowry and the Ford Foundation, 1957–1965," in *Angels in the American Theater: Patrons, Patronage, and Philanthropy*, ed. Robert A. Schanke (Carbondale: Southern Illinois University Press, 2007), 180–181, 184; Sheila Rebecca McNerney, "Institutionalizing the American Theatre: The Ford Foundation and the Resident Professional Theatre, 1957–1965" (Ph.D. dissertation, University of Washington, 1999), 75.

12. "The Foundation and the Arts: The Decade of the Seventies," Office of the President, Records of McGeorge Bundy, Series 1, Box 2, FF.

13. Ibid.

14. Humanities and the Arts was the only Foundation division not to propose a "minority" program in 1966 in its first budget request after Bundy took the Foundation's helm, and its officers later expressed doubts to Bundy about the value of this priority for Ford. Humanities and the Arts, "Planning Budget Request for Fiscal 1967–1968–1969," June 1966, Box 6, Budget Papers, FF; W. McNeil Lowry to McGeorge Bundy, 23 January 1970, Records of McGeorge Bundy, 2, Box 14, FF; Marcia Thompson to McGeorge Bundy, 26 January 1970, Records of McGeorge Bundy, Series 2, Box 14, FF; Richard C. Sheldon to McGeorge Bundy, 22 January 1970, Records of McGeorge Bundy, Series 2, Box 14, FF.

15. "The Arts as Social Development of Minorities," Records of McGeorge Bundy, Series 2, Box 14, FF. In Dallas, the Foundation supported the Dallas Theater Center (Chicano and black), and in Los Angeles it funded the East-West Players (Asian American) and the Inner City Cultural Center (Native American and Chicano). It only worked with these groups after founding or funding exclusively black endeavors, and it provided funding at much smaller amounts than it had for the African American companies.

16. National Affairs, "Proposed Budget: Fiscal Year 1970," 1 June 1968, Budget Papers, Box 8, FF.

17. Ibid. See also W. McNeil Lowry to McGeorge Bundy, 27 February 1967, 67-194, R-1426, FF.

18. McNerney, "Institutionalizing the American Theatre," 147.

19. W. McNeil Lowry to Files, 1 November 1966, 67-194, R-1426, FF.

20. McNerney, "Institutionalizing the American Theatre," 147.

21. John McCarten, "Burdensome Baggage," *New Yorker*, 25 December 1965, 50.

22. Douglas Turner Ward, Robert Hooks, and Gerald S. Krone, "Proposal for the Establishment of the Negro Ensemble Company," 13 February 1967, 67-194, R-1426, FF.

23. Ibid.

24. Peter Bailey, "Is the Negro Ensemble Company Really Black Theatre?" *Negro Digest*, April 1968, 16–19.

25. Clayton Riley, "We Will Not Be a New Form of White Art in Black Face," *NYT*, 14 June 1970.

26. W. McNeil Lowry to McGeorge Bundy, 18 February 1970, 67-194, R-1426, Section 1, FF.

27. Samuel A. Hay, *African American Theatre: An Historical and Critical Analysis* (New York: Cambridge University Press, 1994), 161–162; Douglas Turner Ward, "Lorraine Hansberry and the Passion of Walter Lee," *Freedomways* 19, no. 4 (1979): 223–224; Lorraine Hansberry, "Why the Drum-Beaters Fear Roosevelt Ward," *Freedom*, August 1951, 2.

28. Smethurst, 107, 118; Kevin Gaines, "E. Franklin Frazier's Revenge: Anticolonialism, Nonalignment, and Black Intellectuals' Critiques of Western Culture," *American Literary History* 17, no. 3 (2005): 506–529; Rebeccah Welch, "Spokesman of the Oppressed? Lorraine Hansberry at Work: The Challenge of Radical Politics in the Postwar Era," *Souls* 9, no. 4 (2007): 302–319.

29. Jerry Tallmer, "Black Power: 6. Where Do We Go from Here?" *New York Post*, 24 June 1967.

30. "What We're About . . . An Interview with Artistic Director Douglas Turner Ward," *Playbill*, May 1970, 23.

31. Ibid., 23–24.

32. Sam Zolotow, "Ford Fund Aids Negro Theatre," *NYT*, 15 May 1967.

33. "What We're About," 17; Douglas Turner Ward interviewed by Roscoe Lee Browne, 6 February 1972, Hatch-Billops Collection.

34. "What We're About," 17.

35. *Creating a National Treasure of Black Theatre: The Negro Ensemble Company* (New York: NEC, 1978), Negro Ensemble Company Papers (NEC), Box 7, Schomburg Center for Research in Black Culture.

36. Steve Carter interviewed by Pat Singleton, 20 August 1973, Hatch-Billops Collection, Schomburg Center for Research in Black Culture.

37. Hattie Winston quoted in Wendell Brock, "Denzel Was Here: Negro Ensemble Company Revolutionized U.S. Theatre," *Atlanta Journal-Constitution*, 20 July 2003.

38. Patricia Bosworth, "We Start Out Loving Everybody," *NYT*, 31 December 1972.

39. Judi Ann Mason, "Grambling Coed Named Top Student," *Shreveport Journal*, 8 May 1976.

40. Dan Sullivan, "What's a Nice Black Playwright Doing in a Place Like This?" *NYT*, 5 January 1975; "Negro Ensemble Company Presents *Ceremonies in Dark Old Men*," NEC, Box 24.

41. Milton Adams, "Is Negro Ensemble Co. Ready for Broadway?" *New York Post*, 3 January 1973.

42. Clive Barnes, "Stage: 'The Brownsville Raid,'" *NYT*, 6 December 1976.

43. Jerry Tallmer, "Upstream to the River Niger," *New York Post*, 28 April 1973; Janice C. Simpson, "A Black Theatre Company Keeps the Footlights Burning," *Wall Street Journal*, 26 October 1979; Ines Bello Paris to Samuel Linder, 21 January 1972, NEC, Box 1; Discount Tix [*sic*] Distribution," 31 July [1974], NEC, Box 50; "Theatre Party Infor [*sic*]," 31 July [1974], NEC, Box 50.

44. W. McNeil Lowry to Douglas Turner Ward, 29 June 1971, 67-194, R-1426, FF.

45. W. McNeil Lowry to Files, 1 November 1966.

46. Ibid.; Ford Foundation, "Proposed Revisions in 1975 Budget and Preliminary Presentations of 2-Year Program Budgets for FY 1976 and 1977," March 1975, Budget Papers, Box 10, FF, 40; W. McNeil Lowry to McGeorge Bundy, 18 February 1970.

47. W. McNeil Lowry to McGeorge Bundy, 27 February 1967.

48. Ibid.

49. W. McNeil Lowry to McGeorge Bundy, 18 February 1970.

50. H[oward] K[lein] interview with Gerald Krone, 20 November 1969, RF, RG2, General Correspondence 1969, Reel 25.

51. Ford Foundation, "Proposed Budget, Fiscal Years 1974 and 1975," June 1973, Budget Papers, Box 9, FF, 56. See also Ford Foundation, "Proposed Revisions in 1975 Budget," 40.

52. "What We're About," 23.

53. Turner interview.

54. Negro Ensemble Company, "Revised Request for Grant," 14 June 1971, 67-194, R-1426, FF, 1.

55. Carter interview.

56. D. T. Ward, R. Hooks, and G. Krone, "The Negro Ensemble Company Annual Report: July 1, 1969–June 30, 1970," 67-194, R-1426, FF; Douglas Turner Ward to Marcia Thompson, 24 May 1971, 67-194, R-1426, FF.

57. NEC, "Annual Report July 1, 1971–June 30, 1972," 67-194, R-1426, FF.

58. Larry Neal interviewed by Jim Hatch, 24 January 1974, Hatch-Billops Collection.

59. On the "naturalism" of the NEC's offerings, see Mance Williams, *Black Theatre in the 1960s and 1970s: A Historical-Critical Analysis of the Movement* (Westport, Conn.: Greenwood, 1985), 67; "Creating a National Treasure of Black Theatre."

60. Clive Barnes, "Stage: Walker's Strong 'River Niger,'" *NYT*, 28 March 1973.

61. David Richards, "A River of Rocks and Rapids," *Washington Star-News*, undated clipping, 67-194, R-1426, FF.

62. Mel Gussow quoted in "*The River Niger* Is Moving to Broadway," Box 26, NEC; Roger Dettmer, "'The River Niger,'" *Chicago Today*, 21 December 1973.

63. Douglas Turner Ward to W. McNeil Lowry, 21 July 1972, 67-194, R-1426, FF.

64. Adams. See also W. McNeil Lowry to McGeorge Bundy, 27 February 1967.

65. Judi Ann Mason, "Livin' Fat" [1976,] NEC, Box 58. On Lee's success, see Douglas S. Cramer to Gerald S. Krone, 15 October 1975, NEC, Box 69.

66. Mason, "Livin' Fat."

67. Harry Haun, "Everyone's 'Breeze,'" *Daily News*, 15 July 1975; Harry Harris, "'Breeze' May Start Series about Blacks," *Philadelphia Inquirer*, 28 January 1976.

68. Mason, "Livin' Fat."

69. Walter Kerr quoted in Haun. See also William Glover, "Theatre's New 'Breeze' Light," *New Orleans Times-Picayune*, 9 March 1975.

70. NEC, "Annual Report July 1 1972–June 30, 1973," 67-194, R-1426, FF.

71. Robert Macbeth to W. McNeil Lowry, 18 October 1966, 67-472, R-1866, FF; "Excerpt from BRC Diary with Thomas Dent," 3 November 1966, RF, Box 1335 (A77).

72. Robert Macbeth to W. McNeil Lowry, 27 April 1967, 67-472, R-1866, FF.

73. Robert Macbeth to W. McNeil Lowry, ca. 26 May 1967, 67-472, R-1866, FF.

74. Iris Siff to W. McNeil Lowry, 6 December 1967, 67-472, R-1866, FF; Michael Mabry to Marcia Thompson, 20 December 1965, 67-472, R-1866, FF; "Excerpt from BRC Diary with Thomas Dent."

75. NLT, "The 'Ghetto' Theatre Project" [ca. 1966], RF, Box 1335 (A77).

76. Robert Macbeth to W. McNeil Lowry, 18 October 1966.

77. NLT, "The 'Ghetto' Theatre Project."

78. Ibid.

79. NLT, "Harlem's Theatre, 1967–1968, Inaugural Season," ca. 1967, 67-472, R-1866, FF.

80. Robert Macbeth to W. McNeil Lowry, 18 October 1966.

81. *Black Theatre: The Making of a Movement*, directed by Woodie King, Jr. (New York: National Black Theatre Touring Circuit, 1978).

82. "The Arts as Social Development of Minorities."

83. W. McNeil Lowry to McGeorge Bundy, 11 July 1967, 67-472, R-1866, FF.

84. W. McNeil Lowry to McGeorge Bundy, 22 May 1968, 67-472, R-1866, FF; "Excerpt from NL Diary with McNeil Lowry," 18 April 1968, RF, Box 1335 (A77).

85. W. McNeil Lowry to Files, 4 December 1967, 67-472, R-1866, FF.

86. W. McNeil Lowry to McGeorge Bundy, 22 May 1968; N[orman] L[loyd] interview with Samuel Wright, 4 October 1968, RF, Box R1335 (A77); J. Kellum Smith, Jr., to Robert Macbeth, 17 October 1968, RF, Box R1335 (A77).

87. W. McNeil Lowry to McGeorge Bundy, 19 July 1968, 67-194, R-1426, FF.

88. Ford Foundation, *Annual Report* (1968), 29.

89. W. McNeil Lowry to McGeorge Bundy, 9 June 1969, 67-472, R-1866, FF.

90. Robert Macbeth to W. McNeil Lowry, 22 April 1969, 67-472, R-1866, FF; Howard Dressner to Robert Macbeth, 20 June 1969, 67-472, R-1866, FF; "The New Lafayette

Theatre and Workshop, Inc., 'Disqualified' Contributors for the Years Ended May 31, 1969," 67-472, R-1866, FF.

91. Robert Macbeth to Norman Lloyd, 21 October 1969, RF, Box R1335 (A77). See also Mel Gussow, "Bullins, the Artist and the Activist, Speaks," *NYT*, 22 September 1971; Marvin X, "The Black Ritual Theatre," *Black Theatre*, no. 3 (1969): 21–24.

92. "Statement of Reason and Purpose," ca. 27 November 1967, 67-472, R-1866, FF.

93. Roscoe Orman, *Sesame Street Dad: Evolution of an Actor* (Portland, Ore.: Inkwater Press, 2006), 65.

94. NLT, untitled narrative report, 22 April 1969, 67-472, R-1866, FF.

95. "National Black Theatre Workshop Staff Meeting," 3 June 1969, Box 32, Larry Neal Papers, Schomburg Center for Research in Black Culture; Hardy Holzman Pfeiffer Associates, "Report for New York State Council on the Arts: Theatre Feasibility and Design Study #2 Requested by The New Lafayette Theater," 1 April 1968, RF, Box 1335 (A77).

96. Orman, 59. See also Anthony D. Hill, "Rituals at the New Lafayette Theatre," *Black American Literature Forum* 17, no. 1 (Spring 1983): 34.

97. Errol G. Hill and James V. Hatch, *A History of African American Theatre* (New York: Cambridge University Press, 2003), 391.

98. On Bullins, see Samuel A. Hay, *Ed Bullins: A Literary Biography* (Detroit: Wayne State University Press, 1997). See also Marvin X, *Somethin' Proper: The Life and Times of a North American African Poet* (Castro Valley, Calif.: Black Bird Press, 1998).

99. N[orman] L[loyd] to W[illiam] L[loyd] Bradley, 20 June 1967, RF, RG 1.2, Series 200, Box 304.

100. Hill and Hatch, 392–393; Clayton Riley, "Bullins: 'It's Not the Play I Wrote,'" *NYT*, 19 March 1972.

101. X, "The Black Ritual Theatre," 22.

102. Ibid., 24. See also Hay, 217–225; Hill, 31–35.

103. Woodie King, Jr., "Black Theatre: Present Condition," *Drama Review* 12, no. 4 (Summer 1968): 119, footnote 1; "Reaction to *We Righteous Bombers*," *Black Theatre*, no. 4 (1970): 16–25.

104. W[oodie] King, Jr., to HK, GF, K[enneth] W. T[hompson], KW, NL, 26 December 1968, RF, Box R1335 (A77); Hill, 32.

105. Whitman Mayo interviewed by anonymous, 6 June 1973, Hatch-Billops Collection.

106. Richard Wesley interviewed by Ethel Modey, 26 January 1972, Hatch-Billops Collection; The New Lafayette Theatre, "A Narrative Report of Activities 1970–1971," 22 October 1971, 67-472, R-1866, FF.

107. For numerous letters from other American black theaters to the NLT seeking advice or offering support, see section 3 of 67-472, R-1866, FF.

108. W. McNeil Lowry to McGeorge Bundy, 9 June 1969.

109. Ibid.

110. Ibid.

111. Norman Lloyd interview with McNeil Lowry, 2 May 1969, RF, Box R1335 (A77). See also N[orman] L[loyd] interview with Robert Macbeth, 12 May 1969, RF, Box R1335 (A77); H[oward] K[lein], "New Lafayette Theatre—re Continued Support," 21 October 1969, RF, Box R1335; HK to N[orman] L[loyd], HK, GF, WLB, 27 August 1968, RF, Box R1335 (A77).

112. Howard Klein comments on N[orman] L[loyd] interview with Robert Macbeth, 24 September 1970, RF, Box R1335 (A77).

113. Robert Macbeth quoted in X, "The Black Ritual Theatre," 22; Robert Macbeth to Stephen Benedict, 21 October 1969, Rockefeller Brothers Fund Papers, Series 3, Box 363, RAC.

114. Robert Macbeth to Stephen Benedict, 26 October 1970, Rockefeller Brothers Fund Papers, Series 3, Box 363.

115. Paul Carter Harrison, *The Drama of Nommo* (New York: Grove Press, 1972), 191.

116. Hill and Hatch, 394; Hay, 221–225.

117. Larry Neal quoted in Abiodun Jeyifous, "Black Critics on Black Theatre in America," in *The Theatre of Black Americans*, ed. Errol Hill, vol. 2 (Englewood Cliffs, N.J.: Prentice-Hall, 1980), 135.

118. Neal interview.

119. Ed Bullins, "Black Theatre Notes," *Black Theatre*, no. 1 (1968): 4–7. See also "The Electronic Nigger Meets the Gold Dust Twins: Clifford Mason Talks with Robert Macbeth and Ed Bullins," *Black Theatre*, no. 1 (1968); 24–29; Kushauri Kupa, "A Review of *The Reckoning* by Douglas Turner Ward," *Black Theatre*, no. 4 (1969).

120. Lisbeth Grant, "The New Lafayette Theatre: Anatomy of a Community Art Institution," *Drama Review* (December 1972): 55; Howard Klein interview with Hazel Bryant, 30 October 1970, 24 September 1970, RF, Box R1335 (A77); Mayo interview; Gussow, "Bullins, the Artist and the Activist."

121. Robert Macbeth to W. McNeil Lowry, 3 February 1971, 67-472, R-1866, FF, emphasis in the original.

122. W. McNeil Lowry to Robert Macbeth, 19 February 1971, 67-472, R-1866, FF.

123. W. McNeil Lowry to Files, 10 March 1972, 67-472, R-1866, FF; W. McNeil Lowry to McGeorge Bundy, 20 June 1972.

124. Henry Louis Gates, Jr., "The Chitlin Circuit," *New Yorker*, 3 February 1997, 48.

125. Wesley interview.

126. Eric Bentley to the Editor, *NYT*, 30 April 1972. See also Eric Bentley, "Must I Side with Black or Whites," *NYT*, 23 January 1972.

127. In particular, the Foundation became a key promoter of women's rights, and a woman, Susan Berresford, followed Franklin Thomas as the Foundation's president. On the Foundation's feminism, see Susan M. Hartmann, *The Other Feminists: Activists in the Liberal Establishment* (New Haven, Conn.: Yale University Press, 1998), 132–175.

128. On Ed Bullins's academic career, see http://www.dac.neu.edu/theatre/faculty/ed.html, accessed 23 June 2011. On Richard Wesley's post-NLT career, see http://ddw.

tisch.nyu.edu/object/WesleyR.html, accessed 23 June 2011. On OyamO's academic career, see http://www.music.umich.edu/faculty_staff/bio.php?u=oyamo, accessed 23 June 2011.

129. W. McNeil Lowry to Clayton Riley, 6 July 1970, R-1426, 67-194, FF.

Chapter 6

1. "What the Ford Foundation Omitted," *New York Times* (*NYT*), 31 January 1979.

2. Paul Ylvisaker interviewed by Charles T. Morrissey, 27 September 1973, Ford Foundation Oral History Project, Ford Foundation Archives (FF), Rockefeller Archive Center, 28.

3. Ford Foundation, *Community Development Corporations: A Strategy for Depressed Urban and Rural Areas* (New York: Ford Foundation, 1973), 5.

4. Matthew J. Countryman, *Up South: Civil Rights and Black Power in Philadelphia* (Philadelphia: University of Pennsylvania Press), 83–120; Guian McKee, *The Problem of Jobs: Liberalism, Race, and Deindustrialization in Philadelphia* (Chicago: University of Chicago Press, 2008), 113–210; Michael J. Murphy, "Developing Communities: The UAW and Community Unions in Los Angeles, 1965–1974," *Labor: Studies in Working-Class History of the Americas* 6, no. 4 (2010): 19–39; Kevin Boyle, *The UAW and the Heyday of American Liberalism, 1945–1968* (Ithaca, N.Y.: Cornell University Press, 1995), 161–184, 190–193, 213–216; Robert Bauman, "The Black Power and Chicano Movements in the Poverty Wars in Los Angeles," *Journal of Urban History* 33, no. 2 (2007): 277–295; John Hall Fish, *Black Power/White Control: The Struggle of the Woodlawn Organization in Chicago* (Princeton: Princeton University Press, 1973); Paul Delaney, "In One Part of Chicago, Many Feel Decay Has Ended," *NYT*, 8 March 1975.

5. McKee, 166–173; Countryman, 115–116; Boyle, 214; Gareth Davies, *From Opportunity to Entitlement: The Transformation and Decline of Great Society Liberalism* (Lawrence: University of Kansas Press, 1996), 162–169; Nicholas Lemann, *The Promised Land: The Great Black Migration and How It Changed America* (New York: Vintage, 1992), 194–201.

6. Robert F. Kennedy, *To Seek a Newer World* (New York: Doubleday, 1967), 37, 32, 45, 42, 39.

7. Kennedy, 50. On the self-help appeal of the CDC model, see McKee, 207.

8. On the Ribicoff hearings and policy alternatives to the Great Society, see Davies, 135–156.

9. R. B. Goldmann, "Performance in Black and White: An Appraisal of the Development and Record of the Bedford-Stuyvesant Restoration and Development and Services Corporations," February 1969, 14–16, 22–24, Report no. 001362, FF; Evan Thomas, *Robert Kennedy: His Life* (New York: Touchstone, 2000), 324–326.

10. Thomas, 326.

11. John R. Coleman to McGeorge Bundy, 16 September 1966, Office of the Presi-

dent, Records of McGeorge Bundy, Series 2, Box 17, FF. See also McKee, 135–136; Murphy, 28–29.

12. Goldmann, 16–19; "Economic Development and Administration Planning Budget Request for Fiscal 1967-1968-1969," June 1966, Budget Papers, Box 6, FF; "Public Affairs Program Planning Budget Request for Fiscal 1967-1968-1969," June 1966, Budget Papers, Box 6, FF.

13. Kennedy, 32, 33, 50.

14. Paul Ylvisaker, "What Is New in American Philanthropy" [1966], in *Conscience and Community: The Legacy of Paul Ylvisaker*, ed. Virginia Esposito (New York: Peter Lang, 1999), 277–278. See also "Public Affairs Program Planning Budget Request."

15. Ylvisaker, 277.

16. National Affairs (Urban and Metropolitan Development), "Development and Service Corporation: Reconstruction of the Bedford-Stuyvesant Area," 30–31 March 1967, 67-354, R-1856, FF, 30–31.

17. Ylvisaker, 277.

18. Kennedy, 39.

19. National Affairs, "Development and Service Corporation."

20. Edgar Kahn, "Memorandum," n.d., Thomas M. C. Johnston Papers, Box 2, John F. Kennedy Presidential Library (JFK). See also Murphy.

21. Kennedy, 33, 36, 37–38.

22. Joshua B. Freeman, *Working-Class New York: Life and Labor since World War II* (New York: New Press, 2000), 167.

23. Craig Steven Wilder, *A Covenant with Color: Race and Social Power in Brooklyn* (New York: Columbia University Press, 2000), 175–217; Freeman, 167–183; Goldmann, 3–4.

24. Goldmann, 24–26; Thomas, 318–319.

25. Goldmann, 26–27.

26. Ibid., 18–19. See also Thomas, 325.

27. National Affairs, "Development and Service Corporation."

28. Kennedy, 37, 50, 57.

29. Goldmann, 28–29.

30. Ibid., 39–45; Steven V. Roberts, "Brooklyn Ghetto Given $7-Million," *NYT*, 25 June 1967; Louis Winnick to McGeorge Bundy, 20 June 1967, 67-354, R-1856, FF.

31. Franklin A. Thomas interviewed by Roberta W. Greene, 23 March 1972, Robert F. Kennedy Oral History Program (RFK), JFK, 5.

32. Goldmann, 25–26, 29–33; Thomas Jones interviewed by Roberta W. Greene, 26 November 1971, RFK, 29–34; Thomas interview, 23 March 1972, 1–6.

33. "Brooklyn Groups Charge Meddling," *NYT*, 6 April 1967; Stephen V. Roberts, "800 Demand Vote on Renewal Unit," *NYT*, 7 April 1967; Steven V. Roberts, "City Seeking End to Poverty Split," *NYT*, 8 April 1967; Thomas interview, 23 March 1972, 11–13.

34. Goldmann, 34.

35. Roberts, "800 Demand Vote."

36. Goldmann, 8. The Foundation also sought "tough" men to replace women social workers as black-community leaders. See Karen Ferguson, "Organizing the Ghetto: The Ford Foundation, CORE, and White Power in the Black Power Era, 1967–1969," *Journal of Urban History* 34, no. 1 (2007): 90–92.

37. Winnick to Bundy; Thomas, 341. These presumptions demonstrated white liberal stereotypes about how black power operated in local communities. While black power advocates may have espoused a masculinist ideology, in practice black women, including middle-aged ones, were important and accepted local leaders. See, for example, Countryman, 258–294.

38. "Brooklyn Groups Charge Meddling."

39. For Thomas's biography, see Orde Coombs, "Fear and Trembling at the Ford Foundation," *New York Magazine*, 28 September 1981, 33.

40. Roger Wilkins, *A Man's Life: An Autobiography* (New York: Simon and Schuster, 1982), 90–91.

41. Goldmann, 31. See also Jones interview, 20. White media often commented about Thomas's size when listing his qualifications. See, for example, Roberts, "Brooklyn Ghetto Given $7-Million"; Frank E. Emerson, "A Man Who Keeps Faith in Bed-Stuy," *NYT*, 14 May 1972.

42. Goldmann, 31, 36–37, 40, 117–118; Thomas interview, 23 March 1972, 13, 23.

43. Thomas interview, 23 March 1972, 19.

44. Ibid. See also Bauman, 285.

45. Goldmann, 49–50; Franklin A. Thomas interviewed by Roberta W. Greene, 5 May 1972, RFK, 55. For similar community-development efforts, see McKee, Murphy, and Bauman.

46. Goldmann, 51.

47. Thomas interview, 23 March 1972, 19–20; Goldmann, 18.

48. Thomas interview, 3 May 1972, 43.

49. Ibid., 45. For details of the financial arrangement between Restoration and D&S, see Goldmann, 118.

50. Thomas interview, 23 March 1972, 17; Goldmann, 122.

51. "Meet Our Staff," *Bedford-Stuyvesant Restoration Corporation Newsletter*, October 1969, Black Economic Research Center Records (BERC), Box 16, Schomburg Center for Research in Black Culture; "Meet Our Staff," *Bedford-Stuyvesant Restoration Corporation Newsletter*, December 1969, BERC, Box 16; Goldmann, 47–48.

52. Goldmann, 120, 119, 123–124; Thomas interview, 5 May 1972, 47–52.

53. Franklin Thomas to Sol Chafkin, 17 January 1975, 70-115, R-5451, FF.

54. Barry Stein, *Rebuilding Bedford-Stuyvesant: Community Economic Development in the Ghetto* (Cambridge: Center for Community Economic Development, 1975), 5, 6.

55. Ford Foundation, "Discussion Paper: Budget Plans and Problems, FY 1972 and 1973," March 1971, Budget Papers, Box 9, FF, 2.

56. EBS Management Consultants Incorporated, "Evaluation of the Special Impact Project, Bedford-Stuyvesant: First Analytical Report," 14 October 1968, 67-354, R-1856,

FF, 9–11; Thomas interview, 23 March 1972, 13, 21; Stein, 29–31; Goldmann, 45, 126–127. On the black uplift tradition, see Kevin Gaines, *Uplifting the Race: Black Leadership, Politics, and Culture in the Twentieth Century* (Chapel Hill: University of North Carolina Press, 1996).

57. Thomas interview, 5 May 1972, 67.

58. Stein, 8.

59. Thomas interview, 5 May 1972, 37.

60. Ford Foundation, "Discussion Paper," 7.

61. Stein, 33–34.

62. Suleiman Osman, *The Invention of Brownstone Brooklyn: Gentrification and the Search for Authenticity in Postwar New York* (New York: Oxford University Press, 2011), 82–118.

63. "Community Action," Attachment to Thomas E. Cooney to Social Development Staff, 9 April 1971, Report 011496, FF.

64. Alice O'Connor, "The Politics of Rich and Rich: Postwar Investigations of Foundations and the Rise of the Philanthropic Right," in *American Capitalism: Social Thought and Political Economy in the Twentieth Century*, ed. Nelson Lichtenstein (Philadelphia: University of Pennsylvania Press, 2006), 244–246; Olivier Zunz, *Philanthropy in America: A History* (Princeton: Princeton University Press), 220–231.

65. "Anti Poverty Expert: Mitchell Sviridoff," *NYT*, 14 June 1966; Stanley Levey, "Connecticut Labor Unites for Bowles," *NYT*, 14 January 1950; C. Wright Mills, *The New Men of Power: America's Labor Leaders* (New York: Harcourt Brace, 1948).

66. "Anti Poverty Expert."

67. Ronald Sullivan, "Lindsay Selects Poverty Expert," *NYT*, 6 January 1966; John Kifner, "Giant City Agency to Reorganize Aid to Poor Is Urged," *NYT*, 27 June 1966; Goldmann, 33–34.

68. John Kifner, "Sviridoff and the Poor," *NYT*, 17 August 1967.

69. Ford Foundation, *Annual Report* (1969), 22. See also Alice O'Connor, *Poverty Knowledge, Social Science, Social Policy, and the Poor in Twentieth-Century U.S. History* (Princeton: Princeton University Press, 2001), 232–233.

70. Roger W. Wilkins to Mitchell Sviridoff, 14 May 1970, Records of McGeorge Bundy, Series 1, Box 3, FF.

71. Ford Foundation, *Annual Report* (1969), 27; Boyle, 190, 215.

72. Wilkins, 302–303.

73. Ford Foundation, *Community Development Corporations*, 27.

74. "Community Action," 6. This strategy of coalition was a preferred instrument for elite liberals to end urban rioting, resulting in major efforts like the National Urban Coalition (NUC) and its forty-five local subsidiaries nationwide. The NUC was a major Foundation commitment; Ford provided it with almost $3 million, or 40 percent of its start-up costs, and supported a number of local coalitions. Ford Foundation, *Annual Report* (1969), 27–28.

75. "Community Action," 8.

76. Ford Foundation, "Discussion Paper," 8; Ford Foundation, *Community Development Corporations*, 30.

77. Bauman, 290–291; Murphy, 38; John R. Chávez, *Eastside Landmark: A History of the East Los Angeles Community Union, 1968–1993* (Stanford: Stanford University Press, 1998), 79–81; Delaney.

78. Sviridoff quoted in William E. Farrell, "Bedford-Stuyvesant Group to Build $6-Million Center," *NYT*, 29 June 1972.

79. "Community Action"; David B. Carlson and Arabella Martinez, "The Economics of Community Change," 1988, Report 11648, FF, 56, 57, 76.

80. *LISC: A Private Public Venture for Community and Neighborhood Revitalization* (New York: Ford Foundation, 1980).

81. Adolph Reed, "The Black Urban Regime: Structural Origins and Constraints," in *Power, Community and the City: Comparative Urban and Community Research*, ed. Michael Peter Smith (New Brunswick, N.J.: Transaction, 1988), 167.

82. Ford Foundation, "Discussion Paper," 2.

83. Ford Foundation, *Community Development Corporations*, 30.

84. Ibid., 5–6.

85. Ford Foundation, "Discussion Paper," Annex A, 8. For other examples of this language, see National Affairs, "Proposed Budget: Fiscal Year 1970," June 1968, Budget Papers, Box 8, FF, 13–14; "Community Action."

86. National Affairs, "Proposed Budget: Fiscal Year 1970," 58; Division of National Affairs, "Proposed Budget, Fiscal Year 1969," June 1968, Budget Papers, Box 7, FF, 15.

87. National Affairs, "Proposed Budget, Fiscal Year 1969," 15.

88. Ford Foundation, "Discussion Paper," 3, 4. See also Ford Foundation, "Proposed Budget Fiscal Year 1972," June 1971, Budget Papers, Box 9, 24–25.

89. J. Craig Jenkins, "Social Movement Philanthropy and American Democracy," in *Philanthropic Giving: Studies in Varieties and Goals*, ed. Richard Magat (New York: Oxford University Press, 1989), 292–314.

90. Division of National Affairs, "Proposed Budget: Fiscal Year 1970," June 1968, Budget Papers, Box 8, FF, 59.

91. Thomas E. Cooney to Social Development Staff, 9 April 1971, Report 011496, FF; "Community Action," 11.

92. "Community Action," 6; Ford Foundation, "Discussion Paper," 8; Ford Foundation, "Proposed Budget Fiscal Year 1972," 24–25.

93. Ford Foundation, "Discussion Paper," 1.

94. National Affairs, "Proposed Budget: Fiscal Year 1970," 11.

95. Ford Foundation, *Community Development Corporations*, 8.

96. Enclosure from Eamon Kelly to Robert S. Browne, 24 November 1970, BERC, Box 2.

97. Ford Foundation, "Discussion Paper," 12, 8.

98. Francis X. Cline, "Project Started by Kennedy Aids Slum Business," *NYT*, 12

January 1969; Howard R. Dressner to [McGeorge] Bundy et al., 19 June 1969, 69-530, R-1444, FF; Alfred E. Clark, "$10-Million Given to Brooklyn Area," *NYT*, 12 February 1970; Jeff Diggs and Polly Kline, "Evacuation of Slum Family Bares FHA Landlord Role," *Daily News*, 16 April 1970; Edith Evans Asbury, "Senators Told of 'Blockbusting' in a Financial Conspiracy Here," *NYT*, 2 May 1972.

99. William Borders, "Mrs. Kennedy Tours 'Superblocks' Renovated in Bedford-Stuyvesant," *NYT*, 31 October 1969; Emanuel Perlmutter, "Opening of Bedford-Stuyvesant Theater-Office Building Planned in Month," *NYT*, 27 September 1970; "Restoration's First 'Restore Ball,'" *Restoration Newsletter*, December 1970, BERC, Box 16.

100. On Sullivan's achievements, see McKee, 113–210.

101. Sarah E. Stoutland, "Community Development Corporations: Mission, Strategy, and Accomplishments," in *Urban Problems and Community Development*, ed. Ronald F. Ferguson and William T. Dickens (Washington, D.C.: Brookings Institution Press, 1999), 196-198. See also David J. Erickson, "Community Capitalism: How Housing Advocates, the Private Sector, and Government Forged New Low-Income Housing Policy, 1968-1996," *Journal of Policy History* 18, no. 2 (2006): 167-204.

102. Bedford-Stuyvesant D and S Corporation Board of Directors Meeting Minutes, 5 February 1969, Burke Marshall Papers, Box 40, JFK.

103. See also Bedford-Stuyvesant D and S Corporation Board of Directors Meeting Minutes, 20 April 1970, Marshall Papers, Box 40; Mitchell Sviridoff to McGeorge Bundy, 8 June 1971, R-5437, 70-115, FF.

104. Harvey A. Garn, Nancy L. Tevis, and Carl E. Snead, *Assessing Community Development Corporations: Final Report*, vol. 1 (New York: Urban Institute, 1975), 91-92; "The Unique Fashions and Designs from Corley's Originals," *Restoration Newsletter*, December 1969, BERC, Box 16; "P.F. Creations," *Restoration Newsletter*, April 1970, BERC, Box 16; Bedford-Stuyvesant D and S Corporation Board of Directors Meeting Minutes, 20 April 1970; "Sona Labs," *Restoration Newsletter*, June 1971, BERC, Box 16.

105. "The Design Works of Bedford-Stuyvesant," *Restoration Newsletter*, December 1970, 3-4; Rita Reif, "A Look at Fabrics in Mrs. Onassis's Penthouse," *NYT*, 21 October 1971; Thomas interview, 5 May 1972, 58-59.

106. Bryant Mason, "Jobless Rate in Areas Here Staggering," *Daily News*, 11 August 1974; Stein, 15-16.

107. Garn et al., 65-66; Asbury, "Senators Told of 'Blockbusting'," *NYT*, 2 May 1972

108. Erickson, 171-175; Carlson and Martinez, 6-11; Garn et al., 25-26.

109. Carlson and Martinez, 74; Farrell; Kimberley Johnson, "Community Development Corporations, Participation, and Accountability: The Harlem Urban Development Corporation and the Bedford-Stuyvesant Restoration Corporation," *Annals, AAPSS* 594 (July 2004): 121; David Rusk, *Inside Game/Outside Game: Winning Strategies for Saving Urban America* (Washington, D.C.: Brookings Institution Press, 1999), 34.

110. "Funds, Indigenous Talent and Leadership Can Rebuild a Community," *Amsterdam News*, 19 November 1975.

111. Ford Foundation, "Discussion Paper," 10; "The Multiple Achievements of Exterior Renovation," *Restoration Newsletter,* December 1969, BERC, Box 16.

112. Farrell.

113. Rudy Johnson, "Rebuilt Plant Is a Symbol of Hope in Brooklyn," *NYT,* 2 May 1971.

114. Harry Edward Berndt, *New Rulers in the Ghetto: The Community Development Corporation and Urban Poverty* (Westport, Conn.: Greenwood, 1977), 118–119; Stein, 4–5; John Doar, "Memorandum to David Jenkins," 10 March 1970, Marshall Papers, Box 41.

Epilogue

1. Harvey A. Garn, Nancy L. Tevis, and Carl E. Snead, *Assessing Community Development Corporations: Final Report,* vol. 1 (Washington, D.C.: Urban Institute, 1975), 13.

2. Bryant Mason, "Jobless Rate in Areas Here Staggering," *Daily News,* 11 August 1974; Garn et al., 16; Alice O'Connor, *Poverty Knowledge: Social Science, Social Policy, and the Poor in Twentieth-Century U.S. History* (Princeton: Princeton University Press, 2001), 213–283; Thomas Sugrue, *Sweet Land of Liberty: The Forgotten Struggle for Civil Rights in the North* (New York: Random House, 2008), 514–526; Wendell Pritchett, *Brownsville, Brooklyn: Blacks, Jews, and the Changing Face of the Ghetto* (Chicago: University of Chicago Press, 2002), 239–270.

3. Ford Foundation, "Discussion Paper: Preliminary Budget Planning for FY 1974 and FY 1975," March 1973, Budget Papers, Box 9, Ford Foundation Archives (FF), Rockefeller Archive Center, 12; R. Harcourt Dodds to members of the Racial Policy Issues Ad Hoc Committee, 7 June 1976, Office of the President, Records of McGeorge Bundy, Series 2, Box 18, FF. See also "How Firm a Foundation?" *New York Times* (*NYT*), 26 December 1974.

4. *LISC: A Private Public Venture for Community and Neighborhood Revitalization* (New York: Ford Foundation, 1980); O'Connor, *Poverty Knowledge,* 228–229, 231–237. For a description of how American philanthropy overall responded to this shift, see Olivier Zunz, *Philanthropy in America: A History* (Princeton: Princeton University Press, 2012), 232–263.

5. James Forman, Jr., "The Secret History of School Choice: How Progressives Got There First," *Georgetown Law Journal* 93 (2005): 1287–1319; Herman Gray, *Watching Race: Television and the Struggle for "Blackness"* (Minneapolis: University of Minnesota Press, 1995); Sut Jhally and Justin Lewis, *Enlightened Racism: "The Cosby Show," Audiences, and the Myth of the American Dream* (Boulder, Colo.: Westview, 1992).

6. O'Connor, *Poverty Knowledge,* 233.

7. Ford Foundation, *Civil Rights, Social Justice, and Black America: A Review of Past and Current Ford Foundation Efforts to Promote Racial Justice for Black Americans in Employment, Education, Housing, Political Participation and Other Areas* (New York: Ford Foundation, 1984), 9–10.

8. Early in the 1980s, concerns arose about the emergence of an underclass of "new social dropouts," which preoccupied social scientists and journalists. See Ken Auletta,

The Underclass (New York: Random House, 1982); William Julius Wilson, *The Truly Disadvantaged: The Inner City, the Underclass, and Public Policy* (Chicago: University of Chicago Press, 1987).

9. Kathleen D. McCarthy, "Anti-Delinquency, Great Cities, Gray Areas," May 1989, Report 012158, FF, 61.

10. David B. Carlson and Arabella Martinez, "The Economics of Community Change," 1988, Report 11648, FF, 350–355.

11. See, for example, David J. Erickson, "Community Capitalism: How Housing Advocates, the Private Sector, and Government Forged New Low-Income Housing Policy, 1968–1996," *Journal of Policy History* 18, no. 2 (2006): 194; Joseph McNeely, "Comment," in *Urban Problems and Community Development*, ed. Ronald F. Ferguson and William T. Dickens (Washington, D.C.: Brookings Institution Press, 1999), 123.

12. Kimberley Johnson, "Community Development Corporations, Participation, and Accountability: The Harlem Urban Development Corporation and the Bedford-Stuyvesant Restoration Corporation," *Annals, AAPSS* 594 (July 2004): 111.

13. David Rusk, *Inside Game/Outside Game: Winning Strategies for Saving Urban America* (Washington, D.C.: Brookings Institution Press, 1999), 18. On the neoliberal turn and the CDC's role in it, see Erickson; Alice O'Connor, "Swimming against the Tide: A Brief History of Federal Policy in Poor Communities," in Ferguson and Dickens, *Urban Problems and Community Development*, 109–115.

14. Erickson, 179.

15. Henry Louis Gates, Jr., "Joining the Black Overclass at Yale University," *Journal of Blacks in Higher Education*, no. 11 (Spring 1996): 95–100.

16. John Kifner, "From Brooklyn Restoration to Ford Foundation: Franklin Augustine Thomas," *NYT*, 30 January 1979.

17. Dennis A. Williams, "A Key Black Appointment," *Newsweek*, 12 February 1979, 39; Kifner; Orde Coombs, "Fear and Trembling at the Ford Foundation," *New York Magazine*, 28 September 1981, 33.

18. Joshua B. Freeman, *Working Class New York: Life and Labor since World War II* (New York: New Press, 2000) 256–305; Jerald E. Podair, *The Strike That Changed New York: Blacks, Whites, and the Ocean Hill–Brownsville Crisis* (New Haven: Yale University Press, 2002), 186–205; John Mollenkopf, *Phoenix in the Ashes: The Rise and Fall of the Koch Coalition in New York City Politics* (Princeton: Princeton University Press, 1994); Robert W. Bailey, *The Crisis Regime: The MAC, the EFCB, and the Political Impact of the New York City Financial Crisis* (Albany: State University of New York Press, 1984); Miriam Greenberg, *Branding New York: How a City in Crisis Was Sold to the World* (New York: Routledge, 2008).

19. Roger Starr quoted in Kim Moody, *From Welfare State to Real Estate: Regime Change in New York City, 1974 to the Present* (New York: New Press, 2007), 76. See also Joseph P. Fried, "City's Housing Administrator Proposes 'Planned Shrinkage' of Some Slums," *NYT*, 3 February 1976.

20. Jacob Wortham, "Black Politics in New York: Where Has All the Power Gone?" *New York Magazine*, 23 April 1979, 41.

21. Ibid., 43, 42.

22. Ray Mack and Edward Sylvester, "Pattern for Social Change: An Evaluation of the MARC Fellowship/Internship Program," August 1969, Report 002298, FF, 16; Ford Foundation, *Civil Rights, Social Justice, and Black America*, 9.

23. Global Forum on Women and Social Change, *Strengthening Our Attention to Diversity: Recommendations from Foundation Staff* (New York: Ford Foundation, 2004), 2.

24. Ward quoted in Wortham, 43.

25. Guian A. McKee, *The Problem of Jobs: Liberalism, Race, and Deindustrialization in Philadelphia* (Chicago: University of Chicago Press, 2008), 195; Joy Elliott, "New Wheel at Ford," *Black Enterprise*, April 1979, 19.

26. Ron Edmonds quoted in Derrick A. Bell, Jr., "Serving Two Masters: Integration Ideals and Client Interests in School Desegregation Litigation," *Yale Law Journal* 85, no. 4 (1976): 490. Bell's cautionary tale was particularly apt for the Ford Foundation in the 1970s. Its strong support of legal education for minority students helped to serve its emerging interest in public interest law, in which, as the officers in charge of this program put it, the public interest was not defined by "traditional client demand, but to a problem in which [there is] a perceived social need," presumably defined by the lawyers or their patrons. Gordon Harrison and Sanford M. Jaffe quoted in Gareth Davies, *See Government Grow: Education Politics from Johnson to Reagan* (Lawrence: University Press of Kansas, 2007), 177.

27. Global Forum on Women and Social Change, 2.

28. Michael B. Katz, Mark J. Stern, and Jamie J. Fader, "The New African American Inequality," *Journal of American History* 92, no. 1 (2005): 76–77.

29. U.S. Census Bureau, *Statistical Abstract of the United States* (Washington, D.C.: General Printing Office, 2011), 455.

30. Mary Brucker and Merrimon Cuniggim, "Affirmative Action: A Report to the President of the Ford Foundation," 28 April 1975, Report 011001, FF; Ford Foundation, *Annual Report* (1970), 41–44.

31. Thomas M. Shapiro, *The Hidden Cost of Being African-American: How Wealth Perpetuates Inequality* (New York: Oxford University Press, 2004), 92–104; Katz et al., 107.

32. McGeorge Bundy, "The Issue before the Court: Who Gets Ahead in America?" *Atlantic Monthly*, November 1977, http://www.theatlantic.com/past/politics/race/bundy.htm, accessed 16 March 2012.

33. *Regents of the University of California v. Bakke*, 438 U.S. 265 (1978).

34. *Grutter v. Bollinger et al.*, 539 U.S. 306 (2003).

35. David Remnick, *The Bridge: The Life and Rise of Barack Obama* (New York: Knopf, 2010).

Index

Acknowledgments

This book has been very long in coming. In fact I can trace its genesis all the way back to 1990, when I first read about the Ford Foundation's engagement with black power. That original spark of curiosity about this unlikely relationship ignited a flame that still burns bright, fueled by all of the support I have received over the years.

The Social Sciences and Humanities Research Council of Canada underwrote this project, both through seed funding administered through Simon Fraser University and through a multiyear Standard Research Grant. That money paid for my research travel and also supported a remarkable group of undergraduate and graduate students who helped make this project what it is. Joshua Dougherty, Andrea Gill, John Munro, Ian Rocksborough Smith, and Michelle Wood all conveyed intelligence, diligence, and passion for the history of race in the United States, which stimulated my interest and resolve and helped create a vibrant community of young Americanists in Vancouver, Canada.

In New York City I was greeted at the Ford Foundation by its exceptional archivist Alan Divack and the rest of the archive staff, Idelle Nissilla, Anthony Maloney, and Jonathan Green. Without their generous interest and support and the Foundation's openness to researchers, I could never have written this book. After the Foundation transferred its records to the Rockefeller Archive Center and into the hands of its capable and professional staff, Lucas Buresch provided superb service at a distance during the last phases of this project. I found similar munificence at a very different institution, the Schomburg Center for Research in Black Culture. Despite the challenges they face every day working in the New York Public Library system, my experience working with the staff in the Schomburg's research collections was never less than exceptional. I would like in particular to thank manuscript archivist Andre Elizee, whose vast knowledge of the Schomburg's holdings and of African American history introduced me to important new sources and ways of thinking about my subject. James Briggs Murray let me loose in the Schomburg's treasure trove of interviews and audiovisual material pertaining to the Black Arts movement. Finally, Mary Yearwood went beyond the call of duty in identifying illustrations for me.

Numerous colleagues and friends commented on sections of this book, including Beth Bailey, Mark Brilliant, Mary Chapman, David Chariandy, David Freund, William Graebner, Paul Krause, Leslie Paris, and Jon Smith, as well as participants in the Stokes seminar at Dalhousie University and audiences in the history departments of Simon Fraser University and the University of British Columbia. Although they had not read or heard my work, my exceptional colleagues and students in the Graduate Program in Urban Studies at Simon Fraser University opened my eyes to interdisciplinary perspectives on North American cities that allowed me to write a much better urban history than I otherwise would have. The extraordinary Jack O'Dell and Jane Power were always ready to talk about this book and helped set me on the right path. Ever since she learned about my project almost ten years ago, I have benefited from Alice O'Connor's enormous generosity as a reader of my work. Her expertise and wisdom indelibly shaped these pages. Felicia Kornbluh's meticulous reading of my manuscript exposed me to fresh interpretations and important new sources. I am very grateful to Thomas Sugrue and his advice as I worked on my revisions. Working with the outstanding editorial, production, and marketing staff at the University of Pennsylvania Press was an author's dream. In particular, I offer my heartfelt thanks and appreciation to my editor, Robert Lockhart. Throughout this book's genesis, Bob offered me exactly the exceptional hands-on editorial support that he promised during our very first meeting. His enthusiasm and commitment to this project, including his multiple careful and astute readings of the manuscript, kept me going and vastly improved the finished product.

While I have always been interested in this project, the isolation of researching and writing sometimes took a toll. At those moments, my wonderful circle of friends and family revived my spirits and energy. Thanks particularly to Lesli Boldt, Lara Campbell, Luke Clossey, Pete Cramer, Gregg Currie, Sarah Currie, the Feline family, Orlando Frizado, Drew Kiriazides, Helen Leung, Eva Lewis, Patrick Lewis, Susan Nance, Karen "Pomodoro" Ravensbergen, Meg Stanley, Eric Wredenhagen, and all the members of the Sunday night sangha. I have tremendous gratitude for my teachers Anna Baignoche, Mary Balomenos, and Judy Witheford. As always, the Fergusons provided an anchor of love and support, now reinforced by our newest edition, Hollis, who lights me up even when just thinking about her. Thanks, too, to my new family, the Evertons, and especially my in-laws Pam and Bob, whose love and abiding enthusiasm and respect for the academic life sustained me.

Finally, I dedicate this book to my husband, Mike Everton. No words can express how much his love means to me.